2-62

RELIGIOUS EDUCATION AND THE STATE:

Democracy finds a way

By
Sister M. RAYMOND McLAUGHLIN, O.S.B., Ph.D.

The Catholic University of America Press
Washington, D.C. 20017

Nihil obstat:
Reverend John C. Selner, S.S., S.T.D.

Imprimatur:
+Patrick A. O'Boyle
Archbishop of Washington

May 25, 1967

The nihil obstat and imprimatur are official declarations that a book or pamphlet is free of doctrinal or moral error. No implication is contained therein that those who have granted the nihil obstat and the imprimatur agree with the content, opinions or statements expressed.

Library of Congress Catalog Card Number: 67-21368

(ERRATA SHEET FOR RELIGIOUS EDUCATION AND
THE STATE: DEMOCRACY FINDS A WAY)

ERRATA

Page 15, line 7: For rights read right.

Page 54, line 11: For en ure read ensure.

Page 70, line 7: For secondary read country's.

Page 237, line 10: For are read is.

Page 245, line 3 from bottom: For Montellembert read Montalembert.

Page 251, last line: For Legue read Ligue.

Page 277, line 3: For cult read culte.

Page 278, line 3: For heppy read happy.

Page 433, Footnote 3, Chapt. VII: Delete Second Edition.
Change date to 1955; and change p. 376 to pp. 261-265.

CONTENTS

iii

PREFACE

Since the sixteenth century and more particularly since the advent of national systems of education one hundred and fifty years ago, issues revolving around church-state relationships in education have given rise to much discussion, controversy, and struggle. The problem has proved especially acute in highly pluralistic societies. What role, if any, should religion have in public education? What relationships should the state establish with the church-affiliated schools? In our own country the issue refuses to die although some educational writers shy away from it and a few constitutional commentators would shelve it by declaring that the question has been settled once and for all by the First Amendment. Many thoughtful Americans, however, are of the opinion that the religion-education issue has never been adequately solved and that our present policy on the matter is in need of re-evaluation, and this without necessitating any changes in the First Amendment itself.

Relevant to the dialogue on the question is an inquiry as to how other democracies have handled the issue. The purpose of the present volume is to show how our Western allies came to grips with and solved the problem that still plagues us. A historical approach has been taken because practically all the democracies had to face the issue at one time or another within the past century and struggle through to settlements which, in the case of the majority of the countries studied, met the desires of their people on the matter. As liberty-loving as we and as solicitous for the rights of the religious conscience -- in fact, for these precise reasons -- the Western democracies found it possible and advantageous to give religion a role of importance in their state systems of education and to aid the church-related schools financially.

If there is a thesis in this work it is that the religion-education problem can be settled through democratic processes in a way that gives complete and <u>practical</u> recognition to parents'

v

rights to direct the education of their children and that pro-
tects every child's right to share without discrimination in the
general benefits accruing from taxation. That it can be done
is proved by the fact that it has been done, and this without
impairing to the slightest degree religious liberty or the sacred
rights of conscience, as the present volume demonstrates.

The author's interest in the problem resulted from first
hand acquaintance with the financial difficulties encountered by
church-related schools in their efforts to maintain excellence,
and, secondly, from her experience in teaching courses in
Comparative Education at The Catholic University of America
and the discovery of the paucity of information available on
comparative difficulties and solutions connected with the religion-education issue.

With the exception of Australia, the author has had an
opportunity to visit all the countries dealt with in this investigation. Over the period of a year, schools were visited and
interviews held with state and private school officials and with
specialists on church-state relationships.

It was inevitable that the author's commitment to the
Christian view of life would be reflected in the interpretation
of facts pertinent to the study. This does not change the facts;
rightly is it expected that their presentation be absolutely reliable and objective. The author, however, acknowledges that
the various solutions to the religion-education issue have been
viewed and appraised in a Christian perspective. At the
same time the author disclaims any pretense of representing
an official view of any kind and assumes entire responsibility
for the opinions and evaluations expressed. No claim to completeness or finality is made. Much had to be omitted because
of space limitations. Opinions on technical questions of law
were avoided.

The book has been written with the general reader in
mind. The question dealt with lies beyond those of narrow
professional interest. At the same time it is hoped the book
will serve as a useful reference for college courses in comparative education, educational history, and other courses
dealing with matters of current interest.

The author's debt of gratitude is an extensive one. It is

not possible to list the names of the many persons who have contributed toward the completion of this work, but prayerful thanks go out to them all. Sincere appreciation is expressed for assistance and materials provided by the staff members of: the Mullen Library of The Catholic University of America; the Library of Congress; the embassies of Australia, Belgium, Canada, France, Great Britain, Ireland, the Netherlands and West Germany, all in Washington; the Belgium Information Center, the British Information Services, Cultural Services of the French Embassy, all in New York City; the Ministries of Education in all ten Canadian provinces; Citizens for Educational Freedom, St. Louis; the Catholic Education Council, London; Union Nationale des A.P.E.L., Paris; Union Internationale Pour la Liberté d'Enseignement, Paris; Secretariat d'Études Pour la Liberté de l'Enseignement et la Défense de la Culture, Paris; Service d'Editions et Vente des Publications de l'Education National, Paris; Ministerie Van Onderwijs, Kunsten En Wetenschappen, The Hague; Het Rooms-Katholick Centraal Bureau Voor Onderwijs en Opvolding, The Hague; Federation Nationale de l'Enseignement Moyen Catholique, Brussels.

The author is very grateful for the generous assistance rendered in various ways by: Mr. R. A. O'Brien and Mr. H. Cunningham, the Catholic Education Council, London; Dom Passmore, Downside Abbey School, Stratton-on-Fosse, England; Mother Richardson, Digby-Stuart Teachers' College, Roehampton, London; Sister Veronica, St. Paul's High School, Edgbaston, Birmingham, England; Sister Gregory, O.P., St. Thomas School, Marsh Lane, Stanmore, London, N.W.; Very Reverend Patrick F. Quille, Cathedral House, Edinburgh, Scotland; the administrative officials of Sacred Heart Teachers' College, Craiglockhard, Edinburgh and Notre Dame Teachers' College, Dowan Hill, Glasgow; Mother Mary Lenore, S.P., Providence Motherhouse, Kingston, Ontario; Sister Basil McCormick, St. Bride's College, Littledale, St. John's, Newfoundland; William J. Weeden, Director, Office of Education, Commonwealth of Australia; Very Reverend Fergal McGrath, S.J., Rathfarnham Castle, Dublin; Very Reverend Andre Godin, S.J., Centre International d'Études de la Formation Religieuse,

Brussels; M. Paul Frankhard, professor, University of Louvain, Belgium; Mr. Bresser, The Catholic Central Bureau of Education, The Hague; Dr. K. Peters, Head, Department of Documents, Ministry of Education, Arts, and Sciences, The Hague; M. Edouard Lizop, Secretaire General, Union Internationale Pour la Liberté d'Enseignement, Paris; Very Reverend Monseigneur Bressolles, Director, L'Oeuvre Pontificale de la Sainte Enfance, Paris; Abbe C. Gratel, Secretary General, Direction Diocesaine pour le Monde Scholaire et Universitaire, Paris; M. Majault, Musee Pédagogique National, Paris; Mother Marie Garnier, R.S.C.M., Cours Marymont, Neuilly-sur-Seine, France; M. Guy Bonnefoy, Marist Lycee, Sierck-des-Bains (Moselle) France; Mother Marie Assumpta, O.S.B., Regina Laudis Monastery, Bethlehem, Connecticut; Miss Mary McLaughlin, Washington, D. C. The author takes this opportunity to express sincere gratitude to her superiors, Reverend Mother Athanasius Braegelman, O.S.B. and Reverend Mother Martina Hughes, O.S.B., who allowed time to make the writing of this volume possible.

Acknowledgment and thanks are due to the publishers who granted permission to use copyrighted and other materials: American Council on Education, Washington, D. C.; The America Press, New York; Cambridge University Press, New York; Catholic Education Council, London; The Catholic University of America Press, Washington, D. C.; Clomore and Reynolds, Ltd., Dublin; "Current Affairs Bulletin," Department of Adult Education, University of Sydney, Sydney, N.S. W., Australia; Columbia University Press, New York; Dent and Sons, Toronto, Ontario; Fordham University Press, New York; W. J. Gage Limited, Scarborough, Ontario, Canada; Harcourt, Brace and World, Inc., New York; Harvard University Press, Cambridge, Massachusetts; Heinemann Educational Books, Ltd., London; Het R. K. Centraal Bureau Voor Onderwijs en Opvoeding, The Hague, Holland; Holt, Rinehart and Winston, Inc., New York; Houghton Mifflin Company, Boston; Longmans, Green & Co., Limited, Harlow, Essex, England; Loyola University Press, Chicago; Lumen Vitae, Centre International D'Etudes de la Formation Religieuse, Brussels; The Macmillan Company, New York; National

Catechetical Centre, London; Ronald Press Company, New
York; Routledge and Kegan Paul, Ltd., London; The Ryerson
Press, Toronto; The Tablet, London; University Tutorial
Press, Ltd., Cambridge, England; Joseph F. Wagner, Inc.,
New York; West Publishing Company, St. Paul.

S. M. R. McL.

INTRODUCTION

A LOOK AT THE HOME FRONT

An unsolved educational problem harasses our country. Its resolution is becoming increasingly urgent. The core of the issue concerns the role which religious and moral training should play in American education. Correlative questions bear on the function of the public school in dealing with religion and on the relationships of the state to religion-oriented schools. Although the problem has been partially obscured recently by the current debate on integration in the schools, the question, in the long view, has elicited more discussion than any other issue. It has given rise to high controversy, which has entered into presidential, state, and local elections. Thousands of articles, hundreds of books have been written on various aspects of the problem and from diverse viewpoints.[1] Unnumbered speeches and debates have set forth the variant positions taken on the subject. Controverted questions relating to the issue have repeatedly been referred to the courts for adjudication. Dissatisfaction and tension have been the perennial fruits of the apparent inability to reach an equitable solution.

Whence rose the problem? Our nation had its foundations, all historians agree, in the Christian ideals and traditions of Western Europe. The first schools on American soil were those established by Catholic missionaries in Florida and the Southwest. The English and other settlers along the Atlantic coast gave religion a role of primary importance in their schools, practically all of which were church-related. True, the religious cataclysm of the sixteenth century, which broke asunder the unity of Christianity and initiated a multiplication of sects, had left a trail of religious rivalries, intolerance, bitterness and even hatred. This inheritance, unfortunately, was also carried by the colonists to the New World, where it produced seeds of new rivalries, antagonisms,

1

and persecutions. Nevertheless, the schools continued to maintain their religious character throughout the colonial period even in the case of common schools which the governments established here and there.

National independence brought no sudden changes in educational practice. Under the Federal Constitution education became a responsibility of the respective states. The religious purpose continued to predominate on all levels of education.

Nor did the passage of the First Amendment affect the religious teaching in the schools. The documents of the period testify that the First Amendment was interpreted to mean quite simply what its words imply: the federal government could make no laws respecting an establishment of religion nor could it interfere in any way with the individual's freedom to believe and worship as his conscience dictated.[2] Both the debates in which the Founders argued over the precise manner of wording the First Amendment and the actions of the early leaders in Congress indicate that the specific purpose of the Amendment was to secure the fullest religious liberty for all; the prohibition against an establishment was simply a means toward that end. The Founders well knew from their own experience how established churches in the colonies had interfered with the religious liberty of many good people. Accordingly they were determined that the federal government should not be permitted to adopt an official religion, that is, that it should not be able to favor one church more than another or discriminate against any one or more churches; for this restriction, the Fathers were convinced, would more effectively safeguard the freedom of the individual conscience.

There is no hint of an "impregnable wall" between church and state. Even the word separation does not occur. A study of the legislative history of the Amendment shows that the federal government could maintain relations with the various churches and even aid them if it did so impartially; that it could, and did, cooperate with the religious forces of the nation. There is no historical reason to assume that the authors of the First Amendment intended to oppose the role of religion

in the schools, or anywhere else. On the contrary, these
same men in drawing up the Northwest Ordinance a few years
earlier had declared: "Religion, morality, and knowledge
being necessary to good government and the happiness of man-
kind, schools and the means of education shall be forever encouraged."[3]

As a matter of historical fact, the schools throughout
the early period of the nation's existence were frequently
aided by public funds while they instructed their pupils in religion, morality, and knowledge, these elements being
regarded as necessary in securing happiness for the individual
and responsible citizens for the country. The religion taught
was generally some form of Protestantism. Here and there
a few Catholic schools also received funds. For the most
part, however, the publicly-supported schools were to all intents and purposes Protestant denominational schools.

As the number of Protestant denominations increased
and the religious homogeneity of the population correspondingly decreased, disagreements arose as to what religion should
be taught in the schools. Rivalries and bickerings prevailed
among the sects. The particular brand of Protestantism having a majority in a given area usually managed to get its
tenets taught in the school, a situation which resulted in great
dissatisfaction among the other sects. To settle the disputes
in Massachusetts, Horace Mann advocated state-controlled,
non-sectarian schools. A law passed in 1827 forbade the use
of sectarian textbooks in the common schools. Later, as
chairman of the State Board of Education, Horace Mann waged
a vigorous battle to have the law enforced and to strengthen
state control over the schools. His success, if not overwhelming, was notable and it stimulated similar efforts in other
states. Non-denominational schools began to appear in greater
numbers; many church-related schools were absorbed into the
state systems. A watered-down religion of natural truths was
taught and the Bible was read in these public schools. Entrenched traditions die hard, however. The majority sect of
an area often continued its efforts to have its own doctrines
emphasized, so religious rivalries and dissensions did not
entirely cease.

Then, during the second quarter of the nineteenth century a new factor entered into the arena. Immigrants from Germany and Ireland, many of them Catholic, began arriving in the country. The number of Irish immigrants, particularly, increased greatly in the 1840's and succeeding decades. The majority of them settled in the larger cities of New York and Massachusetts. Catholic in faith and wretchedly poor, they were despised by their more affluent Protestant neighbors. For them, however, their faith was their greatest treasure and they were determined to preserve it at all costs, as they had done for centuries under British tyranny in Ireland. Naturally, they found the public schools, whether totally Protestant in spirit, Protestant-oriented, or neutral, unsatisfactory as schools for their children. Indeed, the atmosphere of these schools was often openly hostile to everything Catholic.

Practically all existing educational institutions, neutral or Protestant-oriented, were aided by public funds. It was only natural, therefore, that the Irish should ask for financial aid to help them provide the kind of schools they wanted for their children. Their appeal aroused to white heat smoldering anti-Catholic animosities. Protestant groups which had opposed each other now joined forces to present a united front against what they regarded as a common danger. In the fear lest Catholics obtain funds for their schools, some Protestants who had stood firmly for denominational schools now joined the public school propagandists in the battle to prevent the application of aid to Catholic schools. An historian of the episode describes it thus: ". . . a new danger appeared, in the presence of which the opposing parties ceased their wordy conflict, and, combining their forces against the common enemy, solidified opinion in support of the non-sectarian public school." [4]

Opposition to Catholics took organized form in the openly intolerant Native American Party, which presented as its aim resistance to foreign influence in the United States. Its hostility was directed mainly against the Catholic Church and her parochial schools, which the organization regarded as foreign institutions. The Nativist movement was succeeded in the 1850's by the Know-Nothing Party with similar aims and tactics.

Bitterly anti-Catholic, both organizations spread misunderstanding and hatred. They entered the political arena, where
they strove to have their negative sentiments enacted into laws
which would limit the civic rights of Catholics and impede the
work of the Church. By dint of emotion-producing slogans and
political machinations, they exercised a powerful influence in
bringing about the pragmatic resolution to the church-state relationship in education which finally evolved in America during
the middle decades of the last century.

The controversy over religion in the public schools and
aid to church-related schools was fought out bitterly and conclusively, particularly in New York and Massachusetts. It
raged in New York for several decades after 1806. The
schools in New York City at that time, though supported to a
great extent by public funds, were conducted by the Public
School Society. The title was misleading since the sponsoring
society was a private, philanthropic group. In theory, its
schools were non-sectarian; in practice, they were strongly
Protestant in orientation and generally anti-Catholic in spirit.
Catholics of the city asked for a share of public funds to conduct their own schools. Several Protestant denominational
schools and two Catholic institutions were at the time recipients of funds, but the majority of Catholic children had to
attend the schools of the Society. The answer of the City
Council to the appeal for funds was to cut off public aid from
all schools except those of the Society.

Thereupon, under the leadership of Bishop Hughes and
utilizing political weapons, Catholics organized a dignified and
vigorous campaign to obtain what they felt was a matter of
strict justice. In this they were accorded the moral support
of several Protestant groups. Bishop Hughes offered a compromise. The Catholic schools would submit to the same
general regulations under which those receiving public aid
operated and would restrict the teaching of religion to after-
school hours.

The reasonableness and justice of the Catholic proposal
were presented again and again in speeches and writing. It
was all to no purpose. Bigotry broke loose; the cry of "no
popery" was heard throughout the state. Eventually the legis-

lature of New York made the decision for that state. A law
was passed in 1842 creating for the city of New York a Board
of Education, which was ordered to establish a system of public schools; the Public School Society was dissolved and the
schools of the society were taken over by the Board. The
teaching of sectarian religion was forbidden in the public
schools of the state. The law further prescribed that no portion of the school funds was in the future to be given to any
school "in which any religion, sectarian doctrine or truth
should be taught, inculcated, or practiced."[5]   This meant
that Catholic schools were compelled henceforth to maintain
themselves from private resources.

Similarly a bitter controversy on the school question
was waged in Massachusetts through the middle decades of the
past century. The Catholics there were not sufficiently powerful or organized to conduct a campaign in behalf of their cause.
The historian of the Massachusetts episode describes the
course of events in that state as follows:

> . . . the atmosphere of the (public) schools was
> favorable to Protestant Christianity;. . .and when
> the Roman Catholics appeared in numbers suffi-
> cient to demand, with some possibility of success,
> that they be not subjected to what they considered
> a sectarian Protestant religious education, and that
> in lieu of that they be given money for parochial
> schools for the teaching of Catholic doctrines, a
> rising tide of Nationalism united the Protestant
> sects to provide in the fundamental law against a
> possible use of state money intended for common
> schools. But it was more a matter of expediency
> than principle, for care was taken to exclude col-
> leges from the prohibition.[6]

A coalition of political factions succeeded in having a
convention called to revise the state constitution, the most
significant change being a provision to prohibit the appropriation of public money to church-related schools. The new constitution failed of adoption at the election of 1853. Two years

later while a Know-Nothing legislature was in session, a proposal prohibiting aid to church-related elementary schools was presented again as an amendment to the existing constitution. It passed the legislature and was approved by the people in 1855. The refusal to include in the prohibition sectarian colleges and academies, which were almost exclusively under Protestant auspices at the time, indicates quite conclusively, as historian Smith points out, that the issue was decided not on its own merits, but on a bias in which intolerance, fear, and expediency triumphed over principle. The same legislature passed an act making Bible reading compulsory in all public schools in Massachusetts.

The school issue was fought out with more or less bitterness in other states as well, with similar factors entering into the settlement. The actions taken by New York and Massachusetts, however, set a precedent for the rest of the country. As new states were admitted into the union after 1858, they inserted into their state constitutions provisions which limited public funds to state-controlled, non-sectarian schools exclusively.

The historical facts indicate that expediency and anti-Catholic feeling had been predominant factors in determining the church-state policy in education upon which America had embarked, a policy which cleared the path for the eventual domination by secularism and was in general satisfactory only to those indifferent to religious education.

State systems of education were gradually organized. Most of the church schools which had been controlled by Protestants were eventually absorbed by the public school systems, for the secularization process was gradual. The teaching of Protestant doctrines, saying Protestant prayers, singing Protestant hymns were often continued for many years in the public schools. On the other hand, Catholics, for whom education on a basis of Catholic doctrine was a sacred demand of conscience, had no choice but to undertake in their poverty to build and maintain their own schools, a task they assumed with courage and determination. That success accompanied their efforts is testified to by the continual growth of the system to the point where today it provides accommodations for

over fourteen percent of the total school population of America.
There have been and still are many Americans who view
as an "unhappy compromise" the educational policy which the
states had, in a sense, bungled into. A distinguished authority on church-state law declares that all sides lost:

> Catholics lost their subsidies, and henceforth were
> forced wholly to support their schools. The Protes-
> tant denominations lost the teaching of their religion
> in the public schools, which henceforth were con-
> fined to purely secular subjects. ('The public school
> pupils lost a large part of the moral restraint which
> religion alone can impart. The churches lost many
> who should have become faithful members, and the
> state finds its burdens increased and its citizenship
> degenerating.[7]

In the opinion of many, the policy runs counter to the best of
American traditions; it has no basis in principle, they hold,
and only by distortion can it be said to be embodied in the intended coverage of the First Amendment. What is needed
today, many thoughtful Americans are saying, is a re-exami-
nation of the whole issue in the light of reason, in the warmth
of charity and justice, and on the sound foundation of principle.
The basis of our unsolved problem rests in the first
place on the pertinent provisions of state constitutions and
statutes, formulas which, though variously phrased, are seen
to contain two complementary elements. In effect, they first
forbid the teaching of doctrinal religion (usually referred to
as sectarian teaching) in tax-supported schools; and, secondly,
they prohibit the appropriation of public funds to schools in
which such doctrines are taught. Today the vast majority of
the religion-oriented schools -- over ninety percent -- are
under Catholic auspices.
The pertinent provision in the constitution of Illinois is
fairly typical of those found in other state constitutions:

> Neither the general assembly nor any county,
> city, town, township, school district, or other public

corporation, shall ever make any appropriations
or pay from any public fund whatever, anything in
aid of any church or sectarian purpose, or to help
support or sustain any school, academy, seminary,
college, university, or other literary scientific
institution, controlled by any church or sectarian
denomination whatever; nor shall any grant or
section of land, money, or other personal property
ever be made by the state or any such public corporation, to any church, or for any sectarian purpose.[8]

The prohibitory clauses, in their over-all effect, have
resulted, first, in secularized public school systems; and
secondly, in economic restraints on the church-related schools
which have militated against their achievement of a desired
excellence and curtailed indirectly their legitimate expansion.
These effects, many Americans maintain, impair parental
rights to choose freely the school their child will attend, restrict religious freedom, and are, in fact, violations of distributive justice.[9]

Although the constitutional provisions, as a rule, left
the door open for teaching non-denominational religion in the
public schools, it was soon found that it was impossible to
draw up a common denominator of religious truths that would
be satisfactory to all parents, or even to a considerable number. One tenet after another had to be eliminated, until
eventually all religious teaching was abandoned in most schools.

As we have seen, the preservation of religious liberty
as guaranteed by the First Amendment to the Federal Constitution did not enter as an argument into the nineteenth century
controversies which resulted in the prohibitory clause of the
state constitutions. Not until after the passage of the Fourteenth Amendment (1868) were the freedoms of the Bill of
Rights, including the principle of separation of church and
state, made applicable to the respective states. It is only
within recent years, however, that the chief emphasis has
been placed on the first clause of the First Amendment and
that the "no establishment" concept has been given such a

highly comprehensive and exaggerated interpretation by the United States Supreme Court that its original purpose, many eminent authorities on constitutional law maintain, has been twisted and distorted out of all recognition.[10]

The first instance occurred in 1947 in the Everson case involving a New Jersey law which permitted the transportation of parochial school children on tax-paid buses.[11]   The Court's decision upheld the transportation of children along with those going to public schools as a child welfare service, but a new doctrine was expressed in the dicta of the majority opinion and vehemently set forth in the dissenting opinion of Judge Ruteledge. A hitherto non-existing "wall" was erected between church and state in the United States: "The First Amendment has erected a wall between church and state. That wall must be kept high and impregnable. We could not approve the slightest break. . ." And the Court declared further: "The 'establishment of religion' clause of the First Amendment means at least this: Neither a state nor the Federal Government can set up a church. Neither can pass laws which aid one religion, aid all religions, or prefer one religion over another."[12]

The doctrine of the "wall" became the basis of the decision in the McCollum case (1949), which dealt with the so-called released-time program for religious instruction as it was conducted in Illinois.[13]   The Supreme Court declared the practice unconstitutional as a violation of the establishment clause. The wall, the Court held, had been pierced:

> Here not only are the State's tax-supported public school buildings used for the dissemination of religious doctrines. The State also affords sectarian groups an invaluable aid in that it helps to provide pupils for their religious classes through use of the State's compulsory public school machinery. This is not separation of Church and State.

A volley of criticism followed this decision, coming from sober authorities on constitutional law and from the

grass roots. The Court, it was said, had assumed the role
of a super-board of education; it was engaging in law-making
rather than in law-interpreting.[14]
   The broad doctrine on the coverage of the establishment
clause was modified somewhat in the Zorach V. Clausen case
(1952), which also involved the released-time program.[15]
The issue arose in New York where religious instruction was
given on other than public school premises. New York's
practice was upheld by the Supreme Court, and in the dicta of
the majority opinion the separation principle was slightly
liberalized. The First Amendment, the Court declared,

   . . . does not say that in every and all respects
   there shall be separation of Church and State.
   Rather, it studiously defines the manner, the
   specific ways, in which there shall be no concert
   or union of dependency one on the other. That is
   the common sense of the matter. Otherwise the
   state and religion would be aliens to each other--
   hostile, suspicious, and even unfriendly.

The Court listed the numerous practices wherein the Federal
government recognized the Creator: prayers in our legislative halls; appeals to the Almighty in the messages of the
Chief Executive; "So help me God" in our courtroom oaths,
and the many other references to God in our laws and public
rituals.
   The Court concluded:

   We are a religious people whose institutions suppose
   a Supreme Being. . . When the state encourages
   religious instruction or cooperates with religious
   authorities by adjusting the schedule of public events
   to sectarian needs, it follows the best of our traditions. For it then respects the religious nature of
   our people and accommodates the public service to
   their spiritual needs. To hold that it may not would
   be to find in the Constitution a requirement that the
   government show a callous indifference to religious

groups. That would be preferring those who believe
in no religion over those who do believe.

Yet in 1962 the Court seemed again to revert to the
more extreme view of separation. The case involved a twenty-two word prayer composed by the New York regents which
acknowledged dependence upon God and asked His help. The
recitation of the prayer was voluntary in the New York public
schools. The practice was struck down by the Supreme Court
as an establishment of religion by the state: ". . . we think
that the constitutional prohibition against laws respecting an
establishment must at least mean that in this country it is no
part of the business of government to compose official prayers
for any group of the American people to recite as a part of a
religious program carried on by the government." [16]
Angry nationwide resentment followed the high Court's
ban on the New York school prayer. Actually the ordinary
American citizen saw in the decision a symptom of a radical
change that was running through the whole structure of American society. He was alarmed because he felt that this change
was not a natural evolution but an innovation engineered by a
small minority of secular-bent agitators determined to remove
all theistic influences from the schools.

Along the same line of thinking, the Supreme Court a
year earlier (1961) had rendered an opinion which had possible
bearings on school issues that might be decided later, though
the case itself did not originate from a school controversy. [17]
A Maryland law requiring belief in God as a qualification for
holding certain public offices was challenged. The opinion of
the Court, delivered by Justice Black, contained this statement:
"Neither a State nor the Federal Government can aid those religions based on a belief in the existence of God as against
those religions founded on different beliefs." The atheism
of Mr. Torcaso, who brought the suit, was, therefore,
equated with the "religions" protected by the First Amendment.
Conceding the right of atheists to exercise their unbeliefs,
many Americans were inclined to believe that it was highly
conjectural that the authors of the Bill of Rights intended atheism to be considered as a "religion" protected by the First

Amendment. Certainly, the opinion of the Court in the Torcaso
case runs counter both to that given in the Zorach case referred
to above and to an opinion handed down in an earlier decision
in which the Court declared that this is a religious nation and
that the Constitution and statutes are to be interpreted upon the
supposition that nothing inimical to religion is intended.[18]
Still earlier in Mormon Church V. United States, the Court had
held that polygamy was contrary to the spirit of Christianity
and of the civilization which Christianity had produced in the
Western World. The Court clearly indicated that the tenets of
the Christian religion were part and parcel of American civilization.[19]

Against the background of the new way of thinking on the
part of the Court, that body's ruling on Bible reading and recitation of the Lord's Prayer in the public schools (1963) came
as no surprise to the American people. These were practices
which had been carried on in public schools for over one hundred and fifty years and currently were permitted in about half
of all the public schools in the country. At issue were two
cases: Bible reading and the Lord's Prayer in Maryland's public schools and Bible reading alone in Pennsylvania's public
schools. In both school systems students whose parents objected to the exercises could be excused. The Maryland case
was appealed from the State Supreme Court by a Baltimore
woman, a professed and militant atheist. The Court's opinion
struck down the practices in both states as violations of the
establishment clause.[20] Delivering the opinion, Justice Clark
quoted with approval this interpretation of the First Amendment:

> The Amendment's purpose was not to strike merely
> at the official establishment of a single sect, creed,
> or religion. . . It was to create a complete and
> permanent separation of the spheres of religious
> activity and civil authority by forbidding every form
> of public aid or support for religion.

Reaction against the decision was less passionate than
that which followed the New York prayer ban because the de-

cision had been fully expected. Yet much quiet firm disapproval was expressed. Concern was shown by some observers
that the Court was permeated with secularism and that the public schools were to be the "pulpit of the religion of secularism." Congress produced a flurry of bills to lessen what
sponsors saw as a damage to the nation's underpinnings. In
January, 1964, a congressman announced that the latest count
showed 131 joint resolutions on prayer and Bible reading in the
public schools were pending before the House Judiciary committee. Fifty of these resolutions proposed a Constitutional
amendment to override the Court's rulings on prayer and Bible
reading in the public schools. Legal scholars and newspaper
columnists called attention to the undue stress on the "no establishment" principle and the corresponding under-emphasis
on religious freedom, pointing out that the effect of this unbal-
anced stress on one element of the amendment to the exclusion
of the other had been to favor freedom from religion rather
than freedom for religion.

Furthermore, the emphasis on separation and its exaggerated interpretation by the Court was seized by the militant
secularists as a handy crutch to support their opposition to any
and all possibilities of aid to church-related schools. Leaning
on the crutch, such groups have, for example, opposed any
reference in the public schools to the Christian meaning of
Christmas or Easter. A manger scene at Christmas is taboo
from their standpoint. Fringe benefits -- bus transportation,
health services, free secular textbooks for parochial school
children -- are opposed as violating the separation principle.

Briefly, then, the official policy in America in regard to
religious education in the public schools and the relation of the
state to church-connected schools as set forth in state constitutions, state laws, and judicial interpretations of the First
Amendment amounts to a practical denial of the importance of
religion in education and in American life. This effect is augmented by the unflagging efforts of a small but vociferous minority who oppose all and every form of cooperation between
the state and religious groups. As they are at present constituted, public schools, which are educating about eighty-five
percent of American youth, cannot make provision for religious

instruction although many parents desire it for their children. The released-time program operating in many states provides a palliative practice. It is good as far as it goes, but those experienced in its workings can verify its limitations as an effective means of religious training. Moreover, church-related schools must struggle against odds to survive and to maintain excellence. The rights of parents to educate their children as their conscience dictates is impaired; distributive justice is ignored. In the opinion of many perceptive Americans this dual defect in our educational system constitutes the foremost educational problem in America -- national in scope, of grave import, persistent, unsolved. The problem in its dual aspects deserves closer analysis.

The Two Aspects of Our Educational Problem
        Consider the first aspect of our educational policy. Public education in the United States is committed by law to the general principle that the teaching of doctrinal religion must be excluded from the curriculum and, as we have seen, the trend has been toward the absolute exclusion of all religious references from the classroom. Either a sort of religious vacuum is created in the public school, or more generally, secular humanism (nature abhors a vacuum) is substituted for the rejected religion.

        But secularism, it has been said, is itself a viewpoint on religion -- a view which holds that one's beliefs can be excluded from the affairs of daily life; that religion can, with impunity, be separated from the educational process; that morality based on humanistic motives, to the exclusion of the supernatural, is all sufficient for the moral training of youth. An example of this view is found in a report of the National Educational Association entitled "Moral and Spiritual Values in the Public Schools," which states: "By moral and spiritual values we mean those values which, when applied to human behavior, exalt and refine life and bring it into harmony with the standards of conduct that are approved in our democratic culture." [21] Episcopal James A. Pike, commenting on the decision of the Supreme Court in the McCollum case, is quoted as saying: "Humanitarian secularism -- by default -- is now the established religion of the United States."

There is, besides, grave danger of the policy of exclusion
becoming anti-religious in effect. A committee of the American Council on Education appointed to study the function of the
public schools in dealing with religion states in a report:
". . .to be silent about religion may be, in effect, to make the
public school an anti-religious factor in the community. Silence
creates the impression in the minds of the young that religion
is unimportant and has nothing to contribute to the solution of
the perennial and ultimate problems of life." [22]

It has been pointed out, too, that in the trend toward the
exclusion of all religious manifestations from the public
school, the emphasis has been on public schools as solely
instruments of the state. This position ignores the fact that
the public schools are cooperative enterprises of both parents
and the state, a principle which American tradition has recognized and implemented by putting the details of school control
in the hands of a local Board of Education, popularly elected.
Unfortunately, too many American parents seem willing to abdicate their primary rights in education and heedlessly assume
that this important function is the states' concern only.

These indictments brought by many thoughtful Americans
are not meant to imply that the public schools are solely, or
even mainly, responsible for the vast numbers of religious
illiterates who go forth from their portals each year, lacking
fundamental moral and religious principles to guide them in
their personal and social duties. Many other factors in our
society have contributed toward this unhappy situation, primarily remissness in the home. At the same time those
competent to judge have admitted that there is little evidence
that the public schools, as at present constituted, are to any
appreciable extent assisting the young toward an appreciation
of the meaning of religion or providing a solid basis for the development of moral character. The main responsibility rests
with the home, but obviously all too many homes are failing to
meet their responsibilities. Left with the question "Why?"
some concerned Americans are asking if the fact that the parents themselves have been victims of a secularized education
has contributed to this social disaster. Secularism in schools,

they reason, almost certainly breeds secularism in life.

We turn now to the second aspect of the state's educational policy. An impressive number of reliable authorities on constitutional law hold that the state's policy of withholding absolutely all public aid to religiously-oriented schools is actually an infringement of the religious freedom guaranteed by both the Federal and the state constitutions. It is also, the critics hold, a violation of distributive justice.

Their reasoning is as follows: The state compels parents through compulsory education laws to send their children to school. It recognizes the private schools as satisfactory for meeting the compulsory education requirements. But, then, as a sort of anti-climax, the educational policy of America, based upon state constitutional provisions and United States Supreme Court decisions, places upon parents who choose to exercise their parental and religious rights by sending their children to a religion-oriented school a severe economic penalty -- a double financial burden. They must pay for public schools, which they do not use, and for the religious school they desire for their children.

Catholic parents are cited as an example. They hold as a matter of religious conviction that moral training based on a solid foundation of doctrinal religion must constitute an integral element in the educational process. Their church-related schools, comparable in all secular aspects to the public schools, were educating in 1965 over six million children on the elementary and secondary levels. These religious-minded parents must build and maintain from their own resources the schools wherein their children are to obtain the kind of education they want for them -- an education that considers the whole child, his religious and moral development as well as his intellectual, social, physical, and civic needs. For their purpose the public schools, as at present constituted, are unsatisfactory. Yet, it is pointed out, Catholics must help maintain them through tax payments from which they receive no return.

The double burden, the reasoning continues, though willingly assumed in view of the sublime purpose served, is an onerous one. In practice it amounts to a penalty imposed upon

parents who are simply fulfilling a parental responsibility
arising from the natural law and exercising a legally guaranteed right to direct the education of their children in accordance
with religious convictions. Herein, the argument concludes,
lies an infringement of religious liberty because a guaranteed
liberty in this instance is exercised only at the price of a
penalty. To attach a penalty to the exercise of a freedom
would seem to limit it in fact, if not in theory.

True, many sincere Americans do not go along with this
reasoning. Yet a review of the literature on this admittedly
controversial issue reveals that no adequate answer has been
made to the argument. There is a tendency for opponents to
fall back on slogans: "separation principle"; "the wall";
"against state constitutions." But slogans, it is countered,
are not convincing arguments; they side-step logic. The
question to be faced squarely is: Do, or do not, the state
constitutions contravene basic rights?

Other opponents attempt rebuttal with statements such
as: If Catholics want their own schools they should pay for
them. Articulate Catholics and Protestants interested in
church-related schools reply that they do want their own
schools, but they hold that they, as tax-paying citizens,
should have turned back to them some part of their school
taxes to help support these schools, which are performing a
public service, as are the public schools.

The advocates of public support for church-related
schools push their argument further, showing that they are
also indirectly hindered in the legitimate expansion and development of their system of schools. New schools must be
built and old ones remodeled and enlarged to meet the needs
of an expanding school population. The movement to suburban
areas has affected patrons of parochial schools as well as public boards of education. Thousands more religious schools
are needed. They must be built and maintained at contemporary standards of efficiency. The financial burden involved is
often too great to be undertaken, especially since these same
citizens must also share the burden of financing vast programs
of public school expansion. Needed parochial schools remain
unprovided and those built are inadequate for the increasing

enrollments. Grades have to be lopped off, children, against their parents' deepest desires, must be sent to the public schools. This situation, the argument concludes, amounts to an implicit legal restraint upon parents, who, because of the double financial burden, are unable to provide the kind of education which their religious convictions demand for their children. Thus the procedure acts as a practical infringement on the exercise of both parental rights and religious liberty.

The argument further holds that our present educational policy violates distributive justice -- the obligation of the state to distribute its benefits without partiality. Unwittingly, a State Council of Churches, a Protestant organization, some time ago abetted the argument by exposing the fallacy of the policy. In a memorandum issued in Albany, 1959, the Council took the position that when a parent removes a child from the public school and places him in another "he renounces any further claim upon equal educational opportunity -- and with it, any further claim upon the tax money of the state for direct or 'fringe benefits' support" (emphasis added). The parent who sends his child to a religion-oriented school, on the other hand, maintains that in doing so he is simply exercising recognized rights -- parental and religious -- and continues to pay his taxes; that he makes no willing renunciation of his rights as a citizen to share in benefits from public taxes because of his exercise of other rights. He has simply been deprived of them, and he wonders on what logical basis he must lose his right to claim equal educational opportunity for his children or to share in other benefits procured through public taxes. Do Americans, he questions, lose rights by exercising rights? Is that Democracy? To fall back on the crutches, "separation," "the wall," "unconstitutional," he maintains, simply begs the question.

When POAU asks: "Should a Protestant have to pay for Catholic schools?", the parochial school user answers: "No, Mr. O'Brien does not ask for Mr. Archer's taxes to support his school; he merely asks that he receive a return from the taxes he pays to support the kind of school his religious convictions demand for his children."

The issue, of course, is not so simple. We are governed under laws and constitutions and the constitutionality of aid for church-related schools cannot be ignored. A considerable number of reputable authorities do hold that the First Amendment does not prohibit indirect aid to the cause of religion.[23] They point out that religion has always been aided indirectly by the federal government. The list of such aids is a long one. Among other items it includes: the payment of salaries for chaplains in Congress and in the armed services; the G. I. Bill of Rights, according to which the veterans used government-provided funds to pay tuition fees to church-related colleges and universities; the allotment of grants and low-interest loans under the National Defense Act to the same institutions; and finally, the Elementary and Secondary School Act of April 11, 1965, which permits denominational schools to receive indirect benefits. Both the federal government and the respective states have always indirectly aided the churches and religious organizations by exempting them in most cases from the payment of taxes. Indeed, instances of direct state aid to church-related schools were frequent throughout the nineteenth century.[24]

Today, however, the states' constitutional provisions, which, as we have seen, prohibit aid for sectarian purposes including aid to church-oriented schools, seem to be the crux of the issue. Many sincere Americans are of the opinion that in our highly pluralistic society no other policy could be adopted without the possibility of its engendering sectarian strife. But equally sincere Americans point out that there is another angle to the problem which has not received the attention it should. The real question in this matter, they hold, is not whether the states can indirectly aid religion, for actually they have always done that, but whether the states, under the First and Fourteenth Amendments, can indirectly penalize the exercise of recognized rights. Or, putting the question another way, may a state deprive its citizens of benefits accruing from taxes because they have exercised a right, in this case, chosen a religion-oriented school for their children? They admit a conflict of interest here: on the one hand, the possibility of indirectly aiding religion through aid to the religion-oriented

school; on the other hand, the possibility of jeopardizing fundamental human freedoms and impairing distributive justice
by the denial of such aid. This latter aspect of the issue has
never come before the courts for review but several legal
authorities and a considerable number of ordinary citizens
maintain that, as a fundamental aspect, it should be so reviewed.

The primary duty of the state, it is argued, is to safeguard the rights of its citizens -- not to deny them without
cause or render them difficult to exercise. Parents have from
nature the obligation and right to educate their children according to their conscience. The laws and courts have recognized
this right and guaranteed to protect it. Why then, the sponsor
of church-related schools asks, should a citizen who is loyal
to his religious convictions be deprived of his right to share
taxes when he sends his children to state-approved parochial
schools, which, as a matter of fact, predated the public
schools? The policy, he reasons, not only infringes on religious liberty but violates distributive justice, denying a citizen
his right to share in state benefits without a just cause.

It should be noted that efforts have been made and implemented to ameliorate the situation for church-related schools
by practices which seemingly fall short of the ban on aid,
direct or indirect. Such is the "shared-time" or "dual-enroll-
ment" plan in which pupils divide their time between the private
and the public school. The pupils of a Catholic high school,
for example, will attend classes in chemistry, physics, home
economics, industrial arts, and agriculture in a near-by public
high school, taking the rest of their courses in their own
school. The National Catholic Education Association in 1965
reported that 251 Catholic elementary schools and 182 Catholic
high schools had shared-time programs.[25]   About the same
time a National Education Association report stated that
"shared time is being watched with mixed emotions. Some
persons are optimistic and hopeful; others are cautious and
doubtful." [26]

Periodically the school issue in its aid aspect gets the focus of national attention. This occurs especially when the question of federal aid to general education comes before Congress, as it has off and on during the last forty years. The question elicited much attention during the 1963 session of Congress, when, at the recommendation of the late President Kennedy, efforts were made to provide huge sums of federal money for the construction of public school buildings and for the payment of teachers' salaries. Private and church-related schools were to be excluded from the benefits.

There were two sources of opposition to the bill. Passage of the measure would have marked the first instance of federal aid for general purposes to public elementary and secondary schools. The American tradition, backed by the Federal Constitution, has been to keep control of the sensitive area of education closer to the parents, that is, on the state and local levels. Experience has shown that the tendency in this country is for "control to follow funds." The one who pays the piper, calls the tunes. Accordingly, many Americans opposed the measure, fearing that with federal funds would come federal control, or at least more control than was desirable.

Other Americans objected to the measure in the form the President had proposed as a violation of distributive justice and held that it was inconsistent with the aims set forth by its advocates. Catholics led this opposition but a considerable number of other Americans recognized the justice of their claims. Many of these citizens also opposed the whole idea of federal aid to education for the reasons mentioned above. They argued that if federal aid was to be given, if it was really necessary for general educational purposes, then all the children of the nation should share in the benefits, especially since the President gave as the raison d'etre for the measure the need to raise educational standards and maintain them at a high level. If that was its aim, why, Catholics and others asked, overlook or discriminate against the fifteen percent of the school population who attend church-related schools? Such discrimination would nullify the objectives to be attained.

In addition, the sponsors of the church-related schools

called attention to the fact that they were already doubly taxed. The huge federal appropriation would call for higher federal taxes, unless one naively believed that the federal government plucked its money from trees. Higher federal taxes would add to the financial difficulties of religiously-minded citizens who were not using the public schools and would not therefore benefit from federal gratuities. Distributive justice would be further violated in their regard. The additional burden could easily cause a breakdown in the whole scheme of church-related education. Hundreds of thousands of Catholic children would be forced to seek admittance into the already crowded public schools. How then would these schools be benefited if they were forced to take on a vast number of additional pupils?

Although there was much discussion on the issue, no direct or logical answers were made to these arguments. The usual defense was to fall back on the slogans "unconstitutional," "opposed to separation principle." Yet highly recognized authorities on constitutional law saw no violation of the Federal Constitution in allowing parochial schools to share in federal gratuities in an indirect manner, such as was applied in the G. I. Bill of Rights. They pointed out that the main purpose of the First Amendment is to safeguard religious liberty, that the "no establishment" provision is a means, not a hindrance, to that end.

As a matter of fact, innumerable citations can be quoted from the statements and writings of competent authorities on the subject, all to the same effect: the First Amendment means just what it says. It is intended to protect individual freedom of religion and not to penalize it or put a price on it. The Amendment should not therefore be made the constitutional basis for the secularization of our culture. Wilber Katz is quoted as saying: "Separation ordinarily promotes religious freedom; it is defensible so long as it does, and only so long." [27]

The fact is that bills restricting federal aid to public elementary and secondary education have repeatedly failed to get the support of a majority in Congress, and the religious issue has been a factor, though not the only one, in the failure. This situation finally resulted in the passage, April 11, 1965, of a compromise measure which has been received by Catholic educational leaders with mixed emotions. The legislation has three main provisions:[28]

1) One billion dollars to public school districts under a formula based chiefly on the number of children in school who come from families earning less than $2,000 a year. The grant would cover half of the cost of education for each eligible pupil.

Parochial and other private school pupils in the same low income bracket would benefit by extension to them by local public school districts of shared services or facilities. Public school districts are required to take these children into account when making plans to aid needy students.

2) About $100 million would be provided to buy textbooks for pupils, materials, and volumes for school libraries and some instructional equipment. All would be owned by a public agency, such as the local school district or library, but they could be lent to children attending nonpublic schools.

3) Another $100 million would be used to establish educational centers to benefit both public and private school pupils with cultural enrichment programs and other special services. Public agencies would operate these centers, but the legislation requires that private school educators and others from outside the public schools take part in planning for them.

While Catholic authorities realized that the legislation provided very little financial help, quantitatively considered, for the hard-pressed Catholic schools, they felt that it established an important precedent. For the first time these schools were recognized as an integral part of the American educational system.

It would seem that one consideration to be drawn from the history of the whole federal aid issue as it relates to elementary and secondary education is that the time has come for Americans to lay aside outdated and emotionally based prejudices; to examine the issue on its own merits; to seriously endeavor to find a way to protect freedom of choice in education which, on the one hand, would conform to the "no establishment" clause, but just as certainly would avoid attaching a financial penalty to an exercise of the individual

right to freedom of religion. Walter Lippman asserts it is
surely "not beyond the wit of man" to resolve the religious
issue in Federal aid for church-related schools.[29]

Aside from its legal and constitutional aspects the educational issue may be approached from a broader, practical
viewpoint, weighing its implications for our traditional values
and the welfare of the nation. There are many thoughtful
Americans who are convinced that our educational policy in
regard to religious education in its two aspects runs counter
to solid American traditions, is undermining the religious
foundations on which our government was built, and to that
extent is jeopardizing the welfare and security of the nation.
We are a religious people, they maintain, whose institutions
suppose a Supreme Being. The United States Supreme Court
itself has made this declaration on several occasions.

History bears out the fact that Western culture, which
is our patrimony, is a product of the Christian centuries.
Faith in God and in the reality of eternity forms the foundation of
our democratic society. The Declaration of Independence,
our official documents, our courts of justice, our great statesmen have given expression to our dependence as a nation upon
God and to our urgent need of religious convictions and high
moral principles as the basis of our democratic way of life.
As a religious people, thoughtful Americans are saying, the
nation must view with apprehension any evidence of a drift
away from the spiritual ideals which have made it strong.
The men who projected the great experiment of government
by free men under God gained for us the liberty we now enjoy.
They cannot preserve it for us. It is up to each generation of
citizens to safeguard the foundations upon which American
democracy rests.

What is then to be done? Should religion be taught in the
public schools? If so, whose religion? How can religion in
the public schools or aid to church-related schools be fitted
into our constitutions and laws? Obviously, given the pluralism of religious beliefs in the United States, no one set of
doctrines could be taught to all. Moreover, it is not the function of the state to teach religion; that function belongs primarily to the home and church.

We face a dilemma, but not an insoluble one. The problem is to achieve cooperation between the state and religious
groups -- a problem admittedly complicated in the United
States by the very highly pluralistic character of our society.
The dilemma is how to reconcile government cooperation with
the principles of religious liberty set forth in the First Amendment, which, now applicable to the state, forbids an "establishment of religion." The right to worship in accordance
with the dictates of one's conscience -- or the right to disbe-
lief -- is our most cherished freedom. There must be no
plan or "cooperation" which would jeopardize religious freedom. But we have seen that our existing educational policy
does in practice, if not in theory, violate religious liberty and
impair distributive justice.

Our Western allies have faced the same issue. They
have worked out, or are in the process of working out, solutions which seem to give satisfaction to their people. They
are as devoted as we are to the cause of religious freedom.
Perhaps no one solution of these democracies fits our situation
or answers our needs. But in view of our dilemma it will be
worthwhile to look at each very closely.

Chapter 1

GREAT BRITAIN FINDS A WAY

Our relationships with Great Britain are friendly, mutually beneficial and long enduring. Her solution of the religion-education issue accordingly is of particular interest to us.

Like America, Great Britain wrestled with the problem for many years. After a century of temporizing attempts to reach a solution, predominantly Protestant England has arrived at an arrangement which both Anglican and Catholic churchmen and the people in general hail as coming close to the ideal. The issue in England was brought to a settlement by reasoned considerations of calm churchmen and practical statesmen wherein the principle of justice to all children of the nation weighted the balance. Remnants of old religious rivalries and intolerance proved too weak to obstruct the forward movement. Ironically, the England which three and a half centuries earlier had bequeathed to us the legacy of religious intolerance and dissension and which still retains an established church has gradually succeeded in drying up the well-springs of religious discord. In our own country, where it might be hoped complete tolerance would find its most secure refuge, the destructive forces of religious prejudice still retain strong roots and their most noisome progeny -- bigotry -- can still on occasion succeed in crippling the cause of justice.

England has kept the best of her old educational traditions. She has retained a rigid regard for fundamental parental rights, a recognition of the unique function of the churches in conducting schools, a thorough dislike for highly centralized and bureaucratic control along with a consistent policy of wide localized authority. There has been an unfailing acknowledgment of the important place which religious and moral instruction has in the educational process.

But England has also made adjustments which changing times demand. She has recognized the need for the state to supplement private educational effort by establishing a national system of education and has strengthened the system by setting up a Ministry of Education to be the central coordinating and planning authority. She has broken down the old class divisions of secondary schools for the classes only and elementary and vocational schools for the masses.

The British people saw no occasion for conflict between a national system of education and a strong system of private and church-controlled schools. On the contrary, they acknowledged that private initiative in education, besides being a legitimate and natural expression of liberty, was highly beneficial to the nation. They recognized the obligation on the part of the state to encourage and aid financially private and church efforts in the educational field while leaving the voluntary agencies free to carry on their work without inhibiting regulations or interference.

We find several common elements in the issue as it appears in our country today and as Great Britain came to grips with it in the nineteenth and twentieth centuries. In both countries a historical legacy of religious misunderstanding and prejudice amounting at times to bitterness and hatred tended to obscure the real issue. The two nations are equally committed to the principle of religious freedom and the sacredness of the individual conscience. England has gone far in achieving a solution to the question of church-state relationships in education. We still struggle with the issue.

This is not to suggest that America take up the British arrangement. There are basic constitutional differences in church-state relationships between the two countries and the multiplicity of religious sects in the United States aggravates the difficulty of reaching a solution. Undoubtedly, we must find an answer to the problem suited to our peculiar circumstances and consistent with our policy of separation of church and state. In the pursuit of this it would seem that an acquaintance with the British arrangement and the struggle involved in achieving it will not be devoid of interest to Americans and may, in fact, prove uniquely useful.

We and our British ally are the inheritors and bearers of the ideals of Western civilization which has its roots in the Judaeo-Roman-Christian tradition. Her solution can be best understood in its historical context.

History's Record: Vicissitudes and Progress

England has a proud record of schools and scholarly at-
tainments which goes back to the country's early history. As
elsewhere in Western Europe, the first schools were the creation of the Church and took their rise at the same time as the
introduction of Christianity into the island. The historian
Dent remarks that English education was born in the Church.[1]
By the thirteenth century a widely spread system of schools
from elementary to university was in existence. Practically
all education was under the jurisdiction of ecclesiastical authority. The authoritative and painstaking research of A. F.
Leach demonstrates that opportunities for elementary and
secondary education were fairly widespread and that all classes
had the opportunity to attend a secondary school.[2]   Respect
for the rights of parents in the choice of education for their
children likewise characterized English medieval education.
A decree of Parliament in 1406 A.D. declared that every parent, regardless of his situation in life, was free to send his
son or daughter to any school in the realm that pleased him.[3]

A point in English history came when the brilliant progress of the preceding centuries was halted. One historian
refers to the sixteenth century religious catastrophe as "a
colossal and ultimate blunder consequent upon many lesser
blunders."[4]   We confine our attention to the effects of the religious Revolt upon education. The vast system of schools
built up with assiduous care and sacrifice during a period of a
thousand years was swept away in the cataclysmic destruction
which followed the break of England with the Catholic Church.[5]
The monasteries were plundered, the monks expelled. The
monastic schools were closed. The Chantry Acts of Henry
VIII and Edward VI suppressed the chantries with their
schools. Confiscation of Church property and the exile or
imprisonment of religious priests practically abolished most
of the grammar schools.[6]

Harsh penal laws were enforced against Catholics who
remained steadfast in the faith of their fathers. They were
forbidden to conduct schools, to teach in schools, to send their
children to school, or to send their children abroad for educational purposes.

The Church of England took control of what was left of opportunities for learning. Although some secondary schools were refounded and a few new schools were opened, all historians agree that the losses of the Revolt were not made good for a long time.[7] Little attention was paid to elementary education. The historian Dent states that systematic provision for this level virtually ceased for a century and a half.[8] Penal restrictions against the education of Catholics and other dissenters remained in force for almost three centuries.

Gradually elementary education fell into the hands of private individuals who in character and attainment were often unfit for the task. The educational situation, especially among the poor, was intolerable. In the early part of the eighteenth century an extensive system of charity schools developed in London and elsewhere. They provided free education for the poor, managing at the same time to perpetuate religious strife and misunderstanding. Characteristic of the intolerance of the schools' sponsors is the remark of a Dr. White Kennet, who in a "charity sermon" asserted that the schools were directed not only against indifference in religion but also against Roman Catholicism. Every charity school, he maintained, was to be "a fortress and frontier garrison against popery."[9] Catholic schools throughout this period were practically non-existent. A number of secondary and higher institutions had been established on the continent to which courageous Catholics sent their sons.

At the beginning of the nineteenth century general educational conditions in England were intolerable. Two voluntary societies, one representing the Church of England, the other representing Protestant dissenters, conducted the only schools available for the poor. These were proving to be inadequate in quantity and inefficient in quality. Finally in 1833 the government reluctantly made the first allocation of public funds for elementary schools by a grant of 20,000 pounds to the two societies. In 1839 an additional 10,000 pounds was allotted, and thereafter the grant became an annual one. The tenets of the sponsoring denomination were taught in its schools.

The few existing Catholic schools did not share in these first financial allotments. In the meantime, the Catholic

Emancipation Act, 1829, had rescinded most of the penalties against Catholics. Though a legal and theoretical expression of toleration, the Act did not and could not destroy the long existing prejudice and hostility which lived on in the hearts and minds of Englishmen. Catholics were despised socially; their religion was scorned. The great majority of them were Irish poor who had immigrated to England during the preceding two centuries. The principle of schools providing an education based solidly on the Catholic view of life never ceased to be an ideal toward which they aspired. By dint of great courage and sacrifice they built schools wherever it was at all possible and every year after 1829 saw the establishment of new ones on every level from infant to secondary.

An influx of Irish immigration during the famine years, 1845 to 1848, greatly augmented the Catholic population. Catholic leaders in 1845 took a decisive step by bringing before Parliament the justice of allowing Catholic Poor Schools to share in school allotments. Their efforts produced minimal results. An Act passed in 1846 included Catholic schools in its operation by providing personal grants to teacher-pupils, that is, to apprentices between the ages of thirteen and eighteen.

The financial needs of the Catholic schools remained urgent, and Catholic leaders continued their efforts to obtain a more equitable share of the educational funds. An Act passed by Parliament in 1847 allowed Catholic schools to share in the educational allotments -- the first instance of direct state aid for Catholic schools in England. A milestone in the solution of the school issue had been reached. The Catholic Poor Committee, representing the Catholic Church, now paralleled the two Protestant church societies on educational questions of national interest.

With the restoration of the Catholic hierarchy in England in 1850 the smoldering embers of religious intolerance and bigotry were activated to full fury, but the calm dignity and fine statesmanship of Cardinal Wiseman in his reasoned appeal to the Englishman's sense of fair play did much to turn the tide. The turmoil slowly subsided and the Catholic school system continued to grow and prosper. In 1851 there were 311 Catholic schools in England.[10]   Nonetheless, the sacrifices of all combined were proving insufficient to meet the ever increasing needs. Many Catholic children were either not in school at all or were forced to attend the schools of the Protestant societies to the possible detriment of their faith.

It was becoming highly apparent that the general educational situation of the nation was badly in need of reform. All the educational facilities in the country were provided by the voluntary schools. These were founded and maintained by private funds obtained in a variety of ways, supplemented with only meager state subsidies. In 1858 a national committee was appointed to "study the state of education in England and to consider what measures, if any, are required for the extension of sound and cheap elementary instruction to all classes of people."

The committee made its report in 1861, disclosing some intolerable conditions. Educational reform was imperative. It came in the Forster Act, 1870, the principal objective of which was to provide schools throughout the country which would make it possible for all children to obtain at least a primary education.

The bill, as originally presented by the Rt. Honorable W. F. Forster, proposed that the country be divided into school districts with ad hoc school boards elected by the rate payers. The boards were to have power to levy a rate out of which, with the help of grants from the national government, the existing denominational schools were to be maintained and where necessary new schools were to be built. The new schools which the boards might build were to have religion taught in them according to the circumstances of the particular area. No financial discrimination on the grounds of religion was to be made. In order to maintain religious equality and freedom, yet preserve popular control and efficiency, Mr. Forster proposed undenominational inspectors and a conscience clause which allowed withdrawal from religious instruction if not desired and forbade discrimination against any religious group or against a pupil because of his religious persuasion. Thus the original proposals of Mr. Forster's bill contained the possibilities of a reasonable solution to the religion-in-education issue."

When the bill came up in Parliament it met fanatic opposition from the Nonconformists, who insisted that all the schools should be undenominational and that the existing denominational schools should pass under the control of the local authorities. They were unrelenting in their efforts to impose their own educational views on the whole country. Politics entered the issue. The Gladstone government feared the power of the Nonconformists and was ready to make a settlement with them. Mr. W. F. Cowper-Temple came forward with a compromise and eventually, after further political machinations on the part of the Nonconformists, a formula favoring their view became Section 14 of the Forster Act, 1870. It provided that "in schools supported from public rates, catechisms and formularies which are distinctive of particular denominations shall not be employed." This meant, simply, that no school at all, existing or future, should be subsidized by public funds if it taught denominational religion.[12]

The Act left England with two systems of elementary schools: one chiefly denominational, called the voluntary system; and a second, the public school system, which excluded all denominational religion. The patrons of the voluntary schools found themselves obliged not only to support their own schools but also to contribute to the maintenance of the board or rate-aided schools of the Nonconformists.

Contemporary dissatisfactions with the "undenominationalism" imposed upon the board schools was widely felt and expressed.[13] A current view appraises it thus:

History shows that 'Cowper-Temple-ism' has never been the real wish of this country at large; that it was not the genuine wish of the Government in power in 1870 until, as a result of political manoeuvres, by Dissenters, it was forced to change its mind in order to remain in power; that it was not Cowper-Temple's own idea of a solution of the political warfare; that it was simply and solely the Dissenters' idea parliamentarily imposed on the whole country by a small party in Parliament.[14]

The Cowper-Temple clause still determines religious policy in the county schools.

The historical facts show that the new policy inaugurated by the 1870 Act initiated an endless struggle between the state and the agencies of the voluntary system to retain their denominational tenets as opposed to the non-sectarianism in the board schools and to be given their equitable share in the local rates toward which their people had contributed.

Catholics began anew their struggle to maintain their schools. A share of local rates was denied them. Financed by grants earned by the pupils and paid to the managers, by tuition fees and voluntary contributions, the schools progressed steadily. By 1882 there were 1,562 under inspection.[15]   But the problem was always there: not enough schools; insufficient funds.

Repeated appeals were made by the voluntary agencies for their rightful share in the rates. The principal opposition always came from the Nonconformists who threatened to abolish the dual system and force all children into the board schools. As a matter of fact, many Church of England schools were losing heart in the struggle to maintain themselves. By 1895, twelve hundred of the Anglican voluntary schools had gone under the boards, sacrificing their denominational teaching for maintenance.

Modifications in the 1870 Act and alleviation for the voluntary schools came gradually. At the beginning of the new century, Mr. Balfour initiated a move in Parliament to remedy the injustices under which they suffered. The resulting Balfour Act of 1902 brought them substantial relief and made other modifications in the existing system. School boards were abolished. Their functions were transferred to Local Education Authorities, popularly referred to as the L.E.A.'s, who were to assist church schools from local rates. Rome, as a contemporary expressed it, was "put on the rates." The voluntary schools were to be maintained; that is, they were to be equipped, teachers' salaries paid, books provided, cleaning and interior decorating cared for out of local funds. But the cost of sites, building, and external repairs were still to be met by the voluntary agencies.

For Catholics this meant that the bulk of the total bill was taken care of from public funds. It represented the most favorable terms so far accorded them and results were soon forthcoming. The general condition and equipment of the Catholic schools were very much improved.

The voluntary schools, however, lost some of their independence in the transaction. While the Act continued the dual system, it put both the public schools and all the voluntary schools which received aid under the authority of the L.E.A.'s. All secular subjects were henceforth under the control of H.M.'s inspectors. Religious instruction was to be given only before or after school hours. Of the six school managers of each voluntary school, the Church was to nominate four and the L.E.A.'s two. Appointment and dismissal of teachers were to be in the hands of the managers but their professional qualifications were to be designated by the L.E.A.

Incomplete as was the justice accorded to the denominational schools by the Balfour Act, the Nonconformists raised a storm of protest against it. Their legislative efforts were directed toward complete government control of all church schools. Bills to effect this were introduced in Parliament in 1906, 1907, and 1908. All were defeated. Up to 1924 some twelve attempts were made to upset the Balfour Act. Gradually the conflict died down, and the traditional view that education in England must embrace a wide variety of opinion gained firm recognition.[16]

The Fisher Act of 1918 extended the school leaving age to fourteen and created the central school for upper elementary pupils. It left the relation of the government to voluntary schools unchanged. An Act in 1921 codified all operative school laws. The provisions of the 1902 Act providing funds for the maintenance of voluntary schools became Section 287 of the Code.

Rising costs after World War I made it increasingly difficult for Catholics to build new schools and improve existing ones. Yet these developments were imperative since the school leaving age had been raised to fifteen and the L.E.A.'s were permitted to grant a certificate to enter "beneficial employment" only after the child reached the age of fourteen.

Building standards had become higher and more exacting. It was the old dilemma: how to provide places in schools for all the children, in this instance, places on the upper elementary level, and how to meet the impossible costs of sites and buildings.

Certain provisions of an Act passed in 1936 were intended to alleviate this difficulty of the voluntary school managers. But to the provisions were attached questionable modifications in the state-voluntary school relationship. By the Act the L.E.A.'s were impowered, but not compelled, to grant from 50 to 75 percent of the cost of building or reorganizing Catholic or other voluntary senior schools (that is for children over eleven years), but not primary schools, where the need for new buildings was actually greatest. The price was considerable loss of independence for the schools accepting. The L.E.A.'s were henceforth to appoint the teachers in such "aided schools" except for certain "reserved teachers," one out of five, who should be of the religious denomination the school stood for. Moreover, in case of Catholic schools, there was to be non-Catholic religious instruction for those whose parents desired it. The schools accepting the terms were designated "special agreement schools." Out of 519 proposals put forward on these lines only 37 had been put into effect before the outbreak of World War II. Further implementation of the Act was then interrupted.

Reform Gets Underway

At the outbreak of World War II, the educational situation in Britain left much to be desired. It was at the height of the conflict that the country took its most revolutionary step toward educational reform in the famous Butler Act of 1944. Amendments were added in 1946 and 1948. The complete reorganization of education in England and Wales which the Act effected was concerned primarily with the non-religious aspects of education rather than with the specific issue of the church-state relationship, which is our immediate concern. However, this also underwent considerable modification. The nature and significance of these latter changes are best understood in the light of the whole program of reorganization.

Previous educational legislation in Britain had been directed toward a greater democratization of education; yet, through it all the two-tract system, discriminating between the classes and the masses, had been retained. Although surveys and reports at various times had pinpointed existing deficiencies in the system and offered possible solutions, it took the exigencies of war to bring into clear focus the fact that the country was being deprived of the full use of its human resources because much intellectual and technical potentiality was being "plowed under" by an outmoded educational system. Only a small percent of English youth, drawn largely from the upper class, had been completing grammar school; fewer still entered the universities.

Nothing but a complete reorganization of the whole system in a way that would provide every child with an opportunity to advance as far as his abilities permitted could rectify the deficiencies. War had presented the country with the final, irrefutable argument. How urgent the reform was felt to be is realized when one considers that it was planned and carried out in the fury of the Battle for Britain while bombs were crashing down upon England's cities and rural districts.

The bill embodying the changes aimed at several elements of reform considered to be fundamental. The central educational authority was to be strengthened, preserving at the same time local initiative. Leaving age was to be raised to fifteen as a condition of effective secondary education, which was to become a continuation of primary education. Appropriate types of secondary education, free to all youth and adapted to differing degrees of ability, were to be provided. Opportunity for "further education" for working youth was to be supplied. In these changes, voluntary and independent schools were to be preserved "in so far as they could be made effective."[17]

The people were aroused in a variety of ways to an appreciation of the need for reform and were informed of the means to be taken to achieve it. Series of surveys and reports, information disseminated through newspapers, professional discussions, meetings and lectures were all utilized. On the general objectives of the reform no great opposition or difficulties were met as the bill progressed through Parliament. But on the questions relating to voluntary schools and religious instruction in public schools pronounced differences in viewpoints were encountered.

Mr. R. A. Butler, president of the Board of Education and author of the bill, was aware of the variety of opinions that the provisions of the bill would need to satisfy. There were three interested groups. The Church of England was divided. One section demanded the continuation of denominational, voluntary schools with complete public support. An increasing number, representing both the Anglican hierarchy and the laity, seemed satisfied with the non-denominational instruction given in the county schools. The Free Churches, or Nonconformists, were firmly and volubly for the abolition of voluntary schools and the retention of undenominational religion in all schools. There was a coalition of segments from the National Union of Teachers, the Trade Union Congress, and the Workers' Educational Association which favored abolition of the voluntary schools.[18]

The Catholic body, unchanging in its view of the fundamental purpose of education, stood firmly for the preservation and extension of the voluntary schools. Resting on the principles of the natural law, the Catholic claim was twofold: first, that the parent has a right to have his child educated according to the sacred demands of his conscience -- a right no power on earth can validly withhold; and, secondly, that the exercise of this right to follow his conscience should not cost one parent more than another.[19]

The Catholic hierarchy had formulated these traditional educational principles in a Joint Pastoral, June, 1942, which stated: "Religious education, to meet the wishes of the parents, should be available to all school children, and on such conditions that the general education of the child shall not suffer in any way from its parents' insistence on religious education."[20] Indeed, Catholics were asking: Do not, in fact, these principles constitute the essential criteria of religious freedom? A century earlier all denominations relied on them and insisted upon their implementation. But in 1944 Catholics found themselves almost alone in maintaining that the principles of the natural law should be the basis of any solution for the school issue.

As a settlement of the problem the Catholic hierarchy favored an arrangement along the lines of the Scottish system, provided that the same safeguards for the religious character of the schools were granted as had been granted to the Scottish Catholics.[21] In particular terms the Catholic position was stated in the formula: "Catholic schools for Catholic children with Catholic teachers." In 1870 the formula went on to add "and under Catholic control." These last four words were dropped in 1944 since the precedent of Scotland in 1918 had shown that it was possible to have truly Catholic schools even though they were administered by public educational authorities.

The Board of Education under Mr. Butler had looked into the Scottish system in anticipation that Catholics might ask for it as a solution for England. The members decided against it on grounds both historical and administrative. England, they stated, had a tradition since 1870 of banning denominational religion in public schools; Scotland, on the contrary, had been traditionally denominational. Moreover, denominational schools in England were too numerous to make the Scottish system workable. Mr. Butler was adamant in his stand that the Scottish "Concordat" was out of the question as a settlement for England, declaring that the "solution must take different lines here and cannot ignore the principles embodied in the Cowper-Temple clause of the 1870 Act."[22] He proceeded to go on with his own plan and to explore estimates of costs for Catholics under its operation.

Mr. Butler's plan was incorporated into the education bill that was presented to Parliament. The bill offered the voluntary schools one of three possible settlements. First, negotiations begun under the 1936 Act could be reopened and if completed such schools would be known as "special agreement schools." Only schools which had begun negotiations before the War, however, were eligible under this plan.

A second possibility existed where the managers of a voluntary school were unable to pay half the cost of alterations and improvements in order to bring facilities to required standards. In such a case, the local government was authorized to

assume the entire financial obligation and the control of the
school passed to the L.E.A. The educational authorities were
impowered to appoint two-thirds of the school's board of managers and to pass on the appointment of teachers with the exception that one out of five, the head-teacher excluded, could be
"reserved," that is, must belong to the denomination concerned.
The L.E.A. might also dismiss teachers. Non-denominational
religion according to an agreed syllabus was to be provided for
those who desired it. Denominational religious instruction was
allowed but for not more than two periods a week. These
schools would be known as "voluntary controlled."

Obviously, this plan involved practically complete loss of
independence on the part of the denominational school which
elected it. For Catholics it gave no guarantee that their
schools, submitting to the conditions, could retain that Catholic
character essential for the achievement of their primary purpose. This arrangement was, therefore, completely unacceptable to Catholics.

A third possibility existed where the managers were able
and willing to pay in full for sites and building of new schools
and to meet half the cost of necessary alterations and improvements on existing schools. The state would then supply the
other half and pay maintenance costs, including teachers' salaries. The school would retain its denominational independence, with the L.E.A. appointing only one-third of the school
managers. Schools electing this arrangement would be known
as "voluntary aided." Independent schools, those receiving
no public aid, were allowed to continue as hitherto without interference.

Only a limited number of Catholic schools were eligible
for "special agreement" status; the second plan was, as has
been noted, completely unsatisfactory; Catholics concentrated
on securing concessions within the framework of "voluntary
aided." They made efforts to obtain grants of three-quarters
of reorganization costs (instead of half) and, in view of already
soaring building charges, asked for a "ceiling" on costs, that
is, any difference between an established post-war cost and
later increases should be paid by the Treasury or by means of
interest-free loans. These pleas were rejected, but during

the course of the Parliamentary debates loans were permitted
to the bishops at four and a half percent and redemption
charges, which were estimated at 430,000 pounds per year.

The Butler bill passed Parliament and on August 3, 1944,
received Royal Assent, and thus became the law of the land.

The Butler Act, 1944

The Act was comprehensive in its scope, providing for
a complete reorganization of the British educational system.[23]
Greater simplicity and unity of administration were secured
by substituting a Ministry of Education with its head having a
seat in the Cabinet in place of the old Board of Education. At
the same time variety and freedom, traditionally so characteristic of English education, were retained.

The new legislation set out to give every child and youth
in the country an education suited to his individual abilities
and aptitudes, irrespective of social or economic position.
The old two-tract concept was replaced by a continuous system
of education in three progressive stages; primary, secondary,
and further. All post-primary schools (beginning around age
eleven plus) were to be called secondary schools, a term formerly reserved for the grammar school. Secondary schools
were organized to suit the aptitudes of three types of students.
There were grammar schools with an academically slanted
curriculum leading toward university work; secondary technical schools for pupils with aptitudes for mechanical and
technical work; and modern secondary schools (ages eleven
plus to sixteen) for those of average ability and for those who
intended to enter practical or vocational work. For all types
of primary and secondary schools maintained by the L.E.A.'s,
fees were abolished. Examinations and other records at
eleven plus were to determine what type of secondary school
each child would attend. Attendance was made compulsory
from the age of five to fifteen, and as soon as possible to sixteen. Further education included all part-time and full-time
education above the secondary level. The Act reaffirmed the
provisions of part-time schools up to age eighteen. It extended
the social services to be provided by the L.E.A.'s.

In the area of religious instruction the Act contained some

new and unique features. A daily corporate act of worship
was made obligatory in all maintained schools, that is, in all
county and all voluntary schools, "controlled" or "aided."
Moreover, in these schools daily religious instruction was
likewise compulsory. The religious instruction in county and
voluntary controlled schools was to be undenominational according to an agreed syllabus. However, in the controlled
denominational schools, denominational instruction was allowed
but not for more than two periods weekly, before or after
school hours. The traditional conscience clause, dating back
to 1870, remained in force, permitting parents who so wished
to withdraw their children from the act of worship and from
religious instruction. Teachers, likewise, might refuse to
attend religious worship or to give religious instruction.
Their attitudes on this could be considered when appointments
were made.

The Act continued the provision of 1902 by which voluntary schools were maintained up to approximately 90 percent
of total costs. Mr. Butler's three plans which set forth the
conditions imposed upon the denominational schools for receiving full or partial public payments for building and reorganizing costs have been described. His ideas had been incorporated into the Act almost unchanged.

From the Free Churches (Nonconformist) there arose
no great cries of dissatisfaction over the Act. True, they had
not succeeded in obtaining the liquidation of the voluntary
schools, but they still had their undenominational religious
instruction in both the county and in the voluntary controlled
schools. The Anglicans, after the Act was passed as during
the parliamentary discussion on it, remained divided in their
attitudes. Many seemed ready to accept controlled status,
being willing to sacrifice their denominational teaching for
complete support. The Archbishop of Canterbury welcomed
the arrangement. The agreed syllabus, definitely Protestant
in tone, could be made use of by competent and zealous Anglican teachers. But other Anglicans opposed the Act vigorously,
holding out for distinctly denominational schools and protesting
the financial discrimination against them.

Catholics, as a body, were dissatisfied. Their unchanging principles demanded both the continuation of their schools and a sufficient independence of control that would guarantee their distinctly religious character. For this reason Catholics were bound to be the group to suffer most from the discriminatory provisions of the Act. The bishops had protested to the end against the intolerable financial burden which they foresaw would have to be met. "We wish to make it clear," they declared, "that we have never accepted, do not now, and never shall accept the bill as it now stands." Their demands and argument were always the same: justice and true religious liberty required that Catholic children have the opportunity to attend, on terms of equality with other children, properly constituted and properly staffed schools to which their parents could send them with a clear conscience.

As it stood, the Butler Act presented Catholics with a dilemma. On the one hand, they faced the loss of independence through a school's inability to pay half the reorganization costs. On the other hand, there was the actual financial outlay involved if the schools were to continue in existence and maintain their integral character as Catholic schools. True, the public authorities were to continue to pay approximately ninety percent of maintenance costs, no small subsidy, but looked at closely the financial outlay left to be defrayed by the voluntary schools was frightening.

One-sixth of the Catholic schools had been destroyed by bombs; a large percentage had been partially wrecked. The new regulations made many other schools outmoded. Catholics would have to pay the entire cost of sites and buildings for the many new schools that were needed. They would have to pay half the cost of modifying the existing maintained schools, half the cost of rebuilding on new sites, half the cost of substituted schools, half the cost of accommodating displaced pupils, from a quarter to half the cost of special agreement schools under the 1936 Act. These demands were to be met at rapidly rising post-war prices for land, materials, and labor.[24] On top of all this, Catholics were paying their share of taxes to pay for the reorganization of the county and controlled voluntary schools, which in conscience they could not use. This was the other horn of the dilemma.

Catholics were, as a whole, in the lowest economic group, a fact which made the financial burden more grievous. Vast sums were to be raised by this poor minority all because they wished to exercise a natural right and meet a religious obligation. In other words, the autonomy needed by Catholic schools to preserve their essential Catholic character had to be purchased at a crushing price.

The government's own estimate of the outlay was based on an all-round increase of thirty-five percent over 1939 costs, amounting to ten million pounds in the next twenty-five years. Catholic leaders emphasized that this calculation was unsound, a prediction which was verified by increases beyond even their gravest fears. Various additional factors entered later into the situation which were not at the time clearly foreseen, but unimaginable rises in building costs continued to be the chief source of concern. In 1945 building costs were forty percent over the 1939 level; by 1948 the increase was put at twofold.

Time also entered as an element in the problem. New regulations demanded that Catholic managers submit to the Ministry a form known as <u>Form 18</u> showing that they were able to pay their share of the expenses of building and reorganizing the schools. Unless the application was made in time the Catholic schools were to be taken over by the L.E.A.'s, built, and given "controlled" status, which meant, practically, that they were lost to the Catholic body.

By 1949 the Catholic bishops were convinced that measures must be taken to ease the unsupportable burden of Catholic parents if the schools were to be saved. In an official statement <u>Ad Clerum</u> issued in June of that year, they pointed out that because of rising building costs and the added financial burden imposed by higher standards of construction which the Ministry had enforced, the Catholic outlay was likely to reach one hundred sixty million pounds. They asked that Parliament in its next session amend the Act to provide a ceiling, that is, a fixed cost agreeable to Catholics beyond which the public authorities would be responsible. They petitioned for emergency help in the meantime.

Then in October, 1949, the bishops proposed a permanent settlement of the whole school question. The dilemma facing them was such that some kind of permanent agreement seemed the only reasonable procedure. Time was running out. Form 18 forced them to decide then and there how far they could pledge themselves to raise the fifty percent cost of reorganization which was demanded for each school to secure for it "aided" and to avoid "controlled" status. Moreover, it was judged that public opinion would be more likely to accept the claim for increased financial assistance if it were presented in the context of a permanent settlement involving mutual compromise.[25]

The settlement proposed was to lease the Catholic schools to the L.E.A.'s, the leasing being optional upon the managers. The rent would be a nominal sum, except where there was a debt outstanding on the school. In such a case, the sum should be large enough to cover interest and redemption charges thereon; and if it were a new school, the rent paid by the L.E.A. should be of sufficient amount to offset the managers' liability. In all leased schools the L.E.A.'s would control the secular instruction and would appoint teachers, but those appointed would have to satisfy the religious authorities as to character and religious fitness.

An election was forthcoming. The Catholic body set to work with determination to obtain a hearing in the next meeting of Parliament. Candidates of all parties found themselves interviewed by delegates of Catholic organizations, who questioned them closely as to their position on the school issue and the proposed settlement. The interview technique was reinforced by an informative leaflet campaign and by countless meetings held before enthusiastic audiences all over the country.

The general attitude of government officials toward the denominational schools had never been unfriendly, much less hostile, either during the discussions on the Butler bill or during the years after its passage. On the contrary, the voluntary schools in England consistently had been accorded an honorable and esteemed place in the total educational system. Now, as the crisis facing the Catholic schools claimed the attention of the government officials, the latters' attitude remained friendly, appreciative, and sympathetic, but they seemed unable to accept the Catholic position.

Mr. George Tomlinson, then Minister of Education, expressed his views in a letter, June, 1949, stating that in his opinion "no new settlement which could be negotiated would be as favorable to denominational interests as that of 1944." At the same time he left no doubt as to his own views on the value of the Catholic schools. In an address at the opening of a Catholic school he declared that "Catholics can rest assured that the Government will respect their rights. Schools like this are the only antidote to many problems facing us in the world today."[26]

On the proposal of the bishops for a permanent settlement, the Minister insisted that redress must come within the terms of the Act. He issued a memorandum on the hierarchy's statement in which he declared that he was opposed to reopening the question of denominational schools in general and to the solution suggested by the bishops in particular. He maintained that their demand for additional financial aid would destroy the basis on which the provisions of the 1944 Act had been made acceptable to the varied interests involved. He indicated that he and other Parliamentary leaders were willing within the framework of the Act to work for adjustments to ease the financial burden of Catholics in preserving their schools. To change the Act, he felt, would run the risk of arousing sectarian strife.

When Parliament convened in 1950 both the main parties, Labor and Conservative, leaning on the Minister's memorandum, officially rejected the bishops' proposals. They argued that the figure of 160 million pounds was an exaggeration and that the amount of help forthcoming for "special agreement" schools had been underestimated. In short the earnest efforts of Catholics had failed to achieve the desired alleviation.

It was felt, nevertheless, that much good had come out of the campaign in that the needs of Catholics had become better known and a more tolerant climate of opinion had developed as a result of the person to person interviews. Through the questions put to them many of the candidates for the first time gained an understanding of the issue at stake in the school question and became aware of the strength of Catholic feeling in the matter.

Education Act, 1953

Obviously the matter could not rest. Their principles unchanged, the needs of Catholics remained absolute and urgent. The bishops decided their case must be heard again and immediately. In October, 1951, they published a statement reiterating the Catholic point of view. [27]

The bishops decided not to press at this time for a permanent settlement of the school issue but to concentrate on one aspect, namely, to secure that Catholic schools did not lose grant aid for what were known as "displaced pupils." The problem was related to movements of population as a result of which many pupils who had been in areas where Catholic schools were already established were now in more or less larger numbers living in places where no Catholic school existed. The 1944 Act had provided grants for such circumstances, but changes in interpretation had been made in the definition of such pupils with the result that Catholic schools were being deprived of aid which had been expected under the Act.

The issue gave rise to considerable controversy. Negotiations and discussions took place between the bishops and the Minister of Education during the years of 1950 to 1953. Catholics were urged to interview candidates prior to the 1951 election for the purpose of getting them to understand the Catholic point of view on the matter. In regard to such interviewing, the Bishop of Brentwood had emphasized that "it must be done in a friendly and helpful spirit, objectively for the purpose of giving information and without contention." He reminded the people that some of their most active support had come from non-Catholic members of the House of Commons who had been persuaded of the justice of the Catholic claims.

All the principal political parties evinced sympathy and interest in the matter and promised an amendment that would bring redress. The Conservative Party, for example, published a statement of policy in October which declared:

The voluntary schools, through the inspiration of
their teaching, give something vital to our national

character and have a great and essential part to
play in education. The Conservative Party has
always striven to keep them outside and above
politics. . . When returned to power, a Conservative Government will go forward, as they
have already promised, with the negotiations
necessary to adjust the present difficulties in a
way that will be of lasting benefit to the Voluntary
schools.

Likewise the Labor Party, then in power, and the Liberal Party published statements indicating favorable attitudes toward
the demands of Catholics.

The general election was held on October 25, 1951, resulting in the defeat of the Labor Government and a victory
for the Conservative Party and associates. After prolonged
negotiations centering on the question whether the amendment
relative to displaced pupils should be retroactive or not, an
education bill was drawn up. It was given its second reading
in the House of Commons, December 8, 1952. Four of its
clauses were designed to assist the voluntary schools.
Clause I extended the definition of "displaced pupils" in a
manner favorable to the Catholic demands, but its specific
use of the term "proposed schools" ruled out retroaction.
Further discussion followed. The Minister of Education opposed retroaction. In the end an amendment was carried
against the Minister by a vote of 26 to 18. The bill was
passed in June and Royal Assent was given on July 14, 1953.[28]

According to a report in the Commons in February,
1955, the grants paid for Catholic "displaced pupils" between
1952 and 1955 amounted to 687,241 pounds.[29]   Several minor
relaxations were provided Catholic schools by Parliament or
by the action of the Minister of Education in the years following 1953. On occasion attention was called to the financial
burden carried by Catholics to preserve their school system.

Education Act, 1959
The negotiations culminating in the 1953 Act brought
alleviation from those immediate difficulties relating to dis-

placed pupils. The Catholic hierarchy, however, pointed out
on several occasions that their proposals on that matter had
not touched "the main burden to be bourne by the Catholic
community in providing the schools to which Catholic parents
can with a good conscience send their children." They emphasized repeatedly their determination "to press for a just,
full, and permanent settlement to the Catholic school question." The 1953 Act fell far short of reaching that goal. The
main burden of raising millions of pounds each year to keep
up with the absolutely necessary building demands remained
unsolved.

Catholic leaders therefore deemed it imperative that
negotiations with government officials go on and that efforts
to inform the members of Parliament, candidates for office,
and the public be continued. The case for the Catholic schools
was a strong one. With a knowledge of the true facts, it was
felt, in most instances would come conviction. The 1950
elections campaign had proved the usefulness of that procedure.[30]

The financial crisis and credit restrictions which affected
the whole country in the winter of 1957-1958 greatly increased
the anxiety of Catholic leaders. Interest rates on loans had
been raised to seven percent. In concrete terms that meant
that 1,000 pounds borrowed today would amount to an ultimate
payment of 2,430 pounds over a period of thirty years. A
point was nearing where the Catholic body could not carry the
crushing burden.

On March 5, 1957, Right Reverend Andrew Beck, Bishop
of Salford, met with the Minister of Education and raised with
him the double questions of immediate relief to continue the
building program on the charts and a possible long-term settlement of the whole school issue. For the first problem the
Minister was confident that loans under the Education Act of
1944 could be obtained. On the long-term settlement, the
Bishop had suggested that an adaptation of the arrangement for
"special agreement" schools should be extended to all types
of voluntary schools, the voluntary body contributing 25 percent of the cost, while 75 percent would be contributed either
through the L.E.A. or directly by the Ministry of Education.

On this suggestion as a final settlement the Minister was highly doubtful.

These proposals, nevertheless, were incorporated by the bishops in a Memorandum, which was sent to the Minister, March 7, 1957. Steps were then taken throughout the country to organize interviewing committees in the constituencies to explain to the members of Parliament the local difficulties and financial obligations with which Catholics were faced and to inform them that the Catholic authorities were considering proposals for a 75 percent grant which would be put forward as a practical solution to the problems of the voluntary schools. The hierarchy's suggestions reached a wider public in an article in The Times Educational Supplement for July 5, 1957.

A speech delivered in October by the Cardinal Archbishop of Westminster expressed the fears and hopes of the Catholic clergy and laity at the time. "We continue to hope," he stated, "that the gap in inequality may soon be removed. In the last ten years Catholics have already paid 14 million pounds beyond their rates and taxes. . . . If it is not intended to give us full equality at present owing to the financial difficulties of the country, we would be happy if we could be given a flat rate of 75 percent grant for our schools as a further installment toward that complete equality which is denied us." He explained that the situation was so serious that although the hierarchy was adverse to making the question a matter of politics every effort would be made to give the members of Parliament full and exact information. With a knowledge of the facts, he contended, it was hard to believe anyone with a true sense of what is right could fail to see the justice of the proposals.

There was a considerable body of opinion in the Church of England that went along with the Catholic hierarchy's proposals. Bishop Beck met with the Anglican Bishop of Peterborough who expressed concern that many Anglican schools would be forced to become controlled.

The Minister of Education remained friendly and sympathetic but hesitated to promise a successful outcome. He seemed to attach much importance to the opposing Nonconformist views and the necessity of adhering to the "1944 settlement." The logical tactic, it then seemed, was to continue efforts to disseminate the facts relative to the crisis facing voluntary schools so that a public opinion of sufficient strength to guarantee a favorable reaction would be assured. Discussions, meetings, interviews with members of the Cabinet, with members of Parliament, with teachers' organizations, with ordinary people were carried on continuously by various representatives of the Catholic body. Pamphlets and leaflets buttressed the personal contacts.

An important step forward in the negotiations was taken in February, 1958, when a meeting of the Education Committee of the Conservative Party (then in control) was called to hear the case for the voluntary schools. A Catholic and an Anglican bishop presented to the members of the Committee the problems of their respective schools and their suggestions for a solution. Bishop Beck, representing the Catholic body, pointed out that, aside from the question of justice, the government was due to gain financially by an increased grant, for, if help were not given, current building plans would break down and the whole cost would fall on the Exchequer.

The Bishop of Peterborough presented the Anglican case for increased grants. The Anglicans, he contended, could not provide more than 13 million of the 17 million pounds required for their building program. Controlled status in his opinion was not the answer to the Anglican problem. He doubted whether many of the controlled schools would survive as noticeable Christian schools in twenty years' time if they did not "have the stiffening which a proportion of aided schools would give them."

A similar meeting took place with the Labour Party Education Committee. Bishop Beck, who again represented the Catholic position, argued along the lines presented earlier to the majority party. The Labour members evinced interest and sympathy.

Efforts were made in all these manipulations to keep the issue from becoming a party political issue. Bishop Beck, however, had warned that reluctant as they were, the members of the Catholic hierarchy might feel compelled to allow the question of Catholic schools to become a matter of politics, especially as they were disturbed that so much weight seemed

to be given to the negative Nonconformist opinion on the issue
of denominational schools. If justice were not done, he contended, the Catholic body was prepared to use all legitimate
means to insure that "their point of view was understood and
considered and accepted."

As a result of these preliminary discussions, an increase
of grant, possibly up to 75 percent, seemed highly probable
for the reorganization part of the building program, but any
grant for new schools still remained doubtful. Yet it was imperative that assistance for new schools be forthcoming. An
increase in the birthrate and the movements of population to
suburbs necessitated building on a scale unforeseen in 1944.
Since the war the number of pupils in Catholic maintained
schools had increased by 100,000. The problem was particularly acute in regard to new grammar and technical schools.
Moreover, in the many new housing areas, crises were immi-
nent since if Catholics failed to hold sites and build schools
they would not get the opportunity in the future of taking up the
projects. Anxiety was increasing, but through it all courage
and determination were never lacking.

Meanwhile there was some evidence that Nonconformist
opposition was lessening. A survey concerning Nonconformist
opinion among the rank and file of Free Churchmen showed
that on the whole the lay element would not be opposed to the
Catholic proposals. Reports suggested that a large number
of Nonconformist lay folk were unaware of the problems and
when it was put to them they showed considerable sympathy.
As to clerical reaction, there was no unanimity, but sufficient
evidence existed to indicate that there would be considerable
opposition from that source. Nevertheless, it represented a
small minority view and many voluntary school proponents
were inclined to think that when the politicians and House
members spoke of "considerable Nonconformist opposition"
they were taking political shelter.

The more serious secular press gave consistent support
to the Catholic cause. On May 6, 1959, an editorial in the
Yorkshire Post expressed the view that "the Church Schools
have earned the right to be given generous help while retaining
their distinctive character. . . The country needs more, not

less, of the kind of provision for which the advocates of church schools are prepared to work and sacrifice."

Definite results from the prolonged efforts were at length forthcoming. In March the Minister met with the Hierarchy's deputation and placed before it a compromise proposal which he had been authorized to make by his colleagues in the government. The propositions fell short of what had been asked but, nevertheless, marked a big step forward in easing the financial burden which the Catholic body had been shouldering. The proposal offered:

(1) To raise the rate of grant on projects eligible as the law then stood from 50 percent to 75 percent;

(2) To give 75 percent grant on new aided secondary schools needed to match voluntary aided primary schools of the same denomination that existed at the time, or schools to replace them.

The compromise which was offered left the entire cost of new primary schools and new secondary schools, not "matching" or "completing" an existing primary school to be paid for by the Catholic body, besides the 25 percent of reorganization costs for the other categories. The hierarchy's request had been for a flat 75 percent grant on all voluntary school building. There was some disappointment, but the offer was accepted as being the best obtainable at the time.

A bill embodying the proposals was introduced into Parliament June 11, 1959. Preliminary discussion had insured that there would be no political opposition. The bill did actually receive a remarkably friendly welcome in the House of Commons. In general the climate of opinion throughout the country was favorable and press comment almost everywhere supported the Minister's action.

As had been expected official Nonconformist reaction was generally critical, even hostile. One publication wrote of the bill as a "betrayal of our Protestant inheritance in the face of unwarranted clamour from a Roman Catholic minority." Another article in the same paper threatened that if the bill passed "then Free Churchmen will do all in their power to defeat the Tory Party at the election."

The debate on the bill following its introduction and second reading in the House was remarkable for the tolerant and
sympathetic attitude manifested by practically all speakers.
The denominational issue was scarcely referred to; in all the
debates the emphases were on fairness to the child and the
benefits of the measure for the nation. In introducing the bill
in the House of Commons the Minister, Mr. Geoffrey Lloyd,
pointed out that "the Government's object is to enable the intentions of the Act of 1944 to be fulfilled in the altered circumstances of today and thereby to en ure that the children in
aided schools have as good facilities for education as those in
county and controlled schools." [31]

The response of Mr. Clement Davies is fairly typical of
the opinions that were freely expressed:

> The principle of the dual system was accepted by
> us all in 1944 and it would be wrong if, at this stage,
> we failed in making the administration and even the
> intention of that Act incapable of fulfillment. Un-
> doubtedly there have been very great changes in the
> way of increased costs, increasing population, and
> of course, the still greater one in the scope of edu-
> cation and, therefore it is right that provision
> should be made to meet that increased cost and
> these increased difficulties. The paramount ques-
> tion, without a doubt, is the welfare of the child
> and his future, which depends upon his education. [32]

Approaching the issue from the angle of parental rights,
Mr. Gilbert Longden reached the same conclusion. He referred to the fact that the 1944 Act provided, as a general
principle, that all children should be educated in accordance
with the wishes of their parents: "If that is so," he reasoned, "we must face the fact many parents, and not by any
means only Roman Catholic parents, prefer that kind of
Christian teaching which they have begun to give to their children in the home should be continued in the school. . .
There are more parents for whom the agreed syllabus is just

not good enough." He maintained that parents should be able
to have their wishes in the matter fulfilled and that to achieve
this the 50 percent grant was not enough.[33]

In an appeal to the opposing Free Churches, Dr. Horan
King stated:

> Britain has learned to separate religion from politics
> more so than any other country in the world. That
> separation has been good both for religion and for
> politics. . . . There are all creeds on both sides
> of the House and in all political parties. To spark
> off old and deeply felt religious points of view and
> make party politics out of them would do harm to
> politics and education and to religion itself. To say
> this is not what the Free Churches in their letter
> unkindly thought-- that this is political expediency.
> It is a recognition by both sides of the House that
> the dual system is the law, and that it ought to work
> justly and efficiently. If it is creaking in any way,
> if it is imposing burdens which impair educational
> advance, unless we are prepared to scrap the law,
> we have to play honestly by the dual system and give
> all children outside State schools the chance of
> equal opportunities with those inside. I ask my
> fellow Nonconformists to accept the bill in the
> spirit in which it is proposed.[34]

In the second reading of the bill in the Upper House,
Lord Hailsham explained that in his view it was essential in
relation to the measure to reconcile four major principles:
the right of the parents, the interest of the state, the interests
of the teachers, and the welfare of the children. The proposal
would, he said, "avoid the danger of putting the children too
low in the scale of importance."

In the course of the debate several adverse statements
were made by members speaking in behalf of the Nonconformist viewpoint, but as a whole the passage of the bill through
both Houses of Parliament took place without serious contention and without division. The Act received Royal Assent

July 29, 1959.

The statute gave substantial financial relief to the hard-
pressed Catholics and they were grateful for the good will
shown by the large numbers of non-Catholics both inside and
outside Parliament. The Act, like the original bill, left unchanged the obligation of the managers of aided schools to pay
in full for new primary schools, many of which were badly
needed, and to pay for the new secondary schools to develop
from them. The Times of June 12th, 1959, noted this point and
suggested that since the situation would remain unsatisfactory
until this deficiency was remedied it could be expected that
Catholics would seek further legislation on the matter.[35]   The
Times' statement expressed accurately the viewpoint of Catholic leaders. Nowhere among the Catholic community was the
arrangement acknowledged or accepted as a final statement.
The bishops still maintained that in justice the whole cost of
Catholic school buildings should come out of public funds as did
the whole cost of the rest of the school system. In any case,
Britain had taken another step on the long and arduous path toward the goal of complete freedom of the religious conscience
and of equity for all her children.

The trend toward liberalization was to continue. In April,
1966, the government's share of the cost of building new schools
was raised to 80 percent. Grants for making improvements in
existing schools were also increased. The remarkable aspect
of these latest developments in the aid issue was the fact that
they were due to the united efforts of all three religious groups,
reflecting therefore, a new interfaith harmony in Britain.

British System in Operation

The county schools comprise the public school system,
strictly speaking, and include somewhat over half the total
number of schools in England and Wales. They are built,
maintained, and controlled by the L.E.A.'s and give nonsec-
tarian religious instruction. The voluntary schools are those
which are provided, that is, owned by voluntary bodies -- a
church, a diocese, a religious order -- and give religious
instruction according to the tenets of the providing church.
The secular instruction given in both county and voluntary

schools is supervised by the L.E.A. The voluntary schools are again classified as voluntary controlled and voluntary aided, depending on the amount of public aid received and a corresponding degree of control exercised by the L.E.A. Distinct classifications are given to two other types of voluntary schools, the "direct grant" and the "special agreement." The differences among these types are analyzed below. In addition there are "independent schools," which are not in receipt of any grant from the Ministry of Education or an L.E.A.

The county schools are built and completely maintained by public funds, local and national. About 55 percent of local expenses in education is met by grants from the national government. The schools are free and open to all children who apply. The L.E.A.'s appoint all teachers. In 1964 the system had 18,891 out of a total of 28,835 primary and secondary maintained schools and enrolled 5,434,840 pupils out of a 7,033,696 total. [36]

The law orders that all maintained primary and secondary schools must open each day with an act of corporate worship and that regular and systematic religious instruction must be given. In county schools the worship must be undenominational in character and the instruction in accordance with an agreed syllabus drawn up for each local area by a statutory committee representative of the various interests concerned. The conscience clause of 1870 has been retained and, at the request of parents, children may be excused from both the act of worship and the religious instruction.

What in practice is the act of worship? The concept behind the law seems admirable: the school children in a corporate manner are to acknowledge their belief in and dependence upon God. Britain does not subscribe to a laïcized public school. But the pluralistic character of the schools presents difficulties. Nowhere does the Act specify a Christian service although this seems normally taken for granted. The service often consists in Bible reading, hymn singing, or perhaps a short sermon. As a rule, it is conducted by the school headmaster; occasionally local clergymen or even pupils are invited to take a leading part. If the school has a chapel the act will be conducted there, but if none is available,

as is usually the case, the service is held in another appropriate location. Rarely, a neighboring Protestant church is used.

The headmistress of one comprehensive secondary
school in giving a concrete description of the procedure in her
school illustrates the difficulties encountered.[37]   On five
mornings out of six an undenominational Christian service is
provided, about two-thirds of the pupils and staff opting out of
this assembly. Jewish and Catholic children meet separately,
each group worshiping with teachers of their own faith. One
day in six there is a combined service of an undenominational
character, which the mistress maintains is unsatisfactory as
an act of worship: Christian children miss reference to
Christ; Jewish children dislike singing unfamiliar hymns. She
concludes that the comprehensive school, catering for all
children of a multi-religious neighborhood, has a very difficult
task to perform "if it takes religious education seriously and
yet tries to conform to the regulations which forbid denominational teaching."

Opinions differ on the value of the religious service in
the county schools. A report of a research committee summarized its findings in the statement: "We should be wilfully
blind if we denied the existence here and there of indifference,
carelessness, or even insincerity, but we should be distorting
facts as far as they are known to us, if we did not assert with
confidence that the predominant desire is to worship God in
spirit and in truth."[38]

The regular religious instruction ordered by the law in
all except voluntary aided schools must not be "distinctive of
any particular denomination" and is to be in accordance with
an Agreed Syllabus compiled or adapted for each area by a
specially selected committee. The law has provision for the
composition of the committee and the manner of drawing up
the syllabus. Accordingly, each L.E.A. has convened a conference in which was represented the Church of England, other
important non-Catholic religious groups in the area, teachers'
associations, and the L.E.A. itself. The syllabus is to be
used as a guide for the teacher in all county schools in the
area and in voluntary schools when necessary.[39]

Many of the syllabi were adapted from a small pamphlet

entitled "A National Basic Outline of Religious Instruction,"
which had been formulated in 1944 by a composite committee
on the national level, including representatives of the L.E.A.'s,
the Anglicans, and Free Church societies. What view of the
religious instruction in the county schools does the "Outline"
give? The content has been determined by such considerations
as the need of each child to become familiar with the Bible and
his need for moral and spiritual training based on the principles of Christianity. It also emphasizes the influence of Christianity on the lives of people, on the social culture of a country, and on the development of Western civilization.

These concepts have value, but some observers have
pointed out that they are more concerned with by-products of
religion than with religion itself. One critic, for example,
in reference to a section entitled "The development of the concept of God in the Bible and in Christian thought" remarks:
"This is no doubt excellent as a term assignment for a Christian teacher in guiding a class of Christian boys and girls; am
I making needless difficulties if I say that it could equally
serve as the heading for historical lectures given by somebody
who had no belief in God at all."[40]   And in connection with the
word "problem" in the topic "Problems of the Bible" the critic
asks: "Is it fair to point out that the word 'problem' can be
interpreted very differently in the minds of a Christian believer
or of one who is (say) a Unitarian or perhaps agnostic? . . .
It does seem a little non-committal, doesn't it? As if, those
who drew up the 'Outline' felt compelled to leave loop-holes
everywhere for the teacher who doesn't believe himself, but
prefers to take his share of the Scripture lesson." The
critic wonders whether the "Basic Outline" has really any good
news to tell the children to whom it ultimately is addressed.[41]
In general the outline keeps close to the old idea of religious
instruction being a Scripture lesson. And probably to counter-
act the incredible ignorance of the New Testament manifested
by some of Britain's children, a discovery made in the war
years, it lays considerable emphasis on the events in the life
of Christ. Many of the local syllabi follow a similar pattern.[42]
A London plan outlines lessons based on the Old and New Tes-
taments. The borough of Bristol adopted a new syllabus that

begins with Bible stories in nursery school, moves on to a
treatment of the Old Testament in primary schools, and concludes in secondary schools with a consideration of the Gos-
pels and Acts of the Apostles.

The law demands that religion classes be given equal
status with other subjects in the curriculum. Regular inspection of religious instruction by H.M.'s inspectors is provided
for in all schools which abide by an Agreed Syllabus. The
classes are taught by lay teachers who have presumably
specialized in religion but are not formal representatives of
any particular denomination. Still the course is pretty much
what the teacher makes it. Much is left to his initiative. An
Anglican who has given much consideration to the question of
religious instruction in the schools sums up his views by
stating that "we must conclude, and we find it confirmed by
experience, that only within the worshipping society of a
church can anyone, young or old, learn what Christianity in
its fulness is. That is why we work so hard for our own
schools, and hold by the denominational principle." He adds
that if religious teaching is to have its proper effect, its
underlying spirit "must touch every part of the schools' life
and all the subjects taught in it; a faith and an interpretation
of life, built into the very being of the society. . ."[43]

In the operation of the conscience clause, the parents
may withdraw their children from the act of worship and the
religious instruction and insist on no substitution. The
L.E.A. may also allow parents to withdraw their children
and send them to another county or voluntary school for religious worship and instruction of a kind that they desire their
children to have. A special arrangement applies if a voluntary
school or church of a particular religious denomination to
which parents of children belong is not near the secondary
county school which the children attend. Then the L.E.A.
may provide facilities for instruction and worship in that denomination within the county school, so long as the denomination and not the L.E.A. bears the responsibility for any cost
involved. The plan does not seem as a rule to have worked
satisfactorily because of difficulties in grouping and problems
of time scheduling, and records show the privilege is rarely

used.[44]

So much for the place of religion in Britain's county
schools. The British, it is evident, hold steadfastly to the
principle that religion must have a role in education; not at
any time in the history of the country has opposition against
the idea arisen.

Turning our attention now to the voluntary schools, it
will be recalled that the 1944 Act gave the voluntary bodies,
which for the most part were the Catholics and the Anglicans,
a choice of two alternatives. Should the managers of these
schools be unwilling or unable to pay half the cost of alterations and improvements necessary to bring the buildings up
to the required standards and to keep them to those standards,
then the L.E.A. would assume all financial obligations. By
the same token, the school would come under the control of
the L.E.A., which would appoint all the teachers, subject to
some reservations; the Agreed Syllabus would be taught, except for two hours a week which could be given to the denominational teaching of the electing body. Under the arrangement
the premises remain the property of the group providing them
but all building and maintenance costs are assumed by the
L.E.A. This alternative was totally unacceptable to Catholics, whose religious conscience could not permit such imposed limitations on the religious character of their schools.
Although there were divided views among Church of England
leaders regarding the suitability of controlled status, eventually the majority of Anglican schools elected this alternative.
Such schools are referred to as voluntary controlled.

Precisely, what price does the church pay to be freed of
financial obligations? The answer is practically entire loss
of independence, as the title itself suggests. The voluntary
controlled school is subject completely to the L.E.A. regulations in the same manner as county schools. It must be open
to all children; it is not permitted to refuse a child because
he does not go to the Sunday school or church of the sponsoring body. Two-thirds of the managers or governing board
are appointed by the L.E.A. and the remaining third by the
school foundation. The managers correspond roughly to an
American Board of Education except that in England and Wales

each county and voluntary school must have its own set of
managers. Obviously, control remains with the L.E.A.,
which appoints the majority. The L.E.A. has power to appoint and dismiss teachers; but the foundation, which is generally the Church of England, has the right both to a voice in
the appointment of the headmaster or headmistress and to be
satisfied concerning the appointment of one-fifth of the teaching staff, who as "reserved" teachers are to be of the same
religious denomination as the voluntary body and must give
the sectarian instruction for not more than two periods a week
for those children whose parents desire it. Apart from the
denominational teaching, the religious instruction given in the
school is according to the Agreed Syllabus drawn up for that
area and taught by teachers appointed by the L.E.A.

As in the county schools, each day begins with a corporate act of worship. Controlled schools have surrendered the
right to hold denominational worship on the school premises,
so the observance, as in county schools, may not be distinctive
of any particular religious denomination. The conscience
clause, of course operates.

The second alternative offered to church-related schools
was based on the principle: less control -- less aid. If the
managers were able and willing to pay half the reorganization
costs of bringing the schools up to specified standards, they
could keep their denominational instruction and appoint the
teachers. The schools accepting this plan are classified as
voluntary aided. Since controlled status was out of bounds
for Catholic consciences, not a single Catholic school elected
it. Catholics were determined both to keep their schools and
to preserve intact the religious character essential to them.
If forced to pay a price for this adherence to parental rights
and the dictates of their religious conscience, as the historical
survey has shown, they could only try to meet the cost, not
necessarily consenting to the injustice. A considerable number of Church of England schools did likewise.

What, precisely, is the present extent of public help
given the "aided" schools and what is the extent of their financial liability? Voluntary aided schools are maintained by
L.E.A. and Ministry grants, that is, current day by day costs

are paid. This includes aparatus, furniture, supplies, inside
repairs, teachers' salaries, janitors' salaries, and a percentage of the cost of external repairs. In newer schools, and
depending on the generosity of L.E.A.'s, visual and auditory
aids to facilitate and improve teaching are provided, including
slides, film strips, projectors, and movie machines. Teachers' salaries, according to an established scale, are paid to
religious personnel in the same manner as to lay teachers.
It is estimated that public aid covers approximately 93 percent
or more of the total maintenance costs.

Available are grants up to 80 percent to meet the costs
of remodeling, repairing, or enlarging existing primary and
secondary schools when such modifications are deemed necessary by the Ministry and to build new secondary schools,
where there are none, to match existing primary schools (for
ages up to 11+. In certain cases where a new school is in effect a substitute for, or a continuation of an old one, or must
be built because movement of population to another area has
brought to that area a substantial number of displaced pupils,
the 80 percent grant toward building costs is made. When a
school cannot be modernized it may be transferred to a new
site and rebuilt by the managers or governors, aided by an 80
percent ministerial subsidy. In this case the L.E.A. pays
for the site of the building. The Act also provides loans to
cover the remainder of the costs (20 percent) spread over
fifteen to twenty years.

Voluntary aided schools participate equally in health and
meal services. Health services provide medical and dental
inspection, and treatment where needed. The milk and meal
service provides daily a free ration of milk, equivalent to
half pint, and cooked mid-day meal at small cost. The cost
is remitted in necessitous cases and when necessary other
refreshments and clothing are provided.

Rooms used for medical and meal purposes; provision,
extension, and upkeep of play fields are paid for by the L.E.A.
If the nearest appropriate school is three miles or more
from a child's home the L.E.A. must by law provide transportation to and from school; for children under eight years
the limit is two miles. Generally the L.E.A. pays the child's

fare by public transportation or it hires buses if the numbers warrant it. The L.E.A. is empowered to provide free board- ing facilities when it deems it necessary. Vocational and placement guidance services are available to aided schools.

Obviously Britain is concerned about the welfare of all the nation's children and the idea of denying benefits to boys and girls because parents desire a religious education for them according to their beliefs receives no countenance. There still persists, however, the attitude that a price, lim- ited though it be, must be paid for independence in the matter of religious teaching. What price must the voluntary aided schools pay?

New primary and new secondary schools, buildings and sites which do not come under one of the categories listed above as eligible for grants must be paid for by the foundation sponsoring them. There is also the 20 percent balance that must be paid on the hundreds of primary buildings undergoing renovation and the numerous new secondary schools eligible for the 80 percent grant.

During the 1960-1961 period, some 108 Catholic schools at an estimated cost of $30,800,000 had to be built. Even with the 80 percent grant then allotted for some of these the cost to Catholics was still $14,000,000.[45]   The education committees of England and Wales, an assembly of the county boards of education, stated that expenditures by Britain's Catholic community would be $84,000,000 in the twenty year period ending in 1965. "This is some measure of their zeal and single-mindedness," the committees said in a booklet, Church and School, "and there are many other denominations who regard their achievement in silent wonder."[46] The total cost of the Church's school building effort since World War II was estimated in 1960 to be more than $162,000,000.

Then there is the approximately seven percent of running costs, specifically those encountered in making external re- pairs. It has been put like this: if a school window is broken from within the building, the L.E.A. pays; if broken from without, the managers pay.

Disputes have occasionally arisen from the unwillingness of the L.E.A.'s to agree that a new Catholic school was needed

or in regard to paying transportation costs of Catholic children
to a new and distant school. In a number of instances the
L.E.A.'s wished to transfer the child to its own secondary
school. Regarding some of the provisions on aid, the L.E.A.'s
are empowered, but not compelled to act; an L.E.A. unfriendly to a voluntary school can therefore refuse the permissible
aid. As a whole, however, the L.E.A.'s are reported to be
eminently fair and relations between them and the Catholic
authorities are friendly and pleasant.[47]

As we have noted, British policy still relates the amount
of public aid granted to a church-related school with a required
surrender of independence. What has been the price paid by
the voluntary aided schools, mostly Catholic? Has it been too
great? It does not seem to be so held. The voluntary aided
schools have retained complete independence in what is really
essential: the religious character of the schools remains absolutely unimpaired. Religious instruction and training are
completely under the control of the managers or governors;
the sensitive area, teacher selection, remains in their hands.

What control is exercised by the public authorities? For
a clear understanding of the relationships of the aided schools
to the public authorities some knowledge of the general administrative set-up is helpful. In England and Wales every
county and voluntary primary school must by law have a board
of managers of not fewer than six persons. Every county and
voluntary secondary school must have a board of governors
of such number as the L.E.A. for the county schools, or the
Minister of Education for the voluntary schools, shall determine. For voluntary aided and for special agreement schools
two-thirds of the managers or governors must be foundation
members, that is, representatives of the body which provides
the school, one-third representatives of the L.E.A. For
voluntary controlled schools, it will be recalled, the proportion is reversed. Obviously, then, control of the schools remains in the hands of the foundation, which selects the majority of managers.

In a typical Catholic voluntary aided school the parish
priest is always a member of the board. If the school is
conducted by a religious congregation, two members of the

community are also on the board, but not those on the teaching staff. There will be at least one non-Catholic, appointed
by the L.E.A. The principal of the school, although not a
member of the board and without a vote, is present at the
meetings and has considerable influence.[48]

In the crucial matter of teacher selection, the religious
character of the school is safeguarded. All teachers are appointed by the managers or governors. The L.E.A.'s retain
the right, reasonable it would seem, to decide the number
needed and to pass on the professional qualifications of teachers selected. The L.E.A. may also dismiss or prohibit the
dismissal of a teacher except when the managers may themselves demand the withdrawal of a teacher who has failed to
give the required religious instruction efficiently and suitably.
Beyond these provisions, vitally essential in preserving the
religious character of the school, the voluntary aided schools
are more or less under the control of the L.E.A.'s and the
Ministry. The L.E.A.'s regulate such matters as the number
of days in the school year, the length of the school day and of
class periods. Reports on attendance, finances, and other
matters must be sent in to the authorities regularly.

The L.E.A.'s see that the aided schools are up to required building standards. They regulate secular education.
H.M. inspectors, representing the Ministry, may inspect the
schools at any time and must do so at least once a year.
Once every five years complete inspection by a group is conducted. Reports on the inspections are sent to the Ministry.
Besides, there are county inspectors, one for each subject.
Inspectors supervise new teachers doing first year apprenticeship teaching. Religious Sisters have been selected to examine the work of young teachers, but not to inspect schools.
Children in primary schools at eleven plus take the examinations set by the L.E.A., the results of which decide what
stream each will enter in secondary schools. No fees may
be charged by the aided schools.

The extensive powers conferred on the Ministry by the
Education Acts may affect the aided schools favorably or adversely. The Minister may accept or reject proposals for
new voluntary schools and decide whether schools are to be

aided as transferred, substituted, or displaced pupils schools, and so determines whether or not they shall be eligible for grants. The Ministry decides disputes between the L.E.A.'s and managers or boards of governors. It may make loans for capital expenditures, or refuse them. As a whole Catholic officials report they have found the Ministry to be fair and sympathetic.

The Catholic Education Council, with headquarters in London, acts as a coordinating agency for the Catholic schools of England and Wales, most of which have aided status. Its general purpose is to assist and promote Catholic education in the country. A full-time attorney handles the legal side of contracts between the Church authorities and the government. In general, a spirit of cooperation and helpfulness characterizes the relations between the Council and national and local authorities.[49]

The law leaves the managers and governors entire control over all religious aspects of the aided schools. The corporate act of worship is, of course, required but in Catholic schools it can be performed in complete accord with Catholic beliefs and practice. Catholic prayers are usually recited and hymns sung. On occasion, such as holy days of obligation and patronal feasts, the pupils attend holy Mass in the parish church or school chapel.

Religious instruction in Catholic doctrine and principles is given daily for about one hour by a teacher whose qualifications for this responsibility has been determined by an examination. The religious teaching is inspected by a diocesan board appointed by the bishop. Inspection must take place at least once a year. There are set syllabi and set examinations, both oral and written. The Agreed Syllabus of the area must be taught, if parents of any children in attendance desire it. In practice, few non-Catholics attend Catholic schools.

Principals and teachers state they feel no restrictions or difficulties in keeping the schools Catholic in the full sense of the term. The L.E.A.'s direct, in fact, that secular instruction must not prevent the giving of due time every day to religious instruction. The content of the religion class may be integrated with daily lessons in the secular subjects. There is no hindrance to maintaining the nuances that help create a religious atmosphere in school and classroom. Crucifixes and religious pictures hang from the walls, sacred images may adorn the hallways, devotions suited to the varying liturgical seasons have a place in the program. Holy days of obligation may be free days. Although no series of distinctly Catholic textbooks has been developed in England, an approved list has been prepared from those available and the teacher is free to adjust them to Catholic needs as circumstances warrant.

Should it happen that a parent living in an area where no denominational school of his persuasion has been established desires his child to attend such a school, Section 106(1) of the law requires that the resident L.E.A. shall pay to the Education Authority of the locality where the child attends the school of the parents' choice the costs of the pupil's education, including the use of ancillary services connected with education.

In 1964 there were 2,116 voluntary aided schools under Catholic auspices, with 563,370 children enrolled. Anglicans had 3,045 schools caring for 377,524 pupils.[50]

A distinct group of voluntary aided schools are designated as special agreement schools. This category arose out of an agreement made under the Education Act of 1936 whereby the L.E.A.'s were impowered, but not compelled, to make grants of 50 to 75 percent of the cost of alterations and improvements and for building new voluntary senior schools, that is for children between the ages of 11+ to 15 years. Under the agreement the appointment of teachers came under the L.E.A.'s except in the case of reserved teachers, who were to give denominational instruction. In regard to the latter, the managers and governors were to have a veto if they were unsatisfied with the candidate's fitness and competence to give such instruction. In other respects the composition of the boards, the responsibility for religious instruction and for alteration and additions to school buildings was to be the same as for aided schools. No tuition fees could be charged. At the outbreak of World War II some 509 agreements had been initiated, but few of these had been completed.

The 1944 Act made the agreements renewable, that is, those initiated before 1939 could be completed. The number of this type of school therefore is limited; the category is closed. In 1964 there were 155 special agreement schools with 67,902 pupils. Catholics had 119 with 54,212 pupils; the Church of England, 33 schools with 11,986 pupils.[51]

In another classification distinct from the voluntary schools are those designated as direct grant schools. From the viewpoint of relationship to government, they seem to oc-cupy a place midway between the maintained and the indepen-dent schools. Most of them are secondary schools of the grammar type. These schools receive no funds from the L.E.A.'s, but are given a grant based on the number of pu-pils, directly from the Ministry. The L.E.A.'s are repre-sented on the governing boards. The grants are made with the condition that not less than 25 percent of the places be of-fered free to pupils from maintained primary schools, who are chosen by the board of governors or selected and paid for by the L.E.A.'s. A further 25 percent of the places must be put at the disposal of the L.E.A.'s as reserved places. The fees of pupils filling the reserved places are paid by the L.E.A. concerned. Tuition, the amount having been approved by the Ministry, may be charged for the remainder of the pu-pils in the school. The list of direct grant schools is closed. There are in all 179 schools of this type. Catholics educate 36,640 pupils in 57 schools, most of which are conducted by religious orders.[52]   Many direct grant schools have estab-lished reputations of excellency, a large number of their pupils being qualified by examination for entrance into the uni-versities.

Outside the system of maintained schools are the inde-pendent schools. They ordinarily receive no grant from either the Ministry or the L.E.A. and depend upon tuition fees or private sources for support. They are completely under the control of the sponsoring body, but are subject to registration and inspection by the Ministry. If found unsatisfactory, they may be closed. England's famous Public Schools such as the Protestant Eton, Rugby, Harrow and the Catholic Downside, Ampleforth, Beaumont, belong to this class. They may apply for a full inspection by the Ministry and if the report is satis-factory the school will be included in the Ministry's list of

schools recognized as "efficient." Most of these schools are
of the resident type and prepare their pupils for entrance into
the universities. An L.E.A. may request a place in one of
these schools and if granted the fees of the pupil will be paid
by the L.E.A. There are 4,251 such fee-charging schools
with approximately half a million pupils, or six percent of the
secondary school population.[53]   Catholic schools in this category number 587, educating about 114,000 pupils. Independent
schools may arrange with the L.E.A. to participate in both
the School Health and the Milk Services. Incidentally, it may
be noted, junior seminarians receive direct grants from the
central government up to the age of eighteen.

Finally there are the special schools for mentally or
physically handicapped children and orphans. The central
government or local authorities maintain schools of this type,
some of which are staffed by religious personnel. In 1954
Catholics had 54 special schools caring for 4,791 children.[54]

Approximately 70 percent of the Catholic children in
England and Wales are in Catholic schools. In 1964 there
was a total of 3,517 Catholic schools of all types with a pupil
population of 824,688 children.

Church-related or voluntary teachers' training colleges
participate equitably in public grants if recognized as efficient
by the Ministry. There are some fifty grant-aided voluntary
colleges out of a total of 156. Eleven of these are under
Catholic sponsorship; about 24 are conducted by the Church
of England. Virtually the whole of the maintenance costs and
up to 75 percent of the costs of approved building projects are
reimbursed by way of a grant from the Ministry.[55]   Students
entering the teacher-training institutions, including the voluntary colleges, can get help from their L.E.A.'s toward living
costs. The amount of each grant is calculated according to
the income of the student or his parents. The maximum grant
covers the total cost of board and tuition fees, plus an allowance for personal expenses and the cost of traveling to and
from home. Day students get a cash grant to cover maintenance at home instead of boarding fees. A minimum grant of
fifty pounds per year is paid irrespective of income.

The control of voluntary colleges is in the hands of the

sponsoring body, by whom teachers are appointed. Teachers,
however, must possess set professional qualifications. There
is no interference by the public authorities in the internal
management. The school has complete liberty in matters of
teaching methods and textbooks, but examinations are set by
the L.E.A.'s or the university with which the college is affiliated and students must pass to qualify for teachers' certificates. The L.E.A. and the Ministry have the right of inspection. Inspections may also be made by the university.
Administrators of the voluntary colleges state that their contacts with the associated agencies are helpful and friendly.
They find the inspectors eager to promote efficient teaching
and fair and positive in their appraisals.[56]

The British Appraise their Solution

Perhaps few Englishmen would state categorically that
Britain has found the ideal and only adequate solution to the
church-state relationship in education, but most feel satisfied
that the country is working towards the one best suited to its
values and traditions. Many would agree that what Cardinal
Vaughn wrote in a letter to The Times in 1895 still applies.
"The basis of a popular system of education," he stated, "will
never be satisfactorily laid until religion ceases to be a bar to
equality of treatment in the matter of state payment for elementary and compulsory education."[57]

The progress toward that goal by Great Britain is seen
as the more remarkable when one considers the rugged terrain
of religious bitterness and intolerance over which the nation
had to travel, and the effort to overcome those barriers on the
way has been the measure of that progress. One can only admire the frankness of an editor writing in the Times Educational Supplement, who, after flatly stating that the only
grounds for resistance to denominational schools must lie in
enmity to the denomination concerned, says, "Such enmity
was the stuff of the nineteenth century controversies." The
extent of the progress made in overcoming this obstacle is indicated by the writer's further statement:

While some few prejudices doubtless still survive

from those days, it is difficult to imagine that any
real enmity still exists. To most men of liberal
temper today, it would seem deplorable if the education of the Roman Catholic children in their own
voluntary schools were actually hindered by Christian bodies of another persuasion. There are those,
of course, represented by the secularist correspon-
dent who wrote saying, 'I am opposed to paying
taxes for the religious education of school children.
The point is that every child's education today is by
law religious. As the national system enjoins religious education, there seems less reason for
refusing any Christian body the right to order that
education in his own way.[58]

Bishop Beck, writing after the passage of the 1959 Act,
notes that "a different climate of opinion with regard to voluntary schools exists throughout the country. The Nonconformist conscience no longer has strength to awaken opposition. In
the negotiations preceding the 1959 Act, we found on all sides
not only sympathy for the efforts which Catholics have made
to build schools during the post-war period, but a recognition
that our case rests on sound educational grounds with the twin
supports of parental rights and natural justice."[59]   More recently the Anglican Primate of England declared, "The ending
of bitterness between Protestantism and Catholicism in our
times is little short of miraculous."[60]
     This factor, namely, the melting away of religious rival-
ries and prejudices and the arrival at understanding and willingness to base a solution on principles of justice, freedom,
and child welfare -- something beyond tolerance -- has been
the vanguard in the process of solving the church-state relationship in education. It would seem to deserve studied attention in view of the fact that the same goal still seems out of
reach in a few Western democracies.
     The British arrangement, to the degree that it has neared
the goal of complete religious freedom in education, conforms
to the principles of the natural law, which is the foundation of
English common law. These principles regulate the relations

among the basic societies -- family, church and state -- and
hold that the state must safeguard the primary rights of family
and church in the education of children.

Britain is not neutral as regards religion and nonreligion
but officially recognizes the necessary role of religion in the
lives of the people and its importance for the welfare of the
country. It recognizes that the nation, as a nation, should
acknowledge its dependence upon Almighty God and it implements this view in the schools by the compulsory act of worship and religious instruction. At the same time the "Conscience Clause" safeguards religious freedom. The unbeliever
or dissenter has the right to follow the dictates of his convictions and to withdraw from both observances. The law leaves
sacred the inner realm of conscience. It is interesting to note
the delicate balance maintained here among what might ordinarily be conflicting elements -- an Established Church, compulsory religion in the schools, and religious freedom -- a
balance, it is true, easily disturbed.

Above all, British tradition and law give recognition to
that fundamental principle of the natural law which holds that
parents have the inalienable right to direct the education of
their children. Section 76 of the 1944 Act states explicitly,

> In the exercise and performance of all powers and
> duties conferred and imposed on them by the Act
> the Minister and local education authorities shall
> have regard to the general principle that, as far as
> is compatible with the provision of efficient instruc-
> tion and training and the avoidance of unreasonable
> public expenditure, pupils are to be educated in ac-
> cordance with the wishes of their parents.

British tradition has led to a variegated system of
schools. Has the proliferation of types resulted in any weakening of educational efficiency? On the contrary, Britons
assert, the amicable competition, the initiative which the
policy fosters have led to greater efficiency. Moreover, it
illustrates that characteristic aptly fitting a democracy and
anathema to totalitarianism -- the encouragement of diversity

in unity.

In accord, too, with the principles of the natural law, the state, while recognizing the primary rights of church and family, exercises a reasonable control over education which is directed toward safeguarding the child's rights, promoting efficiency, and advancing the general welfare. Here, again, we see a nice balance between control and freedom.

Distributive justice has been secured insofar as the state distributes its benefits, accruing from taxes collected from all the people, among all the schools without permitting the religious-orientation of the school to be a bar to an equitable share. Here the British arrangement fails to achieve complete equity. A penalty, small though it may be, is still placed upon parents exercising their right to give their children an education according to their beliefs, the penalty being equal to the amount they must pay to exercise that freedom. The burden continues to work hardships on religious-minded parents, and so in addition to distributive justice being violated parental rights in education are also impaired. A right exercised at the price of a penalty is not a fully recognized right.

Some critics have pointed out that the 1944 Act was illogical in that it withheld grants for new voluntary schools and thereby discouraged their extension, while at the same time it gave its blessings to the dual system. It encouraged denominational teaching and at the same time hindered it by the penalty of financial inequality. Subsequent legislation, as we have seen, has mitigated this anomaly to some extent. It has been asked, too, on what basis of logic or equity does the pattern of equating the size of the grant with relinquishment of freedom for dogmatic teaching rest. It can scarcely be justice, or religious freedom, or welfare of the child or of the nation! On what then?

The compulsory act of worship and undenominational religious instruction in the county schools have evoked various reactions. Some observers feel the practices are commendable in theory but leave much to be desired in practice. The original error, many hold, is the Cowper-Temple formula of 1870, which, in compliance with the wishes of the Nonconformists, fastened the undenominational teaching upon the county school, while it ignored the desires of the majority. In the opinion of many sober-minded Englishmen, the formula continues "to support the religion of the agreed syllabus to the detriment of others." It has failed to promote religious freedom, for it favors those who want their children to receive an undenominational education while it prejudices those who want dogmatic truths taught.[61]

Questions about who does the teaching of religion have also frequently arisen: Is he a believer? If he is not, more harm than good can result, says one Anglican bishop. He adds,

> Real Christianity can only be taught by believing Christians. . . How long shall we tolerate the monstrosity of allowing unbelievers (and there must be many) to teach Christianity to our children. No wonder there is a mass of apathetic irreligion; no wonder there are juvenile delinquents. . . Surely it is time somebody pricked the monstrous bubble for England's sake and her children's.[62]

The Bishop of Durham agrees that "we must face facts. . . that there is at present a grave lack of competent believing teachers.[63]

The headmaster of Westminster City School suggests as a remedy that the wishes of the parents be ascertained on the matter and religious teaching be provided for those children whose parents desire it. "Let this instruction," he states, "be of a denominational character if the parents wish it. . . and let it be given by the local clergy and ministers, admitted to the school on equal terms and for this express purpose."[64]

As to the moral teaching of the agreed syllabi, questions are also being raised. Commenting on the Crowther Report, which among other aspects of English education concerned itself with religious instruction in the county school, Bishop Beck points up some weaknesses in reference to moral training. "The committee assumes," he says, "that the function of education is not to instill principles of conduct but to be a reflection of the prevailing attitude of society." [65]   This criticism arises from a statement of the report which contains this sentence: "Education can only function within the broad directions of right and wrong which society gives." [66]   The Bishop expresses the Catholic view and at the same time summarizes the situation in regard to the voluntary aided schools; he holds, as the Church through the ages has maintained, that an effective religious education must be the integrated product of home, school, and community, and the training of the child involves the influence and atmosphere of the whole school. "But," he remarks, "it is just those schools where serious effort is being made to achieve these conditions which are, financially, most seriously penalized at the present time."

Again, well-intentioned as the daily act of worship was intended to be, not all Englishmen are satisfied. As one commentator has observed, "It can have little lasting Christian value since it is based on what, in its latent meaning, is a very un-Christian principle that one religion is as good as another." [67]

Has Britain's insistence upon religion in the school borne fruit in the moral and religious life of the nation? No scientific study has been made (for that matter, none is possible) which purports to show the relation between religious practices in the schools and the moral climate of the nation. The factors involved are complicated and do not yield to facile investigations. It is generally acknowledged that Britain is witnessing (as are so many areas of the modern world) a moral and religious decline accompanied by greater manifestations of secular and materialistic views of life and conduct. Crime and juvenile delinquency are on the increase. Various inter-related factors are mentioned as causes, chiefly the breakdown of wholesome family life. No one could expect the schools alone to hold back the tide, but some observers see in the undenominational teaching with its inherent weakness a factor which is, at best, impotent to build up, at worst, an element in the current decay. Nevertheless, it may be noted, the rate of crime and juvenile delinquency in England falls far below that of the United States. The fact that religion has officially been given a place in the school program on equality with secular subjects would seem

to hold out a promise of better times to come, once the weakness of the present formula is remedied.

Britain is committed to the policy of safeguarding her
traditional values. Greater unity and contentment among the
people has resulted from the effort to adapt educational legislation to the wishes of the people. The laws have gone far
toward enabling each child, regardless of what school he attends or what his social or economic status may be, to receive
as much education and the kind of education for which his
ability and his interests fit him.

The nation has been benefited. The denominational
school remains as a bulwark of traditional morality and values.
As a newspaper writer remarked, "The country needs more
not less, of the kind of provision for which the advocates of the
Church Schools are prepared to work and sacrifice. Denominational suspicions or rivalries are apt to seem petty beside
the problems that confront all who wish to see Christian doctrine and virtues progress in the contemporary world."[68]

A final point may be noted. Britain showed, in general,
the same liberality and respect for religion and conscience in
her dealing with the schools in her colonies. As an example
of Britain's policy, we may take the case of Malta. The
colonial government aided private Catholic schools and provided a Catholic public school system for the overwhelming
Catholic population. The official report of the British Colonial
Office stated that "Maltese children have the right to attend
free government schools which are Roman Catholic." There
were 114 of these, with 56,189 pupils. The private schools
had a total enrollment of 17,497 pupils. The government
gave per capita grants annually to the private schools which
partially supported them. There are virtually no secular
schools on the island. The people do not want them.[69]

Chapter 2

Scotland's Solution:
"AN UNQUALIFIED SUCCESS"

Scotland's solution to the school issue, which has received wide and enthusiastic acclaim, was reached in 1918.
After almost fifty years, it is being proclaimed "an unqualified
success" by religious, educational and civic leaders.[1]

Although the same Parliament legislates for the three
areas -- England, Wales, and Scotland -- the administration
and organization of education in the latter country are under
the control of the Scottish people. Their solution of the religion-education issue varies significantly from the dual system
which was retained in England and Wales. The interested inquirer may be curious as to why these two allied countries
have arrived at totally different resolutions of the church-state
relationship. The answer is to be found in the unique characteristics of the Scottish people and in the history of their nation.

A Glance Backward

Interest in education and appreciation of democratic
ideals in regard to education have characterized the Scottish
people from the early centuries when Christianity was first
brought to the land by Irish missionary monks. During the
thousand years or more between the beginnings of Christianity
in the country and the period of the Protestant Revolt there developed in Scotland under the supervision of the Christian
Church a complete system of schools from primary grades to
the university.

Scotland also claims that it was the first of any European
country to enact a law to make education compulsory. A
statute in 1496 ordered that all barons and freeholders "put
their eldest sonis and airs to the sculis." There they were
to stay until they had completed grammar school and thereafter
"to remane thre yers at the sculis of art and Jure sua that thai
may have knowledge and understanding of the lawis."[2] A fine
of twenty pounds was to be paid to the king for failure to comply with the law. No record is extant of anyone's having paid

the penalty, and it is unlikely that the law was ever rigidly enforced. Nevertheless, the statute remains the first instance
of a government's entering the realm of educational legislation
and is another illustration of Scottish concern for education.

Throughout those one thousand years the Scottish monasteries were centers of religion, culture, and progress. Even
today, as one historian has remarked, they bear evidence "in
their ruins to their once educational influence in the land." [3]
It was taken for granted that education was an essential activity
of the Church and that the religious and moral formation of the
student was the most important element in the educational
process. Church authorities approved school foundations,
appointed teachers, and prescribed curricula. State authority
cooperated by giving grants to aid scholars; the nobles and
burghers helped support the schools by endowments. [4]

But this brilliant promise of scholastic attainment was
to be eclipsed for over three centuries. Scotland was not to
escape involvement in or be spared the dire effects of the
religio-political upheaval of the Protestant Revolt. The religious Revolution was formally initiated in Scotland by an Act
of Parliament in 1560. Through the teaching and influence of
John Knox, a personal friend of Calvin, the Reformed Church
or Presbyterianism, the Scottish counterpart of Calvinism,
became the established religion of Scotland.

Almost immediately there followed a period of religious
persecution for those who refused to conform to the new creed
and of destructiveness for existing educational institutions,
both efforts being aimed at the extinction of the Catholic Church
in the land. A series of iniquitous penal laws were enacted
which proscribed all Catholic teaching and rendered impossible
the training of young men for the priesthood. Banishment or
death was decreed for those who did not conform. Catholics
whose faith meant more than home or security were forced to
flee to remote areas of their own country or to foreign lands.

Education was dealt practically a death blow. In order
to destroy effectively the Catholic Church, the "Reformers"
set out to destroy the schools under its direction. Elementary
schools by the hundreds disappeared. Some few grammar
schools survived, but all the higher schools attached to monas-

teries and to collegiate churches outside the larger towns disappeared.[5]

Learned men from the universities went into exile. The
higher institutions together with half the collegiate church
schools and many of the parish and burgh schools were confiscated by the Protestants for their own use, but, because of
lack of teachers, the new owners were unable to conduct
schools in the buildings which they had seized. As a result,
all the seats of higher learning fell to a low ebb, and throughout the succeeding three centuries higher academic life stagnated.

Art and culture also suffered. The Calvinist spirit ab-
horred the idea of appealing to the soul by presenting the
beautiful through the senses. Monasteries, cathedrals, collegiate churches and the schools were stripped of all ornaments
and in many cases completely ruined. Progress in ecclesiastical architecture ceased. Music, too, which the Christian
schools had emphasized, came under the ban. In fact, no art,
however noble and elevating, was countenanced. What centuries of Catholic labor and love had built up was soon destroyed.

Catholic clergy and teachers who had not fallen as immediate victims to the rigor of the penal laws fled to the continent. Some few remained and managed secretly to help and
encourage the faithful, but such efforts were highly dangerous.
The children of those Catholics who did not escape were compulsorily educated as Protestants. So complete was the attack
on the Church that according to one historian there were only
fifty Catholics left in Glasgow and environs by the middle of
the seventeenth century, and in all Scotland there were only
14,000 Catholics, of whom 12,000 were living in the Highlands
and the islands of the Outer Hebrides where it was difficult to
enforce the harsh penal laws.[6] Here and there in the Highlands a few Catholic schools were established. By the close
of the penal times about twenty elementary schools and one
seminary had been established. In addition schools were
founded in foreign countries, notably France, Belgium, and
Italy, where loyal Scottish Catholics could send their sons to
be educated in an atmosphere at once Catholic and national.

In justice to Knox it should be said he did try to save

education in Scotland, but without success. To destroy proved easier than to construct. He set forth in his <u>First Book of Discipline</u> a scheme of education which was intended to restore the Scottish school system and to bring it into conformity with his own religion. According to his plan, Scotland was to have a complete national system of education extending from the primary school to the university. The plan rested on the Genevan idea of close union of church and state, with the church the dominant partner. He would have the church compel all parents to rear their children in "learning and virtue" and he would make the church directly responsible for providing and supporting schools for all classes and both sexes.[7] Close coordination was to be maintained between the schools of different grades.

According to Knox, education was not to be the privilege of a class but the right of all, with an opportunity for each to develop his special capacities. Admission to the university was to be granted to a student only on evidence of proven ability. The democratic ideal is further seen in his view that there should be but one system of education for the son of the laird and the son of the laborer. Poor but capable children were to be maintained by the state. On the other hand, Calvinistic intolerance and rigidity are seen in the provision that systematic instruction in the "reformed faith" was to be given compulsorily in all schools and to all pupils.

Knox had hoped that his Presbyterian schools would be supported from revenues derived from confiscated Catholic properties, but these properties were seized by the "robber barons."[8] For this, and other reasons, his plan failed to materialize. Several centuries were to pass before Scotland was to regain its educational inheritance. Despite the failure of his plan, Knox's proposals embodied the ideals and the elements of a school system toward which Scottish education was gradually directed. At the same time the intolerance intrinsic to early Calvinism was by degrees mitigated, and so Scotland began to move forward to the 1918 solution which culminated in the restoral of its pristine educational traditions.

Parliament made many efforts between the sixteenth and the nineteenth centuries to improve educational conditions, but despite all attempts, the situation in relation to the schools continued to be bleak. Many parishes had no schools. When one was found it was only too often a hovel conducted by an incompetent master or mistress, who eked out an existence on a pittance. Yet in the efforts made to establish a system of education for Scotland are to be discerned many of the features which were eventually to prevail. The democratic ideals of a one tract system and of education for all were implicit in the projected legislative measures. Religion and moral training were given a role of importance. No cult of undenominationalism developed.

The nineteenth century ushered in changes which affected all aspects of life, including education. With the Industrial Revolution came great industrial development for Scotland. The population of the country increased greatly but was unevenly distributed, tending to concentrate in a few big towns. Large numbers of Irish immigrants were adding to the increase and bringing to the fore the issue of parental rights and freedom of choice in education. Many children as young as eight and nine years were working long hours in the mills and factories. The parish system was proving itself insufficient for the needs of the nation and lacking in the elasticity necessary to meet changing conditions. New legislation both of a general and of an educational nature was needed.

Foremost was the necessity of removing the disabilities imposed by the penal laws upon Catholics. Toward the beginning of the nineteenth century the number of Catholics on the mainland to the south and west was rapidly increasing. Irish immigrants came pouring into Glasgow and the other industrial towns, bringing with them the treasure of their Catholic faith and the determination to preserve it at all cost. The hedge schools of Ireland had been a product of that determination. By 1814 there were 10,000 Catholics in Glasgow alone, and in 1847 at the time of the famine in Ireland the number had increased to 50,000.[9] As a result of Protestant contact with their Catholic neighbors, Calvinistic intolerance began to weaken somewhat and the Scottish people's traditional sense of justice began to reawaken. However, another hundred years was to pass before justice could claim a clear victory.

In 1779 a Catholic Relief proposal was introduced in Parliament, but opposition was still so great the bill had to be withdrawn. In 1793 a Catholic Relief Act was passed which brought some mitigation of the penal laws. Catholics were allowed to acquire possessions and dispose of real and personal estates in Scotland, but they were forbidden to hold certain offices, for example, that of schoolmaster. Finally, the "Act for the Relief of His Majesty's Roman Catholic Subjects," passed in 1829, removed most of the penal restrictions. Subsequent statutes repealed practically all disabilities.

For Catholics, who now formed a significant portion of the population, education except on a basis of Catholic doctrine and moral principles was inconceivable. Since there were no Catholic schools in the large industrial centers where the Irish had settled, Catholic parents were forced to send their children to the parish schools. These were to all intents Presbyterian parochial schools and in them the Catholic faith of the children was subject to insult and ridicule.[10]

Eventually a Catholic School Society was organized and steps were taken to ease the situation. By 1825 five Catholic schools had been established in Glasgow. Help came from here and there. Funds and books were provided and progress was made despite many difficulties. Staffing was the chief problem. Many schools used an adjustment of the Lancastrian system, pupil-teachers assisting the school masters and mistresses. Gradually religious teaching congregations came to the rescue: some from Ireland, others from the continent. These took over existing schools and established new ones, providing teachers who had been trained in the communities' novitiates and colleges. However, their numbers were too few to supply the ever-increasing need.

Though the Catholic schools were no doubt unsatisfactory in most respects, they compared favorably with other elementary schools in Scotland during the period under consideration. Still the task of restoring anything like a complete system of Catholic education in Scotland was going to prove long and arduous.

Deep faith and a spirit of sacrifice kept the Catholics plodding on. Little by little a creditable system of Catholic voluntary schools developed. The schools had to be built and maintained without aid from the Scottish government, although after 1846 many of them received some help from parliamentary grants. By 1866 there were twenty-three Catholic schools in Glasgow alone.

Scottish education in general was in such an unsatisfactory condition that a Royal Education (Argyle) Commission was set up to inquire into its working. A thorough survey of all the schools in Scotland was made. Finally in 1866 the Commission reported its findings and offered recommendations. The private venture schools were condemned outright. The parish schools (Presbyterian) were shown to be in most respects highly inefficient. The Catholic voluntary schools fared somewhat better in comparison. In fact, on many aspects of these schools the Commissioners made favorable comments. In any case it became obvious that national interest necessitated reform in education. The Commission recommended that an education authority be established to take over control of the parish schools and that the gap be filled by rate-aided voluntary schools."

An impetus toward implementing the proposed reform came from the fact that an Act of 1868 had given the vote to the working class. Better educational opportunities for this group became a necessity. Reform came in the Education (Scotland) Act of 1872. The Act abolished the authority of the Reformed Church over the schools. School boards to the number of 984 were set up in every parish and burgh in Scotland and to them was transferred the control of all parish and burgh schools. The main purpose of the legislation was to give all children an opportunity to learn at least to read and write. Attendance at school was made compulsory from the ages of five to thirteen. Parental defaulters were to be prosecuted and fined.

A one-tract system of schools for the sons and daughters of both laird and worker was to be established and all children were to have the right to attend. Voluntary classes were to be given in the evening for those over thirteen. Each board was permitted to levy a local tax upon the people within the area. Catholics were obliged to pay this imposed rate whether or not they took advantage of the education offered. To provide unity and to administer the grants, the Act set up a control authority for education called the Scottish Education Department. The Department was given the authority to conduct annual inspections of schools and to legislate through a code of minutes, which, after the approval of Parliament, had the force of law. The Education Department deserves much of the credit for the successful developments in Scottish education from 1872 to the splendidly organized system of today.[12]

An Act passed in 1892 provided a sum of money for secondary education and a committee was set up in each county and in the five large cities to distribute grants. In 1908 the powers of the boards were extended to provide boarding schools, transportation facilities, medical examinations of pupils, and food and clothing for needy cases. It should be noted that these provisions were permissive but not mandatory in their application to Catholic schools. Whether or not Catholic pupils were to benefit by them, depended on the good will of the local board. Barry cites the example of a Glasgow board which resolved to give free books to Catholic pupils, but before its decision could be carried into effect a newly elected board rescinded the provision of its predecessors.[13]

How did the 1872 legislation affect the voluntary schools and the issue of religious instruction in the board schools? Church schools had the option of transferring and becoming public or rate-aided schools. While almost three hundred transferred, more than nine hundred preferred to retain their status quo. Sixty-six of the seventy-two Episcopalian schools and all sixty-one Catholic schools continued as voluntary schools.[14] By 1910 practically all of the Presbyterian schools had gone under the boards; the number of voluntary Episcopalian schools had fallen to fifty-seven, but the number of Catholic schools had risen to 220.[15]

As to religious instruction in the board-controlled schools, the Act left the boards free to give any kind of religious teaching they might locally agree upon. A conscience clause allowed parents to withdraw their children from this instruction if they so desired. These provisions were contained in the Preamble of the Act, which read in part:

> And whereas it has been the custom in the public
> schools of Scotland to give instruction in religion
> to children whose parents do not object to the in-
> struction so given, but with liberty to parents
> without forfeiting any of the advantages of the
> schools, to elect that their child should not re-
> ceive such instruction, and it is expedient that
> the managers of public schools be at liberty to
> continue such instruction.[16]

The Act further stated that every school receiving any public
money should be open to children of all denominations.[17]

It will be noted that the Scottish provisions for religious
instruction in the public schools were in contrast to the practice which had been established in England by the Cowper-
Temple clause in 1870. That clause, it may be recalled,
barred any distinctive denominational influence in the county
schools. No religious catechism or religious formulary
which was distinctive of any particular denomination could be
taught in the schools. Thus was established the dual system
which was to prevail in England, while denominationalism
remained the practice in Scotland.

The doctrines of the Reformed Church continued to be
taught in the board schools as before they had been taught in
the parish schools. The practice became an issue in the
board elections of 1872. The outcome of the voting showed
the attitude of the people on the question. A quarter of the
total number of the board members elected were clergy. As
a result, religious instruction remained an integral part of
Scottish public education. In a few instances the instruction
was limited to reading the Holy Scripture, with explanation by
the teacher. In the majority of the cases it meant instruction
in the Shorter Catechism, a compendium of Presbyterian doctrine which had been agreed upon by the Assembly of Divines
at Westminster in 1634 and approved in 1648 by the General
Assembly of the Church of Scotland. However, in those areas
where Catholics predominated, such as the West Highlands
and the Outer Islands, Catholic school boards were elected
and the Catholic religion was taught in the schools. In some

cases, Presbyterian teachers were also employed who gave
instruction to the Presbyterian pupils. On the other hand, in
the industrial cities and towns where more recently the Irish
had been settling, the religious needs and desires of these
"dissidents" were in general ignored, if not scoffed at.[18]

Difficulty only spurred the Catholics to greater sacrifice
in their efforts to build and maintain their own schools. Their
position is brought out clearly in a report by one of the inspectors in 1878 who described the situation as follows:

> The effect of the Act on the Roman Catholic and
> Episcopalian schools has been, if anything, to
> give a fresh impetus to their existence. They are
> now the only existing church schools, pure and
> simple, but it must not be supposed that they are
> the solitary remnants of denominationalism. In
> point of fact, the machinery by which our national
> system is worked is mostly denominational. The
> mass of Scottish people are Presbyterians and for
> these the national schools may be said to exist,
> just as the Roman Catholic and Episcopalian, re-
> spectively, exist for their denominations. The
> public schools are to all intents and purposes de-
> nominational schools. Public and Presbyterian are
> practically interchangeable terms.[19]

This situation in the board-controlled schools explains
why Catholics refused to come into the national system at this
period. The enormity of their problem in building, equipping,
and maintaining their own schools in a manner comparable to
the standard of the board schools is realized when one considers their poverty and the fact that they were also taxed for the
support of the national system. Yet, considering the danger
to the faith of their children in the Protestant, often hostile,
atmosphere of the public schools, they dared not sell their
children's birthright for a mess of pottage. It is some measure of their faith and courage that in the forty years between
1872 and 1918 they built grant-earning schools at the rate of
forty every ten years.[20]   The voluntary schools according to

the Act were to receive Parliamentary grants conditioned on
the examiners' being satisfied with the efficiency of the secular instruction given in them. Some Catholic leaders, however, were hesitant to accept the grants fearful of governmental control and others found it difficult to meet the conditions
requisite for receiving aid. In all Scotland in 1918 there were
226 Catholic elementary schools.

In the meantime the tide of educational progress in Scotland moved steadily upward. Primary education was made
free up to the age of fourteen, upper classes were added to the
course, secondary school committees were created, and
secondary educational opportunities expanded. All these improvements meant increases in tax rates. The patrons of the
voluntary schools faced correspondingly greater difficulties
in keeping their own schools up to ever higher standards,
while paying the increased rates leveled by the boards from
which they received no benefits. A bleak period lay ahead for
the Catholic schools.

Inevitably a point was reached when the growing demand
for accommodations and better equipment could not be met.
Many of the Catholic school buildings were in poor condition
and others were completely out of date. The where-with-all
to make improvements was lacking. Moreover, there was a
serious shortage in the supply of qualified Catholic teachers
and, although those employed were dedicated and hardworking,
they were poorly paid. Provisions for Catholic secondary
education were totally inadequate. Many talented youths never
got beyond the primary level. The few who did get as far as
the senior secondary schools, which were fee-supported and
conducted largely by religious congregations, were from the
wealthier families, but even most of these children left at
fourteen without completing the full course.[21]

A survey of the Catholic schools in Glasgow conducted
early in 1918 brought their unsatisfactory condition into clear
relief. An analysis of the situation there, which its author
maintains was typical of all Scotland, is quoted below:

Of our fifty elementary and supplementary
schools nearly half were out of date and required

either to be superseded or remodeled to meet the latest requirements. Nearly 5,000 pupils were accommodated in our schools in excess of effective places for them according to the latest regulations. Only two of the Supplementary Centres had adequate science equipment. Of the six schools following a full secondary course only two measured up fully to modern standards of accommodation, and in all six there were less than 300 pupils in the post-intermediate classes for a Catholic school population in the city of 40,000. That Glasgow could be considered fairly typical of the conditions in Catholic schools over the whole country, with notable exceptions, is borne out by the reports of Inspectors covering other areas in the west. . . . [22]

Such was the situation in regard to Catholic education toward the end of World War I. Nevertheless, Catholics still recognized as valid the decision of their forebears in 1872: at whatever price, education for their children must be based on a foundation of the doctrines and principles of their faith. The board-supported schools, which they helped maintain but could not use, catered to the religious wishes of the Presbyterians. Catholics felt in all justice they too were entitled to share in the rates and voiced their complaints in no uncertain terms. They were not alone in expressing dissatisfaction with the state of education in Scotland. Municipalities were demanding a wider unit of administration than the old parish area; teachers, Catholic and non-Catholic, complained of low salaries. Educational leaders were pointing out the need to broaden the content of, and to enlarge the opportunities for, secondary education. Civic leaders were beginning to see both the injustice and the harm to the nation of leaving so large a proportion of children as attended the voluntary schools with poorer opportunities than were provided those attending public schools.

In 1914 a deputation representing the Catholics of Scotland -- ecclesiastics, clergy and laity -- had met with Mr. Robert Munro, Secretary of State, to explain their concern for

the depressing situation in their own schools and their grievance in not receiving what they felt justice demanded, namely,
a share in the rates so that they would be able to maintain
their schools at recognized standards. They received an interested and sympathetic hearing. Chances looked hopeful.

Then World War I broke out and the nation found itself
absorbed and its energies drained off in those pressing matters which war entails. But the education question was not
entirely forgotten. In the midst of the war, in 1917 Scotland's
traditional concern for education and ancient sense of fairmindedness came to the fore. Time was taken out to consider
reform measures.

The position of Catholics on the educational question was
given powerful support by the Education Institute of Scotland.
The group had appointed a committee of outstanding teachers
to survey the whole field of Scottish education with a view to
educational reform after the war was over. The committee
report made these significant points in regard to the voluntary
schools: that it could not be claimed that any system was truly
national which did not safeguard the interests of such schools;
the administration of education by the state should be such
that no child would be penalized because of his parents' religious beliefs; an effort to remedy adverse conditions affecting
the voluntary schools was imperative; as a reasonable solution
the voluntary schools should be eligible to receive financial
aid from local educational authorities which, the committee
suggested, should replace the existing school boards.[23]

An educational reform bill for England had been introduced in Parliament and had passed into law before the war
was over. A similar bill for the reform of Scottish education
was introduced in the House of Commons on December 17,
1917, by Mr. Munro. The bill aimed at a general reform of
education in the country. We deal here, however, mainly
with those aspects of the measure which relate to the voluntary
schools and religious education. These matters were embodied largely in the now famous Section 18 of the Act as finally
passed.

Section 18

In the original bill Section 18 attempted to settle the problem of the voluntary schools by proposing to give voluntary school administrators or trustees the right to transfer such schools to the local education authorities. Thenceforth they should be controlled as regular public schools and their efficiency thus secured. To safeguard the denominational character of the schools, the provision was made that just as much time should be devoted to religious instruction and observance as had been customary before the transfer and the religious authorities would have control over the appointments of teachers.[24]

Although it was Mr. Munro who introduced the bill, many others behind the scenes had a share in framing the compromise solution. Among these were: Sir John Struthers, Secretary of the Scottish Education Department; and the Catholic hierarchy in consultation with the Catholic Education Council of Scotland, composed of clergy and laity. The guiding mind, however, was the then Apostolic Visitor to Scotland, Monsignor W. F. Brown, later Bishop of Pella, who advised and directed the Catholic members of Parliament entrusted with the framing of Section 18.

The full text of the bill was printed in the newspapers and was discussed everywhere in Scotland. The proposed settlement relating to the voluntary schools was of greater concern to Catholics, for, while by now the Episcopal schools were very few, the original sixty-one Catholic elementary schools had increased to 226. The question for Catholics to decide was: Could they be assured that the element that mattered most -- the religious administration of their schools and the religious basis of their teaching -- would be preserved? No financial advantage that might be gained could compensate for jeopardizing the religious character of the Catholic schools. If Catholics transferred their schools to the local authorities in order to secure financial upkeep and material equality, they demanded adequate guarantees that this essential element of the child's education would nevertheless be safeguarded.

A number of Catholic leaders feared to hand over their

schools to the authorities, who traditionally were little in sympathy with them and sometimes even hostile. Consequently,
some members of the hierarchy and a number of the laity,
particularly in the Glasgow area, sought to find a solution
short of transfer. There were also other misgivings: Would
Catholics have opportunities to be represented on school committees or boards of management? What provision would be
made for opening new schools? Would the religious teachers
now employed in the Catholic schools be given proper consideration?

Criticism also came from Protestant sources -- from a
different point of view, of course. The United Free Church
of Scotland objected to the idea that the voluntary schools,
although maintained by public funds, would not be completely
under the control of the public authorities. Moreover, it was
argued, the provision for sectarian teaching at public expense
would introduce the "pernicious practice of religious tests and
disabilities and perpetuate and encourage the sectarian
spirit." [25]

Mr. Munro prepared patient answers to all objections.
His position on the voluntary school issue had been stated
clearly earlier in the controversy:

> The solution of the problem is to take over the
> denominational schools, and to place them under
> the same management as public schools -- on
> terms. Those terms are that teachers in the
> transferred schools should be approved by the for-
> mer managers of the school, or by their represen-
> tatives, both in respect of faith and character, and
> that religious instruction should continue to be
> given according to the use and wont of the former
> management of the school. That appears to be a
> fair and just arrangement. It is of course criti-
> cized by Protestants and by Catholics. Neither
> party considers that the arrangement goes so far
> as they would like. . . . I have a sense of justice
> . . . and desire to improve the educational outlook
> of all children in our land, whatever their parentage

may be. I therefore appeal to all parties to study
these proposals on their merits, without prejudice,
bigotry, or heat. . . . [26]

The gist of the Secretary's purpose was expressed in the
House of Commons when he introduced the measure. His hope
was to secure for all children in Scotland "their natural birthright of equality of educational opportunity."

The pros and cons of the plan continued to be cautiously
weighed and debated by Catholics for almost a year. On the
face of it, the offer was tempting to that body harassed as it
had been for years by the financial difficulty of maintaining
from their own resources a system of schools adequate to
their needs and comparable to contemporary standards.

Those favoring the proposal argued that educational
costs would continue to rise and greater difficulties would
have to be faced in the effort to meet the growing needs and
higher standards. Moreover, if the plan were rejected, the
small grants the voluntary schools had been getting would in
all probability cease. The difficulty in obtaining qualified
teachers would increase, and untrained persons would have to
be taken into the classrooms. On the positive side, it was
argued that many advantages for Catholics would be derived
from the proposed arrangement: their financial problem
would be ended; their children would have educational opportunities equal to those of other Scottish children; their schools
would be adequately equipped and on a par with the public
schools; their teachers would be qualified and receive adequate remuneration; most important, the religious basis of
the teaching and the Catholic atmosphere of their schools
would continue as always and the teachers employed would
have to meet the approval of the Catholic authorities. [27]

On the other hand, there was no denying that risks were
involved. What if an unfriendly government should come into
power? What if unsympathetic, or even hostile attitudes
should predominate among the members of the educational
authority? Was there not risk in becoming a part of a system
predominantly Protestant? To these misgivings, Monsignor
Brown always answered: "Trust your fellow-countrymen."

Catholic leaders were eventually faced with the grave responsibility of making a decision. Yet the hierarchy hesitated. Finally, they appealed to Rome for guidance. The counsel given by Pope Benedict XV through the Apostolic Visitor, Monsignor Brown, was conveyed to the people of Scotland in a letter written by the Archbishop of Glasgow. The message stated in part:

> As you are aware, there has been difference of opinion regarding the new Education Bill which is to be brought before Parliament at the next meeting. Our position in regard to the Bill has now been made clear by instructions which we have just received from Rome--that the Holy See, considering all the circumstances, is not averse to our entering the National system, on condition that there shall be guaranteed all that is required by the Catholic conscience for the education of our children in conformity with what has been on many occasions required by the Head of the Church.[28]

Doubts and hesitance ceased. Catholics united in their approval of the bill and in efforts to secure such guarantees as were necessary. Amendments to the bill were drafted and, having been laid before Mr. Munro, received his approval. The amendments made the arrangements relating to religious instruction more definite and satisfactory and provided for the appointment by Catholic authorities of a supervisor of religious teaching for each school. Provision was made whereby future new schools could be transferred to the local educational authority. The right of Catholic authorities to approve teachers on religious ground was further safeguarded.

The viewpoint of Catholics on these amendments was stated by Mr. Boland, a member of the House of Commons. He explained that Catholics were determined to preserve the religious character of their schools and in this respect the selection of the teachers was a vital matter. The Catholic authorities should have the right to list the names of teachers who, in their view, would be suitable on religious, moral, and educational grounds. The local authority would have the power to object on educational considerations. Mr. Boland emphasized that it would be unfair and unworkable to put on the Church representatives the odium of objecting on religious grounds to a teacher first selected by the education authority.

Some further amendments were made after the bill came before the House of Commons. The supervisor of religious instruction was to serve "without remuneration." He was "to have the right of entry to the schools at all times set apart for religious instruction or observance." This arrangement assured that the clergy who ordinarily looked after religious instruction should continue to do so. Facilities for conducting religious examinations were also provided for.

The measure was steered through Parliament by Robert Munro. On June 22, 1918, moving the second reading of the bill in the House of Commons, he restated his views on the necessity of coming to the aid of the voluntary schools "with adequate guarantees, of course, for the maintenance of their distinctive religious instruction." There was no opposition to any of the provisions regarding the voluntary schools. On October 17, 1918, the bill was read the third time. It was passed "amid the cheers of the House." [29] Four days later it was approved by the House of Lords and received Royal Assent, November 21, 1918.

The revolutionary change had taken place quietly and smoothly. Several factors explain its easy passage. First were the traditional fairmindedness of the Scottish people and the energy and determination of the leaders within and without Parliament in seeing the measure through. The sacrifices made by Catholics in common with their fellow countrymen during the war had knit the people closer together and alleviated to a considerable extent religious misunderstanding and intolerance. Some eighty-one Irish members of the House of Commons had taken over the interest of the Catholics in Scotland. Chiefly, however, was the fact that the government officials were concerned in seeing, as a matter of justice involving the national welfare, that all Scottish children had equal educational opportunities, that no child would be deprived of his civic rights because of his religious views.

The 1918 Act was revolutionary not only from the Catholic viewpoint, but for Scottish education in general. It was intended to bring about all round reform in education by providing a systematic course of education for every child from the ages of five to eighteen. It provided, also, for nursery education from two years to five, and at the upper end higher education for each person to the extent that he could profit by it.

Administration was simplified by doing away with the 1,000 school boards and substituting thirty-five county and five urban education authorities elected by the local voters. Unity was maintained by a central Education Department. The remuneration of teachers was placed on a national basis. The principle was laid down that secondary education should be free and encouraged by grants, bursaries, and travel expenses to deserving pupils. The age of compulsory attendance was raised from fourteen to fifteen years. Attendance at continuation classes up to the age of eighteen was envisaged to provide instruction equivalent to secondary education for young people who could not go to school full time. War and post-war difficulties delayed the implementation of some of the provisions and others have not yet been put fully into operation, but the standard to be striven for has been set.

Section 18 is in the nature of a "Concordat" between church and state authorities. The elements of the settlement are best seen in the text itself of this "Magna Carta" of the voluntary schools, as Section 18 has been called.

Section 18. (1) It shall be lawful at any time after the first election of education authorities under this Act for the person or persons vested with the title of any school which at the passing of this Act, is a voluntary school within the meaning of the Education (Scotland) Act, 1897, with the consent of the trustees of any trust upon which such school is held, to transfer the school, together with the site thereof and any land or buildings and furniture held and used in connection therewith, by sale,

lease, or otherwise, to the education authority,
who shall be bound to accept such transfer, upon
such terms as to price, rent, or other consideration as may be agreed, or as may be determined,
failing agreement, by an arbiter appointed by the
Department upon the application of either party.

(2) (This subsection deals only
with the disposal of any grant due to such school
when transferred.)

(3) Any school so transferred shall
be held, maintained, and managed as a public
school by the education authority, who shall be entitled to receive grants therefor as a public school,
and shall have in respect thereto the sole power of
regulating the curriculum and of appointing teachers: Provided that--(i) the existing staff of teachers shall be taken over. . . and be placed upon the
same scale of salaries as teachers of corresponding qualifications. . . (ii) all teachers appointed
to the staff of any such school by the education
authority shall in every case be teachers who satisfy the Department as to qualifications, and are
approved as regards their religious belief and
character by representative of the Church or denominational body in whose interests the school
has been conducted. (iii) subject to the. . .
Conscience Clause (1872 Act) the time set apart
for religious instruction or observance. . . shall
not be less than that so set apart according the
use and wont of the former management of the
school and the education authority shall appoint
as supervisor without remuneration of religious
instruction for each such school, a person approved as regards religious belief and character
as foresaid, and it shall be the duty of the supervisor so appointed to report to the education
authority as to the efficiency of the religious instruction given in such school. The supervisor
shall have the right of entry to the school at all

times set apart for religious instruction or observance. The education authority shall give facilities
for the holding of religious instructions in every
such school.

(4) (The Department is constituted
final arbiter in any dispute that may arise under
subsection (3).)

(5) After the expiry of two years
from the passing of this Act no grant. . . shall be
made in respect of any school to which this section
applies unless that school shall have been transferred. . .

(6) (Refers to special schools to
which this section does not apply, such as schools
for the deaf, blind, etc.)

(7) A school established after the
passing of this Act to which the Section would have
applied. . . may with the consent of the Department
be transferred.

(8) In any case when the Departments
are satisfied upon the representations made to them
by the education authority of any education area, or
by any Church or denominational body acting on behalf of the parents of children belonging to such
Church or body, and after such inquiry as the Departments deem necessary. . . it shall be lawful
for the education authority. . . to provide a new
school. . . the time set apart for religious instruction in the new school being not less than that so
set apart in schools in the same area which have
been transferred under this Section.[30]

The Act went into effect May, 1919. The transfer of the
voluntary schools took place quietly and with a minimum of
friction. On May 19, at the first meeting of the education
authorities most of the Catholic schools were transferred.
Within the next two years 226 Catholic schools, 50 Episcopal,
3 Church of Christ, 24 unclassified and one United Free
Church school had been transferred to the education authori-

ties.[31]   Little or no trouble arose over the matter of fixing
the prices of the schools. In some cases, the buildings were
sold outright, in others they were leased with rents paid to the
church. Some few, mainly fee-supported boarding schools,
preferred to retain their own management.

The transferred schools were nearly all elementary, although there were a few which combined both elementary and
secondary departments. Other secondary schools chose to
come under Section 9 of the Act. In these cases the school
received aid, provided the teachers were remunerated at a
rate not lower than the rate for teachers of similar qualifications employed by the authority.

Further enactments regarding Scottish education in the
years since 1918 have changed none of the essential features
of the Act. By the Local Government (Scotland) Act, 1929, the
old ad hoc school board system was abolished and the management of the schools was put into the hands of the county and
burgh councils under the control and authority of the Scottish
Education Department. On the new Education Committees of
the councils, church rights in relation to the transferred
schools were to be preserved by the appointment of co-opted
members for the various denominations. At least one each
represents the Catholic, and the Episcopal Church.[32]   Depending on the size of the Catholic population in an area,
another Catholic representative may be appointed. Such representatives are appointed by the ecclesiastical authority.
Before 1929, Church representation on the boards had to rely
on support at the polls. The system was open to danger and
at election times caused unwholesome tension and anxiety.
Although the co-option of two representatives meant a decrease
in the number of Catholics on the Education Committee in the
larger cities, that loss has been compensated for by the
present security and stability of representation.[33]   Moreover,
experience has shown that the influence of the representatives
bears little relation to numerical voting power. Strong representation by a minority can exercise a powerful influence. In
any case, fundamental issues affecting religion are protected
by the 1918 Act and cannot be jeopardized by the views of the
majority, should it have any such inclination.

In 1944 in the midst of World War II, Parliament, as has been noted, passed an education reform Act covering all aspects of education in England. An Act in 1946 applied the reform to Scotland, but the legislation brought fewer innovations because that country had been ahead of England in most educational aspects. The distinctive features of the Scottish system remained unchanged. More important among the provisions of the 1946 reform were those referring to secondary education. The Act made it imperative that every pupil after twelve years should receive secondary education according to his age, ability, and aptitude. No one was to be debarred from secondary education because of poverty. The education authorities were given power to assist in cases of hardship by paying travelling expenses and cost of residence in a hostel or to grant bursaries to pay maintenance and incidental expenses. The Act of 1946 superseded all previous education legislation but Section 18 of the Act contained the exact terms of the same section of the 1918 law.

Education (Scotland) Act, 1918, in Practice

Almost half a century has passed since the Act went into operation. That has given ample time to observe its working and appraise its success. The good will prevailing from the beginning was a hopeful portent of the future, which has not proved disappointing. Bishop Brown's wise counsel: "Trust your fellow countrymen," has been verified by events.

True, as could be expected, there were in the early years after the transfer of the voluntary schools some few voices from both sides of the fence bewailing the new situation. On the Catholic side were a negligent number who still feared that their birthright had been sold. The annual reports of the general assembly of the Church of Scotland indicated some perturbation that the control of religious instruction in the Catholic schools remained in the hands of parish priests. With the passage of time, however, the fears and resentment subsided as the benefits accruing from the new arrangement became manifest. Catholics found that their status as a whole had been raised; the perturbed Protestants turned their attention to other matters.

Just how has the Act operated? The concrete facts of
Scotland's educational system, including the church-state relationship, are an open book for those who are interested.
After the voluntary schools had been transferred to the education authorities by lease or sale, they were henceforth administered in all ways as public schools except for the specific
application of Section 18 in regard to selection of teachers,
religious instruction and its supervision.

The entire cost of building, maintaining, and staffing the
Catholic and other denominational schools has been borne by
the state, while the schools have maintained their denominational character intact. The enterprise has involved large
outlays as the years went on and needs increased. Many of
the school buildings had been in poor condition and others completely out of date. These were torn down, rebuilt, repaired,
or remodeled. In places where no Catholic school existed and
where the number of children justified the establishment of a
Catholic school, a new building was erected. Expanding suburban areas, such as those surrounding Glasgow and Edinburgh,
have necessitated the building of many new Catholic elementary
schools. Likewise, existing secondary schools, both junior
and senior, have undergone modernization and adaptation to
meet the increasingly higher standards required by the Scottish
Education Department.

The schools are completely maintained by the education
authorities. General furnishing and special equipment required
by various departments are adequately, even generously, supplied. An allowance on a per capita basis is given all the
schools for textbooks, writing materials, and other school
needs. The allowance covers books and materials used in the
religion classes. Teachers' salaries are paid on a standard-
ized basis.

Social service benefits which Scottish laws provide for
school children are enjoyed in equal measure by children attending denominational schools. These include free transportation for children who live two and a half miles from the
school, medical service, free milk, and dinners for poor children. Holiday camps, vacation classes, assistance for foreign
travel, educational concerts and exhibitions, youth employment

services are provided without discrimination to Protestant and Catholic children.[34]

Bursaries assist pupils to attend a Catholic or other denominational school at a distance if there is none in their own area and if their parents cannot pay the costs. Bursaries are provided also for abler students to finish the senior secondary course not only when parents cannot pay but even when payment would cause a considerable financial strain. The bursaries are on a sliding scale, from fifty pounds maximum to decreasing amounts for higher incomes. The Scottish view is that no one is to be barred by poverty from any kind or level of education, provided he can profit by it.

Education is compulsory, but parents are completely free, economically as well as theoretically, to choose whatever school they wish for their children. As a result the great majority of boys and girls are sent to the public school of their own denomination, only a few (in contrast to the situation in England) attending private schools where fees are charged. Although all state-supported schools are by law open to all denominations, in practice it rarely happens that a Catholic child attends a non-Catholic school, or that a Protestant child attends a Catholic school, except in a few remote and sparsely populated districts where Catholics are too few to justify a separate school. In these cases, the "Conscience Clause" of the law permits parents to withdraw the child from any religious instruction to which they object. Moreover, if they insist and where it can be reasonably done, the public authorities must supply transportation to a Catholic school or supply the costs of housing the child in a town where a Catholic school exists. The ideal in Scotland is that every child attend a school in which the religion of his parents is taught. Although the ideal is not perfectly achieved especially in areas where the vast majority of the population is Protestant, it remains an objective to be striven for and has, in fact, been almost completely implemented in many of the cities.

For all children compulsory attendance is from the age of five to fifteen. The educational program of the denominational schools is that approved by the Education Department except for the teaching of religion. There is much latitude given to the individual schools in the choice of subject matter and complete freedom is allowed the schools in the selection of textbooks. The headmaster selects the texts from lists sent out by the authorities. Scotland has no specifically Catholic system of textbooks, but the Department's list contains books that have been recommended by Catholic educational leaders and by religious supervisors.

The denominational schools follow the general system of grading or appraisal, which determines whether the pupil will go to a junior or to a senior secondary school after leaving the primary school. The less gifted pupils will be transferred to a junior secondary school for a three year course having a vocational bias. The abler boy or girl goes to a senior secondary school which provides a five-year academic course, leading to the Leaving Certificate, which entitles the holder to entrance into a teachers' college or a university.

Before 1918, provisions for Catholic secondary education were very limited, being confined to thirteen schools in all Scotland, eleven of which were managed by religious congregations. By 1955 there were twenty-five Catholic senior secondary schools, fifteen of which were in Glasgow. In addition there were seventy-seven schools or departments providing junior secondary education for pupils between twelve and fifteen. The great majority of new schools have been built by the education authorities who bought the sites, built and furnished the schools.

In January, 1963, the Scottish Education Department reported a total of 580,342 pupils in primary state schools. Of this number, 120,758 were in Catholic schools; 1,069 were in Episcopalian schools. Of the 274,030 secondary pupils, 47,881 were in Catholic high schools. [35]

"Further education" is the term used in Scotland for all types of education above the secondary level. Two Catholic teachers colleges, one in Glasgow, one in Edinburgh, train Catholic women teachers. A National Committee for Teacher Education, which has adequate Catholic representation, regulates and controls all matters relating to the educational program as such. The buildings in which the colleges are housed remain the property of the religious congregation which conducts them, but a part of the maintenance is assumed by the National Committee and the members of the staff are also paid by the Committee. Students get grants from their local education authority. As a rule, the grant covers all expenses including housing and tuition. The housing grant is paid by the student to the institution; the tuition grant, to the National Committee.

The residential character of the teachers' college affords the prospective Catholic teacher a valuable opportunity to live in an atmosphere at once cultural and spiritual. Religious instruction is directly under the control of the Church and in staff appointments preference is always given to the members of the religious congregations conducting the college or to Catholic candidates when properly qualified. All evidence shows that the Committee makes every effort to preserve the religious character of the college. The accomplishments of the two Catholic colleges are generally recognized and highly esteemed by the educational world of Scotland.

Two ecclesiastical colleges completely controlled by the Church educate boys for the Catholic priesthood. These students, too, may receive bursaries for expenses if the parents cannot afford to pay for them or if there is no Catholic secondary school of equivalent grade in their own district.

There is no Catholic training college for men. Male candidates for the teaching profession train in one of the non-Catholic teacher training centers or at one of the universities. Scotland has no Catholic university. Significant, however, has been the growth in the number of Catholics at the various universities. Prior to 1918, for example, there were very few Catholics attending the University in Glasgow. Since then the number has increased greatly. The teaching profession especially has benefited more than others in the numbers who have graduated from the university. There were few Catholic men teachers before 1918 and the supply of women teachers was insufficient to staff all the Catholic schools. Since then the number of Catholic men and women teachers has steadily increased. In 1951 out of a total of 31,000 teachers in Scotland there were 5,000 Catholic teachers of both sexes, 1,670 of whom were university graduates. The economic and pro-

fessional status of the Catholic teachers has been raised. He
or she possesses the same qualifications as other teachers
employed on equivalent levels and receives the same salary.

A similar policy of fairness and regard for religious
training prevails in the provisions that have been made in the
area of special education for the mentally and physically handicapped. For example, the Sisters of Charity conduct a school
for the deaf and blind near Glasgow. The education authority
provides funds for the maintenance of the children and pays
the salaries of the staff, the members of which are appointed
by the religious congregation. Sisters also conduct an institution at Rosewell for mentally and physically handicapped children under the General Board of Control. The education
authority pays weekly allotments for each child. For less
severely retarded children there are day schools employing
special educational methods suited to lower intelligence levels.
Some of these are Catholic, staffed by Catholic teachers.
They receive, as do other denominational schools, the benefits
of the 1918 Act. Likewise, provision is made for the education and rehabilitation of Catholic delinquent children under
the guidance of religious congregations. The Scottish Education Department pays staff salaries, leases and maintains the
school premises.

Foremost in an investigation of the practical operation
of the Act is the question which was uppermost in the hearts
and minds of Catholics in 1918: Would their schools remain
truly and completely Catholic? The consensus is that in this
vital area the Act has proved eminently successful and satisfactory. The Catholic character of the transferred schools
has remained undiminished.

The provisions of the Act regarding the selection and
appointment of teachers were intended to be the principal
safeguard of the religious character of the schools. Every
applicant for a position in a Catholic school must meet the requirements of the Church as to character and belief before he
or she can be appointed. Criteria by which to judge these
qualifications have been informally set up. Teachers in the
Catholic schools are for the most part lay men and lay women.
In the case of women, applicants would presumably have been

trained in one of the two Catholic colleges where religious instruction is required by law. As is the situation in the lower
schools, religious instruction in the college is directly under
the control of the Church. Students are required to pass a
special examination in religious knowledge before entering the
college. Courses in religious doctrine and practice in religious teaching form part of the normal curriculum for both
graduate and non-graduate students. If achievement is satisfactory to the authorities, the college grants the student a
certificate stating that she has passed an examination which
entitles her to teach religion. This is a certificate of proficiency. But before she can be appointed to a Catholic school,
she must be approved by the Church on religious and moral
grounds. As a rule, this latter, which is a certificate regarding religious belief and morals, is provided by the local parish
priest.

Prospective men teachers, as noted earlier, attend a
non-Catholic training center or a university. Nevertheless,
for them, too, religious instruction is required by law.
Catholic men are taught in special classes by priests appointed
by the bishop. They take courses in philosophy and Catholic
doctrine which include Holy Scripture, Church history, apolo-
getics, and catechetics at Catholic centers near the university
or training center. At the end of each course they must pass
a written examination. A passing grade in six courses and a
general recommendation is necessary in order to obtain an
ecclesiastical certificate approving them as qualified to teach
religion in the schools. This certificate of approval is given
by the Ordinary of the diocese and without it no Catholic male
teacher is permitted to teach in a Catholic school.

After receiving his or her certificate of approval the
candidate applies to the Education Committee for a position.
In practice, the influence of the co-opted Catholic representatives on the Education Committee is very strong in the appointments of Catholic teachers to Catholic schools.[36]   The Church
has the authority to withhold or withdraw certificates of approval. If such action is taken, the teacher would no longer be
eligible for appointment to a Catholic school. Moreover, the
Catholic authorities are under no obligation to furnish to the

education authority the reason for their withdrawal of the certificate. Barry says that no more than six such withdrawals
have taken place in thirty-three years and in every case the
teacher was asked to resign from the Catholic school when
the order, through the Bishop's legal advisor, informed the
authority that the certificate had been withdrawn. [37]

What opportunity do members of religious communities
have for appointment to the Catholic schools when vacancies
occur? This was one of the questions that disturbed some
Catholics in 1918. Members of the religious congregation
which was in charge of a school when transferred are generally given the preference in appointments if otherwise qualified. An authority on Scottish education says religious, both
men and women, are welcome on teaching staffs by the Education Committees. The law could not be worded as to guarantee religious their places, but there has been no trouble on
this score, for religious have all the school positions that
their number can supply. In fact, it has been noted that in
many cases religious are preferred as teachers because of
their beneficial influence on the children.

A difficulty has at times arisen when a qualified Catholic
teacher cannot be found when needed. This situation occurs
more often in the secondary schools. The head teacher and
principal teachers of departments in secondary schools are
required to be honor graduates besides holding the necessary
training qualifications. When no qualified Catholic applicant
for one of these positions is available, it becomes necessary
to appoint a non-Catholic teacher who has the required qualifications. In such cases, the applicant is usually regarded as
provisional, pending the time when a qualified Catholic teacher can be obtained. The fairmindedness of the Committees'
policy is indicated by a provision relating to this problem
which is contained in the Handbook of the Edinburgh Corporation. It states in part: ". . . in no case is a Protestant to be
retained in a Roman Catholic school more than six months
after an application has been received from a Roman Catholic
teacher suitably qualified for the position in question. . ." [38]
It is accordingly seen that the Church's rights in the important
matter of teacher selection have been well safeguarded.

An interested inquirer may ask whether the legal safe-guards have proved sufficient to keep the transferred schools all that the Catholic philosophy of education requires them to be. Are they achieving the primary and immediate aim of Christian education: "to form the true and perfect Christian; that is, to form Christ Himself in those regenerated by bap-tism?"

There is no direct way, nor has any attempt been made, to measure scientifically the Catholic schools' achievement in the religious and moral sphere. Undoubtedly, there are some pupils from the Scottish schools, as from Catholic schools elsewhere, whose lives fail to measure up to the hopes of their teachers. Scotland is not free from the myriad influences to-ward secularism and modern paganism which permeate our Western world today. It might be noted, however, that Scot-land's crime and juvenile delinquency rate as compared with a large number of Western nations is low.

But here we are inquiring as to whether the hopes and demands of the Catholics in 1918 are being fulfilled; whether sufficient opportunity for religious instruction is provided, and whether the hundred nuances that compose a Catholic at-mosphere have been preserved in the transferred schools. Again, the consensus on this matter is vehemently positive; the Catholic character of the schools has been maintained in-tact.

The Act itself requires that "the time set apart for reli-gious instruction or observance in any school shall not be less than that so set apart according to the use and wont of the for-mer management of the school. . ." Since the passage of the Act, the limitation on the time when religious instruction was to be given has been liberalized. In 1946 complete liberty was given to the schools to choose any hour of the school day instead of the periods at the beginning or end. In most pri-mary schools one hour a day is devoted to religious instruc-tion. In secondary schools the period is usually forty minutes daily. In outlying districts where Catholic children must at-tend the general school, provision is made for them to receive instruction in their faith, and usually there is at least one teacher who is Catholic. The religious instruction time can

be used in whatever way the head teacher wishes; the children
may attend Mass or Benediction, listen to a sermon, or participate in a discussion bearing on religious matters. Parish
priests are permitted to visit the class and speak to their par-
ishioners during the religion period.

In addition, a religion supervisor appointed by the education authority with the approval of the bishop has the right of
entry into the classes during the religious instruction. He reports annually through the diocesan inspector of religious
instruction to the local authority as to whether or not religious
instruction is given satisfactorily. Usually the bishop approves
the local pastor to be the supervisor for his own school. Time
is set apart each year for the diocesan inspector's examination
in religious knowledge. This aspect, then, of the Catholic
ideal of education has been working out successfully. Bishops,
priests, teachers and parents have expressed satisfaction.

But the Catholic ideal of education is more inclusive. It
requires that all aspects of the education program be directed
in some manner towards the Catholic schools' ultimate objective -- the formation of the true and perfect Christian. The
whole atmosphere of the school must be permeated by the
spiritual. Has this effect been achieved? An authority on the
Catholic schools states that "quite apart from these official
instruction times, the Catholic life of the school continues in a
vital if sometimes intangible and almost subconscious way."[39]

In practice, almost all the schools open the day with a
prayer; each class period begins with a prayer; and the school
day closes with a prayer. Efforts are made to correlate the
doctrine and principles taught in the religion classes with the
child's conduct and activity throughout the day, in and out of
school, applications being drawn when and where relevant.
The textbooks are selected carefully and the teacher is free to
relate the materials of the day's lesson to a furtherance of the
Christian life of the pupil. A spiritual note runs throughout
the whole curriculum.

Every classroom has its crucifix and holy pictures as
reminders to the child of his faith and dedication. The cele-
bration of the patronal feast of the school is an opportunity for
instruction and inspiration. In Glasgow holydays of obligation

are school holidays. All in all, the evidence would indicate
that the Catholic atmosphere of the transferred schools has
been preserved intact. The agreement entered into by the
state with the Church in 1918 has been honorably kept.

Religion has continued, also, to hold an important place
in the general educational system of Scotland. As was noted
earlier, the practice of teaching the Presbyterian religion in
the parish schools prevailed from the period of the Protestant
Revolt. The 1918 Act made no change in this tradition except
that the clause permitting and encouraging such teaching formerly inserted in the Preamble of the 1872 law was made Section 7 within the body of the 1918 Act.[40]   Generally speaking,
the tenets of the Presbyterian religion are taught in all the
public schools of Scotland. The conscience clause continues
to permit parents to withdraw their children from "any instruction in religious subjects and from religious observances. . ."

The Scottish People Like Their Solution of the Education Issue

An indirect testimony as to the peaceful working of the
Scottish solution is the fact that in the almost fifty years since
it went into effect only two cases involving litigation have occurred. In one case the education authority of a local district
rejected the application of Catholics for a school. Later the
Catholics built the school on their own initiative and had it approved by the central Education Department. The Catholic
authorities then asked to have the school transferred to the
educational authorities. Their petition was rejected. Thereupon they took the matter to the courts and finally to the House
of Lords, which decided in their favor. [41]

In a second case, Catholic children in a district where
there was no Catholic secondary school were being transported
at public expense to a Catholic school in Glasgow. The educational authority decided to avoid the expense by insisting that
the children attend the local public school (Protestant). Catholics thereupon referred the issue to the Secretary of the Education Department. He ordered the local education authority
to carry out the provisions of the Act, that is, to continue
transporting the children to a Catholic school. Later, a Catholic school was established in the district.[42]

But positive evidences of the successful operation of the
Act are more numerous and more convincing. Favorable reactions to the solution Scotland embarked upon have come
through the years from all classes of society -- churchmen,
statesmen, educators, and the rank and file of ordinary citizens. A brief sampling of appraisal will be sufficient to indicate that from the Scottish viewpoint satisfaction has resulted.
A. C. F. Beales, lecturer in education at King's College,
London, states: "There is no slightest doubt but that it has
been a success. Testimony is consistent throughout forty-
five years of its operation." [43]   He quotes the writer J. Grant
Robertson, who summarized the settlement thus: "It must
have seemed to every observer that the better part of Scotland
had conquered the worst; that the nation's famous and honorable zeal for education had overcome the lingering prejudices
of a minority." [44]

Expressions of approval abound in current published
materials. From the viewpoint of Catholics, the Act has certainly proved satisfactory. Their fears of 1918 have been
allayed; their hopes, realized. Writing the the Dublin Review,
an authority on the Catholic position declares that every advantage envisaged by the Glasgow Teachers' Association has
been attained: religion is taught to the children; they do receive equal educational opportunities; the Catholic schools
have equal financial footing with others. Catholic teachers do
receive equal pay for equal work. [45]

In contrast with the situation in 1918, it is pointed out,
the Catholic schools are today in all essentials up to the
national level. The standards and range of instruction are on
a par (some think higher) with those of the general public
schools. Her Majesty's inspectors frequently comment on the
efficiency of teaching, the excellent discipline, the wholesome
atmosphere to be found in the Catholic schools.

The mutual relationships between the denominational
schools and the education authorities, which are implicit in
the arrangement, have contributed toward breaking down religious misunderstanding and intolerance. It is agreed that the
relationships are characterized by reciprocal respect, friendliness, and cooperation.

Pastors and other religious authorities have been relieved of the burden of finding the where-with-all to finance the ever increasing costs of building and maintaining modern schools and paying the correspondingly higher salaries of teachers. They now have more time to devote to the duties of the sacred ministry and to study the problems of modern education with a view toward improving their participation in the work of the schools. A keener sense of solidarity has developed among Catholics themselves.

Catholic parents are relieved from the former pressing burden of supporting entirely from their scarcity their own system of schools while paying taxes for public schools they could not use. Tensions which arose from the injustice they suffered have been alleviated. In many districts, as has been seen, they had been unable to provide secondary education for their children; now it is adequately provided by the state. The schools are better equipped. Catholic parents can rest satisfied that now their schools are equal in all secular respects to other schools and at the same time provide their children with a thorough religious training.

Catholic boys and girls themselves have a status on par with their non-Catholic companions. They have equal educational opportunities without forfeiting their birthright of religious faith and full freedom to live according to its precepts. They are, according to their ability, advanced to secondary schools, to the universities or teachers' colleges, to higher technical schools, and to the professions and executive positions. Thus, the social and economic level of the whole Catholic population of Scotland has been raised. But Catholics do not view these advantages as special privileges accorded to them. All denominations share them. The 1918 Act simply rectified a long existing wrong; justice was given full sway.

Catholic teachers are better prepared. They are better paid than they could be under the former conditions. Their remuneration is on the same scale as other teachers. They have opportunities for promotion; their future is made secure by provisions for pensions upon retirement. These advantages have attracted a higher quality of personnel into Catholic school teaching. All these factors have undoubtedly brought

greater efficiency in the art of teaching. The religious teachers too have profited. They are fully employed, receive
salaries on the national scale, are adequately qualified, have
opportunities for inservice training, and are eligible for pensions.

From the viewpoint of the Education Department and the
local education authorities, the arrangement has worked out
advantageously. With state-aided schools in one organization,
administration has been facilitated and rendered more efficient.
Financing has been simplified, since all grants are made to
the local authorities. Reasonable unification has been achieved
and standard of efficiency raised on all levels of instruction.
Equality of educational opportunity has been made possible for
the whole population.

From a larger viewpoint of the nation, a greater sense
of unity, peace and justice prevails. The nation was the loser
as long as any particular group in the population was discriminated against. The statesmen in re-organizing the Scottish
system of education were cognizant of the harm to the nation
in having a significant segment of the school population without
adequate educational provisions and of the injustice and grievance suffered by that segment in being deprived of benefits
conferred on others. By extending equal educational opportunities to all, Scotland has immensely improved its cultural and
intellectual level. It has now available talent that otherwise
would have been lost through lack of opportunity for development. Foremost, however, among the advantages for the
nation are citizens who have been prepared for civic responsibility on a foundation of religious faith which makes good citi-
zenship binding in conscience and supports it by eternal sanctions.

From a philosophical viewpoint, the Scottish solution is
seen to be consistent with the principles of the natural law. It
recognizes, and provides safeguards for, parental rights to
direct the education of their children and to determine what
school they should attend. It provides without favoritism a
workable means of cooperation between the churches and the
state so that the churches are free and unhampered in providing religious and moral instruction for the child in accordance

with the wishes of parents. At the same time, the Act safeguards the state's right to supervise the efficiency of the
schools and to provide for itself an educated and loyal citizenry.

In the denominational schools are uniquely combined the
interests and functions of church and state, for the state cooperates by supporting the schools and providing for their
efficiency, while the churches control the religious education
of the child. The state by law judges the professional qualifications of the teacher, while the church, equally by law, is the
sole judge of the teacher's religious beliefs and character. In
this way, that most precious of all rights -- freedom to worship God according to one's conscience -- is fully protected,
specifically in that very sensitive area of education. In Scotland, parents who desire a religious education for their children may send them to a school which satisfies their convictions without paying an economic penalty for exercising that
religious right.

Likewise, the solution accords with the principle of
distributive justice, which demands that the state distribute
its benefits to its citizens without partiality. All children
without exception have equal opportunity to develop their capacities and talents. All parents share in the benefits accruing
from school taxes toward which they have contributed. Scotland has an established church, yet grants equal liberty to all
religions.

The Scottish settlement may not be the appropriate one
for the United States, yet our country can find much to admire
in the settlement. Here is a nation that has surmounted difficulties of a kind also inherent in our unsolved problem -- religious pluralism and a heritage of religious misunderstanding
and intolerance. To her credit and for the admiration of other
democracies, Scotland has evolved a solution which meets the
demands of freedom and justice, satisfies her people, and
benefits the nation as a whole.

Chapter 3

CANADA IN GENERAL AND ONTARIO IN PARTICULAR

The commonwealth nations, which developed under the leadership of Great Britain, are spread over the earth's surface. While enjoying complete freedom, the member-nations have voluntarily linked themselves with the British Crown in varying degrees by economic and mutual assistance ties. Some of them, originating in a core of British colonists, have closer ties with England, sharing with her a common language, culture, and to a lesser extent a common religion. Included among the commonwealths are such scattered and widely differing countries as Canada, Pakistan, Nigeria, Australia, India. Yet, in common, they subscribe to a democratic way of life, implementing it with parliamentary governments, free enterprise and increasing technological progress.

Having inherited a patrimony of Western ideals -- love of freedom, respect for the essential dignity and equality of every human being -- what solutions have the commonwealths found for the challenging problems of church-state relationships in education? What role, if any, has religion been given in their public schools? Have they found any difficulty in reconciling aid to church-related schools with the concept of separation of church and state? History reveals that the way to a settlement was in many instances a stormy one and that fact may provoke an interest in an investigation of how our commonwealth friends have struggled through historical misunderstandings and complications to achieve some modicum of success in resolving the issue.

For present purposes, our investigation will be limited to the solutions arrived at by two commonwealth nations, Canada and Australia, whose history and traditions, though varying from ours in a thousand ways, have nevertheless many elements in common. Like America, Australia began as an English colony, and Canada became one. All three nations were greatly influenced by the educational system which existed in England at the time their respective colonists left the mother-country to settle in new lands. During the early history of all three countries, religious and moral training was considered the most important element in the educational program and almost all schools were church-related, church-controlled, and to some extent, church-supported. In all three, state financial assistance was given to these schools as a matter of course. In all three almost immediately environmental factors, including the national origins of the various settlers, began to influence the shaping educational pattern.

Each of the three nations eventually had to face the issue of how it would fit religion into the educational scheme in a pluralistic society; of how it could safeguard the conscientious convictions of those who believed religion must play an integral role in the educational process while not trespassing on the freedom of those who wanted no religion.

All three nations went through a period of struggle and controversy in which emotion and prejudice played a part. Attacks and counter-attacks were made, bigotry flared. Eventually policies were adopted which attempted to resolve the issue. Evaluation is difficult, and a satisfactory arrangement in one state need not be the solution for another.

CANADA

As our close neighbor to the north, Canada's handling of the religion-in-education issue has special interest for Americans. No single solution was reached. Each of the ten Canadian provinces is autonomous in the management of education. Environmental factors varied from province to province. The national origin of the settlers, their language, and their religion became important influences shaping educational patterns. The predominance of French Catholics in Quebec influenced the trend of church-state relationships in that province. In Ontario, British Anglicans and Scotch Presbyterians formed the majority, while Catholics were a minority.

The dual issue of the relation of denominational schools to the state and the advisability and practicality of giving religious and moral instruction a place in the regular curriculum of the public school was a live one for almost a century in

Canada. Although in the various provinces it found different solutions, at the same time fundamental views on the importance of religion in life, which were the settlers' legacy no matter from what part of Europe they came, show up in the diversity of solutions. In all but one province provision has been made for the inclusion of religious and moral instruction in the public elementary schools, and in all but two provinces church-related schools are aided by public funds in one way or another. In some cases, as denominational schools they share directly in public taxes. In other instances, they are incorporated into the regular provincial system while retaining their denominational character. Denominational schools of the latter type are known in Canada as "separate schools."

The first settlements in Canada were made by the French and for over one hundred fifty years the eastern parts of Canada were Catholic in religion and entirely French in language and culture. The Maritime areas began early to receive English-speaking settlers and on the Pacific Coast the English were the first to settle in British Columbia.

In 1759 all of Canada was ceded to Great Britain and from then on English-speaking Protestant settlers began to come into the country in increasing numbers. The first attempt at union among the scattered provinces was made by Upper Canada (Ontario) and Lower Canada (Quebec). The association was achieved in 1841 by the Act of Union, which remained in force until 1867. The union proved to be an uneasy one. Misunderstandings were constantly arising as a result of the differences in religion, language, and culture between the peoples of the two sections. Action in the legislature in relation to schools was frequently deadlocked. It soon became evident that a more solid basis of union was necessary. As a result, political leaders, not only in Ontario and Quebec but also in New Brunswick and Nova Scotia, pledged themselves to work for a federal union of the provinces under Great Britain.

During the discussions on the question the matter of education and denominational schools came to the fore. It was manifest that here was an issue of great concern, the solution to which would require careful deliberation and, undoubtedly, compromise. The Protestant minority of Quebec had long enjoyed liberal separate school privileges, which, however, were due more to the manner of administering the law rather than to any specific law itself. The Protestants were fearful that federation might curtail these privileges and therefore demanded that guarantees be built into the Federal Constitution which would effectively safeguard their rights. In this demand, they were backed by the Protestants of Ontario, who were not so willing to confer the same privileges on the Catholic minority in their own province. Long and lively debates on the issue ensued.

The discussions on this issue and others finally culminated in the passage of the British North American Act, 1867, which effected a union of the four provinces under the British Crown. A compromise dealing with church-state relations in education was contained in Section 93 of the Act. The Canadian provinces were given jurisdiction over education within their own borders except for specific limitations designed to protect the rights of religious minorities to establish and operate their own schools. This section is of such great importance in Canadian educational history that it is quoted in full:[1]

Sec. 93. In and for each Province the Legislature may exclusively make laws in relation to Education, subject and according to the following Provisions:

(1) Nothing in any such law shall prejudicially affect any right or privilege with respect to Denominational Schools which any class of persons have by law in the Province at the Union:

(2) All the powers, privileges and duties at the Union by law conferred and imposed in Upper Canada on the Separate Schools and school trustees of the Queen's Roman Catholic subjects, shall be and the same are hereby extended to the Dissentient Schools of the Queen's Protestant and Roman Catholic subjects in Quebec:

(3) Where in any Province a system of Separate or Dissentient Schools exists by law at the Union or is thereafter established by the Legislature of the Province, an appeal shall lie to the Governor-General in Council from any Act or Decision of any Provincial Authority affecting

any right or privilege of the Protestant or Roman Catholic minority of the Queen's subjects in relation to education:

(4) In case any such Provincial law as from time to time seems to the Governor-General in Council requisite for the due execution of the Provisions of this section is not made, or in case any Decision of the Governor-General in Council on any appeal under this Section is not duly executed by the proper Provincial Authority in that behalf, then, and in every such case, and as far only as the circumstances of each case require, the Parliament of Canada may make remedial laws for the due execution of the provisions of this Section, and of any decision of the Governor-General in Council under this Section.

The British North American Act is Canada's Federal Constitution. There is separation of church and state, but the concept in Canada cannot be interpreted in the broad and often exaggerated sense which recent United States Supreme Court decisions have given the "no law respecting an establishment" clause of the American Federal Constitution.

In Canada, the Constitution guarantees that where a province enjoyed special rights in education before it entered the Dominion, those rights may not be abrogated after federation. In case of disputes about those rights, the Constitution makes provision for appeal to the Governor-General in Council and to the Privy Council in London. In general, then, the right to maintain separate Catholic and Protestant schools was affirmed except in the newer provinces carved out of Dominion territories where no such schools had existed. As a result of this provision, as we shall see, there are separate schools in three provinces, a dual system of public education in Quebec and a multiple system of denominational schools in Newfoundland.

An over-all view of the Canadian system of education provides a helpful background for the understanding of the church-state relationships in the separate provinces.

General Features of Canada's Educational System

The Dominion government is not without influence in the educational field even though it has no direct authority. Besides protecting the rights of religious minorities it has aided education in a variety of ways, performing functions similar to those undertaken by the United States Office of Education. It has provided lands for the support of education and it is responsible for the operation of schools in the territories. It has provided a limited amount of aid for vocational schools and higher education. It undertakes research and statistical activities. The trend has been, as in the United States, towards greater concern with education on the national level.

As we have noted, however, the Dominion Constitution gives to each province the essential responsibility for the establishment and administration of public schools. There are minor differences in the general set-up from province to province, but similarities predominate except in Quebec. In each province (except Quebec) the public school system is headed by a cabinet member, usually called the Minister of Education. He is a political appointee and a member of the provincial legislature. It is his function to determine the broad educational policies of the government. He is responsible to the legislature and, through these elected representatives, to the people.

Each province has a department of education presided over by a deputy minister, who is a professional educator and a civil servant. He supervises the department, advises the Minister on policy, and carries out that policy. The department exercises control over courses of study, examinations, textbooks, requirements for school buildings, teacher training, and legislative grants. Supervision of local authorities is maintained by elementary and secondary school inspectors appointed by the provincial department. [2]

In all the provinces legislation provides for the establishment and operation of schools by local education authorities, who operate under the Public School Act and are held responsible to the provincial government and resident tax payers for the effective fulfillment of their duties. Thus authority in education is shared by the provincial government and the local units, the degree of decentralization being reviewed intermittently. There is a trend to delegate more authority to the local units. [3]

The province and local units also share the responsibility for the support of public education. Some financial aid for vocational education comes from the Dominion government. Provincial grants average 43 percent; municipal and local grants, 50 percent; and federal grants, 7 percent; but provincial grants actually range from a high of 80 percent in Newfoundland to a low of 16.5 percent in Saskatchewan.

Though denominational in character, separate schools, where they exist, are part of the public school system and share in public funds. There are private schools outside the government system in all the provinces. These receive no public aid. They are normally supported by the sponsoring bodies and by student fees.

The observation has been made that in nearly every aspect of education the Canadian practice is "between that of England and that of the United States. Denominational schools and religious instruction within the public school system are found virtually everywhere in England, in some parts of Canada, and virtually nowhere in the United States." [4]

Such is the general plan of education in Canada. But, as the Dominion Constitution provides, education is a distinct function of each province, so variations are bound to occur. For an understanding of the church-state relationships in education, each province must be considered separately. In the discussion that follows the history of educational developments in Ontario is dealt with in greater detail, especially in respect to the background of the separate school issue. The Upper Canadian controversy is but one example of a similar struggle in many countries in the Western world, as these pages testify. The history of the debate on the issue in Ontario has some features that bear a likeness to the controversy that was being waged in the United States about the same time on the questions of religion in the public schools and aid to church-related schools. The outcome of the struggle in the Canadian province is at pointed variance with the resolution of the issue in our country. This fact makes Ontario's story of greater interest to Americans, who are today engaged in debate on the related issue of federal aid to parochial schools.

As for the other Canadian provinces, the present status of the church-state relationship in education is stressed with merely a cursory view of the historical background.

ONTARIO

A detailed study of the historical controversy in Ontario which led to the establishment of the province's policy on church-state relationships in education illustrates the way in which one pluralistic society encountered and overcame both the usual difficulties associated with the solution of this issue and some specific problems peculiar to its own environment. For Canada, Ontario's struggle has particular pertinency since it was a factor leading to the inclusion of Section 93 in the Federal Constitution. This section affected and delimited church-state relations in education for the rest of the Canadian provinces.

When Canada passed into the hands of Great Britain in 1759, what is now Ontario was practically a wilderness untouched by civilization. Colonization did not really begin until loyalists from below the border began straggling northward after England acknowledged the independence of its thirteen colonies to the south. To reward the loyalists and encourage colonization in the northland Great Britain gave grants of land to each family as well as provisions, seed, and farm implements. Nearly three million acres of land were so granted.[5]

Problems of government soon arose and a constitution was drawn up in 1791 for Britain's Canadian colony. By this Constitutional Act, the country was divided into two provinces, Upper and Lower Canada, now Ontario and Quebec.

Though the entire white population of Upper Canada at the time was only about 50,000 and conditions were highly primitive, the settlers as soon as possible gave attention to education. A school was opened at Cataragui (now Kingston) in 1785 and several others were established soon after.[6] These early schools were provided by private means and were generally under church-control. In 1807 an act was passed

establishing eight public schools to be governed by trustees appointed for each district by the Lieutenant Governor.   They
were essentially "grammer" schools, secondary in type.   At
the time nowhere did elementary education receive much attention.

The next step was legislation passed in 1816.   The Act
ordered the establishment of a common school where the inhabitants had twenty children to attend and set forth the manner
of organization and management.   Three persons were to be
chosen by the people of a district to act as trustees and were
given authority to appoint a teacher.   A Board of Education
made up of five members was appointed to supervise the
schools in the eight districts of the colony.

Nothing was said about religion in the Act.   However, in
localities where the majority were Protestants naturally the
teacher chosen by the trustees would be a Protestant.   Likewise in those areas where Catholics predominated, Catholic
teachers were chosen.   And, since the people took it for
granted that religious and moral training was an essential part
of school life, it followed that the child would be instructed in
the faith of the majority along with secular education.   In
some places where Catholics were a strong minority their
reasonable demand that their children be instructed in their
own faith was respected by the majority.   In this early system
of public schools which provided for religious instruction and
showed at least a limited regard for parental rights can be
seen the germ of the separate school principle.

At this time there were only a few distinctly denominational schools which were operating in the larger cities and
towns.   They received no public aid.   An exception existed in
the case of a Catholic school established at Glengarry by
Reverend Alexander Macdonell, who later became the first
bishop of Kingston.   The Anglican church was claiming to be
the established church of the province and was, as a matter of
fact, receiving support from public funds.   The atmosphere
of most of the common schools was strongly Anglican.   Bishop
Macdonell insisted that all denominations be treated alike and
be given their just share of the public revenues for religion
and education.

Strong opposition against the idea of aid to the Catholic schools came from several sources, notably from the Reverend Dr. Strachan, an Anglican bishop and chairman of the provincial Board of Education, which had been established in 1824. His key position gave him powerful influence, and the financial arrangements which Bishop Macdonell had succeeded in securing came to an end in 1835.

In the meantime immigration from the British Isles was increasing. Many among the newcomers were Irish. The question of religious instruction in the schools, though a much discussed issue, remained unsettled. Practically all in Upper Canada agreed that religious training was vitally important. Not many were ready to favor its absolute exclusion from the schools, leaving the responsibility entirely to the home and church. Dr. Strachan would have settled for a monopoly of religious instruction by the Anglican Church. Naturally, vigorous dissent on his proposition was made by the Irish.

There was also the ever recurrent proposal that a common denominator of religious truths, satisfactory to all denominations, be prepared and taught in the common schools. A Dr. Charles Duncombe submitted a report to the Assembly in which he said it was his opinion that essential Bible truths could be taught in common without offense to any Christian, but he acknowledged that however preferable such a plan would be, all denominations might not agree on a common religious training. Since that was the case and religious training was so important, he felt it would be better to have separate schools than to have no religion taught. One thing, he contended, was certain: if religion were banished from the provincial system of education "every denomination would be impaired in its most vital intents." And, he concluded, for one who would be proselyted by a sectarian teacher, ten would be ruined by the vice and irreligion consequent upon the exclusion of religion from the schools.[7]

By 1840 common schools had sprung up in settled areas, built, managed, and supported by the local communities with little aid or direction from the provincial government. There were no longer any denominational schools receiving state aid, although a few private schools under church control and support

were operating. The teacher of the common school was usually a member of the dominant religious sect and the atmosphere
and teaching in the school reflected its influence.

The grammar schools, although theoretically non-denominational and open to all, were in practice taught by clergymen
and under either Anglican or Presbyterian influence. Two
colleges had been established by Presbyterians and Anglicans
respectively and were supported by combined church and state
funds.

Many children, however, were not in school at all. In
1840 about 20,000 attended out of 220,000 under sixteen years.[8]

The British Parliament decided that it was advisable to
grant a larger degree of independence to its Canadian colony
and that a union of the two provinces would secure greater
stability. Accordingly, Upper and Lower Canada were united
under the Act of Union, which received Royal Assent,
February, 1841. Prior to this, each of the two separate provinces had attempted to work out its own ideas on education
under its own legislature limited only by its status as a colony
of the Crown. In Quebec the schools had their relationship
primarily to the Church and parish; in Ontario the relationship
was primarily to the state. Now educational matters were to
be handled by a united legislature.

In July of the year 1841 at the first session of the united
legislature education became the pivotal point of interest. Attention was called to the high rate of illiteracy, especially in
Upper Canada. Solicitor General Charles Day introduced a
bill "to make further provisions for the establishment and
maintenance of common schools throughout the province." To
implement this primary purpose, the bill provided funds for
the establishment and maintenance of schools; it created a
Superintendent of Education and made provisions for local
Boards of Education with Power to assess the inhabitants of
each district.

As originally presented the bill contained nothing relating to separate schools and if passed the measure would have
curtailed greatly the privileges enjoyed by the Protestants in
the Catholic province of Quebec in regard to their denominational schools. To understand the implications of the issue,

it should be remembered that the denominational schools of the
Protestants in Lower Canada were fully supported by government funds as were, of course, the Catholic schools of the
majority. On the other hand, as we have seen, there was no
legal provision in Upper Canada for separate schools for the
Catholic minority.

The Protestants in Quebec had no intention of losing
public funds for their schools and immediately they began to
agitate for the preservation of their school privileges. Petitions were presented to the legislature urging recognition of
religious instruction as an essential part of education, urging
the use of the Bible as a textbook in all public schools, and demanding the continuation of government aid for the Protestant
schools of Quebec. It is of interest to note that most of the
petitions came from members of the Church of England in
Quebec and were re-echoed by their religious confreres in
Ontario. One of the petitions was from the Catholic bishop of
Quebec, who asked that in framing the new legislation for the
improvement of education, the lawmakers take care that it
contain no provision that would "prejudice the interest of Her
Majesty's Roman Catholic subjects." The Catholic bishop of
Kingston made objection to the bill as presented but did not
expressly ask for separate schools.[9]

Because of the opposition to the original bill, a committee
was appointed to study the question. Serving on the committee
were seventeen Protestants and seven Catholics. The group
decided that an acceptable bill would have to meet the demands
of the Quebec Protestants and provide for the continued support
of their schools from public funds. Then, to be consistent and
preserve uniformity, the bill would have to contain similar
provisions for denominational schools in Ontario, which would
be mostly Catholic, since the public schools in that section
were already strongly Protestant in atmosphere. Accordingly
a new bill was drawn up incorporating these ideas in Sections 11
and 16. The bill passed the Assembly, September 18, 1841.

Although the Act was repealed several years later, it
has great historical significance since Sections 11 and 16 introduced a new concept of church-state relationships in education
which was to prevail and affect educational developments in

other Canadian provinces as well as in Ontario.

Section 11 stipulated that any number of inhabitants of a different faith from the majority in a township or parish had the right to choose their own schools and might "established and maintain one or more common schools" under the same conditions and receiving the same government support as the other common schools.[10]   Section 16 provided that the Board of Examiners appointed by the governor to supervise the schools might, in those localities where the schools were separate on a religious basis, be divided into two groups. One group would be composed of Catholics to examine the Catholic schools and the other composed of Protestants to examine the Protestant schools. All separate schools were to be subject to the same regulations as were the common schools. Section 4 of the Act, however, exempted members of a religious order from the examination that had to be taken before teaching in the schools.

The Act of 1841 was the first statutory measure in Ontario to recognize separate denominational schools. It contained the seeds of today's school system in that province. The agitation which resulted in the drawing up of this legislation came almost entirely from Protestant bodies.[11]

Legal provision for separate schools did not insure their establishment in Ontario. Catholics were too few in most areas to fulfill the conditions necessary for making an application. The Act made no provision for scattered Catholics, or Protestants for that matter, who desired a separate school to combine in order to meet the requirements for establishing one. Consequently the Act was practically inoperative in securing Catholic schools. It can be said that the 1841 enactment established the principle of separate schools but did not succeed in laying their foundation.

The Act was not by any means received with unanimity by the people of either section. On the contrary, it gave rise to acrimonious debate. As time went on, it became increasingly evident that an identical type of school system for both Upper and Lower Canada could not meet the conditions peculiar to each area, differing as they did in religion, language, culture and traditions. In 1843 the original Act was repealed for

Ontario and new legislation drawn up.

In the new law the principle of voluntary separation was retained. Three sections of the statute dealt with the religious issue. Section 54 contained a "conscience clause" which prescribed that no child could be required "to read or study from any Religious Book" which should be objected to by his parents or guardians. Section 55 provided that should the teacher of a common school happen to be a Catholic, the Protestant inhabitants were entitled to have a separate school, the initial step being the appointment of three trustees to manage the school. After its establishment the separate school was entitled to receive its share of the public appropriation according to the number of children attending the school. It was subject to the same rules, inspections, and obligations provided by the Act and binding upon other common schools.

In this piece of legislation we find the fundamental principles and most of the policies which guided all subsequent laws governing the separate schools of Canada. Religion was to have a definite role in the educational program. The primary rights of parents over the religious instruction of their children received recognition. The separate schools might be Protestant or Catholic, but the individual Protestant sects were not free to form schools in the sense in which the law used the term.

The separate schools were made an integral part of the public school system. They were subject to the same visitors and regulations as the common schools and were to receive public aid. No special legal favor in regard to schools was granted to the Church of England, which at this time was still claiming to be the established church, or to the Church of Scotland. The policy of allocating large powers to the local units was given a firm hold. Negatively, secularism in education was rejected. It is interesting to note by way of contrast that in 1842 New York City, after a bitter controversy, established the policy of excluding dogmatic religious teaching from the public schools and prohibited public aid to religion-oriented schools.

The experience which followed the passage of the 1841 law was repeated: the legal admittance of certain principles

contained in the 1843 Act did not insure their practical implementation. The law as it stood left the operation of the principles and the execution of rights seriously impaired.
Catholics, the minority group in Ontario for whose benefit the
separate school policy had been especially inaugurated, found
themselves unable to establish separate schools in most of the
instances where they wanted them. The application to establish a separate school had to be signed by at least ten resident
freeholders of the school section. Then the approval of the
Council or local superintendent was necessary. Catholics
were generally poor; few owned property. In many districts
ten freeholders could not be found and the 1843 law, as its
1841 predecessor, made no provision for Catholics from two
or more city or rural sections to combine to form one efficient
school when the Catholics in a single section were too poor or
too few to accomplish this.

Moreover, a separate school for Catholics could be established where, and only where, the teacher of the common
school was a Protestant. It could happen that a teacher was
merely a nominal Catholic, ineffective and unsatisfactory to
the Catholic populace, but even so the law would not permit
the Catholics to make application for a separate school.

Then, if and when the school was established, financial
difficulties hindered its adequate maintenance. Although the
separate schools were to continue to share in the grants for
education made by the legislature, they were to receive no
part of the funds raised for public schools by local taxation.
Yet, the supporters of separate schools were held responsible
for all public assessments which the municipality made. Thus
they were doubly burdened. First they paid for their own
separate school and then for the public school from which they
received no benefit. On top of all this, the separate schools
had to meet all the requirements binding upon those which
were getting twice as much public money. The financial burden was usually too heavy to be undertaken by Catholics.

With these handicaps framed into the law, the Act was
practically inoperative for a long time in many cities and rural
areas. As late as 1850, one estimate gives only thirty-one
separate schools for the whole of Upper Canada. Somewhat

more than half of these were Catholic, the rest Protestant.[12]
Contrary to the opinion expressed by some historians, the
facts show that the absence of separate schools was not due to
the lack of desire for them on the part of Catholics but was
the result of the difficulties involved in establishing and maintaining them. The situation of Catholics in Protestant Ontario
was decidedly unfavorable by comparison with that of the Protestant minority in Catholic Quebec.

The 1843 Act, as might be expected, evoked protests
from both Catholics and Protestants, although for different
reasons. The questions associated with separate schools became a foremost political issue for almost three decades,
giving rise frequently to bitterness and animosity which had
their roots, as a rule, in intolerance.

Several prominent personalities appeared on the scene
and took a dominant part in the debates and educational developments in Ontario during the mid-decades of the nineteenth
century. Chief among these was Egerton Ryerson, a Methodist minister and principal of the Methodist Victoria College.
In 1844 he was appointed Deputy Superintendent of Education
for Upper Canada, a position he held for thirty-three years.
From this strategic post, his viewpoints and activities exercised great influence on developments throughout the years he
held office.

He was strongly opposed to the principle of separate
schools. He regretted that the policy had been framed into
law, but seems to have made an honest effort during his term
of office to administer the provision of the law as it stood.
He was consistently adverse to any extension of the separate
school system and hopefully expected that the existing ones
would die out. He expressed scorn for "popish obscurantism"
but was prudent enough to seek the collaboration of Catholic
ecclesiastics in his educational policies. He did not oppose
private schools conducted by religious communities and supported by themselves, but he did not expect or want them to
expand.

He believed that morality based on Christianity should
have a central place in public school education but held that
the Bible contained a body of common doctrine on which this

moral instruction could be based and as such it should be satisfactory to all Christians, Protestant or Catholic. He conceded, however, that if some people, Catholics in particular,
objected to this instruction they might be permitted to organize separate schools, under due safeguards of stability and
efficiency, but this practice -- isolationism he called it --
should never be allowed to become general.

The teaching of dogmatic religion, in his opinion, was a
function exclusively of home and church. Still, rather than
allow a multiplicity of separate schools to come into existence,
he was in favor of making available in the public schools facilities for representatives of the various religious denominations
to come in at stated times and instruct the pupils of their religious persuasion as parents requested such instruction.
Ryerson proved himself a skilled propagandist and his views
helped shape educational developments for over three decades.

Another of Ontario's opponents of the separate school
system was the liberal leader, the Honorable George Brown,
editor of the bitterly anti-Catholic Globe. He built up a political party of his own on the "no popery" slogan, accusing the
old Reform party of having betrayed Upper Canada to French
Canadian Catholicism. He led the opposition to the separate
school principle with an animus and acerbity rivaling any bigot
on the continent.

Ryerson in an early act of his administration established
in 1846 an advisory Board of Education. He himself selected
the personnel of the first Board, including among its members
church leaders, clerical and lay. Right Reverend Michael
Power, the Catholic bishop of Toronto, was named chairman.
Bishop Power cooperated actively with the educational authorities since he felt that in most areas Catholics were too few or
too poor to maintain an efficient separate school. There is
no evidence that he opposed the separate school principle or
did not recognize the advisability of such schools for Catholic
children, although in the controversies of the 1850's this claim
was made by opponents of the separate schools.

Bishop Power was succeeded in the episcopacy by Bishop
Armand Charbonnel, a French nobleman, who had come to
Lower Canada in 1840. A kindly, zealous ecclesiastic, he

stood with unwavering determination for thoroughly Catholic schools for Catholic children. After his appointment to the Toronto see, he worked resolutely to obtain for Catholics in Upper Canada educational rights equivalent to those enjoyed by Protestants in Quebec. His labors met consistent opposition in the person of Ryerson, whose efforts, on the contrary, were directed toward restraining, not encouraging, the expansion of separate schools. George Brown and his followers, who were out to abolish completely the whole separate school system, fought furiously not only against the efforts of the Bishop but against everything Catholic.

The clash of these opposing views and personalities set the stage in Ontario for a period of violent controversy centering on the school issue. A wave of fanatic intolerance swept the province. Politics and the press were corralled into the arena. For over two decades, but especially in the 1850's, Upper Canada experienced the most bitter political-religious strife in the history of any section of Canada.

We content ourselves here with the facts of the situation without attempting to probe into the underlying causes, but it may be noted in passing that similar waves of anti-Catholicism had struck America twice during the middle years of the nineteenth century -- under the Nativist movement in the 1830's and again in the 1850's under Know-Nothingism. It is possible that sparks from the American conflagration were carried across the border, adding to the fire already burning.

Lines were drawn politically. A considerable number, perhaps a majority, calling themselves the "Clear Grit Reformers" followed Brown in his determination to abolish the separate system. John A. Macdonald, Ryerson and the Liberal-Conservatires comprised a strong minority. Though they had no love for separate schools, they were willing to allow Catholics minimum guarantees in order to keep French Canadian support behind the Ministry.[13]   A smaller minority composed of Catholics and many members of the Church of England stood for separate schools, which, while remaining truly denominational, would have every advantage offered by the common school system.[14]

At the core of the struggle, however, were the two

protagonists, Bishop Charbonnel and George Brown, the one campaigning for laws more favorable to Catholics, the other determined to defeat and destroy. Brown did not attain his main objective, but he did succeed in creating dissension and misunderstanding among the peoples of Upper Canada, and his opponents had to rely on a Lower Canadian majority to outweigh his and his followers' machinations. Bishop Charbonnel on his part did not hesitate to put the utmost possible pressure on politicians to secure the legislation he wanted.

Both the Bishop and Brown relied greatly on the press. The Mirror and the True Witness presented the Catholic viewpoint and supported the separate school principle. The Examiner, The Banner, and Brown's own Globe supported the opposition, exhibiting generally grave misunderstanding and frequently fanatic hatred and outright bigotry. The Catholic clergy were mocked and derided, Catholic ceremonies were ridiculed, and Catholic doctrines were misrepresented and refuted. Protestantism was presented as the only hope of the world. We find, for example, such extravagant statements as the following appearing in The Banner:

> The idolatrous church of Rome has so overlaid the
> Gospel with doctrines of Roman invention that it
> has scarcely the semblance of Christianity, that
> wicked and persecuting Church, which is drunk
> with the blood of Saints, and which is clearly de-
> nounced for utter destruction by the word of God.[15]

It was through the Globe especially that Brown carried on his propaganda, breathing hatred and intolerance. He gave vent to his animosity with such unfounded charges as that which appeared in the April 24, 1852, issue:

> In its very nature, the papacy is utterly opposed to
> civil liberty. It claims to bind all men in the most
> debasing thraldom. . . . It forbids men to enquire
> and form opinion for himself. The priest thinks
> for him. . . What a frightful weapon of tyranny
> the confessional is. . .

His paper was widely read and, unfortunately, influenced the thinking of many Upper Canadians.

There were Protestants, who, though they refused to subscribe to Brown's anti-Catholicism, either honestly feared the separate schools would weaken a plan for general education or were not willing to support the separatist principle because they judged Catholics only would stand to gain from any division of public funds.

Ryerson netted a partial victory for his side in an Act passed in 1850, which, although continuing the separate schools, made it more difficult for Catholics to establish them. The statute raised the number of rate-payers required for an application from ten to twelve. The law also continued the restriction whereby Catholics of different sections were prevented from uniting in order to secure the necessary twelve petitions.

Disadvantageous as the Act was for Catholics, Brown in his Globe immediately expressed strong opposition against it, basing his attack on the fear that the public school system would be destroyed by the multiplication of separate schools.[16] Protests also arose from Catholics under the leadership of Bishop Charbonnel, but their logically presented demands were vigorously opposed by Ryerson. Sharply worded exchanges took place between the Bishop and the Superintendent.

Finally, Ryerson yielded to Catholic insistence and suggested to the Assembly an amendment to the Act which would rectify to some extent the inequality of Catholics' receiving no benefit from municipal taxes. The amendment also broadened somewhat the privileges given to separate schools. Ryerson's amendment passed the Assembly in 1853 as "An Act Supplementary to the Common School Act for Upper Canada."

Under the terms of the Act separate school trustees were enabled to incorporate themselves under the law and were given power to assess for separate school rates or to collect subscriptions from the people. If the supporters of a separate school raised by subscription or rates a fund equal to the public school assessment, they were exempted from contributing to the support of the public schools. However, if they

failed to give to the separate schools an amount equal to the
public school rate, they became liable for public school rates.
Moreover, the exemption extended only to the period during
which parents had children in the separate school. When Mr.
Maquire's children were old enough to leave school, he had
to turn his tax assessment over to the common schools.

Separate schools were not to share at all in municipal
taxes levied for the support of common schools, but, as before,
would share in legislative grants in accordance with average
attendance. In granting the separate school trustees the right
to levy taxes, the amendment inaugurated a new concept in the
separate school principle which was to become a permanent
feature of the system.

The amendment also provided that a certificate of qualification from the separate school board would be sufficient to
qualify a person as a teacher in a separate school instead of
his submitting, as formerly, to an examination by the district
Board of Examiners. If this provision seems surprising, it
should be recalled that training schools for elementary teachers were still very uncommon in any part of the Western world.

The 1853 Act did ease the financial situation of the separate schools to a limited extent, but grave inequalities still
existed. Chiefly deplored was the fact that the administration
of the Act was left in the hands of those who opposed the whole
idea of separatism in education. Catholics continued to press
for a better deal. A memorandum of the bishops of Upper
Canada listed the grievances and brought out the contrast between the situation of the two minority groups -- the Catholics
in Ontario and the Protestants in Quebec. The True Witness
stated the Catholic viewpoint in its declaration that Catholics
would not be contented until "they are placed on as good a
footing before the law as their non-Catholic fellow-citizens of
the same province." [17]

Catholic agitation for justice continued, although ridicule
and denouncement in the hostile press accompanied their efforts. In July, 1853, the Assembly again took up the question
of separate schools in Ontario. A bill was presented by
Honorable E. P. Tache, which contained provisions designed
to mollify the grievances of Catholics. Lines were drawn as

usual. Brown argued against the measure, saying that only
the clergy wanted separate schools, a charge refuted by patent
facts. John A. Macdonald, the Attorney General, stated that
he himself preferred a school system without separate schools;
still since there were people who wanted them, that type of
school should be encouraged and helped to be efficient.

Discussion and debate on the measure were prolonged
during which changes unsatisfactory to Catholics were made
to the original bill in a more or less clandestine manner. In
its amended form the bill passed the Assembly and received
Royal Assent, May 30, 1855. The statute went further than
any previous Act in removing the difficulties which stood in
the way of separate schools. A separate school could be established even where the teacher of the common school was a
Catholic; the number of householders required to sign a petition was restored to ten; provision was made for the uniting
of separate schools to form a common board; the trustees of
the separate school were placed on the same footing as those
of common schools and given the power of disposing of all
school funds for school purposes and of receiving their share
of government grants directly from the Superintendent.

The measure, however, was still not all that the Bishop
had asked for and had been promised. The changes that had
been surreptitiously incorporated during the Assembly debate
made the Act, as the Globe put it, "innocuous as a papatistical
School Bill could well be." In a memorandum Charbonnel
listed the disadvantages: a common school had to be established in a district before any application for a separate school
could be made; supporters of a separate school were obliged
each year to make their declaration of being a separate school
supporter; aside from the legislative grants, Catholics were
deprived of sharing other provincial funds set apart for school
purposes; the election of trustees was annulled if the separate
school was not established within two months.

In a pastoral of 1856 Charbonnel strongly impressed upon Catholics the importance of Catholic education and their
obligation to ascertain the attitudes of political candidates on
the school issue. Efforts to obtain further reforms were continued.

As a result, the education question came up again in the Assembly in 1856. A new bill was introduced for consideration, which the Globe immediately attacked as a plot to destroy the common school system: "When he could not control, the ecclesiastic has always endeavored to crush the knowledge-giving system." [18] At the same time Brown moved in the Assembly that all separate school legislation be repealed.

The issue was now firmly in the realm of politics where for almost another decade the battle continued to be waged with intensity and acrimony. Lines were more definitely drawn. There were many of good will who sincerely sought a solution which would secure religious liberty and justice for all. On the opposite end, the forces of ill-will, religious prejudice, and out-and-out bigotry paraded. Old charges, many times refuted, were hurled against the Catholic Church, the Pope, her clergy, and her doctrines. The cry "no popery" rang out, as it had rung out in America a few years earlier. In the middle ground, there were those who did not like the separate school principle but were willing to make compromises in the interest of provincial harmony.

In the Legislative Assembly, Catholic representatives from Ontario patiently pointed out that they were asking for no more than what had long before been granted to their Protestant fellow-citizens in Quebec. They were supported in their demand by the Catholics in Quebec, who could not see why the same treatment should not be accorded both minority groups. But the voices of opposition, though fewer in number, were more vociferous. The extreme segment demanded no less than the complete abolition of separate schools and whatever measure of secularization of the public schools as was necessary to achieve that end.

The reasonableness of the claims of the separate-school advocates, their quiet determination to work incessantly to obtain their objectives, the obvious animus of many of their opponents -- these factors and others made it clear to all concerned that sooner or later the demands of Catholics would have to be recognized. Otherwise, the harmonious development of the province was endangered.

Nonetheless, the cause of justice and peace was not

easily won. Bills introduced in 1860, 1861, 1862, which undertook to procure needed reform, were shelved.

Finally, the Reform Ministry of John Sandefield Macdonald sponsored a separate school bill, which became the
famous Scott Act of 1863. Richard Scott, a member from
Ottawa, introduced the bill, March, 1860, explaining that the
measure was intended to remove obstructions to the administration of the separate school system rather than extend the
system.

Three years were to pass before the bill became a law,
during which the pro's and con's were discussed according to
the lines previously formed. The division of opinion was not
necessarily Protestant against Catholic, but rather anti-
Catholic intolerants versus those who sincerely desired harmony in the province with justice as far as it could be procured
for all. A Protestant, the Honorable H. M. Foley, for example, defended the bill and argued for the right of Upper Canadian Catholics to have their own schools.[19]   He urged the
Protestants of the province to be as generous and just in dealing with the Catholic minority as the Catholic majority in
Quebec was in dealing with the Protestant minority. He denied
that the separate school principle endangered the common
school system.

The final vote taken May 5, 1863, was 74 to 30 in favor
of the measure. The title of the Act is revealing: "An Act to
Restore to Roman Catholics in Upper Canada Certain Rights
in Regard to Separate Schools." The measure was not all
Catholics had hoped for, but they accepted it as the best that
could be obtained. The True Witness reflected the Catholic
viewpoint in stating that the bill was not regarded as a finality
or that parents' rights in education had been fully conceded.
But it did acknowledge that the measure, as far as it went,
was in the right direction. [20]

Since the Scott Act contains the main features of the
separate school system which operates in Ontario today, its
provisions will be given in detail in the discussion below on the
current operation of the church-state relationship in that province. We note here only those features of the statute which
represent a development of the separation principle. The Act

established the right of Catholics to have their own schools.
It put on a firmer basis the related policies that the supporters
should maintain their schools by taxes levied on themselves
with the addition of legislative grants and that these same supporters would be exempted from the payment of taxes for common schools. The Act reemphasized that the separate schools
were to be subject to the same rules as were the common
schools in respect to inspection, supervision, courses, and
other regulations of the school law. It provided for an appeal
to the Governor in Council from any decision of the Superintendent of Education.

Opponents of separate schools, particularly the editor of
The Globe, vigorously assailed the Act. They predicted that
the separate schools would multiply; that Catholic children
would be sent to them where they would receive no education
worthwhile; that Catholics would continue to make demands
until the common school system was destroyed. [21]

Though Catholics had not regarded the measure as the
ultimate in what could be hoped for, in a sense the Scott Act
had a note of finality. Its provisions were the basis of Section
93 of the Federal Constitution. This section, as we have
seen, guaranteed minority rights in education in perpetuity
and made permanent all the advantages which had been granted
to separate school supporters in the Act of 1863. For Ontario
the Act represents, practically, the fullest development of the
separate school principle. Additions which have been made
since are simply developments expected in a growing system,
rather than essential changes. For example, the Separate School
Act of 1960 has 73 sections as compared with the 28 sections
in 1863, yet the basic features of the system remain the same.

The union of Ontario and Quebec, entered into in 1841,
had never been a happy one. Apparently irreconcilable differences in religion, language and culture often stymied action in
the union parliament. Leaders of the two areas pledged themselves to work for federation as a more workable union. A
convention of delegates from the four provinces met in 1864 to
discuss the question. Progress was made and the discussions
continued.

The school issue soon became pivotal. For many years,

the Protestants of Quebec enjoyed liberal separate school privileges. [22]   They became cautious lest federation might result in a diminution of their prerogatives. Accordingly, they insisted that in any consideration of federation, guarantees for the continuation of the rights they were enjoying would have to be given. If there were no safeguards, there would be no federation. From their viewpoint it was that simple and they were backed in their demands by the Protestants of Ontario, who, though not so generous in their treatment of the Catholics in their province, wanted to make sure that the Protestants of Quebec lost nothing of their school privileges by federation.

The Catholics of Ontario, too, indirectly backed them. They wished to have the federation bind the compact of 1863 in such a way that the rights they had fought for so long would be adequately and permanently safeguarded. In securing this advantage for themselves, the privileges of the Quebec Protestants would be likewise safeguarded.

There were on the other hand those who opposed any and all such guarantees being incorporated into the Constitution. George Brown, though he favored federation, again assumed leadership of the opposition. He took a vigorous stand against the admission of the separate school principle into the Constitution, saying in his usual vein that a separate school system "might gradually extend itself until the whole country was studded with nurseries of sectarianism, most hurtful to the best interests of the province." [23]

The situation became hopelessly entangled. Progress on the union movement was stymied. In the face of such circumstances the political leaders finally became convinced that if a permanent federation was to be effected the rights of the religious minorities of the various provinces to denominational or separate schools would have to be safeguarded by constitutional guarantees. To this end, a compromise would have to be worked out. Gradually the acrimonious debates leveled off. Even George Brown showed reluctant willingness to make concessions. "I admit," he stated in a speech before the Assembly, "that from my point of view this (a constitutional safeguard) is a blot on the scheme before the House; it is, confessedly, one of the concessions from our side that had to be made to secure this great measure of reform. But assuredly I, for one, have not the slightest hesitation in accepting it as a necessary condition of the scheme of the union." [24] He had decided to choose what to him was the lesser of two evils.

When the final vote was taken the Assembly was almost unanimous in support of the separate school clause. For Ontario, in a sense, the Scott Act had become part of the Federal Constitution since it is the basis of Section 93.

Although the Ontario government has enacted many educational laws during the last one hundred years, the legislation has merely elaborated or adapted the concept of separate schools to new situations, but has not essentially changed the basic principle itself. Numerous executive actions and court decisions have clarified its meaning or interpreted its implications for a given situation. A brief survey of the principal modifications follows.

Since the separate schools were subject to the same regulations as the common schools, new educational legislation of a general nature applied equally to both systems. Such, for example, was an 1871 Act which embodied the following principles: free tuition; compulsory education of children up to fourteen years of age; county inspection by qualified persons; and uniform examinations for promotion to high school. The same year the name "common school" was changed to "public school." In 1882, the Education Department inagurated the plan of having separate Catholic inspectors appointed for the separate Catholic schools instead of having the Catholic schools inspected by the ordinary public school inspectors.

It will be recalled that the religious teachers of separate schools had been exempted from any examination as a prerequisite for teaching. In 1906 a decision of the Judicial Committee of the Privy Council ordered such teachers to meet the same professional requirements as the teachers in public schools.

General economic changes necessitated modifications in the law in regard to finances. The Scott Act in 1863 had made provision for separate schools to levy taxes for educational purposes on the property of supporters, which usually consisted

of real estate. It did not make any special provision for the
separate schools to share in the taxes paid by stock companies
and corporations since there were few such legal groupings at
the time. But with the passing of years business management
changed and corporations sprang up, both Catholics and Protestants holding shares in them. These companies were taxed
and part of the funds were given over to public education.
Early laws made no provision for the separate schools to share
in these greatly increasing funds.

It was not long before significant inequalities began to
exist between the funds available for public and for separate
schools, and such financial inequality was bound eventually to
affect the quality of education. Acordingly, in 1886 the legislature passed the Assessment Act, amending the legislation
of 1863. The Act provided that corporation taxes be divided
between the public and the separate schools on the principle
that the investment of Catholics in companies or corporations
was to be considered as Catholic property. The corporations
were permitted, but not obligated, to give to the separate
schools a portion of their taxes which were allocated for school
purposes. This portion was not to be in excess of the proportion of stock held by Catholics in the company. [25]

Obviously the solution embodied in the law was neither
equitable nor practical. Difficulties immediately arose regarding its implementation. A legal attempt to meet the problem of making an accurate division on a religious basis was
made in 1913, but the question of corporation taxes continued
to be the cause of considerable agitation.

One final point in this account of the historical development should be noted. The separate school concept, as the
term is used in Ontario, applies only to the elementary school
level, not to the secondary. Before federation Upper Canadian
schools were classified as grammar and common, the latter
including separate schools. The Canadian grammar school,
like the American Latin Grammar school, was secondary and
classical in character and privately owned and supported.

It was not until 1871 that a public secondary school system got started and these high schools then began to replace
the private grammar schools all over the province. Some of

them, boasting superior accommodations and faculty, became known at collegiate institutes. At first the public high schools were fee-charging, but later, like the elementary school, were free.

Since the separate school legislation had been formulated prior to these developments, secondary schools were not mentioned and separate school supporters were called on to support the public high schools through municipal taxation. Later when boards for secondary education came into existence it was provided that separate school supporters should be represented on them by one or two members.

In the meantime Catholics saw the need for their own secondary schools. True, a few privately-supported schools had been in existence from the early days, but now many more were needed. Catholics claimed exemption from public school rates and maintained that they had a right to share in the provincial grants for secondary education on the same basic principles as underlay the separate elementary system. Relying on the guarantees of the British North American Act, they argued that the law requiring the payment of rates and denying them a share in the grants was "prejudicially affecting their rights in respect to denominational schools."

The question was an open one for a long time. Finally it was taken from the lower courts to the Privy Council for adjudication in the Tiny Township case.[26] Catholics of that area had demanded that the principle of separation be extended through the secondary course. The claims of the Catholics were denied by the higher Court, with the result that today Catholic secondary schools must be maintained by their sponsors, who likewise must contribute to the support of the public secondary schools.

This survey of developments in the church-state relationships in education is not complete without some reference to the statistics of growth. A few sample figures will suffice to illustrate the general character of the growth pattern of the separate school system. In 1850, according to one report, Ontario had 46 separate schools in all, 21 Catholic and 25 Protestant; in 1860 there were 151 separate schools, all Catholic. By 1886 there were 244; in 1912, the number reached

513, all Catholic. The increase was steady, if not spectacu-
lar, during the succeeding years. In 1938, the total number
of Catholic separate schools reached 832, accounting for 18.4
percent of all children in Ontario's elementary schools. [27]

Practical Functioning of Church-State Relationships in Education in Ontario Today

Two aspects of the church-state relationship in education
are considered in the following discussion: (1) the role of religion in the public school; and (2) the relation of the separate
school system to the state and to public education.

PUBLIC SCHOOLS AND RELIGION: It seems best to
quote the official regulations on this matter as they give a
clear and comprehensive picture of the role religion is given
in the public schools of Ontario. Religious exercises, as distinct from religious instruction, are required by law in every
public school. The pertinent regulations read:

> 35 (1) Every public school shall be opened each
> school day with religious exercises consisting of
> the reading of the Scriptures and the repeating of
> the Lord's Prayer or other prayers approved for
> use in schools.

> (2) The Scripture passages, forming a part of the
> religious exercises. . . shall be read daily and
> systematically at the opening of every public school
> and may be chosen from any list of selections
> adopted by the Department for use in public schools,
> or from any other public school list approved by
> the Minister, as the public school board by resolu-
> tion may direct.

> (4) The religious exercises held at the daily open-
> ing of public school may include the singing of
> one or more hymns authorized for use in public
> schools. [28]

Definite provisions are made for religious instruction.[29]
In addition to the time assigned to religious exercises at the
opening of the school day, two periods of a half hour each week
immediately after the opening of public school or immediately
before the closing of school in the afternoon are to be devoted
to religious education. The instruction is given by the regular
teacher in accordance with a course of study authorized by the
Department of Education. Issues of controversial or sectarian nature must be avoided.

However, by resolution of the board, official representatives of any denomination may come into the school to give
the religious instruction to the children of their faith, in lieu
of the public school teacher. In this case, the principal of the
school must arrange accommodations within the school for the
denominational instructors, and should the number of rooms
in the building be insufficient, the principal must arrange for
additional accommodations elsewhere.

A "conscience clause" prescribes that "No pupil shall
be required to take part in any religious exercises or be subject to any instruction in religious education to which objection
is raised by his parents or guardians." His absence is not to
be considered a contravention of the rules of the school.
Teachers may claim in writing exemption from the teaching
of religious education. It is then the duty of the board to
make such other provision as is necessary to implement the
ruling with respect to the teaching of the subject.

A handbook stating the regulations and outlining a program for religious education has been prepared under the
authority of the Minister of Education for the use of teachers.
It summarizes the objective of the program in these words:
"It is therefore a major concern of the school that the children
entrusted to its care shall learn to live in a manner that is socially effective in a democratic society which bases its way of
life on the Christian ideal." [30]

Secularism as a policy for public education is evidently
taboo in Ontario. The Schools Administration Act in listing
the responsibilities of teachers includes among them the duty
"to inculcate by precept and example respect for religion and
the principles of Christian morality and the highest regard for

truth, justice, loyalty, love of country, humanity, benevolence, sobriety, industry, frugality, purity, temperance, and other virtues." [31]

THE CHURCH RELATED SCHOOLS. The term separate school, which came into use in Ontario for historical reasons, is misleading. In the United States, although Catholic schools perform a public function, one rightly can speak of two systems -- the public schools and the Catholic schools -- since the Catholic schools are, strictly speaking, private in the sense that they are not part of the public school system. This is not true of the separate elementary schools of Ontario. There, they are truly an integral part and parcel of the provincial system of education, functioning under the Department of Education in the same manner as the public schools. The term public school in Ontario therefore does not connote the same difference in relation to the separate school as do the terms public and private as used in the United States. We may say the public schools of Ontario are provincial and nondenominational; the separate schools are provincial and denominational. Both types of schools are on a footing of equality before the law. The separate schools of Ontario bear a similarity to the confessional schools of Western Germany.

Negatively viewed, the separate schools of Ontario are not private or parochial, such as we are familiar with in the United States. They are distinguished from the American parochial school system by the fact that they are supported by public taxes, administered by public officials, and subject to public regulations. They have their relation primarily to the state and are not directly under the control of a parish or diocese.

A further difference arises from the fact that the separate system in Ontario extends through the elementary level only. The recognized right of Catholics to have their own publicly supported schools does not include secondary schools.

However, concessions have been allowed as a result of custom. Catholics, desirous of keeping their children in their own schools for a longer period, added one or two years to the elementary schools. They are now permitted to conduct what is called the Fifth Form or Fifth Classes, which does work equivalent or at least similar to the work done in the first two years of high school. Moreover, Catholics may conduct under the separate principle continuation schools, which attempt to give a high school course with minimum facilities -- staff, courses, accommodations. In addition a limited number of high quality private secondary schools, conducted usually by religious congregations, are supported by tuition fees or other private resources.

A few statistical items from the annual report of the Minister of Education give an overall view of the extent of the separate school system today and by comparison with public school statistics one can get some idea of the proportion of the educational work of the province which is carried on by Catholics.

The total number of elementary schools in Ontario, September, 1964, was 6,289; of these 4,859 were public, and 1,430 were Catholic separate schools. The total enrollment in the elementary schools was 1,278,473. The public schools handled 925,068; the Catholic separate schools, 353,405 or over 26 percent of the total enrollment. In addition there was one Protestant separate school, enrolling 177 pupils.[32] Approximately 125 Catholic separate schools have attached Fifth Form. Some of these Fifth Form classes are combined with grades 11 to 13 and are conducted in private secondary schools, although eligible for public funds.[33] The total public secondary school enrollment in 1964 was 395,301. Catholic secondary schools, in addition, were educating 39,230 including children in the Fifth Forms of separate schools. There are 97 Catholic independent schools of secondary type.[34]

Since the separate schools are part of Ontario's educational system and operate under the rules and regulations applicable to public schools, a general view of the administrative set-up is helpful in understanding the relation of the separate schools to the provincial system. The basic features of Canadian education, which have been described earlier, apply with fair accuracy in Ontario. The role of the Dominion government is negligible, since interference is limited to legislation that "prejudicially" affects any rights or privileges which the religious minority enjoyed at the time of union relative to their denominational schools.

Like most of the other provinces, Ontario has a Minister of Education assisted by a Deputy Minister, a chief inspector and an outside staff of inspectors, attendance officers, and a staff of clerical workers.[35] The jurisdiction of the Minister as described in the Act is extensive and it applies to separate as well as to public schools. Among other powers listed, he is given authority to make regulations for: the establishment, organization, administration and government of schools; governing the admission of pupils; the approval and purchase of textbooks; granting diplomas and certificates; prescribing the subjects that shall be taught in grades one to thirteen inclusive; prescribing the powers, duties, and qualifications and governing the appointment of teachers.

The Minister's authority over separate schools is exercised in great part by the separate school inspectors. They are provincial appointees and are paid by the province, each being assigned to a specific territory. Catholics are always appointed for Catholic separate schools.

Essential control, then, is in the hands of the Minister. The actual day by day management of the schools is under the direction of local school boards composed of trustees, who are elected by the Catholic supporters of the separate schools. Thus we see that although the separate schools are under provincial control, their practical administration is in the hands of Catholic trustees representing the Catholic supporters.

The Separate Schools Act, which comprises a chapter of the Statutes of Ontario, deals with all matters relating to these schools and their government. The Act is highly detailed in its prescriptions, the 1961 revision containing 73 sections with many subdivisions.

First the Act describes the procedure to be followed in the establishment of separate schools.[36] The law specifies that Protestants, the Colored, or Catholics may upon the application in writing of five or more heads of families resident in a public school section, apply for a separate school and the Council is to authorize its establishment. Since no Colored and very few Protestants have availed themselves of this privilege, the description which follows considers the law as it applies to Catholic separate schools.

A number of Catholics may find themselves living in a new housing development. Desiring a Catholic school for their children, they proceed to take the steps to establish one as the law directs. They will convene a public meeting of Catholics, no less than five of whom must be householders resident within the section or city. In an unorganized township not less than ten Catholics are required. They elect a specified number of trustees, one of whom delivers to the designated authorities a written notice of the meeting and the names of the trustees. After the petition has been indorsed and several other formalities met, the elected trustees form a legally corporate body known as the Board of Education.

Regulations for the holding of meetings, the election and appointment of officers are minutely set down in the <u>Act</u>, some variations being permitted between city and rural boards. In the urban municipalities, one common board conducts the affairs of all schools. Generally, in rural communities each school will have its own board of trustees. However, provision is made, if convenience and economy are so served, to form a union separate school board of three trustees.

The local board of trustees is responsible by law for the management of the schools. Its duties and powers are specified in detail. The trustees must see to it that school buildings are provided and maintained and that equipment and accommodations are adequate. In the words of the law it is their duty "to take possession and have the keeping of all school property, acquired or given for school purposes." The board has charge of school finances. It must provide for the support of the schools and determine the school tax to which all separate school supporters of the district will be held. These financial duties are considered in more detail below in connection with the whole question of separate school financing.

The trustees have the responsibility to provide legally qualified teachers. They may, and do, select members of religious congregations -- Sisters, Brothers, or priests -- provided, of course, that these are duly qualified. In practice, the religious teachers are nominated by their religious superiors. The trustees must send in an annual report to the

Minister of Education. In short, it is their duty to exercise all other powers and perform all other duties of public school boards as are applicable to the case of a separate school.

Associated with the management of the school is the work of the inspectors and attendance officers. The inspectors are all Catholic. Their duties are the same in respect to separate schools as those of public school inspectors. An inspector is expected to visit each school of his inspectorate and each classroom at least once a year; to assist its teachers to improve their practice; to cooperate with the boards; and to prepare required reports. The attendance officers are appointed by the school board and cooperate with teachers, inspectors, and trustees in the enforcement of school attendance laws.

The rights and duties of teachers are listed in The School Administrative Act and are the same as those of public school teachers.[37] They are subject to the same examinations and receive their certificates of qualification in the manner as do their public school confreres. The provincial teachers' certificates are scaled according to the number of years of academic work, the amount of professional training, and the amount of experience. The separate school teachers, like those of public schools, may if they wish have a system of superannuation, the details of which are formulated by the separate school board subject to general regulations. A similar provision applies to the inspectors.

The educational program outlined by the provincial Department of Education is the same for both separate and public schools. Consequently, the course of studies and textbooks are generally the same for both schools. With regard to textbooks, however, a limited choice is allowed to separate schools. Where suitable Catholic texts are available in specific areas such as reading, they may be chosen by resolution of the Board.

No tuition fees may be demanded by the separate schools. A rental charge for libraries may be made and it is optional with the separate school board to supply free textbooks. The same option exists in regard to free work supplies.

FINANCES. It is in the arrangements which relate to

financing the church-related schools that Ontario's system is unique among the various plans other Western democracies have worked out. Connaughton points out that the financial rights of Catholics relative to their separate schools might be considered as consisting of three elements: 1) the right to support their separate schools by means of public taxation; 2) the right of separate school supporters to be exempt from all taxation for public elementary school expenses; 3) in the right of separate schools to share in all public grants for education.[38]

It is worth examining more closely these rights and the manner of their operation. All details are minutely laid down in the law.

We have taken note of the procedure by which Catholics go about establishing their separate schools. After the board of trustees has been incorporated as a legal body it is ready to do business and must secure the funds necessary to build and support the school or schools to be established. A notice in writing must be given to the clerk of the municipality by every Catholic taxpayer who wishes to support the separate schools instead of the public schools. The notice need not, as was formerly required, be renewed annually. The applicant then becomes a separate school supporter and is by this fact automatically exempted from paying taxes for the support of public schools.

The exemption, it should be noted, extends only to the payment of taxes for elementary schools. The separate school supporter is still liable to pay taxes for the support of public secondary education even though he sends his child to a private tuition-charging secondary school. As we have seen, this point was established by the Privy Council decision in the Tiny Township case in 1928. Moreover, the exemption does not extend to the payment of public school taxes that were levied on him before he became a supporter of separate schools.

A separate school supporter may withdraw his support from separate schools, but if he does he remains liable for rates imposed on him before the time of withdrawal. The law reads:

> A Roman Catholic who desires to withdraw his
> support from a separate school shall give notice
> thereof in writing. . . . A person who has with-
> drawn his support from a Roman Catholic separ-
> ate school is not exempt from paying rates for the
> support of a separate school or separate school
> libraries. . . imposed before the time of his
> withdrawing such support. [39]

These provisions preclude a species of cheating which might
be possible could a person change tax-paying status as soon as
a tax was levied upon him. Thus they protect the supporters
of both public and private schools who might otherwise lose
payable tax income.

The clerk of the municipality files and preserves the no-
tices of intention to support separate schools, enters the
names in an index book and makes out a collector's list being
careful to distinguish between the public and the separate
school supporters and the tax rates of each group.

The remainder of the responsibility for securing local
support for separate schools then devolves upon the board of
trustees and the law gives it due authority to act:

> The board of a separate school may impose and
> levy school rates and collect school rates and sub-
> scriptions upon and from persons sending children
> to or subscribing towards the support of such
> schools, and may appoint collectors for collecting
> the school rates or subscriptions who shall have
> all the powers in respect thereof possessed by
> collectors of taxes in municipalities. [40]

The board, having all the powers of a corporate body, may also pass by-laws for contracting loans and for issuing bonds
for amounts which it deems expedient.

The school trustees must arrange for the collection of
the taxes levied. The law provides that this may be done in
one of two ways. The trustees may appoint for the task a collector who "shall have all the powers in respect thereof

possessed by collectors of taxes in municipalities." On the
other hand, the board may instead request the municipal council to levy and collect the taxes from the separate school
supporters through its collectors and other municipal officers.
The law adds that "any expenses attending the assessment,
collection or payment of school rates by the municipal corporation or any of its officers shall be borne by the corporation,
and the rates or taxes as and when collected, shall within a
reasonable time thereafter. . . be paid over to the board
without any deduction whatsoever."

The right of separate schools to support by taxation and
the right to exemption from public school taxes is supplemented in Ontario by the right to share in the public grants for
education. There are three such grants, provincial, municipal, and county, the provincial being the largest of the three.

In allocating the provincial grants, the government has
devised an elaborate system by which the grants are made to
serve several purposes: they reward local achievement,
stimulate local effort, and at the same time tend to equalize
educational opportunities in the various sections of the province by giving more where more is needed. It is to be noticed
that the legislative grants generally are larger proportionately
for the separate schools because, according to the formula,
the grant is partly based on the poverty of the recipient and
the separate schools, which usually have a lower base for taxation, qualify on that head.

In addition to the regular grants, there are smaller allotments to the separate schools for Fifth Classes, kindergar-
tens, and for special educational projects such as manual
training, home economics, music, art, and medical services.
All provincial grants are contingent on the full compliance
with the laws and regulations and are distributed indiscrimi-
nately according to the provisions of the law to both public and
separate schools. The municipal and county grants are paid
to the boards of schools receiving legislative grants and in the
same proportion as such grants are paid. The separate
schools are not allowed to receive any school money "arising
or accruing from local assessment for public school purposes."

The question of corporation taxes needs special consid-

eration. For the past seventy-five years it has been a controversial issue in the educational area. We have already seen
that at the time the British North American Act was drawn up
few, if any, corporations existed, so the question of the division of school taxes in property vested in such companies did
arise.

Later when corporations came into existence and Catholics demanded a share in the taxes, a law was passed, 1886,
permitting, but not compelling, the corporations to divert a
percentage of their taxes to the separate schools. According
to the pertinent section of the Act, the corporation was to turn
over part of its school taxes to the separate schools, but that
part was not to be greater than the proportion of the companies' properties owned by Catholics. Obviously, difficulties
lay in the way of implementing this provision and the net result
was that Catholic schools did not receive their due share of the
school taxes derived from corporations. [41]

Catholics protested time and time again. Although their
arguments were logical and convincing, the efforts to secure
equitable treatment gave rise for a period of time to bitter
political battles in which, unfortunately, religious prejudice
figured. An amendment to the Act passed in 1936 proved unsatisfactory and unworkable and was repealed the following
year.

The question came before the Courts on several occasions. It was hoped that a decision given by the Supreme
Court of Canada in 1939 was a presage of better things to
come. The case arose when the Ford Motor Company of
Windsor asked to have eighteen percent of the company's
taxes diverted to the separate schools. The allocation, in
absence of exact knowledge regarding the religious affiliation
of the stockholders, was based on a careful estimate of the
proportion held by Catholics. The Windsor Public School
Board objected to this action on the grounds that an estimate,
not the actual percentage, was used. The Supreme Court
handed down a judgment which recognized the right and approved the action of the Ford Company.

It would seem then in the light of this decision that a
corporation, unable to determine the religious persuasion of

its stockholders, may make an apportionment of its taxes for separate schools on an estimate of their religious affiliation, and it rests with those who challenge the division to show that it is greater than the proportion of the company's stock held by Catholics.[42]

In November, 1962, Ontario's Catholic hierarchy again called upon the provincial legislature to pass a measure providing a more equitable distribution of corporation taxes for all separate schools. The Bishops' statement emphasized that Catholics were becoming increasingly concerned about their ability to maintain high standards without a higher share of taxes. The urgency of the demand was sustained by statistical facts, where it was shown that the Catholic separate schools were caring for over twenty-five percent of Ontario's elementary school children, but the assessment basis on which the separate schools drew taxes was in a much lower percentage of the total assessments for school purposes; in fact, barely two percent of the taxes paid by corporations toward elementary school education was going to the separate schools.

The pleas and arguments of the bishops bore fruit. The government took up the matter seriously. It was acknowledged that the principle of allocating corporation taxes on the basis of the number of Catholic stockholders in a firm was impossible to carry out. A new basis to secure equity was proposed. The government outlined a plan to supplement by special grants the revenues of any elementary school board -- public or separate -- which was receiving a lesser proportion of corporation taxes than the assessments paid by its supporters bore to the total municipal assessments. In 1964 this reform measure was embodied in a Corporation Tax Adjustment Grant which places separate elementary schools on approximately the same basis as public elementary schools.

What is to be said about the religious character of Ontario's separate schools? Are they able to measure up to the Catholic ideal of education? From the viewpoint of fundamental philosophical principles Ontario's solution of the religion-education issue is somewhat less than completely satisfactory. Of the three basic societies interested in education two have primary rights: the family in the natural order and the Church in the supernatural order. Family rights are recognized and safeguarded by Ontario's solution only partially. For the child's elementary education, the parents are free to choose the school they wish their children to attend and can provide them with an education which integrates the religious and secular. This is not true of the secondary level.

In regard to the role given the Church in the education of her children, the question of how satisfactory Ontario's solution is remains at least debatable. It possesses many elements of freedom. Although separate schools are not under the direct jurisdiction of the Church, ecclesiastic authorities do control completely the religious education, and the priests of the local parish may and do keep in close contact with the work of the schools. Religious instruction in Catholic doctrine and practice is regularly given without interference on the part of the provincial authorities. Religious teachers may be appointed. They constitute in practice about twenty percent of the teaching staff of the separate schools. A Catholic is always chosen if the teacher is of the laity, and the selection is based on character as well as professional qualifications. The inspectors of separate schools are always Catholic.

The pupil may attend daily Mass when the school happens to be near the church. The nuances that make up a Catholic atmosphere in the school and classroom may be maintained. Some freedom is allowed in the choice of textbooks. There is no hindrance to the integrating of a religious influence into all the activities of the school day, including the secular subjects.

Nevertheless some observers of the Ontario set-up see the educational system as geared to a too exclusive state control. More freedom, they maintain, should be allowed Catholic authorities in the regulation of the separate schools. In their November, 1962, statement to legislators, the Bishops of Ontario asked for more freedom to outline Catholic school curricula and to prepare and select textbooks and to establish Catholic teachers' colleges. Their position was reiterated in 1965.

All Catholics and many other interested citizens are ready to admit that there are some shortcomings and injustices

in the law as it now stands which should be remedied. Foremost among these is lack of provision for separate secondary
schools. Practically all Catholics want their children to attend
a Catholic secondary school. Privately supported secondary
schools do exist, but their use involves what amounts to
"double taxation." Many Catholic parents cannot afford the
burden of tuition fees in addition to the tax rates levied on them
to support public secondary schools. They are accordingly
unable to give their children a secondary education in harmony
with their religious convictions. Such economic restraint
amounts in practice to an impairment of religious freedom.
In their 1962 statement the Canadian bishops declared:

> If it is recognized as public policy in Ontario that
> every person is equal in rights without regard to
> creed, we find it difficult to understand why the
> Roman Catholic segment of this privince is not af-
> forded an equal opportunity to educate its children
> beyond the Grade 8 level. [43]

There is nothing in the Canadian constitution or in Ontario law
to prevent the passage of legislation accepting the principle of
separate secondary education. The Tiny Township case merely held that as the law stood Catholics could not demand funds.
Up to the present, however, the provincial government has rejected remedial proposals.

A difficulty and an inequity arises from the fact that the
law provides that only Catholics may contribute their taxes to
the support of the separate schools. A problem erupts in case
of a mixed marriage. If, for example, a Protestant husband
and a Catholic wife desire to send their children to a separate
school, they may do so, but because the father is Protestant
the law forces the couple to pay taxes for educational purposes
to public schools.

Like secondary education, denominational institutions of
higher learning in Ontario are supported from private resources.
For degree granting purposes, the colleges affiliate themselves
with a public university. Financial difficulties in maintaining
an excellence on par with the publicly supported universities

led one denominational university to resort to an interesting
experiment, in fact, to a transformation unprecedented in the
annals of religious education.[44]   Assumption University, a
Catholic institution in Windsor which had been conducted by
the Basilian Fathers for over a century, was handed over in
1963 to the provincial government -- faculty, student body,
and premises -- to be governed by a nondenominational board
of governors in exchange for complete maintenance. Now, as
the University of Windsor, the institution is state-controlled,
state supported, and secular! The Basilians, however, for
the time being remain in their posts, including top administrative positions. They are convinced that while they have surrendered control, they have retained influence in their key
commitment, namely, in the actual educational process itself.
They have, moreover, been guaranteed six seats on the thirty-
member board of governors. Their salaries are paid out of
government funds, including payments for teaching theology.

Two years after the transfer, 1965, the experiment was
declared to be working successfully,[45]   but years will have to
pass before any definite judgment on the unique arrangement
can be made. Several other Catholic institutions have followed
the example of Windsor. In the meantime, more than a few
among both observers and those directly involved in the experiments have mixed emotions about the transactions, and there
are some who regard them as complete "sell-outs" for
Catholic education.

Ontario has found one way of solving the delicate problem of public support for denominational schools, deficient as
it may seem to some citizens and observers. Nevertheless,
there is inspiration in the fact that Ontario, after a long, and
often bitter struggle with opposing odds, refused to succumb
to the easier way out which secularism offered and, rejecting
expediency, held fast to the principle that religion must have
an important role in education and that the right of parents to
provide the kind of education for their children which their
religious convictions dictated had to be respected in a practical manner. To a great extent the obstacle of religious intolerance was overcome simply by not conceding to its demands.
There are remnants left in Ontario today but they are greatly
weakened.

Chapter 4

Canada: VARIED SOLUTIONS

Ontario's system has been given detailed consideration.
It will not be necessary to examine the history and solutions
of the other nine provinces so comprehensively. The outcome
of the efforts of these provinces to reach a settlement of the
religion-education issue illustrates again how people in a free
society use the democratic processes to accomplish ends.
The way is seldom smooth and the outcomes may vary as to
the completeness with which the claims of justice and freedom
have been achieved. But in a free society efforts toward improvement can continue and that is happening in some of the
Canadian provinces.

QUEBEC

It has been said that Quebec presents one of the best ex-
amples of freedom in education that is found any place in the
world. Be that as it may, the province's solution of the religion-education issue does illustrate a nice balance of control
by the three interested agencies: family, church, and state.
This has been achieved not by union of church and state -- on
the contrary, there is complete separation in Quebec -- but by
practical cooperation among these fundamental societies in the
interest of preserving religious liberty. The genesis of Quebec's educational system is embedded in the history of the
province, which is reviewed here in brief outline.
The earliest settlers of Quebec came from France,
bringing with them the educational traditions of their mother
country. Just as the Church had sponsored education through
the centuries in France, so the Church in the person of dedicated clergy and religious undertook to provide education in
New France. This was long before the cold blasts of rationalism and the fiery explosions of the Revolution had begun.
The amount and quality of education provided in early
Quebec are amazing when one considers the sparse population

and the difficulties of frontier life. The Jesuits had established
a college in Quebec City by 1635; in 1668 a "Little Seminary"
was opened. By 1725 there were at least thirty primary
schools for boys and girls among a population of some 25,000
people dispersed in seventy parishes.[1] Attempts had been
made to provide for the training of teachers. In the late seventeenth century trade schools were founded.

Then came the conquest of the land by Britain and the
consequent severing of political relations with France. In the
confusion which followed, education naturally suffered. The
Canadian bishops remained alert to the need and value of education and Canadian archives abound with evidence of the efforts
which the bishops made to encourage schools in those trying
years.[2] The schools, the bishops insisted, must be Catholic
schools for Catholic children. Their problem had become
complicated by the arrival of English immigrants, all Protestant, who demanded Anglican-oriented schools.

In pursuance of this aim, the Assembly passed an "Act
for the Establishment of Free Schools." In 1801 the Royal
Institution for the Advancement of Learning was established.
It was empowered to acquire and administer lands for purposes
of education. Schools, British and Anglican in atmosphere,
were to be established, which were intended to bring about an
intermingling of the English and the French and gradually wear
down ethnic differences. Teachers were generally imported
from England.

As might be expected, the plan did not operate satisfactorily. A culture deeply entrenched for over a century and a
half was not to be easily uprooted. The French-speaking
Catholics would have nothing to do with these schools. Various
amendments were passed in an effort to make the schools less
English and more acceptable to the French, who comprised the
vast majority of the population. The attempts failed. Finally,
an Act of 1826 allowed each Church Council to establish its
own elementary schools. Here is the germ of the Quebec system. Under the provisions of the law, Catholic schools began
to appear in almost every parish of Quebec. The Royal Institution had disappeared by 1838.

The Act of Union in 1841 reunited Upper and Lower

Canada in what proved to be an imperfect fusion. A common
school law was passed the following year operative for the two
Canadas and containing the principle of separate schools for
Catholics and Protestants. It soon became evident that a uniform law for both divisions was unworkable and the statute was
repealed for Lower Canada in 1845. Significantly, the 1842
Act had firmly established the principle of separate schools in
this part of Canada, a policy never to be refuted by either
province.

Then, in 1846, legislation was enacted which definitely
laid the foundation of the present Quebec system. The Act
provided for two completely separate school systems, one
Catholic, one Protestant, operating under the same law. Although administrative machinery has undergone alterations in
the last one hundred twenty years and amendments have brought
some modifications in details, the Act of 1846 is substantially
the school law of Quebec today. Underlying the whole policy
was the principle that religion was to continue to have a central
role in education in the province. Then, as a means of providing complete religious liberty in a society which had become
religiously pluralistic, Protestants, though a small minority,
were to have equal rights with Catholics in establishing their
own schools. The basic requirement was the presence in a
given area of a group of residents of either faith, large enough
to elect a school board and to provide local finances for their
school. The language question entered into the arrangement
but was subordinate to religion, and it did not alter the division
in respect to religion. Catholics at that time were almost all
French-speaking, Protestants were English-speaking.

As a result of this thinking and the legislation it evoked
two entirely separate school systems have developed in Quebec.
In almost every locality where there are children of the two
faiths there are separate public schools. Protestantism by its
nature tends toward splintering. A limitation on this tendency
as regards the schools was placed by including all non-Catholics under the term Protestant. Although comparatively few
in number, Jews, in time, created a special problem. A law
in 1913 provided that all persons professing the Jewish religion
should, for school purposes, be treated in the same manner as

Protestants. An amendment in 1930, agreeable to the Jews, allowed them freedom to choose the school their child should go to. The majority tended to choose Protestant schools. The English language, rather than religion, was probably the deciding factor.

At confederation in 1867, the British North American Act made permanent the policy which had been established twenty-one years earlier. The Act stipulated that each of the four provinces should retain under the new Constitution any rights or privileges in respect to denominational schools existing by law at the union. Quebec's provisions for its Protestant minority were much more liberal in 1867 than were Ontario's provisions for its Catholic minority. Quebec has consistently retained its liberal policy without modification.

Quebec's System in Operation

At the provincial level is an officer called the superintendent of education, who is titular head of the Department of Education. He is assisted by a French and an English secretary. It is, however, the two committees, constituting the Council of Public Instruction, that formulate policy, supervise and administer all educational matters. One of the committees directs the education of all except Catholics, while the other is in charge of the education of Catholics. Each committee is autonomous in deciding school questions for its jurisdiction throughout the province.

Thus there is in Quebec a system of dual control: a French-language system for Roman Catholics; and an English language system for those not Catholic, with each responsible under a common law for the organization and administration of the schools under its control. The dual system operates from kindergarten through the university. The system does not apply to special technical schools described below, which are under the jurisdiction of provincial departments. There are, in addition, a considerable number of independent schools, most of them on the secondary level.

The Council as a whole may meet to discuss and decide on matters of general policy. As a matter of fact, it rarely so meets in joint session, but the committees meet separately four times a year and the real power resides in them.

The Catholic committee now consists of the superintendent, who presides at meetings, twenty-two ecclesiastics,
including the Cardinal, the archbishops and bishops of the
various dioceses, twenty-two laymen and four members appointed by the government. The French secretary acts as
secretary for the Catholic committee. The Protestant committee is comprised of the superintendent, who ex officio is
titular head, twenty members appointed by the Lieutenant-
Governor in Council, one of whom is a Protestant cleric, and
seven associate members, one of whom represents the Protestant Teachers' Association of Quebec. The English secretary
acts as director of the Protestant committee.

Each committee makes regulations concerning such matters as courses of study, departmental examinations, textbooks, the work of inspection, and the management of normal
schools. They make recommendations for the apportionment
of provincial grants.

Each system has its own inspector-general assisted by
local inspectors. The inspectors visit the schools from time
to time and report conditions to the Department of Education,
but the province has no final authority to compel the local
communities to meet specific standards.

Details of administration are carried out on the local
level. For this purpose the province of Quebec is divided into
school municipalities or districts, each of which elects a
Board of School Commissioners, except in the large cities,
where the commissioners are appointed. The French-speaking school districts are generally coterminous with the
Catholic parishes. The people of a district decide through
their elected school board members what type of school they
want as to religious affiliation and how much they are willing
to pay for it. If there is in the community a minority group
(as to religious affiliation) dissatisfied with the decision, they
may withdraw and form their own school district, provided
there are sufficient pupils to justify the opening of a new
school and a sufficient number of taxpayers to support it.
This process is called "dissent" and the right involved is
carefully protected by law. In practice, in any locality where

there are children of the two faiths, separate schools with
separate school boards, one for each system, have been established.

School board members are elected by the votes of property owners. There is a movement toward liberalizing the
voting privilege by granting it to all parents of school children.
Priests and ministers of Protestant denominations are eligible
for election as commissioners. In Quebec City and Montreal
the commissioners are appointed. For the Catholic School
Board, the Lieutenant-Governor appoints four members, and
the Archbishop three others. For the Protestant School Board,
the appointments are made by the Lieutenant-Governor and the
city council.

The school boards carry out the regulations laid down by
their respective committees. In addition, they choose sites,
erect buildings, and select the lay teachers for the schools.
Religious teachers are appointed by their respective superiors.
The boards must make provision for the attendance of all
children who live within the district and provide transportation
for those who live too far from school to walk.

The boards separately decide on the rate of taxation and
levy the local taxes on the residents. Each board taxes individuals of the same religion as represented by the local school.
It is in this area of taxation that Quebec's system is unique
and completely equitable. The taxes of Catholics go to the
Catholic school board; the taxes of non-Catholics, to the Protestant board. Thus each citizen pays taxes only for the
schools he uses. Edgar Smith pays his taxes to a Protestant
district and sends his children to its school; Leon Robichaud,
his next door neighbor, pays his taxes to the Catholic district
and sends his children to the Catholic school. Both are satisfied with the arrangement; their children are receiving the
kind of education they wish for them. Both families share a
loyalty and devotion to their province and the Dominion and
are good neighbors.

The boundaries of the respective districts need not coin-
cide. The tax rates may be different. One district may desire a higher quality of education than the other; or one district may conduct a high school, the other only an elementary

school.

Revenues from businesses and corporation taxes are
placed in a neutral panel and allocated to the Catholic or the
Protestant districts involved on the basis of the school population in each. This seems obviously to be a simpler and more
equitable arrangement than that of Ontario, where the issue
has been controversial for nearly a hundred years.

In Quebec the funds from taxes covers schools on both
elementary and secondary levels -- again a favorable contrast
with Ontario, where, as we have seen, denominational secondary education goes begging. When and where local taxes are
not sufficient in a district, a subsidy is paid by the provincial
government; in some instances the provincial government has
taken on the whole indebtedness. In 1962 the Lesage government set up a family allowance plan under which ten dollars
per month is given for all children in school up to age seventeen.

The separate school system extends through all levels
of education. Compulsory attendance extends to the age of
fifteen inclusive. The structures of the two systems up to
and beyond this age differ. For Catholics, the elementary
and secondary schools giving the regular course include those
formerly known as elementary, secondary and superior
schools. The Protestants hold to their classification of elementary, intermediate and superior schools.[3] Much of
Catholic secondary education is carried on in classical colleges which are affiliates of universities. Students can earn
a bachelor's degree at these colleges and then enter the universities. The classical colleges are privately controlled
and charge tuition fees, but are aided by provincial grants.
Technical and vocational schools are not under the committees.
They are supported by provincial grants and open to all.

In 1961 there were a total of 7,896 elementary and general secondary schools in the province. Of these, Catholics
conducted 7,526 with an enrollment of 1,039,868 pupils;
Protestants had 370 schools with an enrollment of 119,912.[4]
Of the schools conducted by Catholics 691 were independent.
These, though privately controlled usually by religious congregations, receive provincial grants. Moreover, parents

whose children are enrolled in them may receive payment from their respective school boards for tuition fees.

There are six universities in Quebec. They receive provincial subsidies, though the institutions are completely independent of government control. Two are non-sectarian -- McGill and Sir George Williams College; three are Catholic -- Laval, Montreal, and Sherbrooke; one is Anglican -- Bishop's College. The federal government has offered funds, but up to the present the Quebec universities have refused them, fearing acceptance may lead to some loss of their cherished independence.

The schools under the control of the Catholic committee are not parochial or diocesan schools such as we have in the United States but are truly public schools. Yet they are thoroughly Catholic, measuring up to the requirements that a Catholic philosophy of education demands. Religious instruction is given regularly and holds a central place in the course of studies at all levels. The average proportion of religious teachers is over twenty percent, but the proportion is much larger in the secondary schools. Lay teachers are always Catholic and have been trained in Catholic normal schools. The religious authorities have the exclusive right of selecting all the books having reference to religion and morals. Religious influences permeate every aspect of the life and work of the schools.

Visitors to the schools are impressed by the general atmosphere of industry, order, gentility, and respect for the teacher which is manifested by the students. Deweyism and the concept of "permissiveness," which wrought such great mischief in so many American schools, never had a chance to make inroads in these schools. False philosophies of education are given no entrance.

Religion also plays an important role in the non-Catholic schools. The pertinent regulations of the Protestant committee state that religious instruction must be given in all public schools. In the elementary grades the first twenty minutes of each day is to be devoted to moral and religious instruction as prescribed in the Course of Study and Teachers' Handbook, but denominational teaching is forbidden. The school must be opened each day with the Lord's Prayer and the reading of the Holy Scriptures. The usual conscience clause exempts from both instruction and prayers those whose parents or guardians object in writing.

Where there is only one school in a community, that school is a common school for children of all religious persuasions. It might be under the control of either a Protestant or a Catholic board, depending on the wishes of the people. Any child must be excused from religious exercises and instruction if his parents so desire and, of course, the minority group in the community has a right to "dissent" and establish its own school if the number of residents is sufficient to justify such a procedure.

Two features of Quebec's handling of the religion-education issue must be distinguished in any appraisal made of it. First, true to the traditions of Western civilization, religious and moral training is given its due importance in the educational scheme. There have been no concessions to the secularism of the times. Second, religious freedom in education is guaranteed. The religious rights of the minority -- in this case Protestants and other non-Catholics -- are fully protected.

Are there any evidences that the fidelity to the traditional ideals of the Christian West has borne fruit in the form of a higher level of moral living among the people than is found in other places where concessions to secularism have been officially countenanced? It is difficult to obtain convincing data and comparisons in this area are dangerous. Yet, a few pertinent facts can be presented. To some observers, the inferences are clear. According to the 1962 Canadian Year Book 212 persons in Quebec per 100,000 of the population, sixteen years or over, were convicted of indictable offenses. The figure for the whole of Canada was 307 per 100,000 persons. The divorce rate is very low; juvenile delinquency, though slightly on the increase, is comparatively infrequent. [5]

There are critics of the system both within and without the province, mostly from without, and these, showing a bias toward statism, complain of "ecclesiastical control." There are other critics who maintain that the system tends to intensify and perpetuate ethnic and religious differences. Perhaps this is true, but the system did not originate the differences; the differences were its cause. The present arrangement came about as a consequence of an English-Anglican conquest of a French possession, long steeped in French and Catholic traditions. The differences between the two peoples could not have been overcome by coersive legislation. Any such attempt would have led to bitter and futile struggles. What happened was that the people of Quebec realistically recognized these differences and settled on a just and amicable way, not of eliminating them, but of living with them. Their solution illustrates again the democratic principle of diversity in unity.

There are some built-in disadvantages in the Quebec solution. It costs more to support two systems of schools than to support one, but this limitation must be weighed against the boon of greater religious freedom and the effective implementation of parental rights in education. It has been suggested with logic, it seems, that a "neutral committee" in addition to the Catholic and Protestant committees would ease some of the problems which arise from grouping all non-Catholics under the Protestant committee. The Liberal government of Premier Jean Lesage announced March, 1966, that it will introduce a system of secular schools for children whose parents do not want them trained in either the existing Catholic or Protestant schools.

The general attitude of the people of Quebec toward their province's policy on the church-state relationship in education was perhaps adequately expressed by a former Prime Minister, Maurice Duplessis: "I believe it is an example for all of Canada, and for the whole world." And George Marler, the leader of the official opposition and a Protestant concurred: "As a member of the Protestant minority, I absolutely subscribe to the Prime Minister's views in the same sense."

BRITISH COLUMBIA

We shift now to the opposite end of Canada, geographically speaking, and incidentally meet with a completely opposite type of resolution to the religion-education issue. British Columbia's policy in respect to church-state relationships in education is unique among the Canadian provinces in a sort of negative way and stands in sharp contrast to that of, let us say, its easternmost fellow-province, Newfoundland, where the schools of all denominations are supported by government funds. In British Columbia we find a policy in operation similar to that in the United States. The teaching of sectarian religion is forbidden by law in the public schools and public funds are denied to church-related schools. The principle of separate schools on a denominational basis was never in operation in British Columbia. The explanation of the province's divergence in the area of church-state relationships is partly geographical, but other forces, as we shall see, have been operative.

The influence of Catholic France did not penetrate beyond the Rockies. The earliest explorers of the Pacific lands of Canada were mainly English and Scotch; names like Smith, Tottingham, Fraser, Mackenzie, Vancouver predominated in the frontier days. But there, as elsewhere, the first schools were church-related -- Anglican in this instance -- and recipients of public grants. The first settlements were made on Vancouver Island, then under the political rule of the Hudson's Bay Company. In 1849 Vancouver and New Caledonia became crown colonies.

To provide for the religious and educational needs of the settlers, the Company brought to Victoria the Anglican clergyman, Reverend Robert Staines, who established a church and school in 1853, receiving 540 pounds a year for his services as Chaplain and schoolkeeper.[6] Other schools, generally under the control of the Church of England were later established, each receiving aid from the Legislative Council. Religion and the study of the Scriptures were accorded an important place in the program of these schools.

In the meantime additional colonists, representing a variety of religious denominations, were coming to the wide open spaces of the West. Catholic missionaries had begun to work among the natives of the area as early as 1838. They played an important part, scantily recognized by historians, in the exploration and colonization of the vast reaches of Western Canada and in bringing to these almost inaccessible regions the fruits of civilization, education, and religion. Catholic schools were established and were taught in most cases by the intrepid Sisters of St. Ann, pioneers among the pioneers. No public funds were accorded these Catholic missionary schools.

By mid-century Presbyterians and Methodists were on the scene in considerable numbers, looking askance at the Anglican subsidized schools and fearful also that Catholics would ask funds for their schools. Stimulated partly by this sectarian rivalry, a movement for free, non-sectarian schools was begun. It found an able champion in a John Robson, a Methodist and editor of the British Columbia. The Anglicans were soon won over to the cause and with other Protestants demanded a system of publicly-supported, non-sectarian schools. Expediency triumphed, as it had in the United States. Non-sectarianism seemed to be the easiest answer to religious rivalry, and the principle implicitly denied funds to church-related schools.

The first important educational legislation, an "Act Respecting Schools," was passed in 1865. Section 13 of the statute stipulated that "all schools under the Provisions of this Act shall be conducted strictly upon Non-Sectarian principles . . . and all Books of a religious character teaching denominational doctrines shall be strictly excluded therefrom." However, long-standing traditions could not immediately be discarded and so provision was made for some doctrinal religious instruction. Section 14 of the law stated: "It shall be lawful for the clergy of every Denomination at stated Intervals to be fixed by the General Board of Education to visit such schools and impart in a separate Room Religious Instruction to the children of their respective persuasions."

In 1866 Vancouver was politically united to the mainland and a new education act with an amendment went into effect in 1870. The non-sectarian clause had disappeared, but at the same time no special rights or privileges were given the Catholics or to any Protestant denomination apart from the right to conduct private schools at their own expense. The clause permitting the clergymen of the various denominations to come into the public schools was retained with the added limitation that religious instruction was to be given only before or after school hours.

This law was to have enduring significance. It was the legislation in effect at the time British Columbia entered the federation and became a Canadian province, an outcome effected in 1871. Since the existing educational legislation gave no rights to either Catholics or to Protestants of any sect "with regard to denominational schools," no religious group could claim rights thereafter by reason of the Canadian Constitution. The result was that the non-sectarianism of the public schools and the denial of all public aid to denominational schools was put on a firm basis. In fact, in 1872 the clause permitting denominational religious instruction before or after school hours was repealed. British Columbia has not changed its policy in regard to the church-state relationship in education since that date. As public secondary schools and universities became established the same principle was applied to them.

The situation in British Columbia today can be described briefly. The teaching of dogmatic religion is excluded from public schools, before or after, or during school hours. In the words of the law all public schools "shall be free and shall be conducted on strictly secular and non-sectarian principles. The highest morality shall be inculcated, but no religious dogmas or creed shall be taught. The Lord's prayer may be used in the opening or closing of schools." This section has been interpreted as implicitly excluding private religiously-oriented schools from any share in public funds.

Catholics have built and maintained their own system of schools without public aid, while at the same time contributing their share of taxes to support the public schools. Indeed, until 1957 they paid taxes on their school properties.

The double burden of supporting two systems of schools has been for British Columbian Catholics a heavy one, and only deeply felt religious convictions could induce them to undertake it. No organized agitation has been made to remedy the inequality, but Catholic leaders, with some Protestants joining them, have repeatedly expressed their dissatisfaction with the status quo. Actually no fundamental legal obstacle stands in the way of relief, as recent United States Supreme Court

decisions in respect to the First Amendment do for American
Catholics. The legislature of British Columbia would be competent to repeal the prohibiting clauses and to adopt a system
similar to that existing in Quebec or Ontario, if it were so
minded.

Some minimum redress has been granted the Catholic
schools. In addition to the 1957 law giving province-wide exemption from taxes on property, long practiced in the city of
Vancouver, Catholic schools receive health services and the
pupils are either given textbooks or allowed to rent them.[7]

Catholic schools are legally recognized to the extent that
they satisfy compulsory attendance requirements. No legal
attempts have been made to regulate them as to course of studies, qualifications of teachers, inspectors, or in any other way.

MANITOBA

In Manitoba we witness the development of a policy
somewhere between that of British Columbia and the more
equitable arrangements of the other eight provinces. While
rejecting complete secularism as a solution, Manitoba leaned
toward "statism," evolving a system without separate schools
but making provision for the teaching of doctrinal religion in
the public schools by official representatives of the religious
groups in accordance with the wishes of parents. The failure
of the province to grapple forthrightly with the religion-education issue; the intrusion of ethnic and religious prejudices,
which obscured the basic problem; the dissensions and distrust
which deflected action from the path of justice -- these elements
in Manitoba's struggle bore tasteless fruit in a policy which has
been and remains unsatisfactory to a considerable proportion
of the population.

Prior to 1870 and before attaining provincial status,
Manitoba was under the control of Hudson's Bay Company. All
educational effort during the early period was carried on by
missionaries, the Company encouraging their work with financial aid. The first school was established by the Catholic
priest, Father Provenchew, at St. Boniface in 1818. Other
denominations came on the scene later -- Anglicans, Methodists,

Presbyterians, and later Baptists.

Manitoba joined the Dominion in 1870, the first of the new provinces. At that time the population numbered less than 10,000, some 3,000 of whom were white; the remainder were natives and half-breeds. The Manitoba Act, drawn up in Ottawa and giving provincial status, became the constitution of the new province. In regard to education, the Act repeated the guarantees of Section 93 of the British North American Act. True, no law giving rights and privileges to denominational schools was on the statute books of Manitoba, but in practice such schools had been receiving aid. It was assumed, therefore, that these privileges came under the guarantee which provided that nothing in any law to be passed, "shall prejudicially affect any right or privilege with respect to denominational schools which any class of persons have by law or practice in the Province at the Union."

The provincial government set to work in 1871 to implement the educational principles of the Manitoba Act, and an arrangement similar to the Quebec system was introduced into the province. At the time, the population was fairly evenly divided between Catholics and Protestants. The new law portioned the province into 24 school districts, 12 designated as Catholic, 12 as Protestant. A Board of Education was appointed by the Lieutenant-Governor in Council, half the number Catholic, half Protestant. The board was divided into two distinct sections on a religious basis, each to administer and regulate its own schools.

The arrangement was based on the premise of rather solid settlements -- Catholic and Protestant. Time and circumstances soon brought changes and problems. Cheap and fertile farming land attracted all and sundry. The influx of Protestants was particularly large. The homogeneous character of scattered areas changed complexion. Protestant and English-speaking people soon composed a huge majority. There were some difficulties and more unwillingness in making the Quebec formula work. The law underwent numerous amendments. Gradually a system of separate schools much like Ontario's came into use, though the term itself was not employed.

Other factors intruded themselves on the scene -- agitation which stirred up ethnic antipathies and religious prejudice; dissension and distrust which set Protestant against Catholic; propaganda, which aroused opposition against separate schools and raised demands for a unified provincial system. As in all such circumstances, there was undoubtedly fault on both sides. Opposition to Quebec, to the Quebec system of education, and to clerical influence in education became strong and the issue entered politics. Emotion took the place of reason; intolerance soon held sway.

The culmination was a new School Act in 1890 which brought sweeping changes affecting the whole educational system. In one brief sentence, Section 177 of the Act declared Catholic school districts were to be dissolved. There was to be but one provincial system -- and that non-sectarian. Catholics might continue to conduct their own schools, but they would have to support them completely themselves and at the same time pay taxes for the schools of the public school system whether they used them or not. The drastic action had been taken in spite of vigorous protests of the Catholic minority and the guarantees of both the federal and the provincial constitutions against "prejudicial legislation."

Long years of litigation followed. In the first round of the courts the points at issue were: whether the province through its school districts had power to tax Catholics; and whether the province could refuse in the future to make grants to denominational schools. Two cases were brought to trial in the name of two individuals, one an Anglican, and the other a Catholic. The cases ran the gamut of the courts up to the Privy Council, which decided in favor of the legislation. The action of the province was declared lawful; no rights or privileges of Catholics or Anglicans had been violated.

A second round of litigation began. This time the issue was based squarely on constitutional rights -- that the legislation of 1890 had taken away rights and privileges which had been conferred on the minority by provincial law in 1871. These rights and privileges were protected by clauses in the Manitoba Act, which in turn had embodied in essence the provisions of subsection (3) of Section 93 of the British North

American Act guaranteeing the continuation of denominational schools existing at the time of union or "thereafter established by the legislature." Application could be made to the Lieutenant-Governor in Council from any later act of the legislature adversely affecting such rights.

Again the issue, in the name of one Brophy, went the gamut of the courts up to and including the Privy Council. The judgment was delivered by the Lord Chancellor, January, 1895, in Brophy's favor. In substance, the Court declared that the Roman Catholics of Manitoba had been prejudicially affected in their minority rights and privileges by the school legislation of 1890 and an appeal lay to the Governor-General in Council, that is to say, to the Federal government.

It was now the duty of the Federal government to decide whether the grounds of appeal were valid and to announce its decision to the provincial government. In other words, further action was transferred from the courts to Parliament, that is, to a political milieu where old forces of dissension and prejudice were more likely to be at work.

The Canadian Cabinet, on its part, gave preemptory orders to the Premier of Manitoba to restore to Roman Catholics the right to their own schools, a proportionate share of government grants, and exemption from taxation for public schools. The law was not clear on what steps might be taken or what means the Parliament of Canada possessed for enforcing its decrees on Manitoba.

When the Assembly of Manitoba finally met months later it moved the adoption of a firm memorial to Ottawa refusing to carry out the order and suggesting an investigation of the school situation in Manitoba before and after 1890. Politics, expediency, prejudice had each played a role in the province's response.

A remedial bill on education giving some limited concessions to Catholics was prepared by the central government. Manitoba remained adamant: provincial grants would not be available for denominational schools and all Roman Catholics must pay taxes for public schools. The Ottawa government hesitated to take a firm hand. Thus the matter has rested. Today the provisions of the 1890 law form the basis of Manitoba's educational system.

Catholics, who comprise about one fourth of the total population, have never accepted the arrangement as fair and still maintain that they have been unjustly deprived of their constitutionally guaranteed rights by the legislation of 1890. In lieu of justice and consistent with their educational views, they have, wherever it was possible, built and maintained their own schools. Cardinal Merry del Val was sent to the province by Pope Leo XIII in 1897 to view the situation. Later a papal encyclical, expressing a spirit of both firmness and moderation, was issued to be read in Canadian pulpits. The law of 1890, it held, was "imperfect and insufficient"; Catholics should continue to seek justice, but partial satisfaction should not be refused in the meantime; Christian charity should regulate efforts, but efforts should be made to seek justice; the Catholic schools should be equal to the best in quality of teaching and equipment; there need be no conflict with Catholic demands and the maintenance of an excellent system of public schools.

Catholics have, as a matter of fact, continued quietly and firmly to press for equitable treatment by the government. The issue is still an open one and will remain so until a more just resolution of the church-state relationship in education has been achieved.

A more favorable climate of opinion among people and government than existed in the late nineteenth century is evidenced by recent trends. In 1959, an education commission appointed by the government of Manitoba after a three-year study recommended unanimously that the province give financial aid to private schools, stating that "practical application of the principles of democracy. . . requires that whenever possible the majority be tolerant enough to provide for significant minorities the kind of education they want for their children." Under the commission's formula for private school aid, grants from the provincial government would cover about half of the present capital and operating costs of most private schools.[8]

Following publication of the commission's report, the Manitoba School Trustees' Association urged the provincial

government to give sympathetic consideration to the recommendations that financial aid be given to private schools. The
association is a 51-year-old group representing trustees of
more than 1,200 school districts. The provincial government,
however, up to the present has refused to support or initiate
an effort to implement the commission's recommendation.
Observers of the scene predict that sooner or later action is
inevitable.

Practical Operation of Religion-Education Relationships in Manitoba

The general administrative set-up for education in Manitoba is similar to that of the other Canadian provinces. An
Advisory Board, which meets four times a year, is a distinctive feature of the school system. A Catholic priest, French-
speaking, is one in a membership of nineteen. The powers of
the board have been limited in recent years, being now more
or less restricted to providing for religious and patriotic
exercises. Not statutory, but nevertheless binding, is the
practice of giving fair representation to Catholics in administrative appointments.

There are no separate schools. Segregation by religious
persuasion in public schools during regular class instruction
is forbidden by law. Formal denominational religious instruction may be given during the last half hour of the school day
and children must attend unless their parents object in writing,
in which case the child must be excused. The religious instruction is given in the public school building by local clergy,
Protestant and Catholic, or by some one designated by them,
when authorized by the trustees of their own notion or by petition of the parents or guardians of ten children attending a
rural school or twenty-five children attending a town or city
school. One duly qualified Catholic teacher must be employed
if requested by parents or guardians of twenty-five pupils in a
rural school or forty pupils in an urban school. The same
rules govern Protestants in school districts where they are in
a minority.

Religious exercises, as distinct from religious instruction, are governed by printed regulations, which appear in a

booklet prepared by the Advisory Council referred to above.
The booklet contains prayers, references to scriptural pas-
sages from both Protestant and Douay versions, and hymns
taken from both Catholic and Protestant hymnaries.

It may be asked: Is the period allowed for religious instruction being actually used by religious authorities? The
provincial board of education has not the power by law to com-
mand local trustees to authorize the privilege. That is a
matter for their own decision. Exact statistics are not available, but general evidence indicates that in Catholic communities where there are no parochial schools, the period is regularly used for formal religious instruction in Catholic doctrine
and practice. Perhaps not a fourth of the schools in other
areas make use of it.[9] In 1955 the Advisory Council after the
publication of its booklet had an amendment passed in the
legislature designed to increase the use of the suggestions for
religious exercises. Section 252 of the School Law stipulates
that religious exercises shall be held in every public school
on each teaching day when the school is in operation unless
the local board definitely directs in by-law that the practice
be set aside. The cancellation to be valid must be repeated
each year.

There are in Manitoba at the present time 62 private
schools. Twenty-seven of them are elementary, six secondary, and the remainder a combination of the two.[10]   These,
like the private schools in the United States, are almost all
church-related, the vast majority being under the auspices of
the Catholic Church. They receive no public funds of any kind
and up to 1958 paid taxes on their property. The schools are
supported by tuition fees, or gratuities by religious orders.
All property owners must pay taxes for the support of the public schools whether their children use them or not.

The private elementary schools are subject to state inspection and their teachers must hold provincial teaching certificates. As regards secondary schools, the curriculum and
standards are self-determined, but the province may refuse
to recognize diplomas. All junior and senior matriculation
students in the province are required to write examinations
conducted by the High School Examination Board.

Like most of the other provinces, Manitoba has committed itself to support only one non-sectarian university. Denominational colleges may confer degrees in theology only. Several church-related colleges, including St. Paul's conducted by Catholics, have affiliated themselves with the university. They are supported by their respective denominations.

The Manitoba system in respect to church-state relationships in education can be briefly appraised, as the encyclical of Pope Leo XIII in 1897 put it, as imperfect and insufficient. With the prejudices of the late nineteenth century weakened or dead, there will be no surprise if these imperfections and insufficiencies are soon set aside.

SASKATCHEWAN AND ALBERTA

Saskatchewan and Alberta attained separate provincial status September 1, 1905, under identical constitutions. For thirty-five years before that date the area comprising the two provinces had formed part of the North-West Territories under the central government of Canada; and beyond 1870 stretching back for some two hundred years, the land, much of it a wilderness, was under the control of Hudson's Bay Company, and more remotely under the British Crown. Up to 1905, therefore, the history of educational development in the two provinces is a common story. With provincial status came complete autonomy in educational matters and modifications in educational practice.

While Hudson's Bay Company concerned itself with furs and profits in the early years, Catholic missionaries were building chapels and schools for the Indians and half-breeds scattered throughout the eastern section of the area, which is now Manitoba. The company was so impressed with the accomplishments of the Catholic missionaries that, beginning with the year 1825, it donated twenty-five pounds annually to assist them in their work. From St. Boniface the missionaries spread to the western section of the territories, the first regular school west of Manitoba being opened at Edmonton in 1862.[11]   The Grey Sisters, intrepid and zealous, were soon in the wilderness, aiding the missionaries in the work of religious instruction and teaching in the schools.

In 1870, the Company relinquished its rights to the Imperial Government, and the vast territory was transferred to the
rule of Canada and put under the control of the Lieutenant-
Governor of Manitoba. By a legislative Act in 1875, the
North-West Territories were organized and provided with a
system of government. Provision was made for the establishment of a school system which was to embody the principle of
separate denominational schools. The influence of the Ontario
system, rather than that of Quebec, is seen here, the principle
of separation having already been well established in that province. The framers of the legislation in Ottawa went on the
theory that the same rights and privileges in regard to religious instruction belonged to the people of the Territories as
those possessed by the people of Ontario.

Thus, the educational section of the Act contained the
provision that

> the minority of rate payers. . . , whether Protestant
> or Catholic, may establish separate schools therein
> and in the latter case the rate payers establishing
> such Protestant or Roman Catholic schools shall be
> liable only to assessment for such rates as they may
> impose upon themselves in respect thereof.[12]

At this time the number of white people in the Territories was
very small and about evenly divided between Catholic and
Protestant.

To encourage educational developments, the Canadian
government granted subsidies of lands and money, but it was
not until 1884 that steps were taken to establish a system of
common elementary schools. In the meantime Catholic
schools, as well as those of other religious denominations,
were able to avail themselves of the educational subsidies provided by the Federal government. The Act of 1884 made provision for a school system very similar to that of Quebec. The
territorial school system was to be administered by a Board
of Education composed of twelve members, six of whom should
be Protestant and six Catholic, divided into two distinct sections

on the basis of religion. The united Board had limited general powers, but each section sitting separately had extensive jurisdiction over the organization and administration of its own schools.

The schools, whether Catholic or Protestant, were to be supported both by local taxation and by government grants. Formal religious instruction was permitted "only during the last half hour of the afternoon session." If the trustees so desired, the school might be opened with the Lord's Prayer.

As years went by the proportion of Protestants to Catholics increased. A trend toward limiting the jurisdiction of the separate sections of the Board began. Evidence supports the view that the aim was to restrict control by Catholics of their schools and to put the management of all schools in the hands of a general board. This aim was gradually accomplished through a series of amendments passed in 1885, 1891, and 1892. Manitoba had in the meantime abolished the separate school system entirely and influences from that province made themselves felt in the North-West Territories.

The culmination of the trend was reached in 1901 with an ordinance which amended and consolidated all existing educational legislation. The separate school principle was retained, but the separate boards were shorn of power. The situation in respect to separate schools and religious instruction had been changed from a formula similar to Quebec to a system almost identical with that of Ontario. The Act created a Department of Education with extensive powers. Separate schools were subject to the same regulations as were the public schools in regard to curriculum, inspection, and teacher certification.

Teaching of doctrinal religion was restricted to the last half hour of the school day. The trustees had the power to order the school to open with the recitation of the Lord's Prayer. Pupils could be excused from the religious instruction at the request of the parents. Catholic textbooks were permitted only as supplementary readers.

The boundaries of separate and public school districts were to be coterminous. The earlier legislation had allowed the separate school district to be organized within the confines of two or more public school districts. Now it had to be or-

ganized within the district or not at all. Since Catholics were
in most cases the minority, few in number and scattered, this
provision indirectly but effectively precluded the establishment
of a Catholic separate school in most rural areas.

The trustees of a separate school were allowed to select
a qualified teacher or teachers and to impose upon themselves
such rates as they might see fit for the maintenance of the
school. The amount raised by local taxation would be supplemented by a government grant proportioned to that distributed
to the public school. Any person legally assessed for a separate school was not liable to assessment for any public school
and vice versa. This is the law which was in force when the
provinces of Saskatchewan and Alberta came into being in 1905.

Catholics were dissatisfied. They had been deprived of
the denominational rights conferred by the earlier legislation.
Repeated attempts to have the amendments repealed failed, although their constitutionality was considered doubtful by some
authorities. The Premier of Canada, Sir Wilfred Laurier,
expresses his view by stating that there "can be no doubt that
the legislation which has been passed in the Northwest Territories, and which is now in force, has been somewhat at variance with the principle laid down by the organic law of 1875." [13]

The issue reached its final culmination in the Autonomy
Acts of 1905, which became the constitutions of the two new
provinces of Saskatchewan and Alberta. The original bill relating to the erection of the two provinces contained a clause
on education (Clause 16) which considerably liberalized the
situation of the separate schools. Restrictions on religious
instruction and exercises were omitted and the bill brought the
formula for the establishment and management of separate
schools into conformity with the original law of 1875.

These changes gave rise to acrimonious controversy.
Organized agitation against the concept of separate schools for
Catholics was carried on with a bitter intolerance. The voices
of "statists" were persistent and vigorous, demanding an exclusive system of public schools. Catholics were equally determined to sustain their rights and to oppose all efforts toward
limiting and endangering the Catholic character of their separate schools. Letters were exchanged between the Prime Minis-

ter and the Apostolic Delegate.

The controversy dragged on. In the end advocates of
state control and the forces of intolerance won at least a partial victory. A greatly amended educational clause was inserted into the Autonomy Acts. It followed closely the formula set forth by the 1901 Act, which had reduced the rights of
the religious minority in regard to their separate schools to
an absolute minimum. Stated briefly, the pertinent clause
allowed the right of separation to a religious minority in a
district, whether Catholic or Protestant; it limited religious
instruction to the last half hour of the school day; it gave the
minority the right to elect trustees, who in turn had authority
to appoint the teachers; a limited use of Catholic readers was
allowed in Catholic separate schools.

Section 93 of the British North American Act was applied
to the new provinces with the following substitution for paragraph (1):

> Nothing in any such law shall prejudically affect any
> right or privilege with respect to Separate Schools
> which any class of persons have at the date of the
> passing of this Act under the terms of Chapters 29
> and 30 of the Ordinance of the North-West Territor-
> ies passed in the year 1901. . .

The Autonomy Acts also contained a clause which specified
that no discrimination could be made by the provincial government toward the separate schools in the distribution of any
money for the support of schools.

The Autonomy Acts, which became the constitutions of
Saskatchewan and Alberta, put the question of the continued
existence of separate schools for all time beyond the jurisdiction of the provincial authorities, but it left the separate
schools completely under the control of the Board of Education.
So greatly restricted were the schools as to their denominational character that their establishment seemed scarcely
worth while.

Following the achievement of provincial status, both
provinces began their autonomous career. Further educational

developments and the present status of the church-state relationship in education of each province are discussed separately
below.

Saskatchewan

Despite constitutional guarantees, the continued existence
of separate schools became a political issue in the first election of Saskatchewan. The Conservative party stood for a
"rigid national school system" which looked toward the eventual abolition of separate schools. The Liberals, though adhering to the policy of complete control of the separate schools
by the province, held that the constitutional right of such
schools to exist should be protected. Religious intolerance
and anti-Catholic bigotry were clearly manifested in the campaign. The outcome of the election was a victory for the
Liberals. The educational formula then in force with its separate schools as provided for by the Territorial Ordinances
of 1892 and 1901 was adopted as the basis of the Saskatchewan
school system. Few changes have been made since in the legal relation of the separate schools to the provincial government.

The trend toward secularism in public education, which
was evident in the first political campaign, has progressed,
and agitation for the complete abolition of separate schools
has not entirely ceased. The "Orange Lodge" was active in
the movement and Ku Klux Klan influence from the United
States abetted the activities of the group during the second
and third decades of the present century.

The administration of the educational system in Saskatchewan is in the hands of a central Department of Education
presided over by a member of the cabinet styled the Minister
of Education. He is assisted by a superintendent, deputy
superintendent, a group of inspectors, and by an Educational
Council, consisting of five persons "two of whom shall be Roman Catholic." The Council must be consulted before any
departmental regulation can be adopted. The Department,
subject to the laws of the province, has complete control over
the schools, public and separate. Everything comes under
regulation.

The School Act operative in Saskatchewan today permits the teaching of religion in the public schools during the last half-hour of the school day, during which time "any such instruction permitted or desired by the board may be given." This may be denominational, if the board so decides. The law makes it permissible also "for the board of any district to direct that the school shall be opened by the reading or reciting, without comment or explanation, of the Lord's Prayer or a passage selected from Bible readings prescribed for the purpose by the minister, or both." Any child may leave the room when religious instruction is commenced if the parents or guardians so desire. The Department of Education has prepared a brochure "Bible Readings for Schools," which suggests graded selections.

So much for the law. What in practice is being done in the public schools of Saskatchewan in the area of religious instruction? An official from the Department of Education, 1963, writes:

> In our province school boards may permit religious instruction during the last half hour of each school day in the elementary schools. In predominantly Roman Catholic communities we find this half hour is being used for that purpose. In Protestant districts where the people cannot agree as to the type of religious instruction, there is really very little done and the half hour is not used. However, a large number of schools do open with the Lord's Prayer and often a Bible reading. This type of religious exercise is generally encouraged. [14]

This brings us to a consideration of a type of school which has developed in Saskatchewan, sometimes referred to as a Catholic public school. The educational clauses of the provincial constitution quite deliberately had not encouraged the formation of separate schools. Because there was little advantage to be gained from applying for and maintaining a separate school, Catholics tended, especially in those rural areas where they constituted a majority, to continue in the public schools and to use the half hour allowed for religious instruction for teaching the truths and practices of the Church to the children, almost all of whom would be Catholic. Catholic teachers would be employed; otherwise, as to textbooks, courses, regulations, the schools would be no different from any other public school. In 1912, for example, there were 31 schools of this type, whereas there were only 14 Catholic and two Protestant separate schools.[15]

In some instances the teachers selected were members of religious congregations, wearing the religious garb of their order and perhaps displaying other religious insignia. It is possible, too, that religious symbols appeared in the classrooms. During the late 1920's and early 1930's, these practices were attacked in an organized anti-Catholic campaign backed by Ku Klux Klan influence, which had penetrated from across the border. The government elected in 1930 implemented its election pledges by amending the School Act as follows:

> No emblem of any religious faith, denomination, order, sect, society, or association shall be displayed in, or on any public school premise during school hours, nor shall any person teach or be permitted to teach in any public school while wearing the garb of any such religious faith, denomination, order, sect, society, or association.[16]

In spite of these restrictions on the Catholic public schools, the number of Catholic separate schools has not appreciably increased. In 1930 there were 4,910 public school districts; 23 Catholic separate districts; and three Protestant separate school districts.[17]   In 1955 the figures were respectively, 5,141, twenty-nine, and nine. Recently there has been a pronounced trend toward consolidating of smaller districts in the interest of economy and efficiency. This process accounts for fewer public school districts today. In 1963 there was a total of 2,094 operating school districts; 16 of these were secondary school districts; 48 were consolidated school districts and 1,985 were public school districts.[18]

The advantages of conducting separate schools seem to be still too limited to warrant their establishment to any great extent. The main difference between them and the Catholic public schools is that in the separate school religious symbols may be displayed, and the teachers by law must be Catholic; whereas in the Catholic public school there is no legal guarantee regarding the teacher's faith. Both types of schools must follow an identical course of study.

The separate school districts impose rates upon themselves for the maintenance of the schools and are in receipt of provincial grants, as are the public schools. The question of the distribution of corporation taxes has come up for discussion. An early provision followed the Ontario formula, permissive but not mandatory on the corporations. The difficulties which followed the efforts in Ontario to implement this formula were repeated in Saskatchewan, and amendments and litigation accompanied attempts to adjust the distribution more equitably. The matter is still somewhat confused, but in general when the religious affiliation to the stockholders is not known the taxes are to be divided between public and separate school boards in the same ratio as the taxes of other owners of property.[19]

In the early days of the territory secondary education was entirely conducted by the religious denominations. Later when the province entered the field, the principle of separate secondary schools was not applied. Then, legislation passed in 1907 definitely declared that the rights and privileges of separation did not apply to the secondary level. Some of the secondary schools which were operating at that time continued as private, tuition-charging institutions. They receive no public funds of any kind, but are exempt from municipal taxes. For the most part secondary education in Saskatchewan is today predominantly the concern of the state.

In regard to religious instruction in public high schools, the Secondary Education Act reads:

The board of any district may direct that the school
be opened each day by the reading or reciting,
without comment or explanation, of the Lord's

Prayer or a passage selected from Bible readings
prescribed for the purpose by the minister or both.

The province has undertaken to keep higher education unified and controlled. There is only one degree-granting university, state supported and non-sectarian. Denominational
colleges exist, but they must be affiliated to the university, or
to some other recognized degree-granting institution. Catholics pressed for a degree-conferring college of their own. A
compromise was reached. St. Thomas More College was established on the university campus as an Arts college in a sort
of quasi-federal relationship with the university. The students
may take, for example, their philosophy and history at St.
Thomas and their technical courses at the university.

All teacher training is given at "Teachers' Colleges"
under the jurisdiction of the Department of Education, or in
the College of Education as part of the University of Saskatchewan. This means that all teachers in the province, including denominational personnel such as Sisters and priests, are
trained through the same teacher training colleges." [20]

Alberta

Alberta's guarantee of the existence of separate schools
is identical with that of Saskatchewan. In Alberta, as in the
neighboring province, the question of separate schools became
an issue in the first elections of 1905, the Conservatives opposing and the Liberals favoring the formula as outlined in
Section 17 of the Alberta constitution. The Liberals won overwhelmingly and the separate school concept was accepted once
and for all in the province. And again, as in Saskatchewan,
few significant changes have been made in the laws relating to
the status of separate schools or on the role of religion in the
public education. In general, however, the attitude toward and
the situation of the Catholic separate schools in Alberta have
been more favorable than in Saskatchewan.

The over-all administrative set-up of education follows
the usual pattern. Large powers are centered in the Department of Education, which is intrusted with "the control and
management of all kindergarten schools, public and separate

schools, normal schools, teachers' institutes, and the education of the deaf, deaf-mute, and blind persons." At least two of the five members constituting the provincial Council on Education must be Catholic.

Formal religious instruction may be given in the public schools during the last half hour of the school day. Likewise, the district boards may decide at will whether the Lord's Prayer is to be recited and Bible readings are to take place at the opening hour.

The method of establishing and supporting a separate school has remained practically unchanged. First a public school district must be erected and its boundaries defined. If the majority of rate payers are Catholic, the trustees and the teachers may be Catholic. The religious instruction, which is restricted to the last half hour of the school day, in this case would be Catholic doctrine and practice. From this any Protestant may be excused. The course of studies and textbooks are determined by the public authorities. These schools are similar to the Catholic public schools in Saskatchewan, but the trend in Alberta is strongly toward the establishment of separate schools.

If the Protestant minority in a district such as we have described is not satisfied, it may under the law erect a separate school district for itself, elect its own school board, levy and collect taxes from the Protestants of the district, establish a separate school and engage its own Protestant teachers. Very few Protestant groups have shown an inclination to follow this procedure. They seem content to avail themselves of the public school of the district, even though it happens to be under "Catholic control." The procedure is reversed if Protestants are in the majority. Then Catholics, if not satisfied, may set up a separate school. Thus in Alberta, Catholics may conduct either a "public" or a "separate" school. According to the law the first school to be established in a district is a "public" school with the religious-orientation of its majority.

Catholic authorities have provided an organizer who assists Catholics in a district to set up their separate school. The procedure is similar to that in Ontario or Saskatchewan; a meeting is called and trustees are elected. In Alberta, the religion of the owner of property determines whether his property is assessed for public or separate school purposes. Thus, the taxes accruing from property owned by Catholics will go for the support of the Catholic separate school. The school will also share in the public or provincial grants for educational purposes. Supporters of separate schools are exempt from taxation for the support of other schools.

Alberta grappled with the question of corporation taxes as early as 1910. The Assessment Act was amended and corporations were obligated to make a division of taxes. If the number of Catholic and Protestant shareholders is known, the division is based on that proportion. If it is impossible to ascertain the religion of the stockholders, then the directors must assign the corporation's taxes to public and separate schools in the same manner as other property taxes are divided in the municipality.

The trustees of the separate school may select the teachers, who are to be Catholic in the case of a Catholic separate school. The teachers may be of the laity or members of a religious congregation. Although formal instruction in the doctrines of the Catholic faith is limited to the last half hour of the school day, that restriction does not prevent the integrating of a Catholic view of life and morals into the atmosphere and activities of the whole educational program. Provision is made by the Department of Education for the optional use of Catholic readers in Catholic schools. Teachers conducting separate schools must fulfill the requirements set by the Department as to academic and professional training and be in possession of a provincial certificate.

In one aspect Alberta has departed definitely from the practice in Ontario and Saskatchewan. The support of secondary as well as elementary schools is provided for under the separate school principle. Catholic high schools are supported in the same manner as the Catholic elementary schools by both taxation and provincial grants. How did this come about? The practice has its roots in Alberta's early history when secondary education was fostered by the early missionaries and later by the denominational bodies. These church-related schools received public grants. Prior to 1901 some of the separate elementary schools were adding on more advanced work, teacher training included, with financial support from the territorial government. By 1896 the special grant had become statutory.

The argument for the continuation of public support for secondary education on separation principles was that in Alberta the high school was never clearly differentiated from the elementary school and that the right to support for advanced education was carried over into union in 1905 and guaranteed under Section 17 of the Autonomy Acts. That is actually what happened. High schools gradually replaced classrooms above Standard Five, both in public and separate schools, but they continued to be administered by the school board and supported by municipal taxes and government grants.[21]   Thus in practice they came under the guarantee of the provincial constitution that nothing in any law passed by the legislature should "prejudicially effect any right or privilege with respect to separate schools, which any class of persons have at the date of the passing of this Act."

These separate secondary schools are subject to the regulations of the Department of Education, including restrictions as to the time for the formal teaching of religion.

In addition to the schools described above, there are a considerable number of non-government or independent schools, elementary and secondary. Most of these are church-related and all depend on private sources for support. These schools do not come under the regulations of the Department of Education, but attendance at them satisfies compulsory school laws. They are officially inspected and reports are kept on file but no restrictions are placed on them as regards qualifications of teachers, courses given, textbooks, and so forth.

The only teacher training institution operating in the province is the Faculty of Education of the University of Alberta. All teachers are trained at the Faculty either in Edmonton or Calgary. The province recognizes for certification purposes diplomas which have been obtained elsewhere providing the conditions under which they were obtained are the equivalent of Alberta requirements.

Under the University of Alberta Act no institution other

than the University may grant degrees within the province except in theology. Religious groups have residential colleges
on the campus. [22]

There are currently in Alberta eighty Catholic school
districts of which forty-four operate schools. The remainder
send their children to other separate school districts in which
schools are operated. There are three Protestant separate
school districts operating schools. A fourth such district has
joined a large unit of administration called a school division
which provides school service for the area. The trend in Alberta is strongly in the direction of consolidation of public
school districts into large divisions. Catholic separate districts are eligible to join school divisions, but in no case have
they done so. A comparison of the number of separate school
districts with the large public school divisions is meaningless.
Some idea of the proportion of educational responsibility carried by Catholics in Alberta in relation to the total effort may
be obtained by comparing the number of teachers in each type
of school. In 1963 Catholic separate schools employed 1,491
teachers; Protestant separate schools, 44. The total number
of teachers employed in the Province was 13,342. [23]

How satisfactory are the church-state relationships in
education in Alberta and Saskatchewan? What has been said in
reference to Ontario's solution applies to these two provinces,
where the formula is based on that of the older province.
Alberta has progressed further in recognizing family and
church rights and in meeting the demand of distributive justice
by its extension of financial aid to the separate secondary
schools.

Aside from constitutional difficulties, the separation
concept undoubtedly would not appeal to Americans, either to
Catholics or to the general public. Yet it works well in the
Canadian provinces. The relations between the separate
schools and the Department of Education are cooperative and
friendly. One hears few or no complaints about "divisive-
ness." It is a fact that people do differ in their religious
convictions. That is their privilege in a free society. The
separation principle simply takes realistic cognizance of an
existing situation and makes an adjustment to it which at least

attempts to give parents an opportunity to exercise their natural right to choose the kind of education they desire for their
children without paying an economic penalty for the exercise.

THE MARITIME PROVINCES

The three Maritime Provinces, Nova Scotia, New Brunswick, and Prince Edward Island, may be conveniently grouped
together. They originally constituted but one political entity
and shared in common the vicissitudes of war, conquest, and
political changes. Colonized early by Catholic France, their
ethnic origin was later compounded by Protestant settlers from
England, Scotland, and the United States, a situation which
introduced conflicts in the area of religion, language, and culture, and, consequently in education. The unique characteristics of the resolution of the church-state issue in education
arrived at or, more accurately, accidentally achieved by
these provinces is the fact that the religion-education relationships have their bases in custom rather than law.

The area comprising the Maritime provinces of today
was the first of the Canadian lands to be settled, and there we
find the earliest effort to provide schools. The region was
then called Acadie or Acadia. Prince Edward Island became
a separate colony in 1773; New Brunswick was separated in
1783, and the remaining territory became known as Nova
Scotia -- New Scotland.

The first record of an attempt at a permanent settlement
by the French in Acadia dates from 1603. A settlement was
finally made at Port Royal the following year. The story of
all the early explorations and settlements have one point in
common. Side by side with the explorers, traders, and
settlers went the missionaries. Acadia was no exception. Up
the rivers and into the forests these men of God brought the
blessings of Christianity to the natives and, to the extent that
it was possible, the gift of learning. Later would come the
itinerant teacher and the denominational school, and much
later, governments would undertake the establishment and
control of schools.

The first definite record of a school in Acadia was one

established by the Capuchin friars at La Heve in 1632 or
1633. [24]

After the treaty of Utricht in 1713, France relinquished
to Britain her claims to Acadia. English and Scotch settlers
began to arrive. To attract still larger numbers in the hope
that the area might become thoroughly English, the government gave large tracts of land to ministers and teachers who
established themselves in a given settlement. The society
for the Propagation of the Gospel in Foreign Parts, closely
associated with the Church of England, began work in Nova
Scotia in 1728 "for the instruction of the King's loving subjects
in the Christian religion," and for enabling the children to
read and "to write in a legible hand."

The first education Act in Nova Scotia was passed in
1767. Its principal aim was to debar adherents of religious
faiths other than the Church of England from teaching in the
schools. Although the provisions of the Act were designed to
keep all nonconformists from the classrooms, Roman Catholics
were specifically prohibited under severe penalties. A board
of trustees was established. Only Church of England applicants were licensed as teachers and only they were given
grants of land. Such was the intolerance of the times! Yet
a large majority of the people were French-speaking Catholics.
These refused to use the existing schools and illiteracy
abounded. In 1808 an Act was passed recognizing the principle of public support for education by local assessment on real
and personal property.

Finally, the Free Education Acts of 1852, 1864, and
1871 laid the foundation of the system of public education in
Prince Edward Island, Nova Scotia, and New Brunswick, respectively. All these Acts provided for non-sectarian schools,
with no provision for separate or denominational schools.
Any denomination wishing to have its adherents educated in its
own schools had to provide them at its own expense.

With the passing of the years and a lessening of religious
and ethnic intolerance, compromises were effected whereby
both Catholic and French claims were at least partially met.
The compromises developed without benefit of legislative action.
They were a growth from within, a grass roots product, as it

were. With repetition they became custom, and such they have remained. The non-sectarian principle remained unchanged on the statute books, but custom prevailed in practice.

When Nova Scotia and New Brunswick entered the confederation with Quebec and Ontario to form the Dominion of Canada, what custom had ordained in relation to denominational teaching came, it was supposed, under the protection of Section 93 of the British North American Act. These "customs" as they affect the Maritime provinces individually are examined in more detail below.

Nova Scotia

As has been suggested above, the official educational regulations in Nova Scotia give no hint as to the actual practice in regard to the religion-education issue. Even before confederation, custom had more or less definitely determined the pattern which Nova Scotia was to follow. The law declared public schools were non-sectarian; it recognized no separate school system. At confederation, therefore, denominational schools had no legal status, nor did Catholics press for it. It was taken for granted that the prevailing customs were sufficiently protected by Section 93 of the British North American Act, which became part of the province's constitution.

The issue did not enter politics in Nova Scotia after confederation and the legislature consistently avoided pronouncements, leaving to the decision of the Lieutenant-Governor in Council what in other provinces became a controversial political issue. The attitude was that the educational law merely laid down the minimum requirement in regard to religious training in the schools. This was contained in a list of duties to be fulfilled by teachers: "Encourage in the pupils by precept and example a respect for religion and the principles of Christian morality, for truth, justice, love of country, humanity, industry, temperance, and all other virtues." There was nothing in the law to prevent the local boards from going beyond that minimum, and that precisely was what the local boards were doing.

Several factors in the Nova Scotia situation had facilitated these developments. The local districts, especially in
rural areas, had retained much of their original spirit of independence, the administration of the schools being regarded
as a community enterprise to be assisted by the state with a
minimum of interference. Then, again, a grass-roots sense
of fairness -- perhaps enhanced by a reaction against early
intolerance -- prompted the people to make reasonable adjustments which would take into account the diversity of religious
views and the differences in language and culture within the
province.

Several methods of meeting the diverse views of Catholics and Protestants, each agreeable in its own community
and acceptable to the Department of Education, have emerged.
In solidly Catholic rural areas, especially where the French-
speaking predominate, an emphasis permitted by the local
board is placed upon religious instruction and religious practices which give a distinctly Catholic character to the schools,
although these practices are held before or after school hours.
The teachers are frequently members of religious congregations, wearing the religious garb of their order. The Department of Education raises no objection, and the schools continue to receive financial support in the same manner as all
public schools. No exact statistics are available as to how
many such schools there are, but one observer describes
them as "many."

Another type of adjustment sanctioned by custom has
come into use in the cities and larger towns. In Halifax, for
example, where almost half of the population is Catholic, unwritten local custom requires that of twelve members of the
unified school board at least four must be Catholic. The
members are appointed, six by the provincial governor, six
by the city council, each agency therefore appointing a minimum of two Catholics.

The Catholics of the city have rented to the Board for a
nominal sum old buildings, formerly housing regular parochial schools. The schools have been put under the control of
the Board, follow regulations governing public schools, and
are supported completely by public funds. The teachers,

however, are always nominated by the Catholic members of
the Board and are often members of religious congregations.
The general atmosphere of the schools is Catholic, but religious instruction and religious practices take place either before or after regular school hours. Where a new school is
needed by the Catholics, the Board undertakes to build it or to
aid in its construction. It is then conducted in the manner
described above.

In some of the larger towns, Catholics continue to conduct parochial schools. The public schools remain strictly
non-denominational and open to all. At least one of the trustees, usually five in number, by unwritten law must be Catholic. The trustees see that the parochial school is supplied
with free textbooks, examination blanks, and sometimes they
provide for classes, such as home economics.

Though all of these arrangements come under custom,
they are nevertheless adhered to as loyally as written laws are
obeyed. On the whole, the compromise adjustments work
smoothly. Catholics -- almost all of them -- are in the kind
of school their parents desire for them; the parents are bene-
fiting from the school taxes they pay, and there is nothing in
the Nova Scotia school law which explicitly excludes such arrangements.

Besides these "compromise schools" there are in Nova
Scotia a number of distinctly independent schools, church-
related and mostly Catholic. These receive no public aid.

In higher education Nova Scotia has not limited itself by
law to one public degree-granting institution, as have some of
the Canadian provinces. There are a number of church-related universities that have made noteworthy contributions to
Canadian life. St. Francis Xavier University at Antigonish
has won international fame in the field of extension and adult
education.

New Brunswick

For years prior to confederation some 250 or more
schools in Catholic districts of the province, although teaching
Catholic doctrines and engaging in Catholic practices, were
supported by public funds.[25]   In 1858 the so-called Parish

Schools Act introduced into the public school system for the first time the concept of non-sectarianism. Although the terms "non-denominational" or "non-sectarian" were not used, the policy of non-sectarianism was clearly implied in the section which outlined the duties of teachers. They were directed to take diligent care to impress on the minds of the children the principles of Christianity and to instill in them the virtues consistent with Christian living. The Bible was to be read without note or comment to the children whose parents did not object. The implications of the clause were clear: the instruction given in the schools was to be strictly non-denominational.

But long standing customs cannot be stamped out immediately by legislation, and religion continued to be taught in schools in many areas where the religious consciences of parents demanded it. Otherwise, parents refused to send their children to neutral schools. Sisters, wearing the religious garb of their congregations, were frequently the teachers. This was the situation when New Brunswick entered the Dominion in 1867.

Section 93 of the British North American Act would seem in the intentions of the legislators to have protected the denominational privileges granted by custom in New Brunswick, but their intentions had not been fully included in the wording of the law. In 1871 the legislature put the final touches on the public school system by passing the Common Schools Act, making schooling free, compulsory and non-sectarian. The prohibition against denominational teaching in the public schools was made explicit: "All schools conducted under the provisions of this Act shall be non-sectarian." Denominational schools were excluded from public funds. Teachers were permitted to open and close schools by reading a portion of Scripture from the Common or Douay versions and by reciting the Lord's Prayer, but were not to compel attendance of any pupil at the exercises against the wishes of parents. Regulation 20 forbade the exhibition of emblems and symbols distinctive of any religious organization, either in the schoolroom or on the person of any teacher. Thus teachers wearing the religious garb were excluded from the classroom.

The law clashed with long-standing traditions and deeply-felt convictions. It was opposed to the wishes of the vast majority of the people. The question was raised whether Catholic parish schools did not constitute a separate system under the terms of Section 93 and whether they were not therefore entitled to public funds. A case was taken to the judicial committee of the Privy Council in London. The decision was that the New Brunswick parish system could not in the strict legal sense properly be held to constitute a separate school system.

Catholics at this time comprised over one-third of the population. Under the leadership of Bishop Sweeney they protested against the law and petitioned for redress. They declined to send their children to the non-sectarian schools and refused to pay taxes for schools they could not in conscience use. Some non-Catholics joined in the opposition.

Unlike developments in Nova Scotia, compromise and adjustments did not come easily in New Brunswick. The province embarked upon a period of agitation and controversy, at times bitter, before a more or less stable pattern of church-state relationships took form. The government was not disposed at this time to adjust to the consciences of those who desired a religious education for their children. The agitation continued. In one instance a riot occurred.

Obviously a situation so manifestly at variance with grass-root desires could not indefinitely endure, and the government, faced with difficulties of enforcement, was at last willing to make concessions. Regulation 20 was modified by an addition which declared that "nothing herein shall be taken to refer to any peculiarity of the teacher's garb or to the wearing of the cross or other emblems worn by the members of any denomination of Christians."

Other compromises followed. These actions were taken, however, not by the legislature but by the Cabinet. In 1875, important concessions were granted. Religious instruction was permitted after school hours at the will of the trustees; textbooks were to be prepared or revised to free them from misstatements offensive to Catholics; licenses to teach were to be issued to members of religious orders who possessed a certificate endorsed by the superior of the order; children were allowed to attend any school in a district, an arrangement which gave parents a better opportunity to choose a school having a religious orientation.

As a result of these concessions new schools came into operation which were denominational in practice, while adhering to the letter of the government's compromise arrangements. In villages and towns where the French-speaking predominated, it became customary for the Church to erect a school building and rent it to the trustees for general use. The teachers were Sisters; religion was taught after school hours. The schools were maintained by public funds.

Such customs were strengthened and stabilized by a court decision in 1896. Five Protestants had objected to a compromise arrangement in the town of Bathurst where Sisters were conducting a public school. The school, the plaintiffs maintained, was in reality a sectarian school; its manner of procedure was in violation of the school law. The decision of the Court was against the plaintiffs. The opinion handed down declared that there was no violation of the provisions of the Common School Act against sectarian education in the public schools for school trustees to employ as teachers Sisters of a religious order and that the holding in a schoolroom before or after school hours of Catholic religious exercises did not render the school sectarian.[26]

The pattern of church-state relationship in education in New Brunswick has been more or less set by the concessions of 1875 and the Bathurst decision. The law on the statute books is that of 1871. Its broad interpretation is a product of grass-roots demands supported by the decrees of the Cabinet and the judgment of the Court. The general policy of the Board of Education has inclined in the direction of allowing school trustees considerable discretion in the matter of religion in the schools. Neither successive governments nor the legislature has shown a disposition to narrow the interpretation that has come to prevail. If religion has been given an important role in a school in a particular area and that is what the people want, there has been no inclination recently to make an issue out of the matter.

We summarize by a brief review of the law as it stands today on the statute books and the practice in the schools as government decrees and custom have ordained. The pertinent sections of the Schools Act read:

> Section 110. All schools conducted under the Act shall be non-sectarian.

> Regulation 15, It shall be the privilege of every teacher to open and close the daily exercise of the school by reading a portion of the Scripture, and by offering the Lord's Prayer; but no teacher shall compel any pupil to be present at these exercises against the wish of his parent or guardian, expressed in writing to the board of trustees.

Practice varies somewhat from area to area. In general where Catholics are a majority, school accommodations owned by the Church are rented to boards of school trustees for public school purposes. The rental fee is for school hours only.[27] The school is open to all children, but in practice only Catholic children attend. It is under the jurisdiction of the board and is maintained by public funds like any public school. Corporation taxes are no problem. All goes into the common purse to be distributed by the trustees at will. The teaching staff is composed largely of members of religious congregations. Formal religious instruction is given outside regular school hours, but a general religious atmosphere is maintained throughout the day. In St. John, the largest city of the province, practically all Catholic children from kindergarten through high school are in schools of this type. In Frederickton, the capital, the practice extends only through the elementary grades.

There are a number of church-related private schools not within the public school system. These receive no aid whatsoever from public funds. Denominational colleges grant degrees and play an important role in higher education in the province. Among them are St. Joseph's University at Saint Joseph and Collège de Sacré Coeur at Bathurst, both under

Catholic auspices.

Prince Edward Island

Prince Edward Island entered federation as the seventh
province in 1873. Like the other Maritime provinces, the
Island long had a tradition of a "gentleman's agreement" to
allow public schools to be directed by Catholics or other denominations if the number of students warranted the procedure.
This was the policy in vogue even though legislation in 1852,
which set up a public school system in the province, had declared that the schools established under the statute were to
be non-sectarian.

Section 146 of the School Act in operation today is almost
identical in wording with that of the law enacted more than a
century ago. It reads:

> All schools conducted under the Act shall be non-
> sectarian, and the Bible may be read in all such
> schools, and is hereby authorized, and the teach-
> ers are hereby required to open the school on each
> school day with the reading of the Sacred Scriptures
> by those children whose parents or guardians de-
> sire it, without comment, explanation or remark
> thereupon by the teachers; but no children shall be
> required to attend during such reading unless de-
> sired by their parents or guardians. [28]

Such is the law. Actual practice follows closely the example of Nova Scotia, with whom the Island has always had
close relations. We have noted the three types of response
to the claims of religion for recognition in the schools which
have developed in Nova Scotia. Similar arrangements exist
on the Island, where nearly half the teachers are employed in
one room schools. In communities that are predominantly
Catholic -- and just a little less than half the population is
Catholic -- the small rural schools are for all intent and purposes Catholic in spirit and practice. But no one makes an
issue of doctrinal religion taught after school hours, of the
religious garb worn by the teachers, or of religious symbols

in the classrooms. Many of the schools, especially in the cities, carry instruction through grade ten.

The schools are public, following the regulations and curriculum set by the Department of Education. Public funds support them, pay the teachers' salaries, and provide super-annuation grants to the latter upon retirement. The Depart-ment maintains consistently a liberal attitude toward the reli-gious aspects of all public schools and the high school grades attached to them.

There are three private schools in the province spon-sored by the Catholic Church and four under Protestant aus-pices. These receive no public funds but enjoy certain fringe benefits such as subsidized textbooks.[29] St. Dunstan's University under the control of the Catholic Church serves not only Prince Edward Island but attracts students from other provinces of Canada. Since 1957 it has undertaken teacher-training.

The arrangements in respect to religion in education and parental rights as worked out in the Maritime provinces in the form of a "gentleman's agreement" seem to give a fair degree of satisfaction in these areas of Canada. From the viewpoint of a completely adequate solution of the church-state relationship in education, they leave something to be desired. The restrictions on the teaching of religion fall short of the freedom needed and the non-legal status of the procedures gives them an element of instability. On the other hand, the arrangements considered as an expression of deeply felt con-victions regarding the importance of the role of religion in education and the governments' informal accommodation to these grass-roots demands have something to be said in their favor.

NEWFOUNDLAND

Newfoundland, the last of the Canadian regions to achieve provincial status, entered the Dominion in 1949. Education-ally, as well as politically and economically, Newfoundland stood apart from its neighbors, its development proceeding from circumstances unique to itself. Geographical insularity,

a long, irregular coast line, a harsh climate, a rough interior --these were some of the physical factors contributing toward developments in the island, and, indirectly, toward the
shaping of the educational pattern. More important was the
social situation. Protestant British and Catholic Irish settlers
tended to huddle together in religiously homogeneous groupings,
and thus was set the pattern for the future educational system.

The first settlers were English Protestants. By the end
of the eighteenth century Irish immigrants were in the majority. The Irish were Catholic, poor, resented, and were severely persecuted by the more prosperous British. Both
groups retained for many years their ancient ethnic and religious animosities. Both groups tended to segregate themselves
geographically along the coast and even in the cities. Fishing
was the principal industry.

During the eighteenth century facilities for education
were practically non-existent and the harshness of living conditions, the absence of law, and the isolation of the scattered
areas reduced the settlement to a state of near barbarism.[30]
The first attempt to bring religion and educational opportunities to the people was made by the churches and the charitable
organizations. In 1726 the Society for the Propagation of the
Gospel made an establishment at Bonavista and later extended
its efforts to the larger cities. A few schools were opened.
Next the Newfoundland School Society for the Propagation of the
Gospel, with similar aims and methods, took up the work,
conducting some forty schools between 1830 and 1870. Other
organizations, which aimed primarily to being education to the
very poor, contributed to the cause. One such was the Bene-
volent Irish Society, which, starting on a non-denominational
basis, founded an orphan asylum with a school. The institution became in time distinctly Catholic. Later Presentation
Sisters from Ireland took over the care of the girls, and the
boys' school was given in charge of the Irish Christian Brothers. These two religious congregations made noteworthy
contributions towards the religious and educational efforts of
the colony throughout the nineteenth century, and their work,
including the two original schools, has continued until the
present day.

All educational opportunities were provided by churches or church organizations until 1836. In that year a legislative measure provided for the establishment and support of a system of elementary public schools. It gave financial consideration to the services long rendered by the churches and charitable societies by allotting a portion of public funds for the existing institutions in St. John. The colony was divided into districts. For each of these a board of thirteen members was to be named by the government, the "senior or superior clergyman" of each of the several religious denominations being among those named. It should be noted that in the provisions of this law and its successors the state did not agree that it should bear the full cost of education. In general, the arrangement was that half the cost of erecting schools should be borne by the communities and religious groups concerned. This policy has, in general, been adhered to, although in practice some deviation from it occurs.

By 1838 the government reached the decision that it was necessary to restrict and regulate the power of the clergy in the public schools. Abuses of this privilege had given rise to dissension. No minister was to be permitted to give religious instruction in the schools or to interfere in their management. The public schools were to be non-sectarian, although the term itself was not used.

The implied secularization of the schools, however, did not take root. For their schools the people of the island seemed set on two points: religion must remain in the school as an important element, while at the same time freedom must be allowed to the individual conscience; secondly, public aid should be given without denominational discrimination. How were these objectives to be realized? The Newfoundland solution was simple and direct. Protestants and Catholics would continue as they had been doing to conduct their own schools, teaching religious doctrines according to their convictions, and the state would aid them financially. The denominational principle was embodied in a statute in 1843, which set the framework for the future educational system of the island. There were to be 34 districts, 17 Catholic and 17 Protestant; a sum of 5,100 pounds was to be distributed among them on

the basis of population. Where the sum appropriated was
less than 25 pounds it was not necessary, the Act stated, to
appoint a board, but the government would turn over the funds
to the Board of a contiguous district to administer it.

Other educational acts followed in succeeding years, but
the denominational principle remained unchanged. Always
there was evidence of regard for parental rights and the freedom of the individual conscience. An Act passed in 1853, for
example, set down certain studies as obligatory, including
Scripture reading, but it cautioned that this practice must
have due regard for the religious views of parents.

The situation was gradually to become slightly more
complicated. Other Protestant sects were settling on the island. Methodism, particularly, had taken a strong hold and
later the Salvation Army obtained a considerable following.
In 1876 a divided Protestantism, which included the Methodists,
was recognized by law. The educational Act in that year provided for three types of denominational elementary schools
and for three academies or high schools in St. John. It gave
the colony three superintendents. Funds were to be divided
on a basis of population. The number of superintendents was
later increased from three to four with the admission of the
claims of the Salvation Army.

An Act in 1903 made provision for amalgamated schools.
Non-denominational, these schools were to be established only
in sparsely populated settlements where the total number of
children in the area would not warrant separate schools for
each denomination. The government grant was to be paid the
Board of Education having the majority of population in the
settlement. The teacher, who was to be chosen by competitive examination, might give religious instruction to the children of his own faith before or after school hours; likewise
the children of other denominations might receive religious
instruction under the same conditions. The statute cautioned,
however, that the principle of the denominational school was
to be safeguarded: ". . .the foregoing sections shall not be
construed as interfering in any way with the principle of denominational education which is the law in this colony." [31]
The Act also set up a Council of Higher Education of twenty-

six members. It was comprised of the six superintendents
and the heads of the existing secondary schools, which at the
time were referred to as colleges.

The aftermath of World War I and the depression of the
1930's left Newfoundland in a serious economic condition. The
government was bankrupt. A commission set up by the Royal
Warrant to study the situation decided that the colony should
forfeit self-government, and for the next fifteen years Newfoundland was governed by Great Britain. No significant
changes were effected in the field of education. In 1949, by
plebiscite Newfoundland decided to join the confederation.
Clause 17 of the Act of Union, which contained the educational
provisions, declared that this field was to remain completely
under the control of the new province. There was no suggestion of a possibility of federal interference for any reason.
Section 93 of the British North American Act had been modified
to suit the present sentiments of the Canadian people.

The Newfoundland legislature was to have "exclusive
authority to make laws in relation to education." The denominational system was to be forever safeguarded, since the legislature was denied authority "to make laws prejudicially affecting any right or privilege with respect to denominational
schools, common (amalgamated) schools, or denominational
colleges that any class or classes of persons have by law in
Newfoundland at the date of Union." [32]   The principle of non-
discriminatory public aid for denominational schools of all
levels was put on a permanent basis, the law specifying that
public funds set aside for education were to be distributed to
all schools and colleges "in accordance with scales determined
on a non-discriminatory basis." [33]

Such are the fundamental principles on which church-
state relationships in education in Newfoundland rest. The
system is a nicely adjusted compromise. It may be described
as a denominational system within a public school framework.
It also has been referred to as a partnership between various
religious denominations and the state, exhibiting a balance of
support and control shared by the state and the religious denominations. It is a public school system because in the final
analysis the provincial government controls education and votes

most of the money which makes the system operate. It is denominational because the religious denominations control those aspects of education relative to their purpose. From this viewpoint there are five distinct school systems. The schools, with minor exceptions, are denominational and are under the jurisdiction of the Catholic Church, the Church of England, the United Church of Canada (Methodist), the Salvation Army, and the Pentecostal Assemblies. Today the Catholic population outnumbers the other denominations, comprising approximately 34 percent of the total; Anglicans have 30 percent; and the United Church, 24 percent. The Presbyterians and Congregationalists are few in number and have, for school purposes, joined with the United Church. The Salvation Army, the Pentecostal Assemblies and some dozen other smaller religious groups make up the balance. We will see how the principles are practically applied in the day to day operation of Newfoundland's school system.

An administrative set-up under governmental auspices makes possible coherent and integrated action among the denominational sections. At the top is a Department of Education, headed by a Minister of Education who is assisted by a Deputy Minister. The major denominations must be represented in the Department, which is responsible for the distribution of funds according to law. There are five Superintendents, one for each major denomination. Responsibility for educational policy is given to an Educational Council with the Minister of Education as chairman, the Deputy Minister and the five superintendents as members. The latter act as representatives of their respective denominations to the Department. The Council meets once a month. Within the Department, it sets policies and makes regulations which are applicable to all schools in the province. The Department controls the licensing of teachers, authorization of textbooks, and uniform examinations after Grade IX.

To carry out the policies and regulations of the Council, supervisor-inspectors are appointed by the Lieutenant-Governor in Council, the various denominations being represented in accordance with their size. The trend is away from the concept of "inspection" as the main function to the idea of constructive supervision. The law states that as far as possible the duties of the inspectors with regard to any religious denomination shall be performed by such of the inspectors as are members of that denomination.

The entire province is divided into educational districts each of which is administered by a single denomination except in the case of amalgamated or interdenominational districts. The divisions do not involve a great amount of overlapping since the geographical distribution of the population is quite generally along denominational lines. Formerly the boundaries of school districts coincided with parish boundaries. The present trend in Newfoundland, as elsewhere in Canada and the United States, is toward consolidating and creating larger districts. In line with the trend, Catholics, for example, have widened their districts to include several parishes. There has been a trend among Protestants toward amalgamated districts, especially in the newer and larger industrial regions. In these areas Catholics have insisted on their separate districts.

The Lieutenant-Governor in Council appoints in each district a Board of Education of five or more members of the same religious persuasion as the residents of the district, one of whom must be a "senior clergyman" or other officer of the denomination resident in the district. In making the appointments the government acts only on the recommendation of the superintendent of the denomination in question. Each Catholic school board includes the pastors in the district and two representatives from each parish. One of the pastors is chairman.

The Board of Education appoints the teachers who are always of the same faith as the denomination in question. In Catholic communities, Sisters or Brothers of the various religious congregations are selected, if such personnel is available. In practice, the Board of a Catholic district will usually consult with the principal or religious Superior before making appointments. The district boards collect what they can for the payment of teachers' salaries and the maintenance of the schools but depend largely on government grants. In only a few districts are taxes collected on property.

In some areas the denominational boards operate schools which were built by church funds on church lands. The building may serve both as a school house and a meeting hall for church activities, religious and social; it may even serve as the church building. More frequently a considerable portion of the cost of erecting the school was borne by the local community, usually under the leadership of the local church. The present policy is for the province to pay approximately 70 percent of the cost of new buildings and the proportion may be larger in the case of poor districts. The schools are permitted to charge fees to cover heating costs, but no child may be debarred who is unable to pay.

There is nothing in the law or its application to prevent the widest use of religious exercises and instruction in the schools. There is some variation in the extent to which the opportunities are used. Those conducting Catholic schools maintain that there is no interference in keeping the schools thoroughly Catholic in spirit and practice.[34]   Certainly the five board members and the supervisors, which the law provides, are in a position to see that the place of religion in the school accords with the wishes of the community. Still, protection is given by law to the individual conscience. Section 49 demands that "no teacher in any college, academy, or school aided by money granted under the Act shall impart to any child attending the same any religious instruction which may be objected to by the parents or guardians of such child."

Teacher training and certification is controlled by the Department of Education. Memorial University College, a state controlled institution, provides training for future lay teachers and all male candidates. St. Bride's College, a Catholic institution affiliated with the University, trains Catholic women candidates in accordance with provincial requirements. It is assisted by government grants.

The people of Newfoundland seem satisfied with their system. It is admittedly less economical, less pliable, perhaps less efficient, than a totalitarian system might be. But this is a small price to pay for the boon of complete religious liberty in education and equality of treatment for all children by the state. We do not attempt here to evaluate the concrete effects which a religious system of education has upon the moral life and common well-being of the province. One might

see a relationship in the fact that statistics of crime and juvenile delinquency are low. In any case, Newfoundland has
found a democratic solution to the religion-education issue
suitable to its own needs and desires. It has overcome the
ancient fears, hatreds and intolerances of early days. Though
the children of the various denominations attend their own
schools, there seems to be no evidence that the essential unity
of the little province has been jeopardized. On the contrary
the visitor senses a pride in that diversity among human beings
which a democracy by its nature is intended to preserve.

Yukon and Northwest Territories

The territories are under the control of the federal
government, which also directs education. An agreement by
Yukon territorial officials to provide Catholic separate schools
with support equal to that given public schools in the territory
was unanimously approved by the Territorial Council. Under
the agreement public funds are used for the construction, expansion, and maintenance of separate schools and their equipment and furnishing except "sacred objects." The operating
costs, which are paid with public funds on a monthly per-pupil
basis, include salaries of teachers, janitors' fees, heating,
lighting, textbooks, school supplies, and other normal expenditures.

The agreement also provides funds to build residences
for lay teachers of separate schools. It promises "equality
of treatment for public and separate school children" in such
matters as school bus transportation.

The separate schools, almost all Catholic, are required
to conform to public school policy in curriculum and school
hours except for one-half hour of religious instruction. Items
such as religious hymn books are the responsibility of Church
authorities. Most of the schools are conducted by members
of Catholic religious congregations.

The same practice holds in respect to the schools of the
Northwest Territories. These schools are conducted chiefly
by Catholics and Anglicans. Half of the Indian schools are
residential institutions operated by religious denominations,

but supported financially by the national government.

We have seen that only one Canadian province, British Columbia, had embarked on the way of secularism in education, excluding all denominational religion from the public schools and refusing financial assistance to schools religiously oriented. One other province, Manitoba, though arranging for and encouraging the formal teaching of religion in the public schools by official representatives of the various denominations, has excluded church-related schools from sharing in educational funds. The other eight provinces in one way or another give religion a role in public education and allow the church-related schools to share in public funds.

In general, then, it may be noted that our good friends to the North have approached the religion-in-education issue in a different light than ours. Principle more than expediency seems to have been the guide. Principle was expressed in three concerns: concern that religion be allowed to play its vitally important role in the training and education of youth in the schools, as well as in the home and churches; concern that parental freedom of choice in education be recognized; concern that all Canadian children be treated equally by the state and that none be discriminated against as a result of parental choice of an education in harmony with religious convictions. Not every province, perhaps not one of them, has achieved these ideals fully. But as far as implemented, the aims seem highly consistent with the democratic way of life and politics.

The Canadian people, as a whole, have left behind the ancient misunderstandings and intolerances that were a legacy from a Europe in religious turmoil. There is separation of church and state both on federal and provincial levels. But there is no high, impregnable wall between these two societies, both seeking man's welfare, one in the temporal, the other in the supernatural order. Rather the formula is cooperation and harmony, or at least an effort to achieve them.

Perhaps no one of the various solutions of the religion-in-education issue reached by the Canadian provinces would be acceptable or workable in the United States, but the principles upon which the solutions are based are surely of concern and interest to Americans. They have also expressly a place in the charter of the United Nations.

Chapter 5

Australia: PROGRESS TOWARD SOLUTION

The Australian Commonwealth is a federation of six states, each originally independent. Federation was achieved in 1900. As elsewhere among Great Britain's colonies, historical and environmental factors intermingled in the shaping of an educational pattern. As an outpost of England, it is not surprising that Australia took over from the mother-country it's early educational viewpoints and practices. Such concepts as the importance of religious and moral instruction, church-control, and the "aid-if-necessary" function of the government were operative in the first educational efforts which the colony made. As time passed, however, the unique characteristics of the isolated continent with its vast area and small population imposed upon the educational pattern some special characteristics and created some unusual problems.

The country has rich coastal lands and vast pastoral districts, but the huge interior plateau has little or no rainfall and both aridity and sandy soil make the land unfit for any kind of agriculture. The total population of Australia is about 11,500,000. Fifty percent of the people live in the six capital cities. The other half of the population lives in small settlements and widely scattered communities of the so-called "outback." These environmental factors have led to a highly centralized system of education within each state.

As to that aspect of education which is our primary concern, the church-state relationship, there is special interest in noting both the manner of and the causes for Australia's divergence from the traditions of the mother-country and the contrast between its resolution of the religion-in-education issue and those reached by the Canadian provinces. Perhaps it is more accurate to say Australia is still working towards its solution since much of the current educational literature coming from that country indicates a dissatisfaction with the status quo and a search for a more equitable resolution.[1]

The first settlements were made in New South Wales

213

during the latter part of the eighteenth century. Convicts sent
out by Great Britain composed a large proportion of the early
population. Some of the convicts were hardened criminals,
but many were simply victims of iniquitous laws and political
intolerance. Among the latter were Irish "dissenters" whose
only crime was a firm stand against British tyranny in Ireland.
Eventually, free settlers arrived in considerable numbers and
the transportation of convicts ceased. Nevertheless, conditions in the colony were far from normal for a long time.

The free settlers and the better type of convict, some of
whom were reasonably well educated, brought with them the
culture and educational ideas of their own countries. In time
schools were established which naturally followed the pattern
then prevalent in England. Ecclesiastical control of education
was the current practice, a tradition actually dating back to
the time of St. Augustine in the sixth century. As early as
1793, five years after the first settlement was made, a Church
of England chaplain opened a school for the children of military
officers and of convicts. Within a short time, the well-known
societies associated with the Anglican Church and also a few
private individuals had taken up the challenge and more schools
were established. The government aided these efforts with
small financial grants. Later, provision was made to set
aside two hundred acres for the maintenance of a teacher in
each township. Many children, however, were left without
educational opportunities.

The next step was the establishment in Sydney of a public elementary school of the charity type, which was placed
under the direction of Anglican clergy. Within a few years
several more such schools had been set up. All the schools
taught the doctrines of the Church of England and were supervised by its chaplains. For a long time suitable teachers
were scarce, and the establishment of schools perforce remained haphazard.

Catholics, mostly Irish, had in the meantime come into
the colony in considerable numbers, and these, together with
the convicts of the same national origin, formed a growing
part of the population. The penal laws against Catholics,
still in force in England, were likewise applied with vigor in

the colony. Catholics as felons or simply as Catholics were deprived of all political, civil, and educational rights. Socially they were ignored, scorned, and discriminated against. Priests were unwelcome; the Church was not permitted to function.

The Anglican schools were, of course, completely unacceptable to the Irish, who were committed to the age-old educational ideals of the Catholic Church. The schools which their consciences demanded for their children would have to integrate the doctrines and moral principles of Catholic teaching into the warp and woof of the child's education. The Irish Catholics had suffered for these convictions in Ireland, preferring to keep their children home rather than send them to Anglican schools where their faith ran the risk of destruction. And the existing Anglican schools in Australia were in very fact proselyting agents, the teachers, when an opportunity arose, displaying great zeal in initiating the Irish children and other Catholics in the doctrines and services of the Established Church. [2]

In spite of dire poverty, Catholics made heroic efforts to establish their own schools. Father Therry, the first Catholic priest with a recognized status, arrived in Australia in 1820. [3] Having been refused permission to teach religion to the Catholic children in the existing schools, he established a school of his own. How he maintained it out of his meagre resources, no one knows, but manage it he did. Later the authorities allowed him twopence a week per child, but forbade him to charge any fee.

In the meantime the Catholic Emancipation Act, 1829, had been passed in England, and most of the political and civil disabilities against Catholics were removed. The social and political position of Australian Catholics improved but their poverty remained extreme. Nevertheless, efforts to maintain schools continued. Advances in the number and quality of their schools were made possible by the arrival of the Irish Sisters of Charity in 1833 and the Irish Christian Brothers in 1832, who, as professionally prepared teachers, raised the standards of the Catholic schools to as high a level as existed in the colony. The government contributed to the support of the schools conducted by these religious on the basis of one pound for every pound subscribed by parents. However, in view of the poverty of Catholics, who were generally unable to supply their share, not much benefit was received from the proffered aid.

At the moment, then, the educational picture in Australia followed the English pattern closely. The government limited its activity in education to showing an interest by giving financial help to the various private agencies. Control was still assumed to belong to the church. Subsequent developments may be considered as falling into three uneven phases, each characterized by a widening government interest extending from the establishment of schools with public funds and culminating in government control of education. Concurrently with the increasing government activity there was a decline in the religious character of the schools. From almost completely Anglican-controlled, state-aided schools, the situation changed to one in which all denominations shared equitably in government funds. This development may be characterized as the denominational phase. It was followed by a dual arrangement and finally by a secularized public school system, with government funds restricted to government schools only.

Dissenters from the Established Church began arriving in the colony in significant numbers after 1830. They looked askance at the almost complete control of the schools held by the Anglicans. Sectarian rivalries began to develop and demands for equitable treatment were made. In 1836 New South Wales passed a school act which gave equal status to all religious denominations in the receipt of government funds. This example was followed by several of the other states. Each denomination had the right to appoint its own teachers, subject to state approval. Parents thus had the choice of sending their children to a public, a Catholic, or a Protestant denominational school. Public aid was generally granted to the various denominations on the basis of their representation in the population. Catholic schools in West Australia were debarred from participation in public funds. The grant, as a rule, covered the teacher's salary plus a small stipend per day per child. In some cases, the government gave the land where

the school was to be established and even contributed to the
cost of erecting the schoolhouse. This system characterized
by governmental grants in aid, of land, building and salaries,
with internal management of the schools in the hands of the
churches, continued until 1848.

Unfortunately strife among the Protestant sects continued and the governments stepped up their control of the
schools in an effort to improve the situation. A dual system
was set up. Two separate boards were established: one, a
National Board, to allocate funds to the public schools; another, a Denominational Board, representing all religious
groups, to handle the grants to denominational schools. Both
types of schools were supported from public funds. In practice, the Denominational Board left to each church the control
of its own schools.

The educational situation worsened, if anything, with
the adoption of the two boards. Sectarian contentions and rivalries continued within the Denominational Board. In New
South Wales and in Victoria, the competition among the sects
resulted in a multiplication of schools in the larger districts,
while the outback areas had practically none at all. Rivalry,
too, between the dual boards ensued. The National Board was
accused, apparently with good reason, of fostering disunity
and partiality. It seemingly regarded itself as an opponent of
the Denominational Board with which it was supposed to cooperate. Squabbling went on to the general disadvantage of educational progress. A survey in 1866 found that 100,000 children of school age in Victoria were not attending any school.
A similar situation existed in New South Wales.

A movement to modify the whole system was initiated
as a result of dissatisfaction with the status quo. In an effort
to improve matters, several states established a single controlling body, similar to a board of education, on which the
various religious interests were represented. Again disagreements within the body prevented success. More pronounced
changes were then advocated, the extremists demanding that
all the schools be put under one board, that only non-denominational religion be taught in public schools, and that all
church-related schools be denied a share of public funds.

A number of factors operating on the current scene contributed toward the actualization of these demands. Immigration had continued to bring Protestant non-conformists to the Australian colony. Their numbers were now such that their educational views could have an impact on the developing policies. Among the dissenters, the Baptists and Congregationalists had never been interested in conducting their own denominational schools. Traditionally they advocated non-sectarianism in public schools. In this view, they were joined by Protestants of other sects who regarded themselves as "liberals." All of these, especially the Baptists, became militant advocates of public schools -- free and non-sectarian. They disseminated their ideas far beyond the limits of their respective congregations. Purely secular teaching, untrammeled by sectarian dogmas, would, it was argued, "break down the credal barriers which until then had fostered class hatreds and disrupted social life." Children thus liberated could be sent to the same schools and brought up in the creed of friendliness and justice. [4]

But a more powerful influence in the direction of secularism was a general decline in religion itself and a growing religious indifferentism which made the transition to secularism in the public schools easy of acceptance. The concept of liberalism was having an impact on both politics and religion. In religion, the liberals held that there was no positive truth in the doctrines taught by the churches and that therefore one creed was as good as another. All were to be tolerated, since in the last analysis all were matters of opinion. Liberalism became identified with the anti-dogmatic principle and, obviously, the step toward out and out secularism was a short one. The facts of the situation are difficult to document or describe statistically, but evidence is available in the literature of the period, where the current trends were either deplored or glorified, depending upon the writer's own views on the matter. [5]

Anglicanism, the largest denomination, seemed uncertain, but in whatever direction its influence was bent, it was bound to bear a significant share of the responsibility for shaping the destinies of education in Australia during the nine-

teenth century.[6] In a sense the Anglican leaders found themselves caught in a vise. They saw in the rise of secularism
a new and profound threat to religion. Yet the Victoria Royal
Commission, after an investigation in 1867, had presented
evidence that religious instruction in the state-supported Anglican schools had practically ceased. The schools were
unable to refute the charge. The situation had actually arisen
from the fact that large numbers of children of other denominations were in attendance at Anglican schools. Under the
circumstances, the teaching of Anglican doctrines presented
increasing difficulties, so that finally all attempts to continue
such teaching were virtually abandoned.[7]

Moreover, it began to appear that the Catholic schools
alone would gain effectively from opposition to the secularist
movement, since they would be the principal recipients of any
aid given to denominational schools. Catholics alone had
definite and unchangeable convictions on the role of religion
in the schools and were determined to keep their schools at
any cost. A defense of the denominational school by the Anglicans would put them in an embarrassing position -- on the
side of Rome!

In addition to these developments, a wave of intolerance
against "Rome" was sweeping the land. The Church was
growing in influence and her schools were becoming more numerous. Cries of "Watch Rome; distrust Rome" were heard.
Old columnies against the Church were vented anew. At
meetings held to promote secular education some speakers
challenged their audiences with such rhetorical questions as:
"Do we want the Queen of England to rule this country or the
Pope of Rome?"[8] In 1872 the Protestant Political Association
was organized as a bulwark to stem the advance of what it
termed "the political conspiracy against the rights and liberties of men, commonly called the Church of Rome."[9]

It began to require strong convictions and unwavering
courage to defend the denominational school and to oppose the
growing demand for secularism in the public schools. Some
Anglican leaders did adhere to this position on grounds of religious principles. Others, whose views were similar but
whose courage was weaker, held back. Eventually, the Angli-

can authorities capitulated, throwing the weight of their influence against aid to denominational schools and for state-controlled, non-sectarian public education.

Various factors of a different nature also indirectly assisted the cause. There was obvious need for more uniform standards and closer organization. The secular movement had strong political support and was now further strengthened by the cooperation of many who, however uneasy about the principle itself, felt that it provided a means, perhaps the only means, of getting the job done and of resolving the sectarian strife which had become particularly bitter.[10]

Catholics, although growing in numbers, were not in a position of sufficient strength to make their influence felt to any great extent. While not opposing the entrance of the state as a unifying and stabilizing force for education, they stood staunchly for the preservation of the denominational schools on a basis of equality with the public schools. It soon was obvious to them in what direction the trend was moving and they began to prepare for new and more difficult conditions.

The changes were indeed forthcoming in quick succession in all the Australian states. In 1862 the legislature in Victoria passed an Act establishing a centralized system of public schools, which were to be free and compulsory. In 1872 these schools were secularized and public aid was restricted to them. An education department was set up under the supervision of a Minister of Education. The other states soon followed Victoria's lead with similar legislation: South Australia and Queensland in 1875; New South Wales in 1866, and 1880; Tasmania in 1885; Western Australia in 1893. The details of management of schools passed into the hands of the central boards operating from the six capital cities. The local boards retained a mere vestige of authority.

But traditions were strong and the legislators were unwilling to exclude religion completely from the public schools. They demanded, however, that it be non-sectarian. Concessions were eventually effected in favor of the denominations, some states making it permissible for representatives of the religious denominations to come into the schools to instruct children in the doctrines of their respective sects. The

nature of the changes which were occurring is exemplified by
the legislation passed in New South Wales in 1880:

> In all schools under this Act teaching shall be
> strictly non-sectarian, but the words 'Secular
> Instruction' shall be held to include general re-
> ligious teaching as distinguished from dogmati-
> cal or polemical theology, and lessons in the
> history of England and in the history of Australia
> shall form part of the course of secular instruc-
> tion.[11]

Then, as a compromise concession to the denominations, another section reads: "Religious instruction may be given by
clergymen or Special Religion teachers -- but children receiving it must be separated for that purpose from the rest."[12]
Church schools could continue to exist but they no longer
were to receive state subsidies. Their supporters were held
liable for taxes to support the public schools.

As a result of these developments the number of Protestant denominational schools began to decline rapidly in all the
states. In Victoria, for example, of 367 denominational
schools listed as sponsored by Protestants prior to the passage of the Common Schools Act, 1862, only six were in existence twelve years later. The six remaining were Church
of England schools which had numbered 214 in 1862. The 91
and 62 schools which the Presbyterians and Methodists respectively controlled in 1862 had completely disappeared by
1874.[13]   The Congregationalists and Baptists, who had not
maintained denominational schools and had advocated non-
sectarian public schools so strenuously, found no difficulty in
adjusting to the new conditions. Commenting on the situation
as it affected the other Protestant denominations a recent writer declares:

> It is difficult to remain insensitive to the difficulties
> of the Church authorities in the later phases as they
> witnessed the effect on their schools of a decline in
> religious interest and the rise of popular secularism

which they regarded as inimical but were powerless to prevent.[14]

The new situation posed a serious problem for Catholic leaders who had stood staunchly on principle for the continuance of denominational schools on a par with public schools. Their poverty was extreme. It was not clear how they would be able to maintain their own schools and pay taxes for the public schools which, in conscience, they could not use. Their first efforts were directed toward obtaining some concession from the state but the question was how far could they depart from their principles to obtain it. The principles underlying their position were the familiar ones which had been consistently maintained throughout the Western world where a similar situation had confronted Catholics: the primary right of the parent to direct the education of his children and to send them to a school in harmony with his conscience; the right of the Church to teach; the view that religion is both a doctrine and a way of living -- by far too comprehensive and too important to be left as an appendage to an otherwise secular or neutral system of education. The right of the government to inspect, guard, and foster education was recognized in the Catholic position, as documents of the period testify, but the right completely to control education was consistently denied. These principles were basic to Catholics. How far could they permit constriction of their basic rights in return for financial assistance? Could the Catholic position be maintained in a secular system? It was soon seen that complete loss of independence and the relinquishment of fundamental rights would be the price paid for financial support, as the Protestant denominations had discovered. Catholics were unwilling to pay it. To them, complete capitulation was unthinkable. The alternative was to establish their own independent system of schools and to maintain it at the cost of tremendous sacrifice. This was the only course consistent with their religious principles and Catholics met the challenge with determination, vigor, and courage. In South Australia, particularly, the venture into independence was undertaken with a resolution and zeal which was "to issue finally in a national system and a firm pluralism in Australian education." [15]

The challenge was similarly met by Catholic leaders in the other states of Australia. Throughout the entire country, the schools were given the first place in the policy of the Catholic hierarchy. Like Bishop Hughes' principle in New York City in the 1840's, "the school before the church' became the guiding policy for Australian Catholics. The building of schools took precedence over all else in the development of a parish. The struggle to establish and maintain the Catholic school system, the years of self-sacrifice for laity, religious, clergy, and hierarchy have given to the Australian Catholic Church a sense of unity and a spirit of great courage.[16]   The financial burden was a grievous one and the underlying injustice added a sting, for Catholics were paying also for the public schools, which they could not use although they did not oppose them.

Adequate and competent staffing for their schools posed an additional problem for Catholics. It was solved to a great extent by religious congregations who came from various areas in Europe. These dedicated men and women took their places in the Catholic classrooms until Australia was ready to supply her own needs for religious teaching vocations.

Thus did Australia in the latter decades of the past century turn aside from the practice of the mother-country and the traditions of Western culture and, in so doing, create an unsolved education problem for herself. Of her resolution of the issue, a recent commentator says:

> It is difficult to allay the suspicion that many
> questions were suppressed, rather than resolved
> in secular principle. As early as the forties,
> Glenelg, the secretary of State for the Colonies,
> had deplored the injustice which must follow for
> those with 'such objections to the general plan as
> must practically exclude them from any partici-
> pation in its benefits, and who may yet be unable
> to supply a proper education from their own funds
> exclusively.' (Emphasis the author's)

The writer concludes: "The difficulty has never been resolved." [17]

The autonomous colonies were traditionally jealous of
their independence, but eventually it became obvious that joint
action was necessary in matters that concerned Australia as
a whole, such as immigration, defense, and trade. During
the latter part of the nineteenth century a movement toward
federation grew steadily in strength, culminating in the formation of the Commonwealth of Australia in the year 1900. The
Federal Constitution, like that of the United States, limits the
powers of the Commonwealth government to those specifically
conferred upon it. Education is not one of the listed powers
and consequently the control of educational affairs continued
to be vested in the respective states. The formation of the
Commonwealth, therefore, brought no essential changes in the
educational policy, nor have any significant changes been made
in the basic pattern since 1900.

Although the Commonwealth government has no direct
authority in educational matters, like the Federal government
of the United States, it is greatly concerned about and interested in the education of its citizens. It has expressed this
interest in activities similar to those undertaken by the American government in Washington: research, statistics, and indirect aid. The states have resisted any suggestions that the
central government's power in education be enlarged; they
are, however, not adverse to financial assistance for educational purposes.

Although there are six autonomous systems of education
in Australia, the essential features are similar from state to
state, such variations as occur being of minor importance.
One characteristic of all six systems is a highly centralized
form of administration. In each of the states education is
managed in all its details by a Department of Education in the
capital city. Expenditures are all defrayed from the state
treasury. Little local participation in education is permitted.
Such high centralization has its drawbacks, but in the case of
Australia with its vast outback of scattered and sparsely settled areas the advantages seem to outweigh the disadvantages.
The policy insures a uniform standard of instruction and a

reasonable equality of educational opportunity for all districts.

Organization of Education in Australia

So much for the general educational set-up. In practice, education in Australia is provided by a network of schools which basically constitute a dual system: the public or government schools, and a complex of schools outside the government system which are variously referred to as private, church, independent, or non-government. The latter is the preferred term.

The complex of non-government schools constitutes a very important element in the network of Australian education, providing facilities for almost one-fourth of the total school population. The relationships of these institutions with the public schools are harmonious and well integrated; and though the non-public schools are not directly assisted by government funds, they have, from the viewpoint of scholastic reputation, equal status with those of the governmental system. In fact, the non-government schools seem to have acquired an outstanding position in the total network and are held in very high regard by the Australian people.

Despite denial of government aid, the non-public schools have steadily increased in number and in enrollment, especially during the past twenty-five years. In 1950 there were 7,832 public schools as compared with 1,828 non-government; that is, non-government schools were approximately twenty percent of the total.[18]   In terms of total enrollment, in 1956 there were 1,779,000 children attending Australian schools. Of these 424,000 attended non-government schools, or approximately twenty-four percent of the total. In 1964, the figures were 2,366,474, the total enrollment, and 565,163 in non-state schools. Of the latter, 463,125 were in Catholic schools.[19]

The non-government schools have been variously classified, but for our purpose it will be convenient to distinguish three types -- the Catholic schools, the Protestant-denominational schools, and what for a better term may be designated as independent schools. The latter are conducted by private individuals or corporate bodies, are non-denominational, fee charging, prestige bearing, and resemble Great Britain's great "Public Schools" such as Eton, Rugby, and Harrow.

Most of the church-linked Protestant schools are of the secondary residential type, although in some provision is made for day students. Many of them, like the independent schools, are Australian counterparts of England's Public Schools, but perhaps less exclusive. They have great prestige and charge large fees.

The Catholic Church has built up what is practically an educational system peculiar to itself, including both primary and secondary schools. The system plays a highly recognized role in Australian education incompassing over three-fourths of the total enrollment of non-governmental schools, and almost one-fourth of the total primary and secondary school population in Australia. Concretely, in 1964, of the 2,205 non-state schools, Catholics had 1,827 or eighty-three percent; Protestants had 285, and private or non-denominational school groups, 93 schools.[20]

It is of interest to note that the non-government schools play a less important role on the primary level than they do on the secondary level, although about twenty-three percent of all primary pupils in Australia attend them. Practically all of these children are in Catholic primary schools. In 1955 of 302,835 primary children enrolled in non-government schools, 262,500 or eighty-six percent of the total were in Catholic schools.[21]   Currently, these schools are facing a crisis in demands for entrance which far exceed their ability to expand accommodations proportionately. The Catholic primary schools range from small schools in rural areas and country towns to large parochial schools in the cities. Open to all, the primary schools charge no fees or very low ones, but contributions are made by all who can afford them.

The Catholic secondary schools are large. Some of them, like the Protestant denominational schools, follow the pattern of the English "Public Schools." Over one-third of all secondary students in Australia attend non-government schools, most of which are church-related. Of these over sixty-two percent are under Catholic auspices.[22]   One reason for the larger role played by private schools on the secondary level stems from the fact that the state entered the field of secondary education late, namely in 1900, sixty years after the first indisputably secondary school had been established in Tasmania.

Universities in Australia are either state or national. There are no private or church-operated universities in the country. However, Catholics have established seven residential colleges in connection with the state universities. These have tutorial but not professional staffs. The religious denominations conduct teachers' colleges. To secure recognition for certification, the colleges must become affiliated with a university.

The general organization of Catholic education is on a diocesan basis under the direction of the local Ordinary. In each capital city there is a Catholic Director of Education, who supervises the schools and maintains liaison with the state Education Department and with the University. Each diocese manages its own educational affairs quite independently so that Catholic education in a sense is decentralized.

Church-State Relations in Operation

RELIGION IN PUBLIC SCHOOLS. According to the state constitutions the public schools are free and non-denominational. They have also been described as secularized. However, the latter term is scarcely accurate as applied to the Australian public schools. Although the teaching of the ordinary subjects must be dissociated from sectarian views, a place is provided on the school program for dogmatic religious instruction. Many observers regard the arrangements for religious instruction in the Australian public schools as more adequate and satisfactory than the agreed syllabus in Britain's county schools.[23] Until recently all the states had Acts which allow the clergy or accredited representatives of the various denominations to come into the public school building once a week during regular school hours, usually the hour before dismissal, and instruct the children of their faith. For this instruction the children of the various denominations must meet in separate groups in different rooms. This practice is similar to the released-time program which was declared unconstitutional by the United States Supreme Court in the McCollum Case (1949)

because public property was used for sectarian religious purposes. Australia has separation of church and state but gives
the concept no such extreme interpretations as did the United
States Supreme Court. In the Australian practice there is no
preference for any one religious sect over another; all denominations have the right to use the school building and school
time according to law. As a matter of fact, though exact
statistics on the practice are not available, evidence shows
that nearly all of the denominations do take advantage of the
opportunity.[24]   Catholics make use of it in areas where the
establishment of a parochial school is impossible.

A deviation from the policy of providing denominational
religious instruction in the public schools occurred in New
South Wales in 1963. First, a proposal to make religious instruction a part of the public high school curriculum, urged by
the Anglican Primate of Australia, was rejected by the state's
minister of education. A short time later the education minister decreed that religious instruction was to be deleted from
the social studies syllabus for the state's primary schools.
At the same time a Catholic proposal was rebuffed that would
have allowed children in Catholic schools to spend part of their
hours in state schools for instruction in some secular subjects.
Behind these decisions were the activities of both religious and
secularly-oriented groups: the New South Wales Teachers'
federation, the Secular Education Defense Committee and the
Jewish Board of Deputies. There is no evidence at present
that the action taken in New South Wales is indicative of a
trend affecting the rest of Australia.

In addition to the dogmatic instruction, in five of the six
states teachers are required to give religious instruction of a
general character as part of the ordinary work of the school.
Anything of the nature of denominational teaching is forbidden.
In the states where the lessons are given by the regular teachers, instruction consists of selected Bible readings accompanied in some instances by hymns and prayers of a non-denominational nature. No child is compelled to attend any such
session, but, in practice, about ninety percent do take part.
In Victoria, teachers are forbidden by law to give religious
instruction of any kind.

AID TO CHURCH-RELATED SCHOOLS. By law, non-government schools receive no direct revenue from any government source toward capital costs, maintenance, or salaries of staff. There are, however, a considerable number of marginal services and indirect aids which benefit the schools.

Many scholarships provided at public expense are available for children ready to leave the non-public primary schools. These are tenable for five years at either state or registered non-government secondary schools. They are generally not awarded when parents' income exceeds a specified amount, and the grants vary according to the income and number of dependents. In 1958, as an example, of 300 bursaries awarded on the results of examinations in New South Wales, 120 were taken up in non-government secondary schools.[25]   Further, students ready to leave the denominational secondary schools are eligible for scholarships and bursaries which carry them through the university.

In country districts pupils attending Catholic schools are permitted to travel on school buses which are paid for by the state. Lower rates on trains and buses are available for children from denominational schools. In all states free medical and dental service is given to children in all schools. In Tasmania, South Australia, and Western Australia some grants are given to denominational schools for books and film equipment.

There are in addition a number of indirect forms of aid for denominational schools. The federal government allows fees and other expenses paid by parents to approved private schools on behalf of pupils under twenty-one years of age to be deducted from taxable incomes. A maximum deduction is generally set. The non-government schools are exempted from state sales taxes in some states.

Since 1956 the federal government in Camberra has provided for the payment of interest within closely defined limits on loans raised by non-government bodies for school buildings. One out of every three children in the federal district is in a denominational school, and the government quite logically argued that failure to provide financial aid to these schools would weaken the much needed expansion of secondary school facilities.

Of course, no single one or all of the above indirect aids together are of sufficient economic significance to ease effectively the tremendous financial burden borne by the denominational schools. This is especially true in the case of the Catholic body, since outside the Catholic system the higher fees charged almost entirely pay for the other schools. So the Catholics of Australia, like the Catholics of the United States, are facing a grave crisis. They have reached a point where it is impossible to expand their facilities to meet the increasing demands for enrollment.

RELATIONSHIP OF CONTROL OF DENOMINATIONAL SCHOOLS BY THE STATE. A limited amount of direct and indirect control is exercised over the non-government schools by the state. In most states the direct control involves only schools which have pupils within compulsory school age and the regulations are generally regarded as reasonable and helpful. All schools must comply with building, health, and sanitation regulations. In Western Australia, Catholic and other non-government primary schools must be declared "efficient" by the State Department of Education if attendance at them is to be recognized as fulfilling the requirements of the compulsory education laws. The register must be open to inspection by the compulsory attendance officers.

Victoria seems to have proceeded further than the other Australian states in its attempt to regulate non-government schools. In 1905 the state passed a Registration of Teachers and School Act under the provisions of which all non-state schools had to meet certain requirements as to physical facilities and are allowed to employ only registered teachers who possess specified qualifications in regard to professional training. An Act of 1910 empowers the Minister of Education "to authorize the inspection of any school in order to ascertain whether instruction given is satisfactory." [26] The purpose of these measures seems not to have been to interfere in the actual management of the schools, but rather to make sure that certain essential standards would be met.

There are some indirect controls accepted voluntarily

by both primary and secondary non-government schools. In
primary schools many students take state examinations in order to become eligible for secondary school bursaries and
scholarships. In Tasmania, for example, the examination is
taken at age fourteen. If the child passes he is admitted to a
state high school without payment of fees or is given a scholarship which pays part or all of the fees in an approved non-
state school. In addition, he may be given a living allowance.

A kind of indirect control is exercised over secondary
schools which receive scholarship pupils. As a rule they
are visited by inspectors, not so much to examine the work of
individual teachers as to check on the general organization of
the school, the qualifications and experience of the staff, and
the maintenance of required standards in examinations. The
purpose is to have assurance that the schools are suitable for
pupils who hold government scholarships.

Many of the non-state secondary schools have their students take state examinations, which play an important part
in Australian education. The examinations are prepared and
corrected by external authority. Entrance to the university
is based on the Leaving Examination. The successful pupil
gets a certificate of passing, the possession of which has
great value in obtaining employment.

On the other hand, some of the non-state secondary
schools, instead of having their pupils take state examinations,
apply for accreditation, a procedure which exists in four of
the six Australian states and is extending. The school is
visited by a team of inspectors who survey facilities, qualifications and experience of teachers, standards of teaching,
and records. If the report of the examiners is satisfactory
the school is accredited for the Intermediate Certificate examination which takes place at the end of the fourth secondary
year. This means that the school may conduct its own internal examinations and the Education Department will accept the
headmaster's affidavit that certain pupils may be awarded the
Intermediate Certificate. Later the school may qualify to
grant the Leaving Certificate. The inspections are repeated
every three years.

The non-government schools, especially the Catholic

schools, admit the right of the state to insure standards, seek and welcome the inspections, and find them generally helpful. The relationships between the state officials and denominational authorities are cooperative and pleasant. In general, the non-state schools, both primary and secondary, are left with a wide range of independence and are free to carry on according to their own philosophical purposes and to experiment, if they wish.

The Catholic schools have complete liberty to adhere to the ideals and principles of a thoroughly Catholic education. Religious instruction is given regularly, of course, but the entire program of the school, with no diminution of its secular value, is directed toward the ultimate purpose of Christian education, namely, the formation of the true and perfect Christian. The independent schools and some of the non-Catholic denominational schools do not particularly emphasize religion. Indeed, social reasons have much to do with their services. It has been speculated that in the event of a depression, while the Catholic schools would survive, "non-Catholic parents would find it hard to withstand the attraction of the cheaper and free high schools." [27]

How Satisfactory Is the Australian Solution?

Australia, it would seem, like America is still faced with an unsolved educational problem, although, it must be acknowledged, the problem is less comprehensive and less deep-seated than that of the American States. Moreover, the indications are that its solution will prove to be less difficult.

As the situation stands in Australia today, the basic principles of the natural law are not ignored, even if they are not given full implementation. Parents are free to send their children to the school of their choice and in harmony with their religious convictions. The freedom, however, is limited by an attached penalty -- a double financial burden. The parents must support the schools which their religious consciences demand for their children while paying public school taxes from which they receive no benefit. And here again the principle applies: a right exercised at the price of a penalty

is a right denied.   Likewise, the Church, though free to establish her own schools and to conduct them in accordance with
her mandate received from Christ, must do so under a financial difficulty shared with the Catholic parents.   Australia's
policy, therefore, limits true religious freedom and impairs
distributive justice.

Where the practice exists, the opportunity for religious
instruction in state schools by accredited representatives of
the various religious denominations is a redeeming factor.   In
a pluralist society, perhaps no more satisfactory solution to
the delicate problem of religion in the public schools can be
found.   For those who hold that religion must permeate all
aspects of school life, of course, such an arrangement remains inadequate.   It implies a sort of religious schizophrenia
-- the concept that religion can be separated from the affairs
of daily life.   Australian teachers themselves have complained
that their enforced neutrality in religion and marginal matters
affects their capacity "to meet the questions of the young and
leaves too many important areas of inquiry in unsatisfactory
suspense." [28]

Catholic authorities still press for state subsidies for
their schools.   They educate, as we have seen, almost a
fourth of the country's school population at their own expense
and share in the costs of another seventy percent.   In their
case, to speak of "economic difficulty" is something less than
an understatement.   The wonder is how they have accomplished
what they have during the last ninety years.   One explanation
is the indirect contribution of the endowment of consecrated
lives -- the thousands of dedicated religious men and women
who teach in the schools without asking compensation beyond
mere sustenance.   There is also in the management of the
schools "a special respect for the use of things and a conscious
avoidance of wastage and of pure superfluity," which is com-
patible with the fullest use of the most modern equipment and
techniques available. [29]   More directly, funds have to be
raised in a variety of ways -- weekly contributions of parents,
Sunday collections, rounds of concerts, bazaars, and so forth. [30]

The schools, however, have now reached a point of crisis caused by rapidly increased enrollment.   Between 1946 and

1956 the increase in Catholic schools was sixty-four percent
and an estimated increase of over 108 percent was expected
by 1965.[31]   More lay teachers have been employed, who
must be given salaries corresponding to those of teachers in
the state schools; new buildings and new equipment are ur-
gently needed.   All in all there is evidence that the cost factor is ceasing to be tolerable.

The maintenance of current and predicted commitments
of the non-governmental schools at both primary and secondary levels is generally recognized in Australia to be of national
concern.   A writer recently stated:

> One of the most important realities in Australian
> education is our dependence on our entire educa-
> tional system -- on both Government and all non-
> Government schools. All are deeply involved in
> the resources we must bring to bear on a very
> human task which has become one of urgency and
> magnitude -- that of giving all Australian children
> an education of the quality they both need and de-
> serve. (Emphasis the writer's.) [32]

Besides looking to the non-government schools to supply
places for the increasing enrollment, the government leaders
are well aware of the vital contribution which the church
schools make to the moral well-being of the nation.

Australia has some of the difficulties in the way of a
solution which we have in America.   There are those with
secularist mentalities who see no need for religiously-oriented schools and are ready to oppose any movement toward
financial assistance for them.   Small groups of sectarians
join in the opposition.   The New South Wales Council of
Churches has issued a pamphlet whose expressed aim is "to
defend and maintain the public school system and to oppose
aid for private schools."   There is, however, no organized
group like the POAU in the United States.

Indeed, on the other hand, many voices in Australia are
raised in defense and praise of the denominational schools.
In one place, an Anglican vicar openly supports state aid for

church-related schools, holding that a dual system of education
is necessary "in a healthy democracy." [33]   In another incident,
a Presbyterian General Assembly defeats a motion asking it to
reaffirm its opposition to state aid to denominational schools.
It voted instead to set up a committee to collect information on
the question.[34]   A national Public Opinion Poll in 1955 may be
an indication of the trend of general thinking on the issue.
The poll showed that fifty-one percent of the people questioned
were in favor of state aid to the church schools and that forty-
one percent were opposed.[35]

But assistance is desperately urgent. In July, 1962,
Catholic parents in the Goulburn municipality used a dramatic
method of bringing the extreme needs of their schools before
the public. They decided to close them for six weeks and
send their children to the public schools. Goulburn's eight
Catholic schools have a combined enrollment of 2,200. A
Church spokesman emphasized that the decision came entirely
from the parents and had not been imposed upon them. The
strike expressed the parents' bitter disappointment "at the
failure of the state government, present and past, to recognize
the justice of the claim of Catholics to a share of the public
purse for its education system." The closing of the schools
was also intended to demonstrate to the nation the scope of the
Catholic-maintained education and the fact that the Catholic
schools were integrally associated with the effective state
pattern of education.

On the day assigned for the opening of the strike over
two-thousand children arrived at the already over-crowded
public schools, demanding admission. The demonstration
was effective. Goulburn's public educational system proved
inadequate to absorb the 2,200 Catholic children and after the
first week the parents voted to reopen their schools. Norman
Cardinal Gilroy, Archbishop of Sydney, said in a public address
that Catholic parents must make two points clear to other
Australians: Catholic schools perform the same service as
state schools, teaching the same subjects and teaching them
well. Catholics do not ask others to contribute to the education of Catholic children; they merely want a share in the
school taxes they pay.[36]

Since 1963 a lay organization has carried on the battle for more school aid. Titled, "The Association for Educational Freedom," the group in its aims and methods is similar to our "Citizens for Educational Freedom." Through its efforts and those of others, the status of the non-government schools vis a vis the state seems on the verge of a revolution. In West Australia, a Liberal Premier was re-elected in the spring election, 1965, after promising tuition grants for all high school students. In South Australia about the same time, a Labor Party leader was elected Premier with a promise of free textbooks. The Liberal government in Queensland has dropped the requirement of passing an examination for students receiving tuition grants in private, secondary schools. In New South Wales the Labor, Liberal, and County parties all pledged various forms of state aid to non-government schools and their pupils.

As the situation appears at this writing, further aid for the private schools in Australia seems certain. The only question now is: How much, and for what?

Chapter 6

France: CONFLICT AND COMPROMISE

France presents the image of a nation not yet ready for a final resolution of the church-state relation in education. Movements have been made to ease the situation, but in the opinion of many astute observers these lack a foundation of solid philosophy and involve compromises which tend toward the destruction, rather than the promotion, of true liberty in education. The historic struggle between the State and the Church, between secularism and the Catholic conscience, between anticlericalism and the forces working toward unity and justice are far from ended in France.

France is a nation of contradictions and paradoxes. Intensely nationalistic, stressing patriotism as the paramount aim of her national system of schools, the country remains divided at the very source of unity -- in the things of the spirit. France is not religiously pluralistic in the sense that America or England is. A deeper chasm has cut into her corporate life; she is divided in the very marrow of her soul. Historically, and even now theoretically, a Catholic country, this eldest daughter of the Church has in a considerable portion of her people turned aside from her Christian patrimony. The rejection comprises far greater compass than that which Protestantism represents. The leaders of the Protestant Revolt took with them many of the doctrines of the ancient Church. The French non-Catholic is more likely to be a deist, freethinker, agnostic, or out and out atheist. Since the period of the Enlightenment, numerous Frenchmen -- precisely how large a number is difficult to estimate since many of them still cling to the name Catholic -- rejecting the supernatural, have followed along the thought-patterns of eighteenth century rationalism and its progeny, the numerous "isms" of the nineteenth century -- secularism, positivism, socialism, materialism, communism.

France does not present so much the spectacle of a

divided Christianity as the more pronounced dichotomy of unbelief as opposed to belief, rejection of spiritual authority as
opposed to its acceptance, of neo-paganism as opposed to
Christianity, of hatred as opposed to love. And the forces
that molded or split the French mind also molded or split
education.[1] Not until France is determined to restore her
unity of soul and to put forth consistent efforts on the task will
she be ready to resolve the struggle between those who would
give to the state a monopoly of education and those who seek
true religious liberty, which must necessarily include liberty
for religious education, practically and not merely theoretically. Indeed, not until then can France resume her place in
world affairs as a great nation. History again is the great
elucidator.

A Nation in the Making and Unmaking

The Franks were the first of the pagan tribes to be converted to Catholic Christianity, their leader Clovis having received baptism in the year 496 A.D. Thence the Church began
her work of Christianizing and civilizing -- a task not completed in a day or a year, but over the centuries the work went
steadily on. The blood of martyrs was spilled. Success and
reverses, revivals and relapses marked the progress toward
the making of a great Christian nation. It was France that
largely kept the lights of civilization burning during the so-
called Dark Ages and it was in France that the great blossom-
ing of learning, which characterized the thirteenth century,
bore its most abundant fruits.

Unfortunately, forces of irreligion and disintegration
like rank weeds eventually took root in this favored country
weakening its foundation of Christian tradition and imperiling
its unity of soul. During the eighteenth century, in particular,
these forces gained momentum.

What were these forces and how did it happen that they
succeeded in turning France aside from the fulfillment of the
glorious promise which her Christian patrimony had destined
for her? Actually, a complex intermingling of related but
varied factors was involved. Political absolutism (witness
Louis XIV's: "I am the State"), luxury, moral decay in court

and high ecclesiastical offices were rampant. Power was
abused by both the court and ecclesiastics and the vision to
foresee the inevitable results of their folly was lacking. The
higher society of Versailles, while outwardly professing the
faith, was scandalously un-Christian in its manners and morals.

The unfortunate close link between the court and higher
Church circles brought discredit upon the Church and on religion as a whole. The immediate results were scandal, dis-
content and distrust among the masses, loss of respect for
authority both civil and ecclesiastical. The Church, as well
as the court, laid itself open to furious attack. It has been
said, and there is much to justify the view, that the unbelief
and laicism of France can ultimately be imputed more to the
worldliness of Louis XIV's court than to Voltaire and the
machinations of Freemasonry.

Other destructive factors began operating. Philosophical vagaries of all sorts, repudiating old established traditions
and beliefs, were spawning confusion and error. To a great
extent they had their origin in Descartes' Discours sur la
methode, which, proclaiming the sovereignty of reason, captivated the intelligensia and inaugurated the trend toward
rationalism. The harmony between philosophy and religion
was disturbed. The supernatural was rejected. Everything
was subjected to the bar of reason; what reason could not accept had to be rejected. These attitudes gained strength from
the scandal in high places, but assuming man's natural tendency toward pride and independence, they were capable of spiral-
ing on their own momentum.

In the trail of Descartes' le doute and the welter of non-
Christian philosophies which it spawned, a segment eventually
took more definite form in a movement known as the Enlightenment. It was an irrational movement, though officially en-
throning reason; it was negative and iconoclastic, critical and
individualistic. Primarily, it was a revolt against the established order. Authority was rejected; reason alone was glorified. The truths of Christianity, the moral principles and
worship of the Church became the principal points of attack.

Chief among the leaders of the movement was Voltaire.
A genius of a sort, of indominable vanity and pride, he was

able to express his irreverences, his insults and hatreds in a luminous and scintillating manner which captivated those who had abandoned their faith and attracted others who lacked spiritual stamina. His diatribes and raileries were directed against Christianity in general and the Catholic Church in particular.

Associated with Voltaire was a group of self-styled Illuminati -- Montesquieu, Helvetius, Diderot and others -- equally enamored with the deity they had created, namely, reason. They produced the twenty-seven volume L'Encyclopedia, which, purporting to be a compendium of all knowledge worth knowing, was a veritable summa of rational philosophy.[2] Successors of Descartes, the encyclopedists may be considered the direct ancestors of the modern laïques. The weapons of the Illuminati against authority, Christianity, the Catholic Church, priests, monks -- all that they hated and would destroy -- were sneers, ridicule, satire. Gravest matters were dismissed with a jest; authority was challenged; everything was doubted except their own conceits. Truly, L'Encyclopedia cradled modern laicism.

The destructive influence of the Illuminati was abetted by such writers and satirists as Montaigne, Rabelais, and Rousseau, who were also bent upon discarding the established order and designing new patterns of living for the future. Less radical changes were advocated by the urbane Montaigne. Abuse was heaped upon the school system of France in the sneers and mockery of Robelais' Pantagruel and Gargantua. Rousseau's individualism and naturalism popularized the idea of the citizen free from all authority, from all obligations to society, owing obedience only to his own whims and desires. Here was a doctrine that appealed to those who, chafing under the restraints which moral living demands, only awaited someone to encourage them to give full reign to their passions.

In the meantime and consonant with the rationalistic climate, voices were raised demanding the exclusion of religious instruction from the schools and the establishment of state control over them. Highly influential in that direction was a treatise of La Chalotais, Essai d'Education Nationale, 1763. He advocated an educational system divorced from all religious influence and under the complete control of the state. The

teachers would all be laymen. The state, he held, should
teach a morality based on the natural law. He railed against
the Jesuits and Brothers of the Christian Schools. A year later
the Jesuits were expelled from France.

The Church schools, it is true, had lagged behind the social needs. That was scarcely the fault of the religious orders
or their dedicated teachers. Economic and social changes
called for expanded educational opportunities and a more liberalized curriculum. Teaching personnel and finances were
proving inadequate. A fairminded appraisal of the situation
sees not so much the tragedy of the schools doing so little as
the marvel that they accomplished as much as they did with the
limited means at their disposal. A rational remedy would
have been to aid the schools financially so that they could be
improved. But that was not what the iconoclasts wanted.
Church schools, priests, monks, Christianity, religion were
all anathema and had to be destroyed.

All these forces of destruction in their combined effect
set the stage for the Revolution which finally broke loose. The
subversive ideas, bandied about by the intelligensia throughout
the country, gradually seeped down to the masses. Emotion
took the place of reason and a "reign of terror" was inevitable.

Although reform was sorely needed, the Revolution, irrational in its roots, was incapable of producing necessary
changes. Given its genesis in a vacuum of religious and moral principles and its nurture in an emotionally ignited cauldron
of individualism, negativism, and hatred it immediately degen-
erated into senseless destruction and release of base passions,
the outcome of which was the abolition of religion and the upheaval of civil law. Under the guise of democracy, the Revolution rapidly succeeded to a greater absolutism than the one
it replaced.

Because of the link which had existed between the Church
and the throne, the leaders of the Revolution saw in the Catholic Church an enemy hostile to the ideals of the Republic. The
revolutionary National Assembly abolished Christianity and
belief in God and substituted Liberty, Equality, and Reason as
the only deities of France. All ecclesiastical property was
confiscated and large parts of it sold by the state. Monastic

vows of men and women were no longer recognized. All religious orders and congregations were dissolved and upon the clergy a civil constitution was imposed. The ecclesiastical hierarchy was abolished and steps were taken to bring the administration of the Church in France under the control of the State. Primary education was secularized; the study of religion was replaced by a study of the Declaration of the Rights of Man.

A number of plans for the nationalization of education had been proposed, but the chaos of the Revolution made it impossible to carry out any of them. The Catholic teachers had been driven out; there were no others to take their place. Finally the Daunou Law was passed, October, 1795. It did little or nothing to compensate for the destruction wrought on the schools. Primary schools were to be established only in large population centers and the curriculum was restricted to the rudiments. All primary pupils were to pay fees with the exception of the poorest. It was from this revolutionary beginning that the state education system of France eventually developed.

Napoleon came to power in 1799. The political despotism of his regime was carried over into the realm of education. Napoleon saw in religion and the schools a powerful means of unifying the nation shattered by the frenzy of the Revolution, of strengthening his own power and of consolidating his empire. "Altar and throne" were to be united for his own aggrandizement. His gigantic plan for reorganizing the educational system was therefore simply an aspect of his statecraft and did nothing to improve existing facilities for popular education or to promote just relationships between Church and State.

He recalled the Brothers of the Christian Schools in 1801 and entered into a Concordat with Pius VII the same year. According to its terms the Catholic religion was again legally recognized in France and salaries of the clergy were to be paid by the Republic. The government was to have influence in the nomination of bishops, but the investiture of office was reserved to the Pope. It was agreed that a seminary was to be maintained in each diocese. In this section of the Concordat, however, Napoleon added, without the Pope's knowledge, the "Organic Articles" which in effect made the Church subservient to the state. The articles listed regulations concerning diocesan seminaries which contravened the right of the Church to control the training of its clergy.

Reconstruction of the educational system, which the Revolution had left in ruins, was carried out in a spirit of state centralization. By decrees in 1806 and 1808, Napoleon created and organized the University of France, an administrative body established to control education and having no teaching function as such. The decrees stated that "public instruction in the whole Empire is confined exclusively to the University" and "no school, no establishment for instruction, can be formed independent of the Imperial University, and without the authority of its chief." [3]   Although the state was given control over education on all levels, the University embraced primarily the secondary schools and the universities. Former Catholic secondary schools were turned over to the municipalities to be used as lycées.

At the head of the system was a Grand Master, who with a council of twenty-six members was to control the schools, disperse funds, appoint teachers and school executives. For administrative purposes, France with her possessions was divided into subdivisions called academies, each with its rector and educational council. With a large force of inspectors, all appointed by the Grand Master, to supervise and report to the central authority, the whole apparatus formed a huge bureaucracy. Further unification was achieved by the establishment in Paris of a national normal school for the training of teachers, whose students, in the interests of intensive control, were supported by the state.

No particular attention was shown in regard to elementary education. The primary schools were confided to the Brothers of the Christian Schools under state control. The plan called for no financial aid for these schools, however, nor did it make attendance compulsory on the child. The compulsion was upon the communes, numbering about 37,000, each of which was obligated to provide a school building and a teacher.

The decrees required that in all schools loyalty to the

Catholic religion and to the Emperor be inculcated in the students as a basis of instruction. Obviously, the teaching rights of the Church, though restored, were to be exercised only under governmental authorization and geared toward Napoleonic ends. In the religious instruction, the clergy were required to emphasize an entire section on the fourth commandment which listed duties to the Empire. Napoleon himself had added this section to the catechism that was to be used in all the churches in France.[4] The teachers were ordered to instill into the minds of their pupils "Fidelity to the Emperor, to the imperial monarchy, . . . to the Napoleonic dynasty. . ."[5]

That religion was to be used mainly as a means of securing loyalty to himself and his empire, Napoleon made clear also by utterances and deeds. He held and expressed the view that a firmly established political system was impossible unless the schools taught definite, fixed principles and the child learned from infancy whether he ought to be a republican or a monarchist, a Catholic or a free thinker.[6] Thus Napoleon put the political indoctrination of his subjects as the first end of education.

The highly centralized administrative system which Napoleon established became in 1850 the State Department of Education. State lycées and municipal collèges were firmly built by him into its framework. This is the system that has survived to the present day with only minor changes, which have not modified its essential character.

Napoleon's regime came to an end with his defeat at Waterloo in 1815. For the next hundred and fifty years, bringing us to the present situation in France, with every change of government from republic to monarchy, and from monarchy back to republic, with every reversal from victory to defeat, and from defeat to victory, the nation would be exposed to the struggle of those opposing forces which divide the nation at its core. There were to be compromises between the Catholic and anti-Catholic forces in regard to education, "unhappy compromises," as historian Kane points out, "unstable, shot through with distrust from both parties, breaking down from time to time into open conflict. It was, and is, essentially a conflict between education for this world alone

and education which envisaged this world as only an antecham-
ber of eternity, between pagan and Christian education." [7]
Napoleon's approach to the conflict had achieved no healing.
For that matter, neither have succeeding attempts.

The monarchy was restored (1815-48) and with it came
a policy of social and educational conservatism, counter to the
secularizing tendencies of the Revolution and more favorable
to the Church and her schools. On the other hand, it is possible the restoration served to keep alive the idea of "union of
altar and throne" and, consequently, planted seeds of further
hostility.

The most significant development in the church-state relationship during this period was the passage of Loi Guizot in
1833 while Louis Philippe held the reins of government. The
law ordered every commune to support lower primary schools,
thus organizing a national system of elementary education.
Tuition was free for those not able to pay fees. The Minister
of Public Instruction granted teachers' certificates, but local
officials, including the Catholic curé, were to supervise each
school. Religious instruction was to be given and the curé
could engage religious teachers. Religious bodies were to be
represented on the local school committees. Guizot, the law's
sponsor and a Protestant, paid tribute to the work of the clergy
in providing education in the past and declared that a successful system of primary education required the constant supervision of the clergy.

The law gave the Church liberty to establish her own
schools with the requirement that the teachers hold legal certificates and that the schools submit to state inspection. The
University monopoly over secondary and higher education,
however, was upheld and strengthened throughout the July
monarchy, or reign of Louis Philippe (1830-1848).

After the fall of the monarchy, the Second Republic came
into power (1848-52). Catholics had recovered control over
their primary schools. Now, under the zealous and energetic
leadership of Bishop Dupanloup together with the layman
Montellembert and others, they put forth a vigorous struggle
for freedom to control their own secondary schools. The
Catholic point of view, which simply reiterated the age-old

principles of primary parental and Church rights in education, was clearly and forcefully presented. As a result of these efforts, the Loi Falloux was passed in 1850. The law granted the Church the right to have her own primary and secondary schools with a minimum of State control. The religious teachers had no longer to submit to state examinations to secure their qualification. "Letters of obedience" from superiors were regarded as sufficient. Subventions were given to the private schools provided the sum did not exceed one-tenth of total expenses. A tremendous increase in both number and enrollment of Catholic schools resulted. From 6,464 schools in 1850 there were 11,391 in 1864.[8]

The law provided, in addition, for the local curé to be the supervisor of moral instruction in the state schools; later, the right to approve textbooks which were used in connection with moral and religious instruction was accorded to the religious authorities. Loi Falloux, however, strengthened the powers of the central authority over education by improved administrative machinery. No diplomas, for example, were recognized except those granted by the State.

Under Napoleon II the power of the University of France became almost absolute, the emperor proving himself an autocrat in both the political and the educational realms. While liberty of education was theoretically maintained, the exercise of liberty was hindered by government regulations concerning the opening and directing of private schools.

The Republic was restored after the defeat of France in the Franco-Prussian War. During the period covered by the Third Republic, 1870-1918, the controversy regarding the schools -- essentially a conflict between the Catholic Church and the state, between neo-paganism and Christianity -- blazed anew and with unwonted acuity. Gambetta's party, bitterly anti-clerical, came into power with the elections of 1877. This leader had manifested his attitude earlier, having declared openly in 1871: "Clericalism -- that is our enemy." His government, violently hostile to religious schools and the interests of the Catholic Church, was determined to uproot the influence of Catholicism in the country and to consolidate the Republic by secularizing French institutions, particularly the schools.

The objectives and the overtones of emotional feeling which actuated the group in power were plainly exposed by M. Michelet and M. Quitet. The latter in a preface which he wrote to an edition of the works of Marnix of St. Aldegonde, Protestant author of the sixteenth century, identified his own feelings of antagonism toward the Catholic Church with those of Marnix, and declared: "For my part, I claim the honor of not having desisted for a single day during thirty years to show the incompatibility of Catholicism with modern civilization. Catholicism must fall." [9] This aim, which M. Quitet boasted of, is indeed identical with that which underlies the activities of the ardent laïcists from Gambetta in 1870 to Herriot in 1914, and from Herriot to the anti-clericals of the 1960's.

Undoubtedly many of the bishops and priests favored the monarchy. This political affiliation was natural since the pretenders affirmed their loyalty to the Church and when in power had been fairer to church interests, whereas the republican leaders were in general anti-clerical, if not anti-religious. The bishops were not opposed to the Republic as such. Cardinal Guibert wrote: "I should not insist on political considerations. I am a pastor of souls. . . The republican government, considered in itself, would not meet my hostile prejudices, if it were administered with wisdom and justice." [10]

The anti-clerical movement, a legacy of the Enlightenment, was soon fortified by the infusion of other forces, themselves nineteenth century progeny of the preceding century's rationalism. Among them was the viewpoint labeled positivism which acclaimed science -- natural science -- with its empirical methods to be the only source of knowledge. The Christian religion, the foundations of which were faith and authority, could not measure up to the new criterior of truth and must, therefore, be relegated to the realm of prejudice, superstition, and mythology. The positivists would root out from the minds of men every notion of the supernatural, every idea of God, ignoring the facts of history which testify that Christianity had cradled the arts, science, morality, the law. Indeed, French civilization and culture themselves had been its products. Championed by such leaders as Renan, Comte, and

Taine, positivism captured the thinking of the intelligensia.

Allied also to the enemies of the Church and giving them organization, power and wealth was the ever growing force of Freemasonry -- anti-clerical, anti-Christian, anti-Catholic, bent on the destruction of the Catholic school system as a first means of destroying the Church itself. These were the elements underlying the laïc legislation by which the Third Republic succeeded in secularizing the institutions of France during the next few decades and attempted to make the Church of France a subservient instrument of the Republican government.

The movement had energetic and determined leaders: Buison, Pecault, Steeg, above all, Jules Ferry, who as Minister of Instruction masterminded the policy to liquidate Catholic influence in France. Under his sponsorship there were enacted between 1879 and 1886 a series of measures known as "laïc laws," which favored the public school system and undermined the influence of Catholic institutions. The dominating ideal of Ferry was that education, especially in a democracy, is a function of the state. He did not go as far as to prohibit private schools but insisted that they be entirely under state control and that any delegated power allowed them must be revocable at the will of the state."

Naturally, views and aims of the republican leaders such as these were completely at variance with Catholic ideals of education. Loyal Catholics still comprised the majority of the French population. Why then were they unable to fend off the unfavorable legislation? There was resistance but it seems to have been less determined, less forceful, and consequently less effective than it should have been. On the other hand, the proponents of laïcism were in control of a powerful, highly centralized government. Urged on by strong emotions of fear, distrust, and hate, they were more energetic, more united in their efforts than the Catholics. With slogans, subterfuges, appeals to national sentiments, they succeeded in deceiving many who were too apathetic to search for the facts or too morally weak to stand on their convictions. It was an instance, as Scripture forewarns the faithful, of the children of this world being wiser in their generation than the children of light.

A law of 1881 made primary state schools free and attendance compulsory from ages six to thirteen. The private
schools were not prohibited but were denied public aid; competition with free public schools made their continuance uncertain. A law in 1882 prohibited the teaching of religion in public
schools. Instead, instruction was to be given in civics and
morals.[12]   Finally, in the same year, a measure was enacted
which insisted on complete lay personnel in public schools and
abolished "letters of obedience" by which members of religious
congregations had been permitted to teach in the state schools.
To prepare lay teachers to replace religious personnel, every
department was required to have at least two normal schools,
one for men, one for women.

Henceforth there was to be in France a dual system of
primary education: l'école libre, staffed generally by religious and providing religious instruction in the Catholic faith
and principles; and l'école laïque -- the public school, free
from tuition fees and secularized.

Other anti-clerical measures accompanied the "reform"
of primary education. A decree issued in May, 1880, ordered
the Jesuit order to be dissolved within three months. Religious congregations of men and women which had not been formally authorized by the state were obligated to seek approval
within three months. The state was free to reject such applications. These measures resulted in the closing of 261 religious houses and the expulsion of 5,643 male religious.[13]   A
law in 1884 deprived freedom of association to religious groups.
Practically all church representatives were eliminated from
the Councils of Education.

In the area of higher education, the right of conferring
degrees was given exclusively to state faculties. Church-related faculties could no longer hold the title of university.

Ferry moved in all these drastic measures with a certain
amount of shrewdness, acting on the principle of expediency,
which he expressed thus: Old customs must be considered,
necessary transition observed, and consciences quick to take
alarm treated gently.[14]   Once, however, the early resistance
gave way to reluctant acceptance, the real intentions of the
man were openly exposed. The school, he declared, must be

purged of all prejudices. It must be an agency which will
"mold a society without God or king."[15]

At this stage there was little the helpless masses of
French Catholics could do to stem the tide. Their grievance,
however, was laid open by M. le Comte de Mum, in words addressed to M. Ferry:

> You should know. . . that your name is pronounced
> only amid tears. There are thousands of families
> of laborers and petty officials where, because there
> is no école libre within reach, or because, which is
> more frequently the case, the father's salary, the
> support of the family, would be withdrawn if he did
> not patronize the lay school. . . fathers are obliged
> to send their children to the godless school.
> Mothers weep over it and know that you are the
> cause. . .[16]

A period of respite ensued between 1892 and 1900 due, in
part, to the efforts of Cardinal Lavigeries in stressing recon-
ciliation with the Republic and in pointing out the danger of
forming a specifically clerical party. Pope Leo XIII, in an
Encyclical letter to French Catholics, urged them to take part
in the political life of the state and to accept the Constitution
in order to obtain suppression of the laws contrary to the interests of the Church. Accordingly, Catholics made an effort
to cooperate with the government in the hope that the laïc
legislation might be repealed peacefully. Active anti-clericalism ceased temporarily; the government tolerated unauthorized
congregations and the religious orders continued to conduct
schools.

The truce was brief. Actually the undercurrent of hostility to the Church had not really abated. The Dreyfus affair,
however, provided an occasion for it to erupt in greater fury
because of its brief containment. Alfred Dreyfus, a Jew, had
been convicted of the crime of selling military secrets to Germany. Some Catholic leaders had been active in securing his
conviction. Later, a monarchist was found to be the real cul-
prit. The incident brought down upon the Church the vengeance

of the radicals. It afforded an opportunity for a new and violent attack upon the religious congregations, leading to more
anti-clerical legislation under the ministries of the rabid
Waldeck-Rousseau and Combes, who declared the Church was
a rival power, hostile to the state. The teaching in the
Catholic schools, they maintained, was inimical to the principles of liberty and equality and must be discontinued.

First, under the Ministry of Waldeck-Rousseau, came
the Law of Association of July 1, 1901, which was directed
against unauthorized congregations. A section of the law
made it legal for associations of lay persons to be established
and function freely without governmental regulation, but religious associations were ordered to seek the permission of the
central authority for their right to exist. Article 13 stated
that in the future "no religious congregation shall be able to
organize without authorization given by law which will determine the condition of its functioning. It shall not be able to
found any new establishments, but in virtue of a decree rendered by Council of State." Of 136 congregations which petitioned for authorization in 1903, not a single one was accorded
its request. In 1905 all requests were rejected en bloc.[17]

By Article 14 all the unauthorized orders were excluded
from teaching in either public or private schools. The Article reads: "No one is to be admitted to direct. . . an establishment of whatever sort it may be, nor to give instruction if
he belongs to an unauthorized religious congregation."[18]

The Combes ministry interpreted the law strictly and
dissolved many of the orders. The Council of State decided
finally that of all the religious orders and congregations existing at the time in France only four were to be granted authorization. All the colleges and schools of the unauthorized congregations were either closed or turned over to lay teaching
personnel. Not a single member of the order might remain
in the establishment. Should a Jesuit, for example, be discovered on the teaching staff of any lycée or collège he would
become the victim of all the severities of the law.

That the anti-clerical movement was not only anti-Catholic in its feeling, but anti-religious, is seen in a proposal
made the following year by the Legue d'Enseignement, an

extreme laïcest educational group, that the name of God be
barred in every school book. [19]

The antagonism toward the Church finally culminated in a
July 4, 1904, law which forbade any member of any religious
association, authorized or non-authorized, to teach in any
school, public or private, and required the complete suppression of all religious congregations by the year 1914. Article
2 of the law declared:

At the beginning of the promulgation of this law, the
congregations can no longer recruit new members,
and their novices will be dissolved of full rights with
the exception of those who are destined to form the
personnel of foreign French schools in colonies and
countries of protectorates. The number of novitiates
and number of novices will be limited to the needs of
the establishment. [20]

The decree brought about the closing of 14,404 out of 16,904
Catholic schools. Thousands of religious houses were dissolved and unnumbered religious, men and women, went into
exile.

The following year, separation of Church and state was
made absolute and complete. A law in 1905 annulled the Concordat of 1801, which had formed the basis of the relationship
between the Church and the State for over a century. Public
funds henceforth could not be used for salaries of clergy or be
given to any religious cult or allotted to church-related schools.

The death knell of Catholic education in France had been
officially sounded. The policy inaugurated by M. Waldeck-
Rousseau was brutally executed by M. Combes. Unlike Ferry
and Waldeck-Rousseau, who feared moving too rapidly and
used dissimulation and camouflage, M. Combes and his colleagues in the government, M. Briant, the Grand Master of the
University, M. Viviani and others, openly carried on in Parliament the work of de-Christianization planned by Masonry. The
struggle between Freemasonry and the Catholic Church was,
in their view, a social necessity and a struggle to the death.
M. Viviani declared that modern science had "extinguished the

lights of heaven."

But faith and love in the long pull are stronger than unbelief and hate. The divine mandate of Christ to His Church,
"Teach all nations," was still an imperative. The anti-
clerical legislation had not considered, nor could it destroy,
the ardent zeal, the spirit of self-sacrifice and determination
which animated the persecuted religious and the fervent Catholic laity. On the contrary, these qualities were fired anew by
the anti-religious challenge. Catholic education was reorgan-
ized by the establishment of schools in which were employed
laymen and laywomen or members of the dissolved congregations, who in lay garb continued as best they could under the
circumstances to fulfill the obligation of their religious vows.
Remarkable was the zeal with which the lay Catholics accepted
their role as teachers in the Catholic schools, adapting themselves to the new situation and making the most of it. The
work of teaching now became a new vocation for the laity.

The public powers harassed the schools by restrictions
and planned difficulties. Permission had to be obtained from
state authorities to open new private schools and on the slightest pretext the same authorities might close them. Only the
state could grant the degree which permitted the teacher to
hold a position in a secondary school; textbooks, even catechisms, were censored.

In 1901 the French hierarchy published a pastoral letter
treating of the rights and duties of Christian parents in regard
to the education of their children. The bishops, warning parents of the dangers of the laïque schools, exhorted: "Fathers
and Mothers, you have in the first place the right and duty of
selecting for your children a school where they can be educated
as your faith demands."[21]

The answer of the public officials to what they considered
arrogance on the part of the hierarchy was an increased effort
to strengthen les écoles laïques and greater restrictions on
les écoles libres. Among others, a bill introduced into Parliament was directed against all who disturbed the functioning of
a state school either by entering its precincts or by threats,
and by abuse of authority would induce parents to withdraw
their children or prevent them from participating in the regu-

larly prescribed exercises. Another bill aimed at complete control of the école libre, the illogical argument being that if there was to be liberty of instruction in France, it was certainly not proper to permit instruction other than that of the state to continue without its being duly controlled. [22]

How the Catholic schools survived is a matter of wonderment to anyone acquainted even partially with the harassment and injustices heaped upon them during those trying years. The financial sacrifices of Catholics involved far more than the ones arising from supporting a dual system. Lay teachers sacrificed higher salaries obtainable in other positions. Students sacrificed opportunities for positions in civil service or advancements in the military service, since education in Catholic schools was a barrier to such appointments.

Despite the opposition and restrictions, the Catholic schools not only survived but grew at a rate proportionately higher than did the state-supported schools. During the school year 1910-11 there were in France 14,428 Catholic schools with 960,712 pupils. These figures represent an increase of 130 schools and 26,933 pupils over the preceding school year or nine per 1,000 schools and twenty-eight per 1,000 pupils, whereas the increase in public schools and enrollments for the same period was three per 1,000 schools and seventeen per 1,000 pupils. [23]

The two aspects of the situation -- injustice on one side and courage on the other -- were brought before the legislature by M. de Remel in these words:

> Notwithstanding these summary executions, notwithstanding indirection of speech, notwithstanding the lion's share which you give to the public school; although you defray all its expenses with the money of the taxpayers; although you erect numerous and imposing structures; although you afford ever increasing advantages to the teachers; although you attract the children into the neutral school by a share in the school fund, by free school supplies and by still other inducements; although all these administrative favors are reserved to such as send their children

to the public school; notwithstanding these inequalities, notwithstanding the ostracism with which you
have stigmatized the religious school; when you had
believed that the death blow was given private instruction, it still survived. So widespread in this
country, so lively in the human heart is the love of
liberties, and so noble is the ardor to defend them.[24]

The challenge which persecution and sacrifice presented was
unifying and purifying the Church in France.

On the other hand, secularism breeds secularism. Millions of French children who could not go to Catholic schools
were not merely exposed daily to the religious void of the
public schools, but were more frequently victims of vicious
anti-religious propaganda. It is not surprising under the
circumstances that there was widespread weakening of faith
among them.

In general, to the extent that her children were being
weaned away from the practice of the faith, to that extent
France was losing the stamina and moral strength desired in
her citizens. The dissensions which had torn and divided
French life for more than a century were dividing and destroying the strength and unity of purpose of the nation as a whole,
leaving her unprepared and at the mercy of German militarists
at the outbreak of World War I.

For the moment, the common danger again linked the
people together; a coalition government was formed and the
anti-clerical program was held in abeyance. On August 2,
1914, a ministerial message of M. Malvy suspended the laws
of 1901 and 1904. Exiled members of religious congregations,
both priests and Brothers, were recalled from foreign lands
and missionary countries to aid in the military defense of
France. True patriots as they proved themselves to be, the
religious returned to their native land, their faith and their
love of God ennobling, not diminishing, their love of country.
There they willingly gave their services, and if necessary
their lives, in the cause of freedom, displaying a heroic courage and unselfish devotion which their erstwhile enemies were
forced to acknowledge and admire. It is a matter of record

that the Catholics of France, as a whole, were second to none
in their war effort, whether on the battle field or on the home
front.

This demonstrated an unfeigned love of country and devotion to the Republic, this willingness to fight side by side with
those who shortly before had ridiculed them as enemies of the
Republic, mitigated for the time being the religious animosity
of the anti-clericals.

With the advent of peace in 1919, the government showed
a more lenient, even conciliatory, attitude toward the Church,
although undoubtedly emotionalism and pragmatic motives
played a significant part in the trend. Tribute was officially
paid to the courage of the teacher-priests and Brothers and acknowledgment made of their notable contribution toward victory.
Anti-clericals took part in Catholic ceremonies, funds were
provided to rebuild ruined churches and to aid impoverished
priests. In 1920 diplomatic relations with the Vatican were
resumed. Temporarily a more tolerant attitude toward religious schools was maintained, many of the returned exiles
having remained in France and resumed teaching duties. Les
écoles libres multiplied.

Though anti-clerical laws were suspended, they still remained on the statute books; the teaching priests, Brothers,
and Sisters never knew as the ministry changed hands whether
their existence and their works of charity would be tolerated
or not. There were, of course, pragmatic reasons for allowing recognition for foreign missionaries, namely, to bolster
French prestige and influence abroad; but, it may be noted,
the decrees which granted authorization to mission congregations did not give these Orders the permission to reopen former schools within France.

As a matter of fact, men of insight realized that the toleration was of an ephemeral sort, a sentimentalism in keeping
with the post-war emotionalism. The deep chasm in the heart
of France had not in reality been closed, and while France remained incapable of healing internal dissensions, the victory
of 1918, which actually could not have been achieved without
allied help, remained a hollow one. Internal unity and the
spiritual verve of the nation lagged. The hostility toward the

Church and toward religion was merely being held in abeyance.
The spread of les écoles libres was being viewed with alarm
by their former opponents.

The radicals were returned to power in the election of
1924 under the leadership of M. Herriot, socialist and freethinker. A leftist Cabinet was formed, and there ensued a
period of active anti-clericalism, strongly influenced by Free
Masonry. Instead of directing its energies to needed economic
and social reforms and toward improvement of the country's
international relations, the new government used its power to
oppose those developments which ran counter to its own anti-
clerical program. Chief points of attack were the return and
activity of the religious congregations and the resumption of
relations with the Vatican.

So the old religious strife flared again with renewed bitterness. A center of the trouble was the situation in Alsace-
Lorraine, which had been restored to France after the war.
Over three-fourths of the people of these provinces were
Catholic. They had settled the church-state relationship in
education in the manner prevailing in southern Germany with
confessional schools. Herriot decided to change this and establish a system of secularized public schools. Both Catholics
and Protestants united in protest against the infringement of
their religious liberty. Herriot was obliged to abandon some
of his proposed measures and his government fell the following
year.

The succeeding ministry of M. Poincare restored relations with the Vatican and somewhat restrained the anti-clerical trend. There continued to be, however, a strong undercurrent of opposition to religion, especially in the area of
education; and a determined minority fought furiously for complete control of all schools by the state.[25]   M. Blum gave expression to that attitude in the words: "We conceive that in
the affairs of instruction the State has not only the capacity,
but the exclusive right to instruct."[26]

Influential in furthering and consolidating the anti-religious educational sentiments and policy were many public
school teachers. These teachers had been trained in the
completely secularized -- often irreligious -- Écoles Normales,

and in the large universities of the provinces, and had become
imbued with secularistic, socialistic, and even atheistic attitudes.   They had organized themselves into the National Syndicate of Teachers of Public Primary Schools.   The association
was recognized in 1920 as a trade union and became affiliated
in 1925 with a socialist confederation, the Generale des
Travail, a leftist group.   Opposed to private schools, the
teachers' organization aimed at government monopoly of all
primary education.   It is not difficult to appraise the influence
these teachers had on young minds.

By 1930 anti-clericalism, though not arrogant, was in a
state of active survival.   After the election of 1936, the Unified
Socialist Party became the most important parliamentary group
in the Chamber of Deputies.   Many members of the Party belonged also to the Nationalist Syndicate of Teachers of Public
Primary Schools.   The Party had by this time become close to
communism in its aims and had unanimously adopted the concept of laïcité at a Nantes Socialist Congress, May 29, 1939.
The aims of the group included the extension of lay laws to the
whole of French territory including Alsace-Lorraine; stricter
control of les écoles libres and prohibition of catechism teaching in them except on Thursday; exclusive reservation of public
teaching vacancies to candidates coming from state schools;
abrogation of obligatory presence of members of free teaching
on examining boards for certificates of primary studies; prohibition to open a Catholic school in communes of less than
2,000 inhabitants; control of municipal budgets for purpose of
suppressing aid to les écoles libres. [27]

As a means of obtaining its objectives, the Socialist Party
supported the concept of école unique, a plan calling for a free,
unified school or ladder system, with elementary education
basic to all training for all pupils.   All post-elementary
schooling was to be termed secondary education, and a closer
articulation of the lycées and collèges with the elementary
school was demanded.   Over all the system, strong public
control was envisioned.

Such was the educational situation in France when catastrophe struck, August, 1939.   The country was precipitated
into war, and shortly invaded by Nazi armies.   Once again,

the Catholic people of France, the overwhelming majority of
the population, came forward to give all they had in the cause
of freedom for their country. During the war, the Church offered its institutions to children who in consequence of the
destruction wrought by bombs would have been without homes
or schools. Priests, Brothers, and Sisters gave their services unstintingly wherever there was need.

But the half century of religious strife and neutral education had taken its toll. Moral stamina had been weakened;
the nation was not prepared, spiritually or materially, to offer
adequate resistance and collapse came soon.

A government was set up in Vichy by the occupation
forces under Marshal Pétain, a devout Catholic and ardent pa-
troit. Someone had to take the reins; credit, rather than
blame, is due Pétain; he was no Quisling. In a spirit of justice
and in the interest of peace among Frenchmen, the Vichy
government repealed the anti-clerical legislation of 1901-1904
in regard to religion and religious schools.[28] Subventions up
to three-fourths of costs were provided for private primary
schools where needed and scholarships were granted to pupils.
Members of religious congregations were authorized to teach.
The return of ecclesiastical property to diocesan associations
was effected in February, 1941. In conformity with the
Church's desire for liberalization of the spirit of public education, the government declared pupils should receive one hour
weekly instruction in their "duties to their neighbor, their
country and Almighty God." The schools were ordered to
stress in the teaching of history the entirety of the French effort under all regimes. The concept of école unique was dis-
credited as a scheme for state monopoly of education leading
to social conflict and eventually national destruction.

Although the Church actually fared better during the occupation under the Pétain regime, the hierarchy, clergy, and
Catholics as a whole were among the most active in the underground movement for the attainment of freedom for their
country. Their courage and devotion gave lie to any accusa-
tion that they were opposed to the Republic as such. That they
opposed and would continue to oppose unjust or anti-religious
policies of any government was to be taken for granted.

Victory came again with the aid of allied armies; and again, as far as the internal affairs of France were concerned, victory had a hollow ring. Old dissensions, old weaknesses, instability reappeared in the Fourth Republic, which was set up after 1945. There was incapacity to face the reality of the situation with frankness and humility. A scapegoat was needed for the nation's wounded pride. The resentment felt toward the occupying Nazis fastened itself on Pétain's Vichy regime, and Pétain and his activities became the victim to assuage the nation's feelings of chagrin and humiliation. The procedure lacked maturity and honesty. Pétain had not been responsible for the collapse of France; the country's inner spiritual weakness was the cause.

Instability, lack of unity, inability to resolve pressing issues, characterized the government during the ensuing years. Between 1945 and 1958 there were twenty-five successive governments; of these, only two lasted more than a year.[29] The ministries lacked strength and vision to act decisively and to follow a consistent policy. The instability gradually undermined the prestige of the nation and was responsible for Parliament's lack of popularity, cut off as it was from the people. Disasters followed. France lost Indo-China, giving the communists their opportunity to infiltrate and subvert. The Algerian situation reached a point of crisis where the nation was faced with complete chaos -- or a definite change. The better side of France came temporarily to the rescue. General De Gaulle, intensely patriotic, unyielding, determined, was placed in power.

So much for the political situation. How did the Church and her schools fare in the post-war years? The Fourth Republic in its violent reaction against the occupation and Pétain looked with high disfavor on all the activities of the Vichy regime. Moreover, the perennial opponents of the religious schools had been regarding with alarm and indignation the restoration of the religious congregations, the growth of the Catholic schools, and the corresponding trend away from les écoles laïque. Catholic primary schools in 1945 were providing primary education for more than twenty-five percent of the French children, and the Catholic secondary schools for more

young people than did the state schools. In some areas of
western and southwestern France, state schools were practically non-existent.

For a short period after the liberation of France, Vichy
subsidies for private schools were continued. The issue was
soft-pedaled for a time by the Fourth Republic, the only step
taken being the abrogation of the Vichy laws which had provided
for state payment of salaries of priests attached to secondary
schools and allowed religious teaching on the school premises of state primary schools. In 1946 the French Consultative Assembly refused to extend to the end of the year subsidies
to les écoles libres, but the government over-rode the vote.
A commission was set up to inquire into the private school
situation.

The issue was fought over during the following years,
liberals, anti-clericals, and communists opposing the Catholic
demands for justice to their schools. Finally, all the school
laws passed under the Vichy government were abrogated. The
anti-association legislation was returned to the statute books
and mere toleration for religious congregations prevailed.
The Radical Socialists and communists continued to press for
a single, entirely secular school system and the banning of all
private schools. The French nation, however, was, and has
remained, unwilling to accept a completely totalitarian system.

Actually a double crisis in education faced the nation in
the decade following the war. The French birthrate had risen
rapidly after 1945. The existing public schools were unprepared to cope with the new influx of children, especially since
many buildings had been ruined or scarred by bombing. The
undamaged buildings had not been kept in repair; teachers'
salaries were low. At the same time Catholic schools were
even harder pressed for new buildings, new equipment, and
better pay for teachers. With the loss of subsidies, the question of whether many of the Catholic schools could continue
was seriously discussed. Thus the public schools faced the
possibility of having to receive hundreds of thousands of children into their already over-crowded facilities.

The situation in the Catholic schools was indeed becoming
acute. Catholic parents were attempting to support their sys-

tem entirely from their own resources, while paying at the
same time taxes for the state system. The burden, in view
of the post-war inflation, was unbearable. The cost to Catholic parents over and above their taxes, according to La France
Catholique, was over ten billion francs in 1947 and over fourteen billion francs in 1948.[30]   Some former sources of income
had been lost. The rich, rural Catholic farmers, who were
the traditional benefactors of the schools, had lost great
amounts of money during the war and had been unable to re-
coup their fortunes. The unchecked inflation spiral and the
inequalities of the tax laws prevented the French workers and
lower middle class families from sending their children to
tuition schools. To continue at all, there had to be a squeeze
somewhere.

Unfortunately, but perhaps necessarily, the squeeze was
felt most by the lay teachers, whose salaries fell considerably
below par, amounting in many cases to only half the salary
awarded to teachers in the public school system. It was inevitable that the quality of teaching in Catholic schools should
suffer. Catholic officials regretted the situation and would
gladly have paid higher salaries had they been able to do so.
On the other hand, it should be remembered that many of the
lay teachers regarded their work as an apostolate and were
willing to continue at a sacrifice for the sake of helping to
preserve Christian education and to shelter Catholic children
from the chilling atmosphere of the secularized schools.

Both the French government and the French hierarchy
began to view the educational situation with alarm. However,
because of the violent anti-clerical attitude of the French socialists, communists, free-thinkers and Masons who controlled
the Chamber of Deputies little relief could be hoped for from
the government. Earlier in 1940 Catholics who were vitally
concerned about the education issue -- parents, teachers,
Catholic actionists -- had organized under the title "The
Secretariat of Studies for the Freedom of Teaching." Now,
proud of their services to the national cause, united, determined, and articulate, they began to insist upon their basic
rights and presented arguments for their position.

The educational crisis provided a timely setting. The

Catholic group explained again that they found it difficult, especially so in the post-war inflation, to pay for their own
schools and also the state school tax. They presented figures
on the number of children under their care. They called attention to some parts of France, wholly Catholic, where there
were no public schools at all.[31]   Thus, they argued, the
Catholic school system was rendering a significant contribution
to the country and if this service were to deteriorate because
of lack of funds to secure the services of adequately qualified
teachers, then the nation itself would suffer in the loss of intellectual potential.

Their most effective argument was borrowed from the
communists' book, namely, a right is not a right when its
exercise is frustrated. They pointed to the French Constitution which gives families the right to send their children to
schools of their own choice. Yet the financial difficulties involved in exercising this choice and the consequent possibility
of their children receiving only an inferior education, actually
frustrated the right. The Constitution was in practice contravened and justice violated.

In April, 1951, the hierarchy at an extraordinary session
in Paris elaborated on the acute financial distress threatening
the very existence of the Catholic school system. They declared that the government was overriding the rights of Catholics by establishing what was in fact a monopoly of education
by the state. The moral unity of the nation was to be achieved
through mutual respect for conscience, not through totalitarian
unification.

The Minister of Education had appointed in 1950 a commission to bring in another report on the position of the private
schools. The report verified the facts and supported the arguments of the Catholic groups. The conclusions drawn were
that the public schools were scarcely able to take care of the
children now in them; that the private primary schools had enrollments of over 1,300,000 children and half of all the children in secondary schools. It was a material impossibility for
the public school system to receive all the new pupils and the
other system was poverty stricken, teachers' salaries being
greatly below par.[32]

The question of aid was brought up in the Assembly by
M. Teitgen (M.R.P.), March, 1951. He asked that consideration be given to the possibility of a government subsidy for
private schools which would guarantee minimum professional
salaries for the lay teachers in them. He stated that these
teachers had a right to the same consideration as public school
teachers, yet the private schools were unable to pay even the
minimum. He reminded the Assembly that the state could not
take in the million plus children provided for in private
schools.[33]

The election of June, 1951, centered on the school problem. Cardinal Feltin reminded Catholics and legislators that
they should be prepared and determined to defend "the fundamental liberties which permit man to obey the prescriptions
of God, in particular, the effective liberty for parents to give
to their children an instruction and education conforming to
the exigencies of their Christian conscience."[34]   After the
elections, the Catholic Secretariat could count on more than
three hundred deputies pledged to aid Catholic schools.

Discussions and debates ensued reflecting the widely
varied views of the numerous political parties and organizations which flourish in France. Communists and socialists
were, of course, violently opposed to any aid, standing firmly
for a totalitarian system of education. The position of other
parties was vague; the M.R.P. was in favor. In any case,
the peculiarly involved French political system allowed the
violent anti-clerical minority to out-maneuver any attempt to
frame a bill granting massive direct subsidies to Catholic
schools.

On August 23, 1951, the Minister of Education presented
a compromise plan to help the private schools. Debate in the
Assembly on the question was initiated by M. Barangé with a
conciliatory statement:

> The school question has led to bitter discussion but
> it was brought up only to prevent the closing of pri-
> vate schools due to lack of funds, and to permit the
> rapid improvement of our public school equipment
> to be ready for the ever increasing numbers of

school children.

He proceeded to explain the plan.

The bill proposed that public funds, 1,000 francs, be distributed on a per capita basis each trimester to all students
between the ages of six to fourteen years attending primary
schools, either public or private. In the case of public schools
the funds would be allotted to the departmental councils for the
upkeep of school buildings and improvement of equipment. In
the case of private schools, the funds would be allotted to
Parents' Associations to increase teachers' salaries.

As debate on the measure progressed, M. Plevin urged
both sides to remember how important "it is that no impru-
dence or violence of language run the risk of inflaming passions
that might tear France asunder." The result of the debate
was a compromise, which like the original bill respected the
"separation principle" by avoiding direct aid by the state to
Catholic schools.

The provisions of the compromise were embodied in two
measures. Loi Marie, passed September 21, 1951, by 378
votes against 236, put into the hands of the Minister of Secondary Education a certain sum to be used for scholarships for
deserving students tenable in either state or private secondary
schools if the schools met national standards of buildings,
teachers, hours of instruction, and standard achievement.
Private schools accepting scholarship students were subject to
inspection by the state.[35]   The scholarships, about 1,000
francs per capita, were not to be given to the schools as such,
but to the pupils. Parents in the lower income brackets who
sent their children to private schools were thus enabled to pay
part of the tuition costs and the schools benefitted indirectly.

The second measure, Loi Barangé, which was passed
September 28, 1951, embodied the Minister's original proposition. Its purpose was thus defined: To obtain the immediate
improvement of the material conditions in which public education functions, and to provide a temporary and modest assistance to families and children frequenting private institutions.[36]
The Act provided funds -- 1,000 francs (about $2.00) per child
for each trimester -- to be distributed to all students between

ages six to fourteen attending elementary grades in either
public or private schools. As in the original bill, the funds
for public schools were allotted to the departmental councils
to be spent for improvements. For private schools, the subsidies were given to the Parents' Association of the school and
were to be spent, in order of priority, to increase teachers'
salaries, for construction, for upkeep of building, and for the
purchase of school supplies.[37]   Thus France, after a long
struggle, took a step toward aiding her private schools, practically all of which are church-related.

It could not be expected that the private schools would be
perfectly satisfied. The subsidies helped, of course, but they
were far from sufficient to remedy the financial problem. At
best the Act was palliative. Catholic parents had still to pay
public school taxes, which had increased. It was pointed out
that the law gave equal sums to both systems although the private schools were in greater need; that public education was
the principal beneficiary since the funds could be used for a
wider range of purposes, specifically, for enrichment of
services, whereas their use was more restricted in the case
of private schools.

Several amendments were made to the Act to remedy its
imperfections. Since teachers in France are paid on a twelve-
month schedule whereas the subsidies were based on a nine-
month schedule, on September 15, 1952, the total of the allotment was raised to 1,300 francs (about $2.50) per child each
trimester. The Simmonnet amendment, passed February 7,
1953, regulated more precisely the use of the funds for public
schools. The Gabelle amendment, April 3, 1955, extended
the benefits of the law to all children attending primary private
and public schools, irrespective of the age, instead of the original limitation to children between six and fourteen.

Further Aid, 1959

Once General de Gaulle had returned to power and been
given the authority he demanded, French prestige under his
leadership improved. A new Constitution was drawn up.
Elections were held and a new Chamber of Deputies and Senate
gave de Gaulle an overwhelming majority. Numerous reforms

leading to a strong and stable government were inaugurated.
Order was established in place of parliamentary chaos.
Splintered minorities could no longer block action by the
majority. French currency was stabilized. The voice of
France again counted in world affairs.

With these pressing reforms effected, attention could now
be given to the vexing educational issue, which de Gaulle was
eager to settle once and for all. His view was simply that
justice and the national need demanded that the non-state
schools, which were performing a public function, should be
aided financially to the end that they would be able to carry on
effectively. His attitude, however, as events turned out, indicated no deep appreciation of the Catholic schools as such or
of the necessity of their preserving an independence sufficient
to maintain their essentially religious character. There was
much of the old Napoleonic concept of the supremacy of states'
rights in education.

As Catholics had foreseen, the subsidies provided by the
1951 legislation had not solved the problem of Catholic school
needs. Yet so eager were Catholic parents to send their children to religiously oriented schools, enrollments continued to
mount during the decade of the 50's far beyond the capacities
of the schools to adequately care for the children. Statistics
of enrollment vary somewhat, but any set of figures indicates
that Catholic schools were still providing for over twenty percent of elementary school children and at least half of the students attending secondary schools.[38]

The biggest problem of the 14,000 Catholic schools was
still the lack of funds to pay adequate salaries to 43,000 lay
instructors who were teaching alongside of 20,000 Sisters and
11,000 priests and Brothers. A report prepared in 1957
showed that a lay teacher in a Catholic elementary school
could begin at a salary of 28,000 francs ($60) per month and
work up to a maximum salary of 40,000 francs ($85) per month
after twenty-three years of service.[39] This situation, according to some observers, was driving the better teachers from
the Catholic school system into the service of the public schools
and resulting in a continuing deterioration of the quality of
teaching in the Catholic schools.

Catholics also pointed to the waste of public school funds and the obvious inequality resulting from a dispersion of efforts, when the need, instead, was to coordinate them in order to meet the requirements of a mounting population wave. In some villages with a strong Catholic majority it often happened that two schools would exist side by side: a public school with a handful of pupils, generously supported, while the Catholic villagers exhausted themselves trying to maintain a large school, which, despite, the financial sacrifices of the parents and the dedication of the religious teachers, could manage to give only a second rate instruction.[40]

The Catholic hierarchy and the Secretariat of Studies for the Freedom of Teaching continued to agitate for public aid as a right due to the parents and as a necessity for the welfare of the nation. The needs and arguments were the same as those prior to the passing of the 1951 legislation. They pointed out that the result of the existing situation was that some of the private schools could offer only an inferior education from the material viewpoint. Children attending them were deprived unjustly of the benefits of adequately maintained schools. Parents were frustrated by a situation in which, because of financial burdens, it was practically impossible to conduct efficient non-public schools. If the state recognized the private schools and expected them to exist it should supply them with the means to exist on an adequate level. The grants under Loi Barangé were merely palliative. At best they could only keep the schools in existence. This argument proved highly effective. It appeared in modified form in the Preamble of the 1959 Law.

In substantiation of the fact that parents were indeed frustrated in making the choice of schools, it was pointed out that although approximately one-third of all the children of France were in private schools, there were only one-fifth in elementary Catholic schools; yet a poll of parents' wishes indicated that forty-seven percent wanted to have their children in Catholic schools and would send them there if they could afford it.[41]   The Secretariat pointed out that in other countries Catholic claims for recognition of their rights was being met with success. They particularly mentioned Belgium, where the major parties had signed a pact to end the country's school controversy and grant greater government aid to Catholic schools.[42]

Deputy Mayor Robert of Nantes, then president of the parents' associations, summed up the Catholics' claim in France by saying:

> What do we want? First of all the ability to pay sal-
> aries to teachers in private schools which will keep
> them from poverty. . . We also want the costs of
> our fathers of families to be less heavy. That is
> why we are demanding state aid. Moreover, we
> are rendering a service to the state. Because of
> the growth of the school population of France, there
> is no longer enough room in public schools. Private
> schools, which take about a quarter of the children,
> give very great aid to the nation. It is only just
> that they be repaid for this aid. . .[43]

Repeatedly the hierarchy emphasized the raison d'etre of Catholic education -- that Christian truth and Christian principles should penetrate all human life; that the Christian child should not only understand the truth in an abstract man- ner but that he experience it by seeing it lived and by living it himself; that religion should not only complete, but should also transform and illuminate by its light all the rest of the pupil's studies and activities.

The final outcome of the struggle, however, was probably due less to brilliant argumentation than to the political situa- tion. Aid to Catholic schools was practically assured by the fact that de Gaulle favored it and the Assembly was over- whelmingly de Gaullist. The new premier, Michael Debré, as soon as it was feasible and with de Gaulle's backing, ap- pointed a commission to study the question of aid to les écoles libres. Representations of both public and private education were given places on the commission and tactfully the social- ist, M. Lapie, who had earlier shown a disposition in favor of aid to Catholic schools, was appointed chairman.

Debré tried to move cautiously and to appease the legion

of laïcists and "anti-ists."   A compromise was again envisioned -- direct aid to les écoles libres would be tied up with
increased state control over the schools.   What these concessions were to which the private schools would have to accede
are discussed below.

While the commission was conducting hearings and preparing its report for Parliament during 1959, it deliberately
let out to the press the principal features of the plan it intended
to propose with the twofold purpose of testing out reactions of
the French people and of preparing them for the final proposals
of the commission.   Neither side seemed pleased with what it
heard.

The final report came out in November.   It represented
a factual picture of the educational situation in France, showing the financial crisis of the Catholic schools and their massive contribution to the total educational effort of the country.
It suggested direct financial subsidies to the private schools,
but linked the aid with the right of the government to specific
degrees of control over those aspects of the schools that received disbursements.   The report also offered a proposed
text for a new school law embodying the findings of the commission.   Extremists among both Catholics and anti-clericals
attacked the report as a "sell-out."

The Catholics on the commission, however, had kept in
contact with the hierarchy, who recognized that with the situation in France being what it was some concessions would have
to be made.   They insisted, nevertheless, that the essential
character of the Catholic schools would have to be preserved.
The commission on its part gave the assurance that control of
the essential features of their schools would remain in the
hands of the Catholic sponsors.   This assurance was expressly manifested in Article I of the proposed bill, which stated in
part: "The state proclaims and respects the freedom of education and guarantees the exercising of this freedom to regularly opened private schools."   Thus the details of the plan,
which yielded limited control by the state over the schools in
return for direct financial aid, were given tentative assurance
of acceptance by Catholic educational authorities, although the
authorities were by no means completely satisfied.

What aid, precisely, was to be given according to the
Lapie report to les écoles libres and how was it made to balance with the control conceded to the state? The plan was
based on the principle: more aid -- more control. Varying
amounts of aid were linked with increasing degrees of control.
The private schools could sign a contract covering all its
courses and all its teachers or just particular courses and the
teachers who taught them would enter into contract with the
government. The teachers covered by contract with the state
would receive from the state treasury a stipend representing
the current basic industrial wage paid in France. The school
was to supplement this salary. Local governments were to
be allowed by law to give to the private schools the same
school aid which they usually granted to public schools. Previously no specific law made this concession possible. Local
help would be in the form of bus transportation, free textbooks,
and subsidized lunches. The money from the state and the
help from the municipalities together represented considerable
financial aid to Catholic schools.

What was the measure of control ceded to the state in exchange for this aid? The concession was summed up in the
fourth paragraph of Article I of the proposed law:

> In those private institutions which have entered into
> one of the contracts provided for below, the educa-
> tion placed under contract is submitted to State
> control. The private institution, while retaining
> its individual character, must give this education
> with total respect for freedom of conscience. All
> children, whatever their origins, opinions or be-
> liefs, have access to it.[44]

Thus Catholic schools accepting subsidies would have to open
their schools to all who applied, regardless of origin or religion. Religious instruction would be optional; that is, parents
could have their children excused from such classes by requesting same in writing. Teachers who received state subsidies would have to submit to examination by state inspectors
and meet licensing requirements. Catholic sponsors of

schools, however, would retain the right to hire or dismiss any member of the teaching staff even if the teacher had entered into contractual relationship with the state. The state educational authorities claimed the right to approve the textbooks used in the courses for which the school received subsidies through contract signed by both parties.

These concessions were attached by many Catholics who feared that in their application the necessary independence of the Catholic school would be sacrificed and eventually the law would bring about the strangulation of the Catholic school system. In fact, the Secretariat split over the issue. The members of the Commission insisted that the concessions were the minimum to avoid injecting the old bitterness and animosity into the efforts to have the bill approved.

Indeed, as it was, considerable acrimony entered into the debate. Inside Parliament, socialists, Freemasons, freethinkers, communists, anti-clericals, some of the latter nominal Catholics, were lined up against the measure. Though their combined membership constituted a minority, the school issue was one peg on which the extreme and center left could hang a common policy. Outside Parliament similar groupings joined with scores of public school teachers, aggressively anti-clerical, who led school children in demonstrations against the proposed measure.

The laïc legions contended that the whole concept of the measure was anti-Republican, anti-Constitutional, an attack on the national school system, and a plot of the clerical party. On the eve of the Assembly's deliberation, the state schools under the auspices of the public school teachers' association observed a "day of refusal." Jules Ferry's famous letter to the instituteurs during the height of the church-state struggle in the last century was introduced into the classrooms where its sentiments were commented on and admired.[45]   The teachers led the children in singing an old anti-clerical song:

> Honor and glory to the secular school
> Where we have learned to think freely
> To defend and cherish the republic.

The real battle, however, took place in the Council of
Ministers, presided over by President de Gaulle. The question
of state control and freedom of conscience were matters of
controversy between Catholics and socialists, ranging around
the wording of Article I. Catholics insisted on a form of
words in the Article that would guarantee the essential independence of the Catholic schools. As finally approved the
controversial article stated, somewhat equivocably, that a
school receiving aid shall "present its instructions in a manner entirely respecting freedom of conscience" while at the
same time "keeping its own identity." Education Minister
André Boulloche promptly resigned, ostensibly on a technical-
ity of procedure.

As the Assembly had a massive majority of deputies all
concerned to see that the case for the Catholic schools would
be settled, there seemed no reason to fear that when the text
of the bill had been hammered out in the Cabinet opposition
would arise in the Chambers sufficient to prevent its passage.
So it proved. Despite only lukewarm enthusiasm by supporters and united opposition by socialists and communists, a
special Assembly passed the bill by 427 votes against 71,
December 31, 1959.

The provisions of the law may be briefly summarized
here. Details of its actual operation are discussed below.
Private schools were given several choices. A school could
be integrated into the state system, all expenses would be paid,
and the school would lose its independence. On the other hand,
a school could retain its status quo; that is, choose not to accept government aid. In between these extremes, it could
enter one of several contracts with the government, receive
varying amounts of aid and submit to corresponding degrees
of control by the state. No group was happy about the "settlement." Those who favored it were less than enthusiastic;
opponents were bitter.

The law gave no precise figures on what the new subsidies would be. It merely established the principle that private
schools could get help. It was estimated, however, that it
would cost the state about twenty billion francs ($41 million)
as against the existing six billion francs ($12.3 million). Only

time would tell how adequately the school issue had been
solved, whether the contracts would be used to aid or merely
to curb the Catholic schools. What seemed important was the
spirit in which the new law would be applied. At this date,
seven years after its passage, it is still too early to make a
categorical judgment on the success or failure of the law, but
a view of its operation is revealing.

The French Educational Policy in Operation

According to the French Constitution "the organization
of free, secular public schools on all levels is the duty of the
State." But, comments an official bulletin,

> . . . the state does not have an educational monop-
> oly. Freedom of thought and freedom of conscience,
> the two great fundamental freedoms governing
> French constitutional law, are necessarily accom-
> panied by freedom of education, which confers upon
> the human being, on the one hand the right to choose
> both the form of education which best suits him and
> the teacher who is to dispense it.

How practical this freedom of education is will be commented
on later. Here we note that two sharply conflicting views on
the place of religion in education have resulted in a dual system of education in France. Private schools may be established and maintained by individuals, professional agencies,
or religious organizations. Actually about 93 percent of all
the private schools in France are sponsored by the Catholic
Church with the express purpose of giving the children an education integrated with religious truths and principles. The
public schools, states the Constitution must be gratuit et laïque
(free and secular).

Our purpose in this section is to examine more precisely
first, what function, if any, the French public school system
assumes in regard to the religious and moral training of the
children attending its schools and what effect the professedly
laïc atmosphere of the schools may have on the religious life
of the pupil. Secondly, we will examine more closely the

present relationships of the private schools to the state under
the twofold aspects of aid and control.

For these purposes, some understanding of the French
administrative policy in education is necessary. France has
one of the most highly centralized systems of education in the
world. On the national level is the Ministry of Education
(formerly the University of France) presided over by a Minister, who holds membership in the Cabinet and is the supreme
head of the whole system. For administrative purposes, the
whole country is divided into sixteen academies, each under
a rector, who is the delegate of the Minister and is appointed
by him. The rector heads the regional university and directs
all the educational services and institutions in the academies.
At the level of the departement or county, of which there are
93, the rector is represented by an inspector, who is responsible for the normal school and for all elementary education
within his departement. Each arrondissement or district
within a departement is headed by an elementary school inspector. Reports of inspectors are sent regularly to the
Ministry. This system of school inspection, says an authority on education in France, "keeps the Ministry informed at
all times on the status of personnel, equipment, and general
progress of every last school in the Republic, public or private, kindergarten through secondary." [46]   The state claims
the right to inspect private schools to assure itself that "there
are no breaches of morals, hygiene, and sanitation, and to ascertain that the Constitution and laws are duly respected."

Everyone connected with the public schools, including
teachers, form part of a body of civil servants and is paid out
of the general budget of the state. The Ministry of Education
uniformly fixes courses, assigns textbooks, regulates teaching methods and disciplinary matters, makes appointments and
arranges promotions. It controls and makes out the examinations for the diplomas and degrees, licenses all the teachers
on the university, secondary, and elementary level, except
for elementary teachers in private schools (and then only if
they have not signed one of the "contracts" allowed by the 1959
Act). The state reserves the privilege of granting all diplomas. Diplomas granted by private schools have no official

value.

With such a high degree of centralization it can be readily understood why private schools hesitate to align themselves by contract with the state. Obviously, to the extent that they do, independence is jeopardized. The danger is intensified, as facts of history show, by the ever present possibility of a definitely anti-clerical, anti-religious government getting into power.

A second pertinent feature of the French system is the movement toward l'école unique, the unified school -- a movement against the two tract system and toward the latter concept. It advocates the abolition of parallelism of the elementary and secondary schools. The bars between the two levels should be removed; all post-elementary education is to be termed secondary. One school for all classes is the aim. Despite the acceptability of many of the objectives of the movement, Catholics in general fear that the establishment of l'école unique tends toward a monopoly in favor of state schools.

By law the French public schools are laïc, not merely neutral. Laïcité is the term used for laïcism in operation. The term has connotations analogous to our secularism, but actually has far wider implications than those generally thought of when one speaks of the secularism of the American public school, where the majority of the teachers are believing Christians, the principles of Christian morality underlie ethical teachings and where, until recently, prayers and Bible reading were common practices. The French laïcist holds that religious instruction is exclusively the responsibility of parents and the church; it has no place whatever in the school. Dogmatic truths are particularly anathema. Religious instruction and prayers are prohibited in the state elementary schools. God becomes an abstraction. He is banished from courses and textbooks. The teachers, for the most part, are imbued with the laïcité viewpoint, almost all having been trained in the rigidly laïcest normal schools of the departements.

In practice, according to the view of many observers, teaching in the French public school is frequently based on a sort of natural religion, having its own cult, prophets, and doctrines. The facts of science supply the doctrines. The

truths of religion are unknowable according to M. Bayer, who
wrote texts for the schools. It was Combes who said teachers
in public schools were instructors of a cult nouveau, human
reason having taken the place of revelation.[47]   Indeed, critics
are not few who hold that the atmosphere of the laïc school in
many instances is definitely irreligious and hostile. We quote
the testimony of one witness who has had ample opportunity to
know the situation. He writes:

> It is known that in the so-called 'lay' schools,
> the teaching is either anti-religious or mutilated or
> dessicated by an entirely negative neutrality which
> completely eliminates the highest spiritual values.
> Occasionally the education is steeped in certain ra-
> tionalism which partially sterilizes the germs of
> faith deposited in the children's souls by baptism
> and by the work of Christian formation undertaken
> outside the school. . . The pupils get, at least
> vaguely, the impression that it is possible to under-
> stand everything without the principles of religion
> -- and to lead a good life without any light or help
> from Heaven. God is absent. The world goes on
> without Him.

The author of these lines finally asks: "What is to be said
when the teachers of the schools are professed atheistic mat-
erialists and. . . organized."[48]
    Do the laïc schools make any effort to teach moral prin-
ciples? Or are there any arrangements for permitting the
students to receive religious and moral instruction outside
the school? The Ministry, according to Moehlman, holds that
the only morality which can safely be taught in the public
schools is one which approximates the French concept of the
honnête homme (the ethical man), a man imbued with the best
that moral, if not theological, philosophy has produced.[49]
At best it is a natural morality, formulated independently of
all religious truths, backed by no supernatural sanctions, supported only by the facts of natural consequences and social
approval. The principles may change to suit changing cir-

cumstances. At worst it is the morality of such men as M. Bayet, who wrote: "Good actions are useful actions, that is, such as make us and all men truly happy. Bad actions are harmful actions, that is, such as render us and all men miserable;"[50] and of M. Durkheim, who states: "It must not be said that an act wounds conscience because it is criminal; but that it is criminal because it offends conscience. We do not condemn it because it is a crime, but it is a crime because we condemn it."[51] Human conscience receives from itself the laws of its own activity and science suffices for its observance.

All of this runs counter to the Christian traditions of the French nation, of the facts of history, of common sense. Yet this is the morality of the laïc school. It is taught with deliberation in civics classes and incidentally in any course the student may be taking.

On the positive side, public schools are closed on Thursdays (school on Saturday, though) to give the children an opportunity to receive religious instruction outside the school, usually in the churches. Do the children attend? And how effective are the results? Exact statistics do not seem to be available on attendance but various reports indicate that a fairly large proportion of the children are at the classes, especially in the large cities. Regarding effectiveness, again no exact information is available; most likely, such information is unattainable. The views and opinions of those who have had experience in dealing with the public school children in instruction classes do not present a hopeful outlook. This is the conclusion of one:

> To sum up, rationalism, atheism, utilitarianism
> and practical materialism, more or less gravely
> distort the minds of our children who are also pu-
> pils of secular schools, and render them in various
> degrees impervious to the truths of religion.[52]

The French government has amended its 1959 school law to permit religion to be taught in the state primary schools "under certain conditions." A basic "certain condition" exists

when churches are too far distant. The classes are to be
taught by school chaplains or by the local pastor. In cases of
disagreement over the need for classes, a special committee
composed of public and Catholic school representatives will
make the final decision.

What has been said above refers especially to the public
elementary school. The French law affects secondary schools,
the lycées and collèges differently. Most of these secondary
schools are boarding institutions. The first text of the Debré
law (1959) stated that in secondary schools chaplaincies were
to be established "as of right" in institutions with a proportion
of boarders. The final text, April, 1960, stipulated that the
establishment of chaplaincies in such schools was to take place
only on the demand of the parents of pupils. Moreover, the
arrangements contained in the original legislation that in exceptional circumstances the religious instruction could be
given by other than priests (or other clergymen) was suppressed. The provision that the expenses of the chaplain are
to be borne by the parents demanding the appointment was retained in the final text but it is added that the communes may
vote subventions for the purpose.

The bishops of France have urged Catholic parents to
ask for the religious instruction and pastors have reiterated
the appeal, reminding them that only they are legally entitled
to insist that chaplaincies should be instituted in the schools.

At a meeting of Catholic chaplains in Paris under Cardinal Feltin in 1960, the new law and décrets d'application were
examined. It was noted that the new legislation did not envisage the possibility of permitting religious instruction to be
given by laymen; yet the number of priests available for operating school chaplaincies was becoming more and more insufficient. The chaplains welcomed the provision of the new text
which allowed them to enter almost all educational establishments and meet the teachers. They felt this arrangement
provided an opportunity which would allay many prejudices and
difficulties otherwise present.

We turn now to a consideration of the relationships of the
private schools to the state. A fact of importance to be noted
first is the significant place the private schools hold in the

total educational effort in France, numerically speaking. We
have seen that sets of statistics vary, the government figures
being lower for private schools than those from other sources.
Any set, however, shows that the private schools provide for
a considerable proportion of school enrollments, over one-fifth
in primary schools and almost one-half in secondary schools.[53]
According to statistics of the Ministry of Education for 1959-
1960, there were 10,266 private primary schools, 1,652
secondary schools, and nine Facultes Libres (not dependent on
the state) at: Paris, Aix en Provence, Basançon, Lille, Lyon,
Montpellier, Poitiers, Rennes and Toulouse. Private primary
schools cared for 1,103,000 children as compared with
6,305,000 in state schools; private lycées and collèges had
472,000 pupils, which was more than half the number found in
public secondary institutions. The proportion was somewhat
less in the vocational secondary schools; 138,000 in private
as compared with 303,000 in state vocational schools.[54] The
proportions vary widely from one area of the country to another. In some parts practically all the children are in Catholic schools.

There are a few private schools conducted by Protestants
or Jews here and there, but for the present purpose we may
regard all as under Catholic auspices. The controversies and
problems of the past have centered around the Catholic schools
and the school issue today is their concern.

The French call their private schools les écoles libres,
which term indicates "freedom" from government control as
contrasted with the strongly centralized state system. But
les écoles libres are not entirely without control by the state.
In the first place these schools may not be opened without the
approval of the local mayor, the department of education officials, the academie inspectors, and the Ministry of National
Education. Any level of state authority may oppose the
school's opening, but the decision to oppose may be contested
before a special tribunal.[55] The Ministry inspects the private
schools to assure itself that "there is no breach of morals,
hygiene and sanitation, and to ascertain that the Constitution
and the laws are duly respected."

The teachers and principals of secondary schools must

meet the national certification requirements. The diplomas
granted in private schools are not recognized by the state;
the students can obtain valid certificates only by passing the
state examinations which are taken by all public school pupils
in order to be certified. This means that the private schools
must pattern their course of studies after the state schools
and set the same examinations. All this represents a rather
extensive form of indirect control, despite the official statement that "private schools are entirely free in the choice of
pedagogical methods, programs and textbooks." [56]   How
"free" then -- free from state control -- are les écoles libres?
The term, as the French use it, is scarcely accurate.

Up until 1951 the écoles libres received no public aid.
With the advent of aid came more extensive control. Loi
Marie (1951) entitled the private secondary schools to take
scholarship holders. The scholarships when provided by the
national budget can cover books, equipment, complete board
or, in the case of day students, lunch at school. A commission presided over by the rector of the academie decides on
applicants. Requirements include an economic situation of
need in the family and academic qualifications on the part of
the student, who must begin secondary school at age eleven to
be eligible. The private schools which accept scholarship pupils are subject to inspection by the state. To qualify they
must fulfill the conditions required of public institutions as
far as physical facilities, studies, and personnel is concerned.
In 1958-59, there were 18,537 scholarship students in private
as against 160,019 in public secondary schools, a proportion
considerably less than the proportions of total enrollment in
each type of school.

Loi Barangé (1951), which allots 1,300 francs per trimester per child to parents who have children in private
schools, has, according to reports and opinions of those close
to the situation, been operating as successfully as the limitations of the law permit, without giving much satisfaction to
either the public or the private schools. It has helped the private schools to continue to exist, but has not greatly alleviated
their financial needs. How far can a school manage on an $8
to $10 per capita income? There have been complaints, too,

that the government has not always come through with the allotments. Moreover, only schools established before 1951 are
entitled to the subsidies.

The funds are given directly to the Parents' Association
of each school. Parents' Associations in France are semi-
official groups, not at all analogous to such voluntary organizations as the American P.T.A. They are committees of
parents or patrons whose purpose is to assist the elementary
schools. Every school must have such an association. In the
public schools the committees are usually appointed by the
academie inspector, rather than organized by the parents
themselves.[57]   In the private schools they may be elected or
appointed by the authority of the school.

In general, the Catholic elementary schools have been
getting about twenty-one percent of the funds, which approximates the proportion of their total enrollment. The amount
received, however, has been completely inadequate to remove
the inequality of Catholic teachers' salaries when compared
with those of state teachers.

The Debré Act of 1959 did not immediately abrogate Loi
Barangé. Its Article VIII states:

> The Law of September 28, 1951, will cease to have
> effect three years from the date of the promulgation
> of the present law. Nevertheless, in accordance
> with the opinion of the National Committee of Con-
> ciliation which will have taken into consideration
> the number of institutions which by this time will
> have subscribed to one of the two types of contracts
> described above, the Government may prolong the
> application of this law for a supplementary duration
> not exceeding three years.

The main provisions of the Debré Act have been noted.
It offers the Catholic schools several possibilities: a school
may elect status quo, that is to remain as it is without state
control, except for the general regulations, and without aid,
except for the indirect aid provided by Loi Barangé. Some
Catholic schools having sufficient income to maintain them-

selves have deliberately chosen status quo rather than barter
their independence. A school may elect to be integrated gradually into the state system. In this case, all costs are absorbed by public authority and likewise the school loses its independent character. No Catholic school has elected integration status. Obviously the price is too high. That would
indeed be an unwise purchase if its price should destroy the
buyer.

A Catholic school that desires aid, but not integration,
may enter into various forms of association or contractual
relationships with the state, each being linked with corresponding degrees of control. The school may enter a contrat
d'association (Art. IV of the Law) which covers all or some
of the schools' classes. In this case, the state takes over all
the expenses of those classes covered and the classes must
conform to the program and regulations of public education in
the same way as do those of corresponding classes in public
schools. The teachers are drawn from a government list and
named jointly by the government and by the school authority.
They are either teachers of public education or teachers linked
to the state by contract.[58]   The school electing contrat
d'association will be free to conduct its religion courses as
before, with the provision, however, that attendance at them
be voluntary. The school underwrites the cost of the religion
program.

Since the government assumes all costs in "association
schools" of those courses under contract, tuition may not be
charged for the classes covered, but the school may charge
fees for the courses not covered and for elective courses
taught by a chaplain and for the upkeep of the chapel. The
original law did not lay down the exact amount to be paid the
schools under contrat d'association, but in a series of decrees
formulated later, the government fixed the amount of aid to be
granted to various sections of private education. During the
first year of the contract, the state paid "association schools"
according to the number of students enrolled. The amount
paid for each student varied according to the material expenses
of the school: technical schools which require a maximum of
physical equipment received from $65 to $100 per student a

year, while for purely academic classes the amount was $40 to $70 per student.

An official bulletin describes the contract of association this way:

> Thus, a public education is being given in the midst of a private institution, yet in a private institution which retains its specific character, its originality, its own atmosphere, for it remains free to organize those classes and scholastic activities not included in the contract, and to demand a corresponding remuneration from the parents.[59]

A Catholic school, on the other hand, may enter into a contrat simple or free contract (Art. V of Law). This allows a more flexible relationship with the state. The contract bears upon a part of the school's program. The institution requesting this relationship must meet state requirements as to: length of school term; qualifications of teachers; numbers of pupils; appropriateness of school environment. There is, however, more flexibility allowed in the arrangement of schedules and in methods. The school's directors appoint the teachers with the approval of the government authorities. The state then pays the teachers a salary in accordance with their qualifications as fixed by law. According to later decrees elaborating the functioning of the law, the government pays each teacher one-half the normal salary and underwrites half of all material expenses of the school. The institution must meet the remaining half from fees charged the pupils or from other sources of income. As noted above, in case of both simple and association contracts, the private schools participate in municipal services in the same manner as do public schools. The services include free school transportation, textbooks and subsidized lunches.

Because of the foreseen need of interpretation and application of the law to specific circumstances and the possibility of disagreement between the parties to the contract, the law provided for joint committees of conciliation of twelve members on local, departement and national levels. To these

committees are referred "all litigations concerning the drawing up, interpretation, execution, and renewal of contracts,
and more generally, all difficulties that stem from the application of the Law of December 31, 1959."[60]

The operation of the law has given rise to mixed reactions. Nowhere, however, does there seem to be great enthusiasm. Views pro and con are expressed by Catholics;
heated denunciations are the rule from the laïcest groups,
though the opposition fails to reach the heights of emotionalism which characterized the church-state conflicts of the past.

The Conseil National d'Action Laïque has continued the
demonstrations of hostility which it had shown toward the Act
from its inception and has declared that it will fight until the
law is abrogated. Its techniques consist in a systematic campaign of administrative non-cooperation together with efforts
to sabotage the provisions of the law. It was reported that
laïc-minded school teachers made propaganda in the cause
during school hours and encouraged demonstrations of hostility
on the part of pupils and parents.[61]

A number of leading Catholic spokesmen have expressed
misgiving at the provisions of the law, regarding it as the thin
end of a wedge that will eventually lead to the elimination of the
Catholic schools. The hierarchy has been cautious but willing
to give the law a fair trial. A Plenary Assembly of the French
Episcopate meeting April, 1960, in a communique covering a
variety of subjects stated in relation to Loi Debré that although
"registering its regrets and reserves, the hierarchy. . . desirous of working toward the union of Frenchmen on the school
question. . . accepts in this spirit that Catholic schools should
envisage the conclusion of contracts. In this way there will
be made a fair trial of the law the result of which will dictate
the definitive attitude of the bishops."[62]

The French cardinals, August 15, 1960, called for
Catholic elementary schools to apply for contrats simples and
for Catholic secondary schools to apply for contrats d'associations, but they expressly indicated that the recommendation
was subject to the ruling of bishops in their dioceses. One
bishop recommended school directors in his diocese to enter
into contrats simples and in no case to consider either of the

other formulas. He pointed out that the law "recognizes for the écoles libres merely a momentary role as substitutes." [63]

According to a report of the Minister of Education for 1960-1961, nearly 11,000 of the approximately 14,000 private schools had requested aid under the Debré law. Reports from various French dioceses have indicated that schools which had entered into contracts later withdrew them. There have been complaints that the essential Catholic spirit of the schools under contract has suffered as a result of subtle, or at times not so subtle, interference on the part of state inspectors. Nowhere, it seems, has great satisfaction been felt.

The problem of the Catholic school system in France is still acute. The rising birth rate in France has confronted the Church with the need to raise close to three hundred million dollars for school construction in the next five years if Catholic schools are merely to retain their present proportion of all French students. This was brought out at the annual congress of parents of Catholic school students. The secretary general of the National Union of Studies for Freedom of Education told the Congress that private schooling is doomed to becoming limited to the privileged few unless the burden of constructing and enlarging schools is reduced. The relationship between the state and the private schools in France is evidently in a still unresolved condition.

The School Issue in France: Appraisal

We began by noting the deep cleavage which cuts asunder the hearts and minds of the French people -- a sort of spiritual schizophrenia on a national scale. We saw its historical beginnings in the Enlightenment and Revolution, beginnings which gave rise to struggles between monarchists and republicans, between clericals and anti-clericals, between church and state. These were merely overt expressions of a deeper conflict involving Christianity as opposed to rationalism; indeed, between entirely different views of life and of man's fundamental purpose and destiny. Throughout the conflict the Church did not oppose the Republic as such, but it opposed the republican concept as it was expressed in nineteenth century France, as in truth the Church had to if it were to remain

faithful to its own nature and purpose. Despite lofty-sounding
slogans, the Republic was born in excesses -- brutality, hatred,
rapine, murder, irreligion. It was not possible for a long
time for the Church to separate the excesses from the valid
principles and new institutions implicit in the philosophy of
true republicanism. That can now be done, but it could not
have been done before the twentieth century.

The conflict tended to center largely on the schools; it
became a struggle for the minds of the children. The revolutionists and following them the republicans wanted neutral
schools under state control to "prepare citizens who would be
loyal to republican ideas," which generally meant anti-clerical
and anti-monarchist attitudes. They saw in the Church an
enemy hostile to the ideals of the republic. The Church, on the
contrary, faithful to the mandate of Christ, insisted on her
right to educate her children, as she had done for centuries,
preparing them to become good citizens of both their native
country and of their eternal home. The historic struggle continues in France today, moderated somewhat, less bitter, but
there in its essentials.

Just as a great cleavage exists between the secularist or
rationalist and the believing and practicing Christian, so an
antagonism exists between the two types of schools: l'école
libre, for Christ and country; the other, state-controlled and
laïcist, for this world and country. The key insight into the
relationship between the private and the public school in France
today is that the two systems reflect in a smaller sphere of
action the bitter conflict between two opposing views of life.[64]
In its practical aspects, the struggle today focuses on the dual
questions of the place of religion in the public schools and of
sufficient aid for the Catholic schools so that they may be able
to compete at least on equal terms with the state schools while
maintaining their essential character unimpaired.

France's historical tradition of a highly centralized
government controlling all spheres of activity including education has worked in favor of the laïc, state schools, strengthening them, while keeping the private schools incapable of com-
peting equally with the public school systems, materially
speaking. Aside from that aspect of the highly centralized

system, much adverse criticism of a general nature has been levied against it. True, from a limited practical viewpoint, it is a ruthlessly efficient system. But its efficiency is also its chief weakness. The entire thrust of the educational effort in France is dominated on the teacher's side by getting a "good rating" for teaching and doing what the Ministry in Paris wants. On the student's side the educational endeavor has as its purpose "to pass the examinations set by the Ministry and get a high diploma rating." The Ministry sets "relative ranks" for different levels of success in passing. Thus the true purpose of education, the total development of the truly human person, is subordinated to inferior goals. Both teachers and students are stymied; paradoxically, initiative is stifled in a country where "freedom" is always a popular shibboleth. And, again, the practical danger involved in such centralization is obvious. Were the communists to gain control of the Ministry of Education, a single stroke of the pen could put Marxist-Leninist teaching in the courses, the texts, the examinations and in the whole system.

The Christian philosophy of education judges that the purpose of education is to develop the true and perfect Christian. [65] The development of the perfect Christian involves the full development of the human person. As such, he is a good citizen of earth, as well as of heaven. The person is "a distinct subsisting entity of rational nature." This person is developed rationally through free choices, through goals established by right reason enlightened by faith. Faith does not establish "passing examinations" or "conforming" as the primary aim of education; neither does reason. Thus, this over-centralized system is built on a false purpose. Good philosophy declares that to begin from error leads only to error.

More could be said, and has been said, adversely about France's highly centralized system. But our specific concern at the moment is an attempt to evaluate the relationship of this highly centralized system to the Church in her educational work. How does it measure against a Christian philosophy of education? Take the principle of subsidiarity, called by Pope Pius XII the "Key principle regulating action in society." The

primary right to direct the education of children on the natural
level belongs to the parents; in the supernatural order it belongs to the Church, who through her sacraments and teaching
gives and nourishes divine life. The function of the state in
education is to assist these primary, natural societies in the
harmonious achievement of their purposes. The state is to
supplement, not to supplant them. It is to assist them, financially or otherwise, to fulfill adequately their respective functions toward the full development of the individual, physically,
mentally, socially, spiritually.

The implications of the revolutionary slogan "L'enseignement fonction de l'Etat," which still underlies the government's
attitudes toward education, go beyond the rights of the state
and violate the principle of subsidiarity. The slogan ignores, if it
does not explicitly deny, the primary rights in education of
both parents and the Church. The French state has exceeded
its lawful function in education by abrogating to itself exclusively the task of creating a curriculum, choosing texts, and
setting all the standards of educational performance. This
latter is accomplished through its examination and certification
system. True, the coercion upon the private school in these
matters is not always direct, but the indirect coercion through
refusal to recognize private school certificates and the consequent economic liability for the students results equally in a
restriction on the rights of the private schools to manage their
affairs in harmony with their philosophy of education. Likewise, the financial aid so badly needed, provided by the 1959
law, carries with it a restriction on all Catholic schools which
jeopardizes their raison d'etre.

The contention of its advocates that the extensive centralization of education by the state is necessary for the glory of
France and its well-being is belied by the facts of history.
The system does not seem to have developed in the young citizens the stamina needed to withstand the gigantic attacks upon
the nation's freedom which occurred twice during the present
century. Other western nations, adhering more closely to a
Christian philosophy of education, were able to develop greater
valor. And the instability and near chaos which have characterized the French government for the past eight decades do

not denote a patriotism and responsibility for the general welfare that the lay public schools were supposed to inculcate.

In any case, the fundamental premise is false. It makes
a secondary aim -- the country's glory -- a primary aim of education, which, properly is the full development of the individual.
The true, mature Christian, by the same token, is a good citizen; he is more than likely to be an ardent patriot. France
found her staunchest defenders among the practicing Christians
during her days of trial. The contemporary observer is inclined to ask: Is the inherent weakness of the nation, which
has its source in the spiritual cleavage among its citizens,
being manifested anew today by policies which seem to have
their motive in expediency rather than in principle?

The government boasts of its regard for freedom.
"Freedom of thought and freedom of conscience, the two great
fundamental freedoms governing French constitutional law,"
states an official bulletin, "are necessarily accompanied by
freedom of education which confers upon the human being, on
the one hand, the right to teach others, and on the other hand,
the right to choose both the form of education which best suits
him and the teacher who is to dispense it." What, in practice,
is the quality of this freedom guaranteed by the French constitution? We have referred to the arguments of the French
Catholics in 1951 when demanding aid for their schools: that
a right is not truly recognized as such when it can be exercised
only at the price of a penalty. Catholics in conducting their
schools have done so only under penalty of accepting a double
economic burden: payment of taxes to support public schools
which contravene their philosophy of education, and support
for their own schools from their own resources. The recent
laws of 1951 and 1959 granting aid have not relieved them
completely from the penalty; they must pay for new buildings,
greatly needed, and for a considerable part of maintenance
costs. Moreover, the aid received has been paid for by relinquishment of freedom to conduct their schools as their
philosophy of education dictates. This situation does not add
up to true educational freedom.

It should be noted, too, that the emphasis is on "freedom
of conscience." This is right and proper, unless, at the

same time, it ignores or de-emphasizes other freedoms. In
practice, that is what happens. In the so-called lay schools,
the "freedom" amounts largely to freedom for "free-thinking"
or for rejection of traditional religious truths and religious
authority. The public school student is urged to think for
himself about religion. He is free to reject what he does not
like. Is the primary school child (and almost eighty percent
of French children are in public schools) ready to make judgments for himself on religious matters? Rejecting traditional
dogmas, the laïcist teacher is strongly doctrinaire in his insistence on the laïc viewpoint. And what about the fundamental
right of parents to direct the education of their children in accordance with their religious convictions? Many parents, because of their inability to pay tuition or because there is no
Catholic school available, must send their children to the public schools where they are frequently exposed to an anti-religious or irreligious atmosphere and consequently to loss of
their faith. Most of the French parents, surveys have shown,
want their children in Catholic schools. What, too, about the
freedom of the Church to enter the public schools and instruct
her children in Christian truths and principles as her mandate
from Christ demands?

Philippe de Las Cases in a pamphlet entitled Valeur
Social de la Liberté de l'Enseignement compares the notion
of freedom of education in France with that obtaining in other
democracies, such as Holland and Scotland. He points out
that the latter show a more logical conception of neutrality;
that is, their procedure is to give equal protection and the
same material help to schools of all beliefs. They thereby
protect the rights of the family without absorbing it or substituting for it.[66]

The French school is not neutral. At best it is rationalistic;
at worst, it is openly irreligious. The nation has suffered. Confusion, restiveness, vacillation have characterized France for
many years. The historic split in the nation at its spiritual
core prevents the country from taking adequate steps to return
to France her birthright of Christian traditions. The laïcist conflict continues to divide the French nation. There are two
Frances. In peace the division has wasted energy over issues

on which the people should have been united and diverted attention from pressing social questions. In war it has undeniably weakened both the unity of the nation and its ability to resist attacks from outside, a fact clearly exposed in the two World Wars.

As to the new relationship of the state to the Catholic schools initiated by the 1959 law, it is too early to make conclusive judgments. The principle on which the law is based -- "more aid -- more control" is neither philosophically nor practically sound. With good will, however, on the part of the state authorities, the contracts could work out with a fair degree of satisfaction for both sides. France has need of her private schools and their value is enhanced, not diminished, by their retaining full independence in achieving their specific aims. In them are preserved and cherished the traditions that made France a great nation. In them lies her hope. Comte de Mum echoed what Catholics well knew when he said: ". . . the best guarantee that you can have of our patriotism is our Christian faith, for that teaches us to cherish the fatherland and to devote ourselves to it, and I do not know what lessons you will give the child to teach him love of his country if you do not teach him first love of God." [67]

As best it can be said that the government has at last taken a step toward equity in its relations to the Catholic schools. The Constitution of the Fifth Republic has retained the declaration that France is a laïc state, that is, the government adheres to a policy of neutrality toward all religions. There is no "establishement"; one church cannot be preferred to another. The concept is similar to the American principle of separation of church and state. Nevertheless, France has found it possible to give financial aid to her church-related schools, apparently with no violation of her separation principle. The situation in France and America is not entirely analogous. We have a Supreme Court which interprets the application of the Constitution. France does not. Still Americans may find it worth while to watch this democracy in her efforts to solve the school issue where it is equally acute and perhaps even more emotionally involved than it is in our own country. France has made a beginning, unsatisfactory though it may be.

Chapter 7

Ireland: A CATHOLIC NATION'S SOLUTION

In the foreword to a recently published book on education in Ireland, the writer, who knows the situation well, states that Ireland is one of the few countries "in which the problem of religious education has been happily settled to the satisfaction of everybody concerned."[1] That statement implies a remarkable achievement which surely deserves a closer study in a world in which a vast totalitarian oligarchy has banished religious education in areas covering over half the globe and in which other nations, though committed to religious liberty, are in danger of losing all faith in the supernatural through sheer neglect, while they stall in their efforts to meet the issue forthrightly. The observation has also been made that Ireland, one of the oldest and most solidly Catholic nations, gives the "best deal to the handful of non-Catholic citizens in the matter of schools."[2]

A sane and balanced philosophy, avowedly based on the natural law and on Christian principles, forms the foundations of the Irish system. The Irish people are absolutely sure of their position on the aims and purposes of education. It must be an education that prepares for both time and eternity. The respective rights and functions of home, church, and state in the matter are clearly delineated. Fundamental is the view that education is primarily a responsibility of parents and is foremost a spiritual work. The Catholic Church is recognized as having primary rights in the supernatural order. The state's rights are secondary; its function mainly is to assist and to cooperate with the family and Church, primary societies having primary rights in education. The rights of conscience and desires of parents in regard to the education of their children must be scrupulously considered.

From these principles it follows that the Irish system of education is pre-eminently a denominational system initiated by the churches in concert with parents. There is, therefore, strictly speaking, no state system of education in Ireland, but

293

the fullest cooperation among the agencies interested -- the
family, church, and state -- exists. The function and right
of the state to secure the temporal welfare of society and,
therefore, to insist on efficiency in the schools are fully recognized. Catholics, Protestants, and Jews enjoy equal educational opportunities under the law. Each group establishes its own
separate educational system, which on the primary level is
completely supported by public funds. While in most countries
church-related schools are but an appendage or complement
of a state system, sometimes only grudgingly tolerated, the
peculiarity of the Irish system is that the church-related
schools constitute the only schools, there being none, except
vocational institutes, directly initiated and controlled by the
state or local authorities. Paradoxically, however, the denominational schools in Ireland are called "National" schools.

The Irish educational system can scarcely be said to be a
gradual development, progressing over the years through controversy and struggle to its present form, although that is true
of education in most countries. On the contrary, in Ireland
the fundamental educational principles, which form the basis
of the present system, go back to the earliest years of Ireland's Christian history. These principles, however, could
not be implemented during the long years of British oppression.
For centuries Irish traditions struggled for existence against
the influence of alien thought and government, when the educational policy imposed upon the country was deliberately designed to Anglicize the Irish and to destroy their attachment
to the Catholic Church. The fact that Irish ideals and culture
survived at all is remarkable; indeed, it is a silent tribute to
the nobility of those same ideals and culture and to the fortitude
of the people. Actually it was during the long, harsh period
of her trial and suffering that the country's cultural traditions
were strengthened in such a way that they were ready to direct
immediately her political and educational policy when freedom
finally came. The story of Ireland's travail and final victory
is an inspiring and enlightening one relevant to an understanding of the present unique church-state relationship which underlies her solution of the religion-education issue.

Land of Saints and Scholars

The history of Ireland's culture and schools predates Christianity on the island. It seems fairly certain that an educational tradition existed among the Irish Celts similar to that of Gaul about which Caesar wrote, although the precise state of culture during that early period is difficult to determine. Ireland was never under Roman control and therefore was not adversely affected by the Empire's fall or by the corruption and moral decay which for several centuries had been destroying its vitality. Yet Ireland was close enough to the classical world to absorb some elements of the ancient learning. Sufficient evidence exists to conclude that there were a Celtic literature and Celtic scholars, Bards or Druids, who conducted schools during the pre-Christian period and thus developed and preserved an Irish culture. Scholars from the continent attended these schools.

The account of St. Patrick's missionary labors on the island and the enthusiastic acceptance of Christianity by the Irish in the fifth century are well-known events. During the following sixth, seventh, and eighth centuries Ireland became a beacon of culture, learning and piety for the rest of harassed Europe. While barbarian tribes were overrunning and plundering England and continental Europe, Ireland, which escaped the ravages of the pagan raiders, remained a sort of quiet retreat where learning could flourish and scholars could find a haven.

Undoubtedly the principal factor contributing to Ireland's position as "schoolmaster of the West" during those dark centuries was the rise of monastic schools. Armagh, founded about 457 A.D., was probably the first of the schools although it was not a monastic institution in the strict sense. Here and in several other colleges, St. Patrick had his young men trained and educated for the priesthood. From these schools developed the monastic institutions which, if not actually founded by Patrick, were outcomes of that spirit of faith and love which the saint had planted so deeply in the hearts of his converts and especially in the hearts of his priests. Most of the early monastic schools were founded within the century following Patrick's labors and with them the educational system of Ireland began.

From their beginnings the monastic schools cultivated the arts and literature of the time and they soon became illustrious for the erudition of their teachers and the proficiency of their students. A monastery often embraced a whole tribe, had its own rule, and became the center of ecclesiastical life and administration.[3]   Schools were conducted for both <u>oblati</u>, those entering religious life, and for <u>externi</u>, or outsiders.

The Christian monastic institutions, however, did not replace the old bardic schools completely. These were allowed to carry on their educational work. In actual fact, there was a dual system of education in Ireland at the time, a sort of distribution of educational work. The lay bardic schools formed one system, operating side by side with the monasteries and assuming responsibility for instruction in military science, law, and literature. The monastic schools gave their attention to elementary and secondary education, rarely offering professional studies except theology.[4]   It was only toward the end of the seventh century that the monastic schools began to replace the bardic institutions and the latter were gradually eliminated from the Irish scene.

At the same time the monastic schools were effecting a new flowering of classical culture, interpreted now in a Christian perspective. Science too was given a place in the curriculum, without of course any pretense of empirical techniques. Soon every part of Ireland had its flourishing monastic schools. Open to the laity, they gave free instruction to some, if not to all; women, apparently, were not excluded from the opportunities for education. The excellence of many of the schools drew to Irish shores students from England and the continent. Some monastic institutions had enrollments as high as 3,000.[5]

Besides providing instruction in the liberal arts, practically all the larger monasteries had both a library and a scriptorium for the copying and multiplication of books. The classics, textbooks, sacred literature, the Fathers, and above all Sacred Scripture were painstakingly copied in the scriptorium. The oldest extant Horace is an Irish manuscript preserved now at Berne, and the oldest Ovid is a Cambro-Irish manuscript now at Cambridge.[6]   Saints, as well as scholars, were founders or connected with the Irish monasteries. The list is a long one with names like St. Columba, St. Comgall, St. Finbar, St. Malachy, St. Keven, St. Ninian, to mention only a few.

Perhaps more important than the work accomplished at home were the missionary and educational efforts of the Irish monks in Britain, Scotland, and on the continent, where, as a consequence of the ravages of pagan barbarians, Christianity and learning alike were in danger of extinction. Monasteries were established, many of them becoming famous. Lindisfarne and Wearmouth-Jarrow in England, Luxeuil in France, Bobbio in Italy, St. Gall in Switzerland, and many others carried on the work of re-Christianizing the people and of revitalizing and preserving learning. Eriugena, an Irish scholar and the one great philosopher-theologian of his time, became head of the Palace School of Charles the Bald. In short, all historians agree that Ireland from the sixth to the ninth century was the principal center of learning and piety in the West. Her monks and people had preserved learning during the most dangerous period of Europe's history.

Then tragedy struck the little island that had so long been preserved from the ravages of barbarians. The savage and pagan Vikings began invading Ireland in 795 A.D. and continued the attacks for almost two hundred years. Their most vicious fury was directed against the instruments of religion and letters. Monasteries were plundered, libraries were destroyed, monks were murdered, manuscripts by the thousands were burned. The light of learning on the island was all but completely extinguished; the ancient glory of Ireland ended. Only round towers and ruins stand now as reminders of the country's former brilliance.

Fortunately, by the time of Ireland's decline, her missionaries and scholars had completed the great work of transmission. Learning had been preserved. The continent had been provided with the basic materials out of which the renaissance of the ninth century was fashioned and to it now had fallen the task of conserving and developing letters and the arts.

In the meantime, Ireland's woes were only beginning. She had had no chance to recover from the blow dealt by the

Vikings when in the thirteenth century the Normans invaded the land, destroying and confiscating whatever they could find. Then followed the gradual usurpation of control over Irish territory by Britain, an accomplishment which removed any possibility of Ireland's regaining her former prestige. It was not possible for learning and the arts to thrive in a land torn by tyranny and division. Finally, the prostration of the country begun by the Vikings and the Normans and augmented by the British seizure of lands reached its climax in the violent persecution following the Protestant revolt in England.

The Agony of Ireland

Britain set out with determination to Anglicize and Protestantize her prey across the Irish sea, an overwhelming task were a weak nation involved, an impossible one in the case of a spiritually strong nation, as Ireland proved to be. Catholics and other dissenters from the Established Church were being persecuted in England, but the full fury of the offensive was vented upon the Irish, who resisted with all the spiritual might at their disposal.

By the Supremacy Act of 1537 the Catholic Church, to which all Irish gave their allegiance, was deprived of its land and buildings in Ireland. The Anglican Church was established as the "Church of Ireland" and Anglican ministers were installed in all the churches as pastors. The lands of the great abbeys and religious houses were confiscated and vested in the Crown.

Penal laws enacted the same year forbade Catholics to educate their children either at home or abroad. Catholics were forbidden to conduct schools. Every Church of Ireland "incumbent was obliged to establish a parish school and to instruct and teach the English language to all and every being under his rule." The intent of this ruling was obviously to make the Irish an English-speaking people. The incumbent was obliged also to instruct the children of his parish, practically all of whom were Catholics, in the doctrines of the Anglican Church, with the express purpose of making them Protestant. The law could not be enforced. Catholic parents refused, no matter what the penalty might be, to send their

children to the Protestant schools. Later in 1570 under Queen
Elizabeth, the expedient of creating a "secularized school system" under the control of the Church of Ireland was tried.
The results were the same. Catholic parents would not send
their children to the schools.

The Irish Catholics followed the example of their religious confreres in England and established schools and colleges
in Catholic countries on the continent -- at Louvain, Antwerp,
Lille, Douai, Rouen, Salamanca, Madrid, Lisbon, Rome and
several other places. All the Irish clergy and many members
of the gentry were educated in these schools abroad.

Two measures were then taken by the government to
stop the exodus. Harsh penal laws were enacted forbidding
Catholics to send their sons abroad. The child sent to the
continent for education could not afterwards receive any legacy
or gift, could not sue in law or equity, and forfeited for life all
his goods and lands. Those who aided in his education were
also guilty and were meted out the same penalties.

The second measure was of a positive nature. To keep
the youths at home Trinity College was founded in Dublin.
The preamble of a letter written by Queen Elizabeth establishing the institution stated frankly that its purpose was to stop
the trek to France, Italy, and Spain wherein the students "have
been infected with papacy and other ill qualities."[7] To achieve
the desired end the college at first accepted Catholic students,
no religious test being required. Later, however, under
James I, the political aim of conversion was insisted upon,
and Catholics withdrew from attendance. Several Jesuit colleges were established at this time, but they were quickly
suppressed. Catholics who could afford to do so continued to
send their sons to the colleges abroad.

At the beginning of the seventeenth century, the Irish, in
spite of prohibitions, in spite of, as the poet says, "fire,
dungeon, and sword" were still staunch in the faith of their
fathers. During the reign of James I an Act passed in 1608
was aimed expressly at intensifying efforts to diffuse Protestantism on the island. New "Royal Schools" were established,
which were to recall the people from "superstition and rebel-
lion to the true religion and obedience." These schools, like

the previous foundations, failed utterly in their purpose. Catholics refused to use them. Nevertheless, vast sums of money were expended on them by the government, although they were attended only by a handful of Protestant children. Eventually they became parish schools for Anglican children. Catholics sent their children to their priests for instruction in religion and when possible in the three R's.

As might be expected, illiteracy was widespread, but Catholics, though grieved over the deprivation to which their children were subjected, were convinced it was better than endangering the faith of their children by sending them to the existing schools. At the end of the seventeenth century, British efforts to Anglicize and proselytize had still scored only failures.

England did not give up. A three-pronged attack against Irish insubordination was made at the beginning of the eighteenth century: more stringent penal laws, their strict enforcement, and schools more specifically designed for proselytizing. A price was placed on the head of a Catholic teacher. Priests caught teaching were subject to the death penalty. Since it had been found to be practically impossible to "convert" children living at home with parents, it was decided to take them from the parents and place them in boarding schools in remote localities. Neither priest nor Catholic relation of a child was allowed to communicate with him except in the presence of the schoolmaster. The purpose of the new schools was expressly stated in their charter: "to the intent that the children of the Popish and other poor natives in Ireland might be instructed 'gratis' in the English tongue and in the principles of true religion and loyalty."[8] Catholic parents refused to part with their children and another failure was registered against the machinations of the government.

The Irish, however, wanted their children to be educated and under the circumstances the only way was somehow to provide clandestinely schools which would be acceptable to their religious conscience. The answer was the hedge school, so-called from the fact that it sometimes consisted simply of a few children in the open air concealed behind a hedge along with a teacher who in this most unlikely of places endeavored

to teach them the catechism and perhaps unfold to them the
mysteries of a printed page. Sometimes the school was a
small cabin. Generally there were no buildings, no school
apparatus, no regular attendance. The teacher was a lay
Catholic who had perchance managed to obtain a meager education abroad, from a priest, or perhaps in a Protestant
school. Constantly in danger of being discovered by police or
exposed by an informer, the hedge schools provided the only
training possible to hundreds of Irish boys for over a hundred
years. "Still crouching 'neath the sheltering hedge or
stretched on mountain fern," so a historian describes the
situation, "the teacher and his pupils met feloniously to
learn." [9]

In all the efforts which England put forth to Protestantize
the Irish, it appears quite clear that the Church of Ireland was
not a free agent but a tool utilized by the government to achieve
the subjugation of the Irish people to the British yoke. The
religious aims were in reality subordinate to the political.
The British were determined to force upon the Irish their own
culture and religion. The Irish were even more determined
to remain Irish and Catholic. The whole British scheme was
a failure and led only to bitterness among the Irish toward
their alien overlords, remnants of which survive today.

Toward the end of the eighteenth century a more tolerant
and rational attitude on the part of the British government
emerged. The educational disabilities of the Irish were partially removed in 1793. Emancipation came in 1830 and the
penal laws were lifted, at least theoretically. Catholic teachers were permitted to establish schools under certain conditions and a revival of Catholic education began. Catholic Poor
School Committees were formed. Religious congregations
dedicated primarily to teaching were founded. Among the latter should be mentioned the Irish Christian Brothers devoted
to the education of boys; the Sisters of the Presentation and
the Sisters of Mercy for the education of girls. These and
other communities have been continuously playing an important part in the development of Irish education. Four Catholic
diocesan colleges were opened, and the government even en-
dowed a college at Maynooth for the purpose of keeping the

Irish clerics from going to the continent for their training.

Since Catholic schools had to find the means to support themselves and available funds were scarce indeed, educational opportunities remained limited and many Irish children did not go to school at all. Instead of coming to the aid of the Catholic schools to remedy this situation, the government determined to establish a system of undenominational national schools. A National Education Board was set up under the control of commissioners, one-third, later one-half, of whom were Catholics. Elementary schools were to be built all over the country, most of the costs being met by the government. The curriculum was to be made up of combined literary and moral instruction for mixed religious groups and separate religious classes for Catholics and Protestants on the principle that no attempt would be made to interfere with the peculiar religious tenets of any pupil.[10]

Definite regulations were drawn up for the denominational instruction. Opportunities were to be provided for each pupil to receive such instruction as his parents or guardians approved. The various religious denominations were to meet in separate classrooms under the control of a clergyman or lay person who taught the class in accord with the creed of the children. In all cases no pupil was obliged to be present at any form of religious instruction if his parents objected. Where instruction in a particular creed could not be given in the school, pupils were to have reasonable opportunity for leaving the building and taking it elsewhere. In schools outside the national system, the patrons or managers were completely free to determine what religion was to be taught or whether no instruction at all was to be given. These regulations certainly ensured freedom of conscience and as such gained the approval of Catholics in general.

The neutral moral instruction was another matter. Based on principles of the natural law and given by the regular teacher to combined groups, it raised questions among some Catholics as to its suitability for Catholic children. Most agreed it was satisfactory as far as it went. A set of practical rules for teachers instructed them "to pay the strictest attention to the minds and general conduct of their pupils, and

to omit no opportunity of inculcating the principles of truth,
honesty, and politeness, the duties of respect to superiors and
obedience to all persons placed in authority over them." [11]
The teachers were ordered to exclude from the school except
at hours set apart for religious instruction "all catechisms
and books inculcating peculiar religious opinions."

The plan of the national system of education offered the
Irish people a far better deal than their British rulers had ever
before given them. A half loaf, they decided, was better than
none. So the Act implementing the new plan was, as a whole,
well received by Catholics. There were, however, some
doubts expressed by a few as to how religion would ultimately
fare in such mixed schools. One member of the hierarchy,
the Very Reverend Dr. McHale, Bishop of Tuan, vigorously
opposed the National schools. Other bishops were willing to
give the system a trial. Controversy waged and the issue was
finally referred to Rome in 1840. The Sacred Congregation
preferred that the question be settled in Ireland. The national
system was not condemned; it was left to the individual bishops
to decide whether the system should be introduced into their
dioceses or not. The bishops were warned, however, not to
permit books dangerous to Catholic faith to be used and they
were to see to it that the school property should be vested in
themselves or in their charge. [12]

Though they did not regard the national system as completely satisfactory, the Irish bishops and clergy set about to
give it a fair trial as the best arrangement attainable at the
time. Many of them were of the opinion that a system of education on a mixed basis could not long endure in a country
where the vast majority adhered to the ancient Catholic faith
and where in addition other deep ethnic and cultural differences
set the Irish people apart from the British and Protestant minority. Time eventually proved them right.

Aside from the religious issue there were other factors
which impeded the smooth working of the scheme. In its
operation various policies, sometimes subtly, opposed Irish
sentiment. The English language was used almost exclusively.
The contents of official textbooks were aimed to develop
British rather than Irish patriotism.

A minority of Protestant churchmen favored the National schools and even collaborated with the National Board in trying to establish a truly denominational system. The majority of Anglican ministers, however, could not accept the new situation. They insisted that the Church of Ireland was the established church and that it was its duty to convert the Irish through education. With the disestablishment of the Anglican Church in 1809 all pretense of monopoly of education had to be abandoned.

Gradually changes took place, de facto, if not legal. The National schools eventually became in effect parish schools, either Catholic or Protestant. The management of the schools came more or less completely under the control of the clergy of the different denominations, who had the right of appointing teachers. Generally speaking, the schools were attended by the children of one denomination only, Catholic or Protestant. In this way the national system by degrees absorbed most of the pupils of private schools. A few of the latter did survive, particularly the preparatory elementary schools attached to Catholic secondary institutions conducted by religious congregations.

It is to be noted that the national system provided education only on the elementary level. Secondary schools, referred to in Ireland at that time as intermediate education, existed, but they were all privately owned, controlled, and supported. The schools for Catholic boys and girls were conducted generally by religious congregations. Protestant children attended secondary schools that had developed out of holdings confiscated years before from the Catholics. Those available for Catholic youth were few in number and tuition-charging. Most Irish children could not afford to attend them.

In 1878 the Intermediate Education Act gave a strong impetus to the development of secondary education. The purpose of the Act was to provide intermediate secular education to larger numbers through the introduction of a system of public examinations, on the results of which prizes, medals, and certificates would be awarded to deserving candidates and fees would be paid to the schools.[13] An Intermediate Education Board was established, its chief function being to distribute

the public money according to results on the written examinations.

An element of unfairness prevailed. All the endowments
hitherto enjoyed by Protestant schools were left to them while
the Catholic schools, depending entirely upon private resources,
were compelled to compete with the wealthy institutions for the
prizes and fees. Nevertheless, Catholic secondary schools
established and run by religious congregations became fairly
numerous and their pupils vied successfully for the prizes
against the students in the opulent Protestant set-up.

The system inaugurated by the Act had obvious defects.
By placing great emphasis on examination results, the policy
tended to encourage a narrow type of teaching oriented toward
high rating in the examinations and led to over-pressure on the
pupils. An Irish critic-historian characterizes the limitations
of the system thus: "The formation of character, the cultiva-
tion of taste, the disinterested love of learning not being capable
of being tested by examinations were disregarded in this sordid
race for results' fees." [14]

A series of later Intermediate Acts increased the financial aid to the schools and extended the powers of the Board.
Secondary school teachers were required to have specified
qualifications and funds were set aside for their salaries. [15]

In April, 1833, the Commissioners opened two Model
Schools in Dublin, one for training male teachers, the other
for prospective women teachers. Later more such schools
were established, one for each county district. These institutions were staffed almost exclusively by Protestant teachers.
They were, consequently, viewed unfavorably by the Catholic
bishops and Catholics refused to attend them. The result was
that many Catholic teachers in the schools lacked professional
training. Eventually the opposition of the bishops bore fruit.
Limited funds were granted for the maintenance of Catholic
training schools, far less, however, than was given to the
state institutions. Nevertheless, Catholics, accustomed to
struggle, carried on their work of training their own teachers
achieving, the record shows, notable success.

In 1899 the Agriculture and Technical Act was passed,
making provision for the establishment of technical education.

The Act was to be administered by local councils and financed jointly by the Exchequer and local rates. A considerable number of this type of school were established. They were administered under the control of Committees of Agriculture and Technical Instruction and thus represented a system of education dependent on local rather than central administration and outside of any immediate control of the churches. Religious instruction by chaplains was provided in accord with parents' wishes. This Act set a pattern for agricultural and vocational education which has survived practically without change in today's Irish system.

Education Under a Free Ireland

National consciousness lagged sometimes but never died among the Irish. In the last years of the nineteenth century it displayed renewed vitality, which was manifested in a reemphasis on the Gaelic language and a strengthened determination to achieve national independence. The Gaelic League was founded by Douglas Hyde in 1893 for the purpose of restoring Gaelic as the vernacular language. Sinn Fein, a society of Irish nationalists, was organized about 1905 for the purpose of achieving independence. Finally, after a bitter struggle, the Irish Free State, with dominion status, came into existence in 1921.

For the first time in centuries the desires of the Irish people could now shape the policy of the government. A constitution was drawn up and adopted in 1923. In reference to education the document laid down the principle that all citizens of the Irish Free State had a right to a free elementary education. The Gaelic language was proclaimed to be the national language, while at the same time English was recognized as having a place in official life. A Ministry of Education was set up and primary, intermediate (henceforth to be known as secondary) and technical education passed under its control. Agricultural education remained the concern of the Department of Agriculture.

Many Irishmen were dissatisfied with the dominion status and wished to abolish all semblance of Ireland's subordination to Britain. Under the Fianna Fail administration,

an anti-treaty party, which came into power in 1926, all political ties with Britain were severed and Ireland took her place
as a republic among the independent nations of the world. A
new Constitution was adopted in 1937. The Christian spirit
of the new state is expressed in the opening words of the Preamble to that remarkable document: "In the Name of the Most
Holy Trinity, from Whom is all authority and to Whom, as our
final end, all actions both of men and States must be referred,
We the people of Eire. . ." [16]

Article 42 of the Constitution sets forth the principles
upon which the educational system in Ireland is established:

1. The State acknowledges that the primary and
natural right to education of the child is the Family and
guarantees to respect the inalienable right and duty of
parents to provide, according to their means, for the
religious and moral, intellectual, physical, and social
education of their children.

2. Parents shall be free to provide this education in
their homes or in private schools or in schools recognized or established by the State.

3.a. The State shall not oblige parents in violation
of their conscience and lawful preference to send their
children to schools established by the State, or to any
particular type of school designated by the State.

b. The State shall, however, as guardian of the
common good, require in view of actual conditions that
the children receive a certain minimum education,
moral, intellectual, and social.

4. The State shall provide for free primary education
and shall endeavor to supplement and give reasonable
aid to private and corporate educational initiative, and,
when the public good requires it, provide other educational facilities or institutions with due regard, however,
for the rights of parents, especially in the matter of religious and moral formation.

5. In exceptional cases, where the parents for physical or moral reasons fail in their duty towards their
children, the State as guardian of the common good, by

appropriate means shall endeavor to supply the place of
the parents, but always with due regard for the natural
and imprescriptible right of the child.[17]

In Article 44 on Religion are to be found further principles applicable to education:

7. Legislation providing State aid for schools shall
not discriminate between schools under the management
of different religious denominations, nor be such as to
affect prejudicially the right of any child to attend a
school receiving public money without attending religious
instruction in that school.

8. Every religious denomination shall have the right
to manage its own affairs, own, acquire, and administer
property, movable and immovable, and maintain institutions for religious or charitable purposes.

9. The property of any religious denomination or any
educational institution shall not be diverted, save for
necessary works of public utility and on payment of compensation.[18]

These constitutional provisions determined the salient
features of the educational system which was set up: religion
is positively and effectively integrated with the educational
work of the school; the claims of religious minorities are met
on the basis of justice and complete religious liberty; the primary rights of parents to determine the education of their child
are fully recognized.

There is no established church in Ireland, but the separation principle is interpreted in accord with the Christian traditions of the country. The Constitution states in Article 44:

1. The State acknowledges that the homage of public
worship is due Almighty God. It shall hold His Name in
reverence, and shall respect and honor religion.

2. The State recognizes the special position of the
Holy, Catholic Apostolic and Roman Church as the guardian of the Faith possessed by the great majority of the

citizens.

4. The State also recognizes the Church of Ireland, the Presbyterian Church in Ireland, the Methodist Church in Ireland, the Religious Society of Friends in Ireland, as well as the Jewish Congregations and the other religious denominations existing in Ireland at the date of the coming into operation of this Constitution.

5. The State guarantees not to endow any religion.

Each society is recognized as supreme in its sphere: the state in the temporal order; the church in the spiritual order. Since the functions of both societies converge on the individual, cooperation between them is seen as absolutely necessary. The principles laid down in the Constitution and quoted above show how this cooperation is to be achieved in the field of education where both societies have legitimate claims. Moreover, these same principles show how both church and state yield to the primary claims of the family to decide what kind of education the child is to receive, while at the same time the natural rights of the child to receive an adequate education are protected by the state.

We now examine how these principles are implemented in the actual operation of Ireland's system of education.

How the Irish System Operates

The system of education in Ireland has the general features of the educational systems found in most Western democracies. It has primary, secondary, vocational-technical, and university levels or branches. There is a compulsory education law and a state-administrative set-up to assure the efficiency of the schools through supervisory instruments of the government. As might be expected, however, notable differences arise from the fact that the Irish system has been deliberately planned to harmonize with the philosophical principles of neo-scholasticism. These, as they relate to education, were given definitive form by Pius XI in the Encyclical Divini Illius Magistri (The Christian Education of Youth), 1929. The educational clauses in the Irish Constitution (1937) practically paraphrase the words of the Encyclical.

In the Irish system home and church take the initiative in founding schools; the state encourages and aids these efforts financially and safeguards the efficiency of the schools established. As a result there is the fullest cooperation among the agencies interested: the home, the church, the state. While the state recognizes the primacy of the Catholic Church, which has the allegiance of somewhat more than 97 percent of the people, the rights of the Protestant minority are fully protected. Catholics, Protestants and Jews conduct their respective educational systems, each being treated alike by the state. Although paradoxically referred to as national and undenominational, the schools in Ireland are in fact denominational and voluntary, dedicated to fostering and preserving religion. Only in the sphere of vocational and technical education does the state take a larger part of the responsibility, but even there the denominational principle is preserved through the services of chaplains, and local control is ensured by statutory county and urban committees.

PRIMARY SCHOOLS. Primary education is provided mainly in the National schools, that is, in schools supported by the state. There are also a few private elementary or preparatory schools. These are usually run by religious congregations in connection with a secondary school. They receive no financial assistance from the state, but are supported by fees and funds from other private resources. The National schools are undemoninational according to the letter of the law, that is, they must be open to all children who apply. In practice, however, they are denominational, since each religious body is free to establish its own schools. In general, Catholics attend only Catholic schools and Protestants only Protestant schools except in a few scattered rural areas where, because of the sparcity of the population, the groups may be mixed. There are also separate schools for Jewish children in Dublin. Ireland has no neutral schools from the religious point of view.

Each school must have a manager, who is not the same person as the principal or headmaster. In the case of a Catholic parish school, the pastor is manager. He takes care of finances and relationships with the state, has responsibility

for the maintenance and upkeep of the building, appoints teachers subject to the Department of Education's approval of the
teacher's professional qualifications, dismisses teachers with
the bishop's consent, visits the school and watches that the
"Rules and Regulations for National Schools" is complied with.
The Church retains full control over sites on which National
schools are built. The ownership of sites is vested in trustees
of whom one is the bishop. Managers accept state aid towards
building only in accordance with the wishes of the bishop.[19]
The Protestant schools are managed by the rector or other
Protestant clergymen, who have duties similar to those of the
Catholic pastor.

The state has rights and duties commensurate with its
functions in the temporal order. Parents are required by law
to have their children between ages six and fourteen in regular,
whole-time attendance at a National school or other suitable
school, unless there is a reasonable excuse for not doing so.
One of the excuses accepted is that there is not a school ac-
cessible "to which the parent of the child does not object on
religious grounds." [20]

Insofar as the state is concerned, the administration of
education is vested in the Department of Education under the
Minister of Education, who is responsible to the Dail Eireann
(i.e. National Parliament). The Department publishes a
handbook "Rules and Regulations for National Schools" as a
guide for managers and teachers. A group of school inspectors visit all the National schools to ensure their efficiency.
The inspectors may come at any time and inspect the work of
teachers, lay and religious. Their visits are intended to be
constructive as well as critical. All teachers in the National
schools must be qualified, that is, they must be certified as
graduates of a recognized training college. For recognition
as a National school at least twenty pupils are required, but
exceptions to this rule are made as noted below. The curriculum is that usual in primary schools. The courses of instruction in the various subjects are prescribed by the Minister of
Education after consultation with representative bodies and
educators.

The Department is making an effort to revive the use of

the Irish language through the schools. Wherever it is possible the Gaelic language is to be used as the medium of instruction for all subjects, and all National schools are expected to
work toward that objective. During the school year 1958-59
all subjects of the curriculum except English were taught
through the medium of Irish in 471 National schools, while
the teaching was partly through the medium of Irish in 2,375
schools.[21]

The National schools are almost entirely supported from
public funds. State grants are made toward the building of
new schools and the enlargement, reconstruction, or improvement of existing ones. The normal grant is two-thirds of total
costs. The balance comes from local voluntary contributions.
In special cases the whole cost may be borne by the state.
The salaries of teachers are provided entirely from government funds and are the same for religious as for lay instructors. Grants-in-aid, usually amounting to about fifty percent
of costs, are given towards charges for heating, cleaning, and
maintenance of buildings. Free textbooks and supplies are
provided for poor children. The Department of Health arranges, with parents' permission, for medical inspection of
children and the Department of Security for provision of free
meals in necessitous cases. In all these allocations of public
moneys and services, there can be no question of any discrimination on account of religion. Protestant and Jewish schools
participate in the same manner as do Catholic schools. No
fees may be charged in National schools.

The statutes prescribe that all Catholic children are to
receive dogmatic religious instruction from the teacher every
day and throughout the school course. Yet, paradoxically,
the undenominational character of the school is stressed in the
"Rules and Regulations." Thus the text states: "Religious
instruction must be so arranged that each school shall be open
to children of all communities for secular instruction;" and
"No inscription can be sanctioned which appears to imply that
the school is conducted for the exclusive benefit of the child
of any particular religious denomination." Again we read:

When the secular precedes the religious instruction,

the teacher is required before the commencement
of the latter to announce distinctly to the pupils that
the time for religious instruction has arrived and
to put up and keep up during the period allowed for
such and within view of all pupils a notification
thereof containing the words 'Religious Instruction'
in large characters in English and Irish on forms
supplied by the Department.[22]

Despite all this, the denominational character of the
National school is obvious to any observer. It is most unusual
to find the notice referred to above. The schools are either
Catholic or Protestant. A Protestant child would scarcely
ever be found in a Catholic school and vice versa. Indeed,
the "Rules and Regulations" make fairly certain that such will
be the situation. The text states:

In certain cases where the means of instruction are
not available for the child of a particular denomination in a National school within reasonable distance
of the home, the Minister is prepared to consider
the question of recognizing a school and of making
a grant to a teacher in accordance with the regulations on condition that the average daily attendance
of pupils is not less than ten. In certain conditions,
moreover, as an alternative to recognizing a school,
the Minister contributes towards the cost of convey-
ing the children to a suitable neighboring school.

In 1949, sixty such conveyances were in service for bringing
Protestant children to schools of their parents' choice.[23]
     In all cases, parental rights in deciding on religious in-
struction receive prime consideration. The "Rules and Regulations" state that "no pupil shall receive, or be present at
religious instruction of which the parents or guardians dis-
agree." It follows that a child may withdraw from the religious instruction if the parents wish them to, but actually
such a situation is rather theoretical in Ireland. It would be
difficult to find an instance where parents have made this

request.

The Rules clearly imply that religious teaching is to be an integral part of the curriculum and indeed that religion is to be the very center of school life. The formal instruction is given for at least one half hour each day. This instruction is completely under the control of the clerical manager, priest or minister, as the case may be. Lay headmaster, lay teacher, or religious does the actual teaching, but the parish priest and his curate are strictly bound to visit the classes in their parish and at times to engage in teaching.

But beyond the formal instruction, it is intended that a religious spirit inform the whole of school life. In pursuance of this objective the Department of Education in its "Programmes of Primary Instruction" states: "Though the time allotted to it (religious instruction) as a specific subject is necessarily short, a religious spirit should inform and vivify the whole work of the school." [24]

In 1965 there were a total of 4,848 national schools. Of these, 4,404 were Catholic with 489,448 pupils; 444 were non-Catholic schools, with 12,753 pupils. [25]

SECONDARY EDUCATION. Secondary schools in Ireland are not part of the national system, which has been described above, but are regarded as private institutions. They are owned, managed, and maintained by the churches, religious orders, or, in the case of some Protestant schools, by boards of governors. It should be noted, however, that a considerable number of National schools have "tops," that is, they carry the pupils through a secondary program up to the ages of sixteen or even eighteen. Such "tops" are part of the National system, and, accordingly, are maintained as are primary schools by state funds and are free to the pupils who attend them. These extensions exist especially in rural areas where no regular secondary schools are available.

Pupils attending them are admitted to state examinations for secondary school certificates on the same conditions as pupils from regular secondary schools.

The Irish secondary schools are the equivalent of the British grammar schools. There is no "streaming" in Ireland

as is the policy in England and Scotland. Ireland feels it is
better to let the parents decide what type of secondary school
the child will enter; mistakes may occur, but they can be seen
and remedied. The course is four years in length, carrying the pupil through ages fourteen to eighteen. Somewhat less
than one-half the pupils transfer from primary to secondary
schools.[26]

The program of instruction is prescribed by the Minister
of Education following consultation with the Secondary School
Association. Examinations are set by the state and must be
passed successfully by the pupil to obtain the Leaving Certificate, which admits to the universities. The appointment of
teachers rests entirely with the school authorities, but the
Department's regulations require that schools in receipt of
state grants employ a certain minimum number of Registered
secondary teachers and pay each teacher, if lay, a fixed minimum salary. To be registered a teacher must have obtained
a degree from a recognized university, have had one year of
professional training, and another year of successful teaching
experience in a recognized secondary school, and give evidence
of oral competency in the Irish language. Secondary schools
in receipt of state grants are subject to inspection by the Department's inspectors.

The school managers are required to defray the costs of
providing, equipping, and maintaining the school buildings and
to pay the minimum basic salary of teachers, which in 1960
was 200 pounds per annum, somewhat less than one-third the
salary the teacher received. In practice, higher basic salaries are paid in most schools.[27] The schools receive financial
assistance from the state under two headings. A capitation
grant is given for each pupil in attendance at the rate of seven
pounds for each junior pupil and ten pounds for each senior pupil. Secondly, the state pays to Registered teachers what is
called an incremental portion of their salaries, that is, a salary in addition to the basic amount, which the school pays.
The increments are fixed and the amount varies according to
whether the teacher is married or single, is male or female.[28]
The increments amount to about seventy percent of the total
salary. Special grants are given for the teaching of science,

home economics, and manual arts. No distinction of any sort
is made by the state as between the secondary schools of the
various denominations. All get the same type and amount of
grant whether they are Catholic or Protestant institutions.

Since the total of the state grants is not sufficient to support the schools, fees are charged the pupils, the amount of
which varies, but in all cases the charges are comparatively
low. Competitive scholarships tenable in secondary schools
are awarded annually by County and Borough Councils to children of low income groups. Likewise scholarships covering
university fees are available to worthy secondary school graduates if they are unable to pay.

As in the primary schools, religion is the core of the
secondary school course and of school life. Formal instruction in dogmatic religion is given daily by the teachers, lay or
religious. Constant efforts are being made to improve methods of imparting the Christian message. A syllabus has been
prepared by the bishops for use in the schools, the orientation
of which is Christo-centric. The pervasive influence which,
it is hoped, the religious teaching will have on the pupils is
shown by the general aim of the course: "The person of our
Divine Lord and Saviour should be kept before the pupils as
their teacher and model, as 'the way, the truth, and the life.' "

VOCATIONAL AND TECHNICAL EDUCATION. Voca-
tional education is the function of local Vocational Education
Committees established under the Vocational Education Act of
1930. These committees are obliged to provide a system of
continuation and technical education and for this purpose they
are impowered to establish and maintain schools and to appoint
the teachers and such other staff personnel as may be necessary, subject always to the approval of the Minister of Education. Continuation education generally takes the form of
whole-time courses for young persons who have completed
their primary schooling and includes pre-employment courses.
The schools are built by the government and maintained with
public funds, state and local. The pupils pay low fees and buy
their own books.

The vocational schools are undenominational in that they
are open to all students, but provision is made for religious

instruction by the various religious groups. In practice 95 percent of the pupils are Catholic. The Catholic hierarchy and the
Department of Education have collaborated to foster a vigorous
apostolate of youth. A chaplain is appointed by the local ordinary whose sole work is the spiritual care of the students. He
teaches formal religion courses twice a week, and is spiritual
advisor to the students. He has the same status as other
members of the teaching staff and receives a salary from the
state, or an emolument if his services are part-time.

The religion program in the vocational school is designed
to provide on the widest basis for the spiritual and moral development of the students and to stimulate their interest in the work
of the lay apostolate. Here in the vocational schools is seen
implemented the principles laid down in the Constitution in a
new situation. The chaplain has full facilities to develop his
mission in what is really in this case a state system of education. The state shows its regard for the spiritual needs of the
pupils, of the rights of parents, and of the Church, and of the
moral and spiritual basis of education, without, however, in-
fringing on the primary rights of parents and Church in this
area. The state recognizes the Church as guardian of the
moral law and makes available to it facilities to carry out its
work in the vocational schools.

The attitude of the state is expressed in a pamphlet issued by the Department of Education for the guidance of the
Vocational Committees. "Continuation Education," it says,
"must be in keeping with the Irish tradition and should reflect
in the schools the loyalty to our Divine Lord which is expressed
in the prologue and articles of the Constitution." Commenting
on the immediate purpose of the continuation schools, the
pamphlet points out that

> . . . this makes it all the more necessary to safe-
> guard the general purpose of education which is to
> develop, with the assistance of God's grace, the
> whole man with all his faculties, natural and super-
> natural, so that he may realize his duties and re-
> sponsibilities as a member of society, that he may
> contribute effectively to the welfare of his fellow

men, and by so doing attain the end destined for
him by his Creator.[29]

The relationship expressed by these attitudes and policies,
the Irish maintain, is not union of church and state but rational
cooperation. The same cooperation is shown to the Protestant
churches.

TEACHER TRAINING INSTITUTES. The training colleges for primary teachers from their beginning developed on
a denominational basis. At present there are six such institutions for training candidates for teaching in the National
schools. Three are for Catholic men students; two, for
Catholic women; one, for Protestant men and women.[30]   The
Protestant college, under the auspices of the Church of Ireland,
is located in Dublin and is managed by the Protestant Archbishop. One of the colleges for men is under the Irish Christian Brothers and is intended generally for the training of their
own members. The de la Salle Brothers also have their own
training college. A third college is under the Vincentians but
staffed by laymen. The local bishop is manager. The Sisters
of Mercy conduct the largest college for Catholic women. In
1956 it had 300 students enrolled; 200 were lay women, 100
were religious Sisters.[31]

To be recognized by the state the college must obtain official approval and submit to inspection. The government
makes no regulations relating to time-schedules, compulsory
subjects, and so forth, but these matters are examined by the
inspectors when they make their visitation.

The colleges are supported by low fees paid by students
and subsidized by government grants. The present rate of
grant is normally 115 pounds per student.[32]   Because of its
small enrollment the Protestant college receives a grant in
excess of the normal scale.[33]

Religious instruction in the colleges is completely under
the direction of the bishops who are responsible for the syllabus. A "diploma of Competence" to teach Christian doctrine
is awarded students by the superior of the college on the results of an examination. Managers of National schools are
forbidden to appoint teachers who do not hold this diploma.

HIGHER EDUCATION. There are two institutions of higher learning in the Republic. The National University of Ireland, founded in 1908, is organized on a federal basis, with constituent colleges at Dublin, Cork, and Galway. The National Ecclesiastical College of St. Patrick at Maynooth is an affiliate with recognized status. Each of these colleges has considerable autonomy, but all degrees are given from the National University, which functions from a central office. The other institute of higher learning is the University of Dublin, comprising one constituent college, Trinity College in Dublin.

Both universities are self-governing, autonomous institutions. They receive aid from the state in the form of annual grants, including, from time to time, allotments for capital purposes. In general the state grants cover about one-half of all costs. Fees are charged the students to make up the balance.

Trinity College is Protestant under the auspices of the Church of Ireland. Very few Catholics attend. Theoretically the National University of Ireland is undenominational. In practice it is a sort of Church-State institution. Ninety-five percent of its professors and ninety-nine percent of its student body are Catholic. A considerable proportion of its staff are priests. Chaplains are appointed to care for the spiritual needs of the students and university life is Catholic-oriented. There is an opening Mass of the Holy Spirit and Catholic organizations, such as the Legion of Mary, are fostered. To all intents it is a Catholic university, though not such in name.[34]

Appraisal

The Irish people seem to be completely satisfied with the general plan of their educational system. Relationships between church and state are characterized by mutual understanding and cordiality, with the result that the religion of the home and church enters fully and directly into school life. This is due to public recognition that the child should be educated in accordance with the religious conscience of parents. No citizen is debarred by reason of his religious convictions as they apply to education from any right or privilege or share

in state benefits. At the same time, the Irish Parliament
may not restrict religious freedom. The state must observe
the principle of equal treatment in the matter of schools, all
of which are denominational in character.

On the other hand no one who has observed the system in
operation would claim that the millennium in educational practice has been reached. The limitations, however, do not flow
from the principles upon which the system has been based.
Economic factors have continually hampered the country in its
development, not least in the educational field. Many school
buildings, by any comparative standard, are old and delapi-
dated, improperly heated, and inadequately equipped. But
Ireland is a poor country, wanting in natural resources.
Moreover she has never shared in the largesses of the American government, which have been so generously poured into
other Western nations and also behind the Iron Curtain. The
Irish are aware of the inadequacy of their schools from the
material side and have been discussing the problem since freedom was attained. Some progress has been made; more perhaps could have been done. Practically, it seems true that
results are uneven in regard to the parish schools. When the
priest-manager is efficient and progressive, excellent results
are to be found, but much depends on the individual manager.[35]

It has been said by some critics that the schools are
clergy-dominated. Perhaps so, but in that connection it
should be remembered that the clergy in Ireland are drawn
from the rank and file; they know and understand what the
parents want. During the long years of persecution the Irish
people clung to their heroic priests, loved them, trusted
them. That sentiment is still with the Irish. They themselves
are not the ones who complain of clergy-domination.

The fact remains that the freedom and justice of the Irish
system, its recognition of parental rights, its formal acknowledgment of the important role of religion in the education of
youth give it unique significance worthy of study in a world
that seems to be losing its freedom because, as many astute
thinkers feel, it is forsaking the bulwarks upon which true
freedom must ultimately rest.

NORTHERN IRELAND

Consideration of Northern Ireland's solution of the religion-education issue strictly is not relevant to this chapter since Northern Ireland is now politically an integral part of the United Kingdom. However, historically, geographically, and to a great extent, culturally, it is Ireland and hopes are still extant that the political unity of all Irish territory will some day be achieved.

The northeast section of Ireland is richest in natural resources. During the long period of their domination of the island, this area was heavily colonized by the British. The lands and property of the Irish were confiscated and given to the settlers who exercised a haughty ascendancy over the native population. Persecution against Catholics was carried on with particular severity and eventually the English immigrants comprised the majority of the population. When the struggle for independence was nearing its end and before Britain drew up the treaty granting dominion status to the south under the Government of Ireland Act of 1921, the six northeastern counties were sliced off and given a parliament of their own. In 1921 Northern Ireland came into existence as a separate political unit. It legislates through a House of Commons and a Senate of its own, but certain matters are reserved to the United Kingdom's Parliament, to which Northern Ireland returns thirteen members to the House of Commons. The land comprises about one-sixth of the total area of Ireland and has a population somewhat less than one-third of that of the Republic.

The educational policy for the North was formulated by the Education Act of 1947, but, prior to the passage of that Act and shortly after the partition, Northern Ireland's educational system had been reformed by a series of education Acts which brought it more or less in line with the set-up then guiding education in England. A Ministry of Education was established and all branches of education except the universities were put under its control. A School Act in 1923 substantially altered the system as it had existed when Ireland was a unit. Local Education Authorities were established. The former

National schools became Public Elementary schools. Under
the Act several possibilities for obtaining public funds were
open to Catholic schools. They could transfer to the L.E.A.'s,
accept on statutory school committees of six members, two
appointments by the L.E.A.'s, or they could remain independent and receive no aid. Most Catholic managers chose the
latter alternative, viewing the others as the thin end of a wedge
toward complete control. Rather than run any risks they preferred to assume the full burden of supporting their schools.
An Act in 1930 relieved the burden to a considerable degree.
Teachers' salaries were to be completely paid and also fifty
percent of the charges for heating and cleaning the school
houses. For building new schools and reconstructing old ones
the Ministry was to pay fifty percent of total costs. Then
came the Education Act of 1947 which applied to Northern Ireland most of the reforms which the Butler Act of 1944 had produced in the British educational system.[36] The provisions of
this Act still shape educational policy in Northern Ireland.

There is a Ministry of Education. The Councils governing respectively the six counties and the two boroughs form
the Local Education Authorities, which, as in England, function through education committees. From the viewpoint of
control, the schools may be classified under three groupings.
All primary and secondary schools completely supported and
controlled by the L.E.A.'s are known as county schools, as
in England. Primary and secondary schools owned by private
groups, which are recipients of aid and under only limited
control by the L.E.A.'s are known as voluntary schools. In
addition there are independent schools, not to be confused
with the voluntary institutions. These receive no public aid,
but are subject to state inspection.

There are three progressive stages in the educational
process: primary, secondary and further. Compulsory education starts at the age of five, when the child proceeds to the
primary school. This level terminates at eleven plus, after
which the child enters one of three streams, or types of secondary schools, according to his ability and aptitude: intermediate, grammar, and technical. Intermediate secondary
schools (eleven plus to sixteen) are for children who do not

qualify for grammar secondary. They are the equivalent of the British modern secondary. The grammar secondary schools (eleven plus to eighteen) for those of higher ability are similar to the British grammar school and admit to the universities. The technical secondary (eleven plus to sixteen or eighteen) offers specialized training for young people with suitable aptitude in the technical field. The expenses of county schools -- primary and secondary -- are completely defrayed from public funds.

Religious instruction is compulsory in every primary and secondary school whether county or voluntary and the school day must begin with a collective act of worship on the part of the pupils. A conscience clause applies and children upon application of parents may be excused from both of these requirements. Clergymen or other properly appointed persons may come into the county schools and instruct the children of their denomination during the time set aside for religious instruction. Thus the Catholic priest has the legal right to give instruction to Catholic children in county schools. As a matter of fact very few Catholic children attend the county schools. Children who do not take denominational religion attend classes where an agreed syllabus of Christian doctrine "not distinctive of the tenets of any particular denomination" is taught.

Voluntary schools, the majority of which are under Catholic management, have complete control over the manner of conducting the religious instruction and of the act of worship, which the law enjoins. The schools can be thoroughly Catholic in aim and atmosphere. Most of the teachers in the primary schools are laymen and laywomen. In the exceptional cases, members of religious congregations are the teachers.

The appointment of teachers in Catholic schools is left to the pastor, who by virtue of the office is also manager. The schools are subject to state inspection. There is no interference from the L.E.A.'s. The Ministry determines which textbooks are to be used in the secular subjects, but if Catholic authorities object to any particular text, the objection is taken seriously. Relations with the Ministry and with the

L.E.A.'s are reported to be friendly and constructive.

The voluntary schools, primary and intermediate secondary, receive generous government aid. This includes 65 percent of the cost of the building, equipment, and maintenance; 100 percent of the cost of teachers' salaries; and 100 percent of cost of textbooks, milk and meals. The voluntary schools participate fully in an extensive health service which provides free medical and dental treatment under the administration of the Ministry of Health. If the managers of a voluntary school, Protestant or Catholic, are willing to accept control of a school committee, four members of which are chosen by the school and two members by the L.E.A., the school can qualify for a 100 percent grant for heating, lighting, and other maintenance costs.

There are very few Catholic technical schools, but provision is made in state schools for denominational religious instruction daily during a half-hour period besides the ten minutes for assembly prayer. This contrasts with the two periods a week in the technical schools in the Republic.

Catholic secondary schools of the grammar type are managed by a board of pastors. A per capita grant for pupils in effective attendance is given by the government. Small fees are charged.

Catholics constitute about forty percent of the total population of Northern Ireland. A 1955 report of the Ministry gave 856 voluntary schools to 750 county schools. In terms of pupil enrollment the figures for Catholic children were: 1,023 in county schools; 1,302 in voluntary schools under the 4-2 committees; 84,518 in regular voluntary schools. For Protestant children the figures were: 104,226 in county schools; 9,176 in voluntary schools under the 4-2 committees; 2,810 in regular voluntary schools.[37]

As a whole the system in North Ireland is reported to be working smoothly and proving to be satisfactory to all concerned. It will be noted that the Catholics there have a better deal financially than in England, and the provisions for denominational religious instruction in the county schools seems to be a far more satisfactory arrangement and one more conducive to religious liberty than is the agreed syllabus in the county schools of Britain.

Chapter 8

Belgium and Italy: TRADITION PREVAILS

The Belgian people have had a practically unbroken Catholic tradition for over a thousand years. The sixteenth century religious upheaval left them staunch in their adherence to the old faith. Unfortunately, however, they did not prove themselves to be entirely immune to the anti-clerical influences emanating from eighteenth century rationalism. As a result the modern Belgian is likely to be a devout Catholic, a mere nominal Catholic with anti-clerical attitudes, or at the extreme end, an uncompromising unbeliever. Though the Catholic tradition, in general, has been the predominant force in the nation, long and bitter struggles between the conflicting religious and anti-clerical factions have preceded the "peace pact" which controls the educational policy in Belgium today.

The southern part of the land area which now constitutes the Kingdom of Belgium had come under Romanizing influences, while the northern part was overrun by Germanic peoples. The history of the nation through the centuries is largely the story of annexation from one country to another. Yet throughout the exigencies of political changes there was a pronounced feeling of national unity among the people. In 1830 after a war with the Netherlands, Belgium finally became independent.

The national character, as also the educational system of today, was shaped by the vicissitudes of the country's history. First among the characteristics of the people is a vibrant spirit of liberty, which had its genesis and nurture in those long periods of foreign rule when, resentful of its subjugation, the nation developed an ardent desire for and a deep appreciation of freedom. This passionate love for liberty is the basis of the Belgian Constitution, which guarantees the three great freedoms -- speech, education, and the press. Secondly, the unchanging allegiance of the majority of the people to the Catholic faith and their commitment to its principles accounts for their traditional insistence upon the importance of religious instruction in the educational plan.

Finally, the exigencies of their history has developed in the Belgian people a strong individualism, tenacity of purpose, a shrewd realism together with good humor that can be maintained even in the face of repeated adversities.[1]

But the diversified factors which have entered into the making of the nation have also left the Belgians with clearly marked, and often antagonistic, racial, linguistic, and political differences. The Flemings in the north are predominantly Catholic, Flemish-speaking, and right-wing in politics. The French-speaking Walloons in the south are religiously a diversified mixture of Catholics, anti-clericals, and unbelievers, and politically a medley of Christian Democrats, Liberals, and Socialists. In times of crises, Flemings and Walloons are one in their dedication to preserving the unity, well-being, and prosperity of the nation. At other times, Belgian society may be split into rival political, religious, and linguistic factions.

All this has relevancy to Belgian education, the whole structure of which is one of shrewd compromise. Basic to the system is the concept of educational freedom. Anyone may open his own school or educate his own children as he thinks fit, subject only to safety and health precautions set by the state. An accent on local and provincial influence in determining the details of educational policy balances nicely with central control; and an emphasis on the important role of religious instruction is countered with a recognition of parental right to choose the kind of religious instruction the child shall receive or to withdraw him from all such instruction.

In fact, it was the issue of religious instruction in the schools that, more than any other grievance, precipitated the revolt which expelled the occupying Dutch troops in 1830. William of Holland had set out to impose upon the people of Belgium a complete state monopoly of education, which did not even exempt the training of the Catholic clergy from control. Official decrees made the Dutch language the medium of instruction and excluded religious instruction from the public schools, substituting "common moral principles" instead. These restrictions and regulations ran counter to the

Belgian peoples' most cherished traditions. They refused
adamantly to accept them. Flemings and Walloons, Catholics
and Liberals were alike alienated. The whole country was
aroused at last from mere passive resistance to active revolt
and presented a united front in opposition to the Dutch rule.
The concerted action of all factions achieved the independence
of the country.

A Constitution was drawn up in 1831, proclaiming absolute freedom of worship, of the press, and of education. This
basic law still continues to be, with some amendments, the
first law of the country. Articles in the Constitution in respect to church and state relationships imply that there is
neither complete separation nor complete union. There is
mutual cooperation, but each society remains independent in
its own sphere.[2] The only constitutional reference to education is contained in Article 17 which states: "There shall be
freedom of opinion in teaching; all measures preventing this
are forbidden; the repression of offences shall be regulated
only by law. Public instruction given at the expense of the
State shall likewise be regulated by law."[3]

The two national parties, Catholic and Liberal, were
then and remained for some time in full agreement on the
government's educational policy. Education was to be "free,"
that is, anyone or any group might undertake to establish a
school. Religious instruction was to retain its place of primary importance in the education of the young. In practice,
for the next ten years the whole of elementary education in the
country was confined to church-directed schools and to schools
established by private citizens, both of which were subsidized
by the government.

This uncurtailed liberty and exclusion of all state control
led to some deplorable abuses. Anyone, qualified or not, had
the right to set himself up as a public teacher. Near chaos
developed. The defects of the system -- or lack of system --
called for intervention on the part of civil authorities, not indeed to take over the responsibility of parents, but to guide
and coordinate their efforts towards the development of efficient schools which the good of the child and the welfare of
society demanded.

After years of discussion between Catholics and Liberals
the first law organizing elementary education in Belgium, a
compromise measure, was passed unanimously by both chambers of Parliament. Education was still "free" but each
commune had to have at least one public school in its territory.
However, to fulfill this requirement, the local authorities
could either recognize and make use of an existing denominational school, or build their own public school. The communes
could select the teachers for their schools from the ranks of
graduates of either state-administered normal schools or
state-recognized denominational institutions and give them
their appointments free from any ecclesiastical control. The
communal and state officials had the right to inspect both public and recognized denominational schools, but the church
authorities could exercise complete control over the books
used for religious and moral instruction.

Religious and moral instruction was made a compulsory
part of the curriculum. It was to be given by the regular
teacher under the supervision of the church and according to
his own religious belief and that of the majority of the pupils,
but children of other faiths could be excused from attending
the formal instruction at the request of parents. The Flemings accepted French as the language of instruction in the
schools while the Walloons admitted the principle of "free"
Catholic schools subsidized by the state and operating alongside the public school system. "Free" applied to the schools
meant independent of the state and free from state control.

The phrasing of the statute proved to be open to various
and conflicting interpretations. Some Catholic bishops opposed
the legislation, seeing in the wording of some provisions possibilities that could prove dangerous to the Catholic school
system under a Liberal government. Nevertheless, this law
formed the basis of the Belgian educational system for thirty-
seven years and many of its features survive in the legislation
which underlies the system today.

During the decade of the 1840's the Liberals increased
in both number and influence and the party began to manifest
its latent anti-clerical tendencies more openly. Finally after
1850, under the influence and pressure of the Masonic Lodge,

the uneasy alliance between the Liberals and Catholics collapsed. The Liberals then initiated an open policy of systematic warfare against the Church and Catholic education. In
1879 the party succeeded in obtaining control of the government.

One of the first acts of the new government was the passage of an educational law, 1879, which Belgian Catholics still
refer to as the "Law of Misfortune." The measure, which
was maneuvered through both chambers by a very narrow margin, was the reverse in every respect of the law of 1842.
Religious instruction was excluded from public schools; graduates of free, that is, denominational normal schools, were as
such refused the state teaching certificate.[4] Direction of
education was given to the central government under a Department of Education. Each commune had to have at least one
secularized public school whether it was needed or not. The
right of communal authorities to adopt and make use of an
existing denominational school was abolished. The Catholic
members of Parliament refused to take part in the discussion
of the bill, thereby compelling the Liberals to shoulder the full
responsibility before the nation.

The Catholic masses were at least aroused from their
apathy. Reacting promptly, they organized an orderly but
vigorous campaign in opposition to the law and in favor of religion-oriented schools. The bishops issued an instruction
which forbade Catholic children to attend the secularized public schools. At the cost of great financial sacrifice, free
schools were opened everywhere. More than 2,000 state
teachers resigned, most of them taking up teaching positions
in the Catholic schools. Practically all Catholic children were
withdrawn from the public schools, so that many of them had
only teachers but no pupils. In judging this situation, it must
be recalled that Belgium was traditionally a Catholic country,
not pluralistic, with a strong Catholic culture. The law had
been framed under the influence of fanatic Freemasonry and
represented an open and deliberate attack upon religion in
general and the Catholic Church in particular. In fact, it was
aimed at the gradual de-Christianization of an overwhelmingly
Catholic population.[5]

The efforts of the Catholics were successful. In just one

year, they had established 2,000 schools attended by more
than sixty percent of the country's elementary school population. In five years they had established 3,385 schools and the
vast majority of Belgium children were attending them. In
the elections of 1884 the Liberals were badly defeated and the
Catholic party was brought back into power. The law of 1879
was formally repealed. New educational legislation was enacted which contained many of the provisions of the 1842
statute.[6]

Public instruction was again put under the direction of the
Ministry of the Interior, and the general control of education
was taken from the central government and given to the communes. The communes could either erect their own public
schools or recognize and make use of one or more existing
private or denominational institutions. In regard to their own
schools, the educational authorities could decide whether or
not religious and moral instruction would be part of the curriculum. However, if the commune decided against religious
instruction, the central government could force it to recognize
and subsidize one or more denominational schools, if at least
twenty fathers of families requested it. All elementary
schools, whether communal or free, were entitled to state
subsidies whenever they met the state requirements as to
teacher qualification, curriculum, and examinations.

In 1895 additional educational legislation complementing
that of 1884 was enacted. The central government was
thenceforth to subsidize Catholic schools directly. It was to
divide equally its subsidies between the public schools and all
confessional schools which were willing to accept both an official curriculum and state inspection. The provinces and the
communes were permitted to give additional subsidies to denominational schools. The communal authorities no longer
could exercise the right to decide the question of religious instruction, which was henceforth to be compulsory in all public
schools. It was to be given either at the beginning or the end
of the school day in order to meet the greater convenience of
those pupils who, at the request of parents, were excused
from attending. Later, the Minister of Education in a further
effort to respect the differing religious views of the pupils

interpreted the law as demanding that the general teaching in
the public schools had to be religiously neutral even if only one
pupil was legally excused from attending the formal religion
course.[7]

The Liberals bitterly opposed the new school laws. They
were now vigorously abetted in their opposition by the Socialists who as an organized party had entered the political field
in 1885 and by 1894 had obtained seats in Parliament. Anti-
Catholic provinces and communal authorities undercut the
central government's subsidies to the denominational and private schools by discriminatingly excluding these schools from
all provincial and communal aid. They did all that was possible to eliminate religious influences from the public schools
and to diffuse an anti-clerical and frequently an anti-Catholic
spirit. The bitter feud between the Catholics and anti-clericals continued until the outbreak of World War I.

Despite the opposition of the Liberal-Socialist minority,
who left the chamber floor shouting their disapproval, the
Catholic majority passed a new education law in 1914 which
consolidated previous legislation and elaborated it by adding
several innovations. This law laid the basis of the school
policy which was to endure until 1954. The war interrupted
the implementation of the statute for the duration.

By 1919, with the war over, the old bitterness had died
down somewhat and the controversy over the educational issue
seemed to be a thing of the past. New legislation revived the
1914 law, adding new features without changing the essentials
of the old. Three types of schools were to be subsidized from
public funds: public or provincial and communal schools;
private adopted schools; and private adoptable schools. The
law stated that instruction was to be given free in all these
schools.[8]

Each commune was to have at least one public elementary
school. It was to be controlled directly by the local civil
authorities, who appointed the teachers and drew up the
school regulations and curriculum. Costs were to be shared
by the central government, the provinces, and the communes.
The communes were given permission under certain conditions
to substitute or replace a communal school with an existing

denominational school, "for which the commune optionally assumed some varying expenses." Such a private school was termed a "private adopted" school. The conditions of adoption were defined in Article 15 of the statutes. The school had to be in a convenient place; the teachers had to be of Belgian nationality and possess a state certificate; the school had to follow the academic program required by law and accept inspection by the national government. Religion had to be a part of the school program.

The charges that the commune assumed by such adoption included a supplementary payment on the teachers' salaries which brought them up to the level paid public school teachers. The central government was responsible for the payment of the minimal salary. The commune also gave free supplies to children of necessitous families. In addition the province gave to the adopted school the same amount that it was paying to communal schools. Expenses for heating, light, and upkeep were paid according to individual contracts drawn up between the civil authorities and the adopted schools at the time of adoption. Financially the principal difference between the public and the private adopted was the fact that the owners of the private school received no aid toward the erection of the building or for expansion of the plant and repairs.

The adoptable schools were "private schools which theorectically had all the qualifications for adoption, but which enjoyed no advantages given by contract on the part of the communes." [9] As long as it was not adopted, the adoptable school was not required to give religious instruction. Financially, the adoptable school received the basic teachers' salaries from the national government and medical care and supplies for necessitous children. The province was responsible for school supplies.

One section of the law stated: "The salary of teachers, not married and living in community, of the communal, adopted and adoptable schools is fixed at half the salary." [10] That meant that teachers who were members of religious communities received only half of the basic salary paid by the central government.

The general principle was laid down that there must be

religious teaching in the primary schools. An exception, we have noted, was made in regard to adoptable schools. However, since practically all the adopted and adoptable schools were Catholic schools, religious instruction was actually an integral part of the curriculum. The law invited official representatives of the various religious denominations to come into the schools and give the instruction, but they could delegate any other person, including the regular teacher, to do the teaching. Children whose parents requested it were excused from following the courses. In classes of pupils of different religious convictions the law ordered that the teacher "abstain from attacking the persons or the religious convictions of the families of the children entrusted to their care." [11]

This then was the educational situation in Belgium in 1950. The Catholics were obliged to build their own schools, but the government cared for practically all the other expenses of the elementary schools. On the secondary level, Catholic schools received no financial aid at all, but had to depend on tuition fees and other private sources for support. For technical private schools, at least seventy-five percent of the teachers' salaries were paid by the government. There was a high correlation between the amount of help given and the enrollments in the private schools on the various levels.

In 1950 the Christian Social Party, which had been organized to represent the Catholic position, came into power. Under the leadership of M. Pierre Harmel, the Minister of Education, the government proceeded to develop the public schools to the maximum of their need. The Minister then turned his attention to those two areas in which the private institutions had been neglected, namely, the secondary and the technical schools. The Constitution granted freedom of teaching; but freedom of teaching, Harmel argued, to be effectively safeguarded, presupposes that the non-state establishments are enabled to offer to parents of limited means the same conditions of reductions and gratuities offered by state schools. From the principle of freedom of education evolves the state's obligation to subsidize non-state schools.

Following the precedent on the primary level, the government proceeded to authorize subsidies to the two types

of private secondary schools which would be sufficient to ensure their maintenance. The schools, on their part, were
required to grant a reduction of school fees to parents of
modest means under the same conditions as those offered to
families of children attending the public schools and to pay to
lay teachers salaries equal to those paid to their colleagues
in state schools. The religious groups would still have to
find from private sources the financial means of building, enlarging, or repairing their schools, no small burden in those
post-war years.

Limited as this aid for private schools was, the old animosities from the Liberal-Socialist combination flared anew.
The Socialists accused the Christian Social Party of endangering the government's fiscal policies by its "give-away" program. The anti-clerical campaign was intensified. In the
elections of 1954 the Socialists succeeded in gaining control
of the government through a coalition with the Liberals.
Though the Socialists and the Liberals were diametrically
opposed on many issues, they were united in being systemati-
cally hostile in varying degrees to the idea of religion in education. The coalition proceeded immediately to put through
a series of anti-clerical educational laws under the leadership
of the Socialist premier, Achille Van Acker, and the Minister
of Education, Leopold Collard.

Among other provisions, their educational bill proposed
that the mixed committees representing state and non-state
schools, which had been established to settle problems common to the two types of schools, were suppressed. The state
educational network was to be greatly extended. The state
for financial reasons, it was argued, would be compelled to
reduce the grants given to private schools. The state was not
only to control all the conditions set down for the allocation of
what grants were to be given but also to control the curriculum taught and the standard of efficiency in subsidized private
schools. Grants accorded by the state were to be allocated
in the form of fees directly to teachers, not as heretofore to
the schools. New private schools could be opened only if
they could be proved "economically and socially" necessary.
The lay staff in the private schools were to be protected from

"all arbitrary treatment."[12]   For this purpose an Appeal
Committee was to be created to which all teachers who considered themselves wronged in any way might have recourse.
Another bill proposed that only graduates of state normal
schools could be appointed to teach in elementary, secondary,
and normal schools of the state.

Hostile in spirit and unacceptable as the suggested changes
obviously were, Catholics were convinced that the ultimate aim
of the proposed measures went deeper than their surface meaning suggested.   It was felt that the bill represented an attack
on the traditional freedom of the Belgian provinces and communes by the centralization of educational control in the capital and eventually by the establishment of a state monopoly of
education.   In this way the ultimate aim could be attained,
namely, the formation of Belgian youth according to socialistic
ideals.[13]   The move to cut subsidies was seen as another
means to the attainment of the same objective.   Catholics
would have to charge high tuition fees, which many parents
could not pay; the children would thus be forced into public
schools.   The final outcome of all these changes was nothing
less than the destruction of religious influence in public life
and the de-Christianization of society.[14]

Opposition by Catholics to the school proposals was
prompt and vigorous, taking the form mainly of mass meetings
and demonstrations.   One hundred thousand Catholics jammed
the public square of Brussels on March 26, 1955, in protest
against the bill.   Fifteen thousand paraded for three and a half
hours through the streets of Liège in July.   These and other
demonstrations made it clear to the government that a responsible and popular opposition to the proposed educational reform
existed in the country, a fact which the socialist government
had long persisted in denying.   The bishops spoke out against
the measure because they interpreted it "as evidence of hostility and scorn of Catholic teaching and of a policy destined to
make undenominational and lay teaching predominate in the
country."   The proposed law, they declared, "attacks the
liberty of conscience of the citizens."[15]   Nevertheless, on
July 21, 1955, the Socialist-Liberal coalition managed to complete legislative action on the bill.   The Christian Social Party

members left the Senate in protest before the voting took place. The new law tightened state control over religious schools. It cut subsidies to the elementary institutions by ten million dollars. Under the previous government 25,000 Belgian francs were allotted for each student in public secondary schools, and 8,000 for each student in private schools. Collard cut the private schools' allotment to 3,497 francs. Furthermore, no additional Catholic schools could be built without the express permission of the government. The Minister of Education insisted that the purpose of all these measures was only to help "the growth of education" in Belgium, that no hostility toward Catholics was intended.

The Belgian hierarchy rejected such explanations, however, and denounced the law as a transgression of Belgian traditions and of parental rights. "It attacks," they declared, "the freedom of conscience of parents who have to choose between secular institutions upon which the state has lavished material advantages and the free institutions which will surely impose upon them burdens which will be heavy."[16]

The bishops set up the Family and School Association, the purpose of which was to collect and apportion the additional financial support the Catholic schools would need. Catholics responded with generosity and determination, recalling that earlier episode in their history when in 1879 their ancestors, after the passage of the "Law of Misfortune" had rallied to the defense of their rights and within a year had built new schools to replace those taken over by the government. In 1956 the Family and School Association collected 170,000,000 Belgian francs. Although this sum represented great financial sacrifices on the part of Belgian Catholics, it could scarcely compare with the loss sustained by the government's action.[17]

Catholics indeed tried to make the best of a bad situation but the growing dissatisfaction with it among the people was an indication that it could not continue. Finally both parties to the feud began to realize that the internecine strife was destroying the very roots of the country's educational system and that the time had come to take the school issue completely out of politics and settle the question once and for all. The Belgians' traditional love of freedom and aptitude for compromise came again to the fore.

In this climate of feeling the elections of 1958 brought Gaston Eyskens of the Christian Social Party to head the government as the new Premier. The Premier felt he had received a clear mandate from the voters to resolve the ancient problem of church-state relationships in education. The Socialist and Liberal parties understood well that they had lost the election mainly because of their anti-Catholic policies, and, if for no other reason than political expediency, they were ready to bring about a lasting solution. A series of meetings were held with the representatives of the three parties and of the Church.

Sincere efforts to resolve the issue in a manner as acceptable as possible to all concerned terminated in a settlement referred to as the "School Pact" (Pacte Scolaire). The agreement was reached November 6, 1958, and the bill based on the Pact was passed May 29, 1959, by 191 votes for the pact against two opposing it, the negative votes having been cast by communist deputies.

The Pact, ending the centuries long dispute, laid down the principles on which future governments were to base their policy with regard to the denominational schools. A shrewd commentator has described the Pact as a "beautiful compromise between the maximum requirements of Catholics and the minimum non-Catholics were ready to give."[18] Noteworthy are the words with which the agreement begins: "A generous and spirited policy of educational expansion being one of the principal objectives of every government in future years. . . effective aid should be given to all the forms of education recognized as valid."

The compact was concerned with rights of the public authorities as well as with the rights of parents and of the Church in education. It gave the assurance to Catholics that, regardless of the party in power, their financial situation would remain sound. In addition to settling the church-state relationships in education, the Pact extended free primary and secondary education, enlarged the scholarship system, and made arrangements for teacher placement. The agreement is to last for twelve years and provision is made for its reconsideration at the end of that period.

Belgium's School Pact in Operation

The fundamental principle underlying the whole system of education in Belgium is freedom, that is, the right of parents to have their children educated according to their wishes and conscience. This right, we have noted, is first of all guaranteed by the Constitution, which allows anyone to open a school. The Pact safeguarded this right in several clauses. It declares, for example, that if there is no school of the type desired within reasonable distance of the child's home, the state will be compelled, upon the written request of a number of parents, to open a new school or to refund travel expenses to an existing denominational school, or to admit for grant purposes an existing denominational school whose staff ratio of recognized diploma holders would not, under the new law, qualify it to receive subsidies.[19]

Under the Pact, therefore, and in harmony with Belgium's traditions, there is a dual system: schools built and controlled by the state, provinces, or communes; and schools built and controlled by private groups, which are, in practice, practically all under Catholic auspices. The Pact disregards the old designations of "adopted" and "adoptable" in regard to the private schools. It redefines the schools as "official" and "free." An official school is one founded by the state, province, commune or some other organization of a public character. A free school is one that respects the philosophical or religious views of the parents. The agreement places the schools of the two categories on an equal footing. Fees are abolished up to the age of eighteen in schools subsidized by the state.

The present law prescribes that the curriculum of all public primary and secondary schools is to offer a choice between religious instruction or lessons in lay morality. According to the wishes of parents, a priest or a minister of the appropriate denomination, or a delegate chosen by him, will give the religious instruction during school hours twice a week in any of four recognized religions: Catholic, Protestant, Anglican, and Jewish. The churches also have the right to appoint the inspectors of such courses. Any parent who does not wish his child to attend the religion class may apply for a dispensation, which is readily given. The child will then be obliged to follow a special course of study in what is termed non-sectarian morals.

The provisions relating to primary denominational schools, which are practically all Catholic, are based on the principle that the right of parents to choose the kind of education to be given to their children implies that they have at their disposal and within a reasonable distance a school which accords with their choice and that this choice will not have to be made at unreasonable financial sacrifice.

The Catholic school system in Belgium seeks only to live, not to destroy the state system. Catholics consequently settled for less public aid than that received by the official schools. The state pays the lay teachers in primary schools the standard minimum salary, which local authorities may supplement to bring it up to that of the teachers in official schools. Religious teachers, that is, Brothers and Sisters, in the primary schools receive sixty percent (instead of the former fifty percent) of the salary normally paid to teachers in public schools. Priests and religious teaching in secondary and technical schools, however, receive the full minimum salary, which is increased by fifteen percent after fifteen years of service. All teachers in the free schools share in retirement benefits.

Catholics could easily have had state subsidies for building and remodeling their school but decided against it because of the opening it might give to undue state control. They settled instead for an annual per capita subsidy for operating expenses, which varies according to the type of school. In 1961 the grants approximated: $15 at kindergarten level; $20 at elementary; and $65 at secondary level. Grants for equipment are made up to sixty percent of the cost. Provincial and communal governments are empowered to grant additional subsidies. The National Student Fund, which awards scholarships, bases its decisions on juries of teachers representing all types of schools. Likewise graduates of all schools, official and free, are eligible for the scholarships which usually average about 4,800 Belgian francs a year.

To receive subsidies the free schools have to meet certain reasonable requirements. The teaching staff must hold recognized diplomas and the program of studies must be comparable to that offered in official schools. The Ministry has the right of inspection, but Catholic schools are permitted to have their own body of inspectors, who, however, follow the directives of the Ministry. The object of the inspection is simply to see that national standards are maintained in all schools. Subsidized schools may charge no fees. Religion must be taught for two hours weekly, but this regulation does not bar the Catholic schools from increasing the time allowed for religious instruction or interfere with efforts to integrate Christian principles and atmosphere in all aspects of the school program. A minor point of controversy was settled with the decision that holidays in both systems are to be uniform.

More than half of all pupils in the Belgian elementary and secondary schools are in free institutions and practically all of the latter are under Catholic auspices. The Ministry of Education in 1961 gave the following percentages for enrollments on the primary level: in Catholic schools 51.58 percent; in state schools, 8.24 percent; in communal schools, 40.06 percent. Provincial schools care for the fractional remainder.[20]

In line with the Belgian idea of freedom in education there are a small number of schools completely independent of the state. These receive no subsidies but are supported by fees and income from other private resources. To obtain recognition for their diplomas, they must submit to limited inspection by the Ministry.

Training colleges for primary teachers are operated by the national, provincial, and communal governments, or by private agencies. Most of the private normal colleges are under the auspices of the Catholic Church and are owned and controlled by religious congregations. For the training of elementary school teachers, in 1958 there were sixteen state colleges, five provincial, seven communal, and fifty-three free institutions, practically all Catholic.[21]   The training of teachers for the lower secondary schools is carried on in

some thirty-eight écoles normales moyennes. Of these,
twenty-four were free and fourteen public, but in terms of enrollments, pupils were almost evenly divided between the two
types. Teachers for upper secondary schools are generally
trained in the universities.

The pattern of public subsidies to private schools applies
to the normal colleges also. Religious instruction or classes
in morals are required subjects for all pupils. To insure uniformity in standards of training, all subsidized institutions
are under the general supervision of state authorities. Though
considerable freedom is allowed the private colleges in establishing their program of studies, a degree of uniformity is
achieved because subsidies are granted only for courses approved by the Ministry of Education.[22]

There is no highly centralized control over teacher appointments, as exists, for example, in France. The teachers
are appointed by the authority responsible for the school --
public authorities for official schools and the Church authorities for Catholic schools.

The controversial question of whether teacher positions
in official schools should be filled by graduates of the church-
related normal schools has received a compromise settlement.
The Ministry of Education announced in January, 1959, that in
accordance with the Pacte Scolaire first priority for positions
in the public nursery, elementary, and lower secondary
schools would go to graduates of the public normal colleges.
Similarly, graduates of universities not affiliated with a
religion would have priority for positions in upper secondary
schools, except that the existing ratio between the graduates
of church-related and graduates of non-church-related universities was to be maintained.

At the level of higher education, the state provides two
universities. A "free" secular university is established at
Brussels. Catholics have their own university at Louvain.
While remaining completely independent in the management of
its affairs, the Catholic University of Louvain receives from
the state subsidies up to sixty percent of all costs. Louvain
has 16,000 of the total 38,000 students attending universities.[23]

Is the Pacte Scolaire Satisfactory?

Although the agreement embodied in the School Pact is not regarded as perfectly satisfactory from the Catholic viewpoint, as a compromise measure it fulfills to a great extent the desires of Belgian Catholics, both hierarchy and parents. Moreover, the fact that such an accord was reached is certainly an important and outstanding achievement when one considers the passionate conflict over the school issue which had riven the nation for over a century. In these days of totalitarian intransigence, the Pact provides a valuable study of how a modern democracy can solve a bitterly controversial issue by democratic processes and on the basis of principles of the natural law. It serves as an example, too, of the moderation of the Catholic Church in pressing her demands for justice even in countries where, nominally at least, Catholics are the overwhelming majority.

Recognition of parental rights in education would seem to be the key to the entire solution. The Premier himself in announcing the Pact stated that the chief principle behind it was "the recognition of the parents' right to choose the type of education they desired their child to receive." The function of the state is to see to it that this right can be exercised without attached difficulty or penalty. Thus, the demands of distributive justice are also met. A second key to the solution is regard for the welfare of every child in the nation and not the mere safeguarding of a particular system of schools. The responsibility of Belgian legislation in educational matters is not to a system but to the child to be educated. The rights of the religious conscience are safeguarded. Religious instruction is provided in the official schools for those who want it and in accordance with the parents' religious convictions. Those who do not wish religious instruction may withdraw, but the state in view of its own interests demands that the child receive at least instruction in natural morals. Practically, in the opinion of some observers, the spirit and influence of some official schools tends towards rationalism, but this situation arises not from the Pact itself but from the failure of teaching personnel to observe the neutrality which the Pact requires.

The settlement has taken the school issue out of partisan politics and changed it from a contest between the Church and the state to a matter of general social progress. It has lessened tension among the political parties and among the people of the nation. It accordingly is a presage of renewed national strength. All in all, the Belgian compromise offers an example of educational justice that might well be studied by those nations that have not yet resolved the issue.

ITALY

The area of Europe embraced by what is now Italy has had a long and often tumultuous history. For present purposes the story to a great extent is irrelevant. It need only be noted that throughout the Christian centuries the ideals and traditions of the Catholic Church, if seemingly dormant on the surface, remained strong forces behind the nation's cultural development. Fragmentation into warring city states and principalities characterized the area for over a thousand years. Aspirations towards national unity were awakened towards the beginning of the nineteenth century. The control by the Church of a large section of the country comprising the papal states resulted in the emergence of contending factions, one group opposing papal control and contending for national unity, the other favoring the papacy.

Partial unity was achieved in 1861 by the proclamation of the Kingdom of Italy from Sardinia. In 1871 with the government's takeover by force of the papal states and Rome, Italy emerged as a unified nation and Rome was made the capital of the new kingdom.

As elsewhere in Europe education was traditionally the responsibility of the Church, and in Italy it remained completely such until the last quarter of the eighteenth century. The first attempt at state control was made by Sardinia with the establishment in 1771 of a state system modeled after that of the German Frederick II. After Napoleon's conquest of the Northern provinces, he set up a closely centralized system of education similar to that which he had already established in France.

This provided the model for the first educational legislation in Italy, the Casati law of 1857, on which modern Italian education has been built. A reflection of the French pattern, it was based on the principle that education must be a primary concern of the state. It called for the establishment of a Minister of Public Instruction. Compulsory elementary education was to be followed by various types of secondary instruction in vocational and technical schools and in the classical ginnasi-licei, leading to the universities and teachers' training colleges.

The Church was excluded in principle from educational control, but religious instruction as part of the Italian heritage was prescribed for the schools. It was accorded the first place in the syllabus on the primary level. Non-Catholics and those whose parents declared that they themselves provided for instruction were dispensed. In secondary schools religious teaching was entrusted to an officially nominated Spiritual Director whose responsibility it was to guide the pupils in the fulfillment of their religious duties.[24] In the teacher-training schools religious instruction also was given first place in the program of studies and was entrusted to the professor of pedagogy and ethics until 1861, when a special teacher of religion became responsible for it. This arrangement was made for the purpose of preparing primary teachers who would have to give religious instruction to children in the primary schools.

The administration of elementary education, as in France, was delegated to the communes. Later (1911), because of mismanagement, the responsibility was handed over to the provinces. Private schools were allowed to function only on condition that they met state requirements. The Casati law also called for minute regulation by government of higher educational institutions to the extent that for all practical purpose the universities became organs of the state, subject to a control and uniformity that tended to stifle creativity and healthful growth.

After national unification in 1871, the anti-clerical forces obtained control of the government. There were bitter feelings between those loyal to the Holy See and those who had supported the seizure of the papal states and favored the new kingdom. The conflict between the Holy See and the kingdom led to the selection of government leaders more and more from the ranks of those hostile to the Church. In fact, the Quirinal entertained a certain mistrust of Catholics who practiced their faith openly.

The hostility of the government to the Church was soon manifested in the educational field. Religious instruction was in practice abolished in the urban elementary schools by the Coppino Act of 1877. The law also abrogated the office of Spiritual Director in the grammar schools and teachers' colleges. In 1879 religious instruction was eliminated in the latter institutions. Theological faculties at the universities were abolished. Nevertheless, religion continued to be taught in the village schools until 1908. After that date, the teacher could refuse to teach the subject and the instruction could be omitted if a majority of the local authorities opposed it.[25] In general, education became secularized throughout the land. Not only did all outward religious emblems disappear from the schools, but the very name of God and any allusion to His existence were banished. Even the teachers and professors who were, themselves, practicing Christians had been trained to be silent on religion questions in conformity with the strict liberalism which barred all religion notions from the public schools. If religion were mentioned at all, it was most likely with irony or ridicule only.[26]

After World War I hostility toward the Church on the part of the government was somewhat mitigated. The citizens who had been faithful to the Church had also proven themselves loyal and courageous citizens of their country. The obstacles placed by the Holy See to Catholics' participating in politics were withdrawn, particularly after the formation of a political party with a Christian bias. The success of this party demonstrated that it represented a broader movement than that controlled by the papal party.[27]

The country, however, was exhausted from the war and disillusioned by the results of the Versailles Treaty. Bitter feelings again began to erupt. Neither the group loyal to the papacy nor the government party was strong enough to lead the nation to unity. A post-war economic crisis added a new source of disorder. The government, weak and unpopular, was unable to stem the tide of dissatisfaction and disorder.

The discouraging situation in the country offered an opportunity for anyone promising reform and betterment. It was in these circumstances that Mussolini organized his new national movement of Fascism, a conglomeration of many elements never completely synthesized into a distinct ideology. With his Black Shirts he marched upon Rome, promising to restore both order and the grandeur of Italy on the basis of its great and glorious past. Victory came easily under existing conditions.

It soon became evident that the acceptance of the aim of the Fascists meant acceptance of the state as absolutely supreme. Mussolini appointed Giovanni Gentile, a scholar and philosopher of some renown, as Minister of Education. An opponent of democracy, Gentile was a follower of Fichte and Hegel, accepting wholeheartedly Hegel's idea of the state as a supra-personality. For him, the primary aim of education was to train the child to identify himself with the state and to devote his life to its perpetuation. The state had the right to demand this sacrifice because, according to Gentile, it was identical with all individuals and society within it. It was, moreover, the only link that joined individuals and society. The modern Italian state had a world mission similar to that of the Roman Empire. The historical destiny of the Italian people was to realize this mission through Fascism. These ideals and ideas of Gentile served as the inspiration of Italian life and education throughout the entire Fascist regime, although he himself did not remain long as Minister of Education.

Gentile advocated the teaching of Catholic doctrines in the schools, not because he himself accepted them as true, but because he regarded the Catholic Church as a peculiarly Italian institution and a reservoir of tradition. Hence, although Fascism began with an explicitly anti-clerical program, Mussolini, following Gentile's theory, gave a recognition to religion in education that his predecessors in the government had refused. The Church, however, was allotted only a subordinate position in reference to the state; in fact, the effort was made to have it simply serve the state's purpose.

In 1924 the state invited the Prefects of Study to put public
school premises at the disposal of the ecclesiastical authorities
outside school hours. At the beginning of the school year
1926-1927, about 30,000 pupils in the secondary schools could
receive religious instruction in state school buildings. In the
next year half the school population was following these religion
courses, although they were held in only a few establishments.[28]
It should be noted that at this time Mussolini made the providing of facilities for religious instruction in the state schools
voluntary, not compulsory, on the Prefects of Study.

Finally, after he was firmly established in power,
Mussolini decided that it was expedient to make peace with the
Vatican, a movement that had, as a matter of fact, been on
foot for a number of years. He took into consideration Italy's
strong religious heritage, which he regarded as wise to foster
rather than to destroy. In February, 1929, he concluded a
treaty with the Holy See. The Lateran Treaty, as signed by
Cardinal Gasparri and Mussolini, consists in reality of three
pacts: a treaty between the Holy See and the Italian government concerning the territorial status and rights of the Holy
See in relation to international law; a concordat between the
Holy See and the Italian government regarding the position of
the Church in Italy; and a supplementary financial convention.[29]

It should be recalled that after the seizure of the papal
states by force in 1871, Pius IX and his successors, as a ges-
ture of disapproval of the high-handed manner in which the
unification had been achieved and as a demonstration of their
demand for territorial independence, had made themselves
voluntary prisoners in the Vatican and refused to have any official relations with the Italian government. The Lateran
Treaty resolved that situation. The State of Vatican City,
over which the Holy Father had sovereign jurisdiction, was
created as a political entity recognized in international law.

By the Concordat, religious instruction, optional since
1926, became obligatory in all state primary and secondary
schools for those pupils whose parents did not desire them to
be dispensed. In secondary schools the religion class was to
be held for a period of one hour a week, the instruction to be
given by a professor approved for the purpose by the Ordinary

of the diocese. Priests, for the most part, were to be selected as professors. Full liberty was accorded for the establishment and management of private schools.

Eventually Gentile's ideology proved too unrealistic for
the more practical purposes and military ambitions of the
Fascist government. He was released after two years. Mussolini adhered in a general way to the provisions of the Lateran
Treaty in regard to education, but he began to utilize groups
outside the schools as more effective means towards the
achievement of his aims. The Opera Nazional Balilla, an official Italian youth movement, was organized. It usurped most
of the prerogatives of the schools. The members were en-
listed in the service of the all powerful and beneficent state.
All had to take the oath of allegiance to the Duce: "In the name
of God and Italy, I swear that I will carry out the Duce's orders and serve with all my strength and, if need be, with my
life the cause of the Fascist Revolution." Their motto was:
"Believe; obey; fight."

Mussolini recognized at the same time the necessity of
controlling education in the schools to ensure the success of
his political experiments in Fascism. Central control by the
government was strengthened. All teachers were required
either to be members of the party or to take a loyalty oath to
educate "citizens loyal to country and to the Fascist regime."
Textbooks were rewritten to fit Fascist ideology and aims and
to inculcate loyalty and devotion in their users. Without absolutely prohibiting them, efforts were made to make the
private schools unattractive. The idea of the supremacy of
the state reached its culminating point in 1935 when Casare
de Vecchi, a violent Fascist leader, became Minister of Education. He dissolved consultative educational bodies and
vested all power in the Minister himself.

Like its German counterpart, the Fascist regime and the
education it fostered collapsed at the end of World War II and
were followed by several efforts towards a more democratic
system. A new Constitution was drawn up in 1947. Article
7, which deals with the church-state relationship, declares:

The State and the Catholic Church are each in its

own sphere independent and sovereign. Their relations are regulated by the Lateran Pacts. Modification of the Pacts, mutually agreed upon, do not
require the procedure necessary for the amendment
of the Constitution.

Articles 3, 8, 9, and 20 deal with religious freedom, which is
guaranteed to all, while at the same time the Catholic religion
is recognized as the official religion of Italy.

Remnants of leftist groups which had gone underground
during the Fascist regime united with communists to reassert
themselves. For a while there was concern that Italy might
come under Soviet control. Practicing Christians, however,
were sufficiently aroused and the Christian Democrats succeeded in 1948 in gaining control of the governmental reins.
The Italian Christian Democrat party corresponds broadly to
the Christian Democrats in West Germany, the Christian Social Party in Belgium and the M.R.P. in France. It supports
the policy of the Catholic Church in its desire to permeate
politics with Christian principles. The hold of the party on
the government has been shaky and coalitions with other political groups has been necessary. More recently it has been
forced to form a coalition with the Socialist Party, which formerly had been allied with the communists. These coalitions
have prevented the Party from achieving some of its objectives
and many of its preferences have been compromised. In June,
1964, for example, Premier Aldo Moro and his cabinet were
forced to resign over the question of increased state aid for
private schools, most of which are Catholic. Objections had
come from the Socialists, who claimed that the proposed increase was a violation of an agreement made with Moro's
Christian Democrats when the government was formed seven
months earlier. Two other coalition partners backed the Socialists in abstaining in the vote on the issue. The communist
leader then demanded that Moro and his government resign.[30]

The Functioning of Italy's Educational System
The present structure of Italy's school system is built
on compulsory attendance to the age of fourteen. Administra-

tion is centralized in a Ministry of Public Instruction and a network of state and provincial officers, somewhat in the manner of the French system. On the other hand, the Italian system shows a marked Germanic influence in its historical consciousness of and provision for regional differences and, of course, in its strong Catholic outlook.

On the completion of his primary course at the age of eleven, the pupil may pass to one of two kinds of intermediate or lower secondary schools: the scuola media run on traditional lines or a work-preparatory school, both lasting three years. These prepare for entrance into one of several types of higher secondary schools -- classical, technical, and teacher-preparatory -- the terms of which are from four to five years duration and on completion lead to the universities. In addition to the schools mentioned, there are the non-compulsory scuola materna, for children ages five to six, and a post-elementary course which pupils finishing the primary school may choose instead of one of the lower secondary schools.

The church-state relationships in education are still determined by the Concordat of 1929. Article 36 of the document declares that

> Italy considers the teaching of Christian doctrine in the form handed down by the Catholic tradition to be the foundation and crown of public education and, therefore, agrees that religious instruction should be introduced according to syllabi agreed between the Holy See and the State. Such instruction should be given by teachers approved by the ecclesiastical authorities. Only textbooks approved by ecclesiastical authorities shall be adopted.

Accordingly, religious instruction is given in all state schools in Italy and at all levels, with the proviso that children may be excused if parents desire it or declare that they provide the instruction otherwise. As a matter of practice, practically all the children in the schools attend religion classes.

Plans for the courses, in strictly Catholic form, are

worked out in each diocese by the bishop and school authorities
of the locality. When possible priests or religious are instructors, but because of lack of sufficient personnel, lay teachers,
approved by the ecclesiastical authority, more generally do the
teaching. Lay instructors, who may also be ordinary classroom teachers, must hold certificates issued by the diocese.
Revocation of the certificate immediately deprives the individual of the right to teach religion. All religion instructors receive state compensation at rates comparable to those paid
other teachers. Article 37 of the Concordat states that no
administrative or school activity can interfere with the religion
classes or religious practices. The amount of time given to
religion courses varies with the grade level, from one hour
per week in the first grade to five hours at the fifth grade level.

In addition to formal instruction in Catholic doctrine and
morals, the religious program includes daily prayers, religious music, reading of the Bible, and a study of the lives of
saints as they portray the Christian way of living. Opportunities are provided for participation in religious services and
the making of spiritual retreats. Beyond all this, religion is
expected to be the guiding force and the integrating factor in
the whole school program. Religion penetrates other subjects
such as history and reading. It is the first subject listed on
report cards sent to parents. Closely allied to the course in
religion is one on morals, civics, and physical education
taught as a unit.

Interesting is the official attitude toward religion in the
scuola materna, or kindergarten, as expressed in a decree
issued May 24, 1945:

> In religious instruction the behavior of the child
> during prayers must receive special attention.
> Essential religious ideas must be imparted with
> short stories on the life of Jesus, thus illustrating
> the infinite love of the Great Creator for all things
> created.[31]

Religious teaching is obligatory in all the types of secondary schools as well as in the primary school. One hour a

week is set apart for the instruction. The class is usually
taught by a priest or a religious chosen by the headmaster of
the school and approved by the ecclesiastical authority.
Where necessary lay teachers are appointed as assistants.
The ecclesiastical authority has the right and duty to provide
special training for teachers of religion and also to appoint
priest inspectors. The textbooks used must be approved by
the bishop. The program is agreed upon by the Holy See and
the government.[32] What has been said about correlating religion with other courses in the primary school applies also to
the secondary schools.

All of the above is the accepted theory in regard to religion in Italy's public schools. What is actually the practice?
No survey data are available, but it would seem practice varies from area to area.[33] Much is constantly being done by
ecclesiastical authorities to improve the situation and to make
the teaching more effective in the lives of the students. On
the other hand where communist influence is strong, efforts
are unceasingly made to undermine the religious teaching in
the schools. In some schools communist teachers indirectly,
or even openly, ridicule religious doctrine and practice. If
the regular teacher happens to be an unbeliever, he has it in
his power, though not legally, insidiously to weaken or destroy
the effects of religious instruction. Observation indicates
there is much of this in some areas of Italy.

Besides the public schools there are private primary and
secondary schools in Italy. Almost all of these are under
Catholic auspices. Article 29 of the Concordat states that
"religious foundations of any kind are allowed provided it is
clear that they answer the religious needs of the people and
that they impose no financial burden on the state." The Concordat does not touch specifically on elementary schools
maintained by the Church. A number of secondary schools
are conducted by the larger international religious congregations of men and women. The Catholic secondary institutions
have the same legal status as the state schools and can award
certificates of maturity admitting to the universities provided
their students have taken and passed state examinations successfully.

The private schools depend generally upon tuition charges
for support. Here and there the state, without definite legislation on the matter, has given aid. The Salesian Fathers
operate several elementary and secondary schools to give vocational training to poor children in southern Italy and receive
state grants. The state also maintains nursery schools which
are run by religious. It compels each commune to set up its
own patronage fund for needy pupils in private as well as in
public schools.

Because the private schools are tuition-charging and are
not generally attached to parishes for support and because of
the general poverty of Italy's population, the percentage of
students in Catholic private schools is dropping. Church
authorities point out the danger of a state monopoly in education. In 1961 non-state schools were taking care of only
about 8.7 percent of Italy's school population.[34]   There is no
constitutional provision against giving aid to the private
schools. Italy has no wall between Church and State, but Socialists and Communists resist efforts made by the Christian
Democrats to come to the financial aid of the private schools.

Primary school teachers are trained in a distinct type of
secondary school maintained by the state. In these, as in
other secondary schools, religious instruction is obligatory,
but two hours a week instead of the usual one hour is generally
the practice. Moreover, the courses are designed to prepare
the prospective teacher to give religious instruction in primary schools. Secondary school teachers receive longer and
more intensive training and for them also religious instruction
is included in the required course of studies.

In addition to the courses given in the training schools
and colleges, the Sacred Congregation of the Council has arranged for additional national and regional courses of study
to prepare catechists. The Catholic University of the Sacred
Heart in Milan has a professorship of catechetical pedagogy
for the faculty dealing with the training of teachers. In Rome
there are several schools for women providing opportunities
to study theology, notably "Regina Mundi," which is directly
under the Sacred Congregation of Universities and caters particularly to religious women, although lay women students are

admitted. The most complete and systematic work of preparation, however, is carried on in the regional seminaries. Many of the seminarians, while following lectures, teach catechism classes in the parishes. Several reviews devoted to catechetical teaching are published. Unquestionably, definite progress is being made in better preparation for catechetical work inside and outside the schools.

There are twenty-five general universities in Italy. Three institutions of university rank are under Catholic auspices. Some of the state universities have faculties in Sacred Theology. Article 39 of the Concordat safeguards the Catholic universities and seminaries under the Holy See from state interference. It is provided that degrees in Sacred Theology granted by faculties approved by the Holy See in the universities will be recognized by the Italian state. The same provision is made for certain diplomas granted by the schools of Vatican City. The appointment of professors at the Catholic University of the Sacred Heart in Milan and the Institute of Mary Immaculate connected with it is subject to the approval of the Holy See. The institution called the University of Social Studies established in 1948 receives funds allowed by the government to pay for the education of civil servants.

No one, undoubtedly, holds that the situation in regard to religious instruction in the Italian public schools meets the ideal demanded by Catholic principles. After almost one hundred years of secularism, it was to be expected that for a long time outcomes of the restoral of religious instruction in the schools would be indeterminate. In 1950 and 1955 the results were reported to be poor.[35] Hostility to the new teaching had to be overcome; catechists had to be obtained and prepared. Much progress along these lines is apparent. Students now recognize religion as a vital matter that cannot be ignored either at school or in after life.

The question of aid to private schools remains unsolved. Many religious leaders feel that unless the state is to obtain a virtual monopoly of education in Italy more aid must be forthcoming for the private schools.

Chapter 9

The German Federal Republic:
THE CONFESSIONAL SETTLEMENT

Emphasis on denominational religious instruction as an integral part of the school curriculum has been a practically unbroken tradition in the lander or states which now comprise the German Federal Republic (West Germany). Indeed, there was the same emphasis in the schools of the Democratic Republic (East Germany) until 1945, when the area was put under Russian control and was almost immediately communized. For centuries the principle that the child should be instructed in the religion of his parents was as much a matter of course in the German states as that he should be taught to read and write his mother tongue and this policy held whether the school was state-controlled or was managed by a private group. School controversies were waged during those centuries, but the arguments concerned such issues as the degree of state control over education, the efforts of the state to divert religious instruction to its own purposes, and the question of confessional versus inter-confessional schools.[1] Paradoxically, too, the German states were the first to establish strong state systems of education. Prussia was the leader and model in this development, laying down as early as 1794 the principle that education was definitely the function of the state.

These two historical features -- denominationalism and a pervasive state control -- are still outstanding characteristics of West Germany's educational system. Historians, in tracing these developments in education or, for that matter, other developments in Germanic history, are struck by the fact that invariably conflicts between force and freedom were involved, with the elements of force more frequently in the ascendancy.[2] Again, a brief review of these historical struggles provides a helpful perspective for understanding the unique solution of the church-state relationship in education which is found in Western Germany today.

A Nation is Born

With the collapse of the western division of the great Roman Empire, it was the Germanic peoples who became the
framers of a new Europe. After a period of wandering and
plundering, the various Teutonic tribes finally settled down
and set up throughout Western Europe small kingdoms and
principalities under feudal systems of government. Pagan
and semi-barbaric for the most part, these scattered peoples
became immediately the object of the Church's Christianizing
and civilizing efforts. The Church had apt instruments at
hand for the gigantic task: Benedictine monasticism, uniquely
suitable for this specific purpose; and Celtic missionaries,
still fired with the deep faith and ardent zeal which had been
implanted by St. Patrick several centuries earlier.

Hundreds of monasteries soon dotted the land, each
spreading among the inhabitants within a wide radius the light
of Christian truth and the arts of civilization. Forests were
cleared, and blossomed into gardens; swamps were drained
and became productive farms. The Franks who had settled in
ancient Gaul were the first of the tribes to be converted to
Christianity. By the eighth century the Germans beyond the
Rhine had embraced Christianity and by the thirteenth century
the tremendous task had been completed with the conversion
of the Prussians.

With Christianity came schools and learning. Under the
guidance of the Church, Teutonic vigor and initiative united
with Latin law and order to produce a new culture -- a new
civilization.[3] The synthesis culminated in the Carlovingian
dynasty. Under Charlemagne, one of the great leaders of all
time, the Western Empire, which was to last at least in modified form for over a thousand years, was established. Charles
placed great emphasis on education, ordering schools of all
types to be established and reproving abbots who had been lax
in this regard. But the work was by no means done. There
followed a long period of darkness when the light of learning
seemed to be all but extinguished, and the fire, which Christianity is, seemed to smolder under the debris of ignorance,
superstition, and disorder. But these were appearances only
and the period which historians refer to as the "dark ages"

was not so much a night closing out the light of a brilliant day
as the dawn struggling through to a new and brighter morning.

The light burst through in the thirteenth century. The
German lands not only shared in but contributed much to the
glory of that century. All types of medieval schools from the
elementary to the university flourished. The German monastic schools, particularly, rose to a higher plane than elsewhere. The Church controlled practically all the educational
facilities. Always the spiritual aim predominated; religion
was the integrating element of the entire educational process.
This continued to be true even after Renaissance influence
changed the emphasis from grammar and logic to a study of
the ancient classics.

Force and Freedom in Conflict

The Protestant Revolt had its origin in the Germanic
lands. It is not relevant to the present purpose to go into the
general facts of this explosive movement. No reliable historian denies that reform in the Christian Church was necessary.
The question may be, and has been raised, however, whether
the movement as it developed produced the needed reform.
Viewed from the perspective which time affords it would
seem the term Reformation does not accurately convey the
real nature of the catastrophic events of the sixteenth century
which, in reality, involved a revolt against the authority of
the ancient Church and culminated in breaking up the unity of
Christianity, thus destroying the one bond of unity among the
emerging national states.

Our primary concern here is the effects of the Revolt on
the schools. The immediate result in Germany, as elsewhere,
was calamitous. The historian F. Paulsen declares that the
ten years between 1525 and 1535 resulted in a "depression of
learning and education which is without parallel in history."[4]
In those German states where the Revolt prevailed the thousands of schools which had been conducted by Catholic parishes
and monasteries were forced to close. Learning stagnated.
Luther became aware of the havoc wrought and issued a call
for schools. Efforts were later made under the direction of
Melanchthon to build up a system of Protestant schools. In

this development we have the beginnings of those educational features which, as noted above, characterize the German schools today.

First was a renewed emphasis on denominational teaching. The schools of the Protestants were intended first of all to inculcate the doctrines of the new religion and to nullify the influence of the Catholic Church. Consequently, the teaching of the reform doctrines was stressed. Likewise, in areas where the people had remained faithful in their allegiance to Rome and the Catholic faith, the Catholic schools continued in existence and, as always, in them the Christian truths remained the integrating core of school life.

A second result was the trend to look toward the state for support in maintaining the schools since the churches of the reformers were unwilling or unable to provide the means. The princes and rulers readily acceded to requests for financial aid, seeing in their compliance an opportunity to advance their power in the spiritual as well as in the secular realm. With the support provided came various degrees of control, although at first the schools remained nominally under the supervision of the church officials. Furthermore, with the authority of the Pope denied, it became necessary to find another power to insure the acceptance of the new doctrines that the reformers favored. No other authority of sufficient strength was at hand except that of the civil rulers, so to them in their respective domains was given in Protestant theory the supreme control over religious matters. Thus from its inception, the Protestant church in Germany became essentially a state church. Religion and politics tended to be identified.

The secular rulers recognized that the schools were apt instruments which could be used to crystalize and preserve the spiritual power which had passed to a great extent into their hands. With this end in mind several of the German rulers issued school codes: Saxony and Brunswick in 1528; Hamburg in 1529; Wurtenberg in 1559. The princes in drawing up their codes acted as the heads of the state church in accordance with the doctrine that made the civil rulers also ecclesiastical rulers. Thus it would seem laws regarding education had for their object not so much the instruction of

the people or the promotion of learning as the assurance of
religious uniformity and the strengthening of the rulers' powers. The Treaty of Westphalia in 1648 assured the continuation of the status quo in Germany on the formula cuius regio
eius et religio, the principle that gave the ruler supremacy
over the religion of his subjects. In this manner were created
a system of state-church schools. These Protestant denominational schools of the post-Revolt period in Germany represent the transfer stage from the church school of the Middle
Ages to the state system of today.[5] Although the Lutheran
churches repeatedly proclaimed education to be a church function, the fact remained that the church was a state institution
deriving its educational authority from the state, whose educational power was supreme.[6] Little by little the princes
withdrew the administration of the schools from the church
officials and handed it over to civil officials.

Several German principalities such as Wurtenberg and
Gotha had established state systems of education in the seventeenth century, but Prussia was the first to establish a
national system free of church control and supervision.
Frederick William I (1688-1740) had 2,000 new schools built,
urged better preparation of teachers, and ordered the attendance at school of all children between the ages of five and
twelve. Frederick the Great (1740-1786) took a long step toward the nationalization of education when he made a complete
revision of the school code in 1763. The examination and
licensing of teachers by state-appointed inspectors were provided for, although the immediate supervision of the schools
was left in the hands of the Lutheran clergy.

In 1787 Baron von Zedlitz, who had been school officer
under Frederick the Great, prevailed upon his successor,
Frederick William II, to place the administration of Prussian
education under the control of a central board of experts, the
Oberschulkollegium. The administration of the school was
thus separated from that of the church and the former came
directly under state control even though the clergy were given
a prominent place on the new board.

In 1794 Frederick made a general codification of Prussian
education laws which contained the principle: "Schools and

universities are state institutions. . . Such institutions may
be established only with the knowledge and approval of the
state. All public and educational institutions are under the
supervision of the State and are at all times subject to its
examination and inspection."[7] Thus the principle that education was a function primarily of the state, not of the parents,
was clearly affirmed in 1794.

As the Protestant rulers took over more and more control
of education, the Catholic rulers came to realize that they
could also strengthen their power by making the schools subservient to themselves. In Catholic Bavaria the Elector
Charles Theodore, while leaving the Catholic schools free to
conduct religious instruction, decreed in 1778 that all schools
must be considered as belonging to the state and as such subject to local magistrates. In this manner, through a gradual
process, the state in Germany definitely supplanted the church
in the control of education. Nevertheless, amidst these
changes religion continued to have the chief emphasis in the
curriculum and the right of the churches to instruct was given
recognition. The Lutheran state church in the north and the
Catholic Church in Bavaria and the south continued to exercise
a significant influence in educational matters. At the end of
the eighteenth century all the schools in the Germanys were
confessional schools, that is, state-controlled schools in
which children of one creed were instructed by teachers of
the same creed, the religion of the parents was taught, and
other subjects of the curriculum were likewise confessionally
biased.[8]

In France Napoleon had envisaged a state system of education that would ensure followers devoted to him and to his
empire.[9] Indirectly he advanced the trend toward state control of education in Germany. Prussia was so aroused by her
defeat at the hands of Napoleon and the humiliating terms imposed by the Treaty of Tilsit (1807) that, borrowing a page
from the conqueror's book, she resolved to reorganize the
educational system in such a way that the schools would serve
primarily as instruments of the state. This determination
was intensified by the views and writings of the philosopher
Fichte, who in his "Addresses to the German Nation" stirred

up in his countrymen a fiery patriotism and a resolve to make
their nation a great and formidable power. Fichte proclaimed
that education was to be provided by the state, which was to
allow no competition from the church or the family. The philosopher's plan exerted a tremendous influence on German
education, although it was never completely realized. Under
the inspiration of the intense national spirit which had been
aroused, drastic educational reforms were initiated on all
levels. The Oberschulkollegium was abolished. A Bureau of
Education in the Ministry of the Interior was set up, which in
1817 was raised to the status of a national Department of Education and given the title Ministry of Religion, Education, and
Public Health. Under the leadership of the scholar Wilhelm
von Humboldt a reorganization of the educational system was
effected which made the Prussian schools the most closely organized and complete in Europe. In 1825 provincial school
boards were established to replace the local church school
boards. Thus in law, and largely in practice, the control of
Prussian education was gradually transferred to the state.
The Prussian system became the model for all the other German states.

Amidst these changes there was no thought of abolishing
religious instruction in the schools and Catholic and Protestant
churches continued to have considerable influence in the educational field. The idea that the schools should be specifically
denominational was not challenged until in the wake of the
French Revolution and under the influence of the Enlightenment
it was argued that education was a matter for the community
as a whole and should not be affected by single elements within
it, such as religious organizations.[10]   Thus the concept of a
type of mixed denominational school in which children of different denominations could be educated simultaneously was introduced. In these schools the children were to be instructed
together in all subjects except religion. Teachers likewise
were to be denominationally mixed.

Controversy over mixed denominational versus single
confessional schools was waged for many years during the
nineteenth century in most of the German states, but the mixed
school won recognition in only three areas. In the Duchy of

Nassau it became in 1817 the only permissible type of elementary or secondary school. In the Grand Duchies of Hesse-Darmstadt and Baden it became permissible.

The struggle known as the Kulturkampf began about 1850, lingered to some extent through the rest of the century, and was resumed in an intensified form under Hitler. Built up in its early phase on a myth of Germany's destiny to lead Europe through the use of disciplined force, the movement gained momentum under Bismarck's "blood and iron" theory. Among other aims, it pressed for the complete separation of education from church influence and was directed chiefly against the Catholic Church.

In 1872 Bismarck secured the passage of legislation, the so-called "May Laws," which made at least some of his objectives effective. The Catholic bureaus in the Ministry of Education were suppressed; the Jesuits were driven from Prussia; all schools were withdrawn from church control; the position of school inspector was limited to qualified, non-clerical officials of the state and appointments were to be made by the government. The latter provision was intended as a blow only against the Catholic Church for all Protestant clergy who held the position of inspector were confirmed in office."
A later decree, 1880, struck a deeper blow against the Catholic clergy. It declared that the local priest was no longer entitled to teach religion or inspect the instruction; he could do so only with the consent of competent school authorities and this would be granted only if there were no objections "regarding his attitude to the state." [12]   At the same time school inspectors appointed by the state were authorized to inspect the teaching of religion.

The laws were never completely implemented and ultimately Bismarck had to give way. When Leo XIII became Pope (1878), Bismarck opened negotiations with him and a concordat with the Vatican was arranged.

Up to 1871 Germany had remained a loose confederation of states. After the Franco-Prussian War and under Bismarck's leadership, the states were welded into a unified political whole, the king of Prussia becoming the head of the new German Empire. The Empire was a union of twenty-six states over which the influence of Prussia was dominant. The government was a constitutional monarchy. Many affairs of local concern were left to the control of the states, education being one of these.

The story of the Empire was one of steady and extraordinary growth in economic and national power together with an ever increasing spirit of militant and aggressive nationalism and a rapidly expanding military and naval strength. The outcome of this extreme nationalism was World War I and eventual defeat for the Empire.

The defeat of Germany shattered the economic, political, and social structure of the country. Socialist influence was strong. Eventually a republican form of government was set up. The constitution of the new republic, which was drawn up at Weimar, contained the declaration: "Article I: The German Reich is a Republic; the power emanates from the people." Church and state were to be separated. Religious freedom was guaranteed.

The document contained a number of provisions relating to education. It charged the states with the main responsibility for public instruction, but laid down some definite regulations which the states were obliged to follow. The question of single confessional schools as against mixed-religious schools had come to the fore earlier in debates, with Socialists and Democrats demanding mixed schools and the Center Party, Conservatives, and Peoples' Party advocating the single denominational school. This division among the main parties had resulted in a "school compromise" which was embodied in the Weimar Constitution. Article 149 stipulated that religion was to be a regular subject in the public schools and that it was to be carried out in harmony with the principles of the religious community concerned "without prejudice to the supervisory rights of the state." The participation of children in the instruction was to depend on the decision of parents or guardians. A special Reich law in 1921 decreed that after the age of fourteen the decision was to be left to the child.

Article 144 of the Constitution stated that school inspection was to be entrusted only to full time specialists appointed by the government. The right of inspection by the clergy was taken away. The establishment of private schools was permitted, but such schools were obliged to have the approval of the state, to meet fully the standards of public schools, and were subject to inspection.

Beyond the constitutional stipulations, the states were permitted to issue their own regulations and in these there developed considerable variations in the matter of church-state relationships in education. At one end, in predominantly Catholic areas state teachers provided religious instruction, the control and inspection of which was left completely to the churches. At the opposite end, with varying degrees of mutual cooperation between, were the states in which the churches had no voice whatever either in giving or inspecting religious instruction.

Continuing economic crises finally brought the country into a state of chaos. The hungry, confused masses were dazzled by Hitler's promises of a restored and powerful Germany, of jobs for unemployed, and of a brilliant new paradise for all in the not too distant future. In 1933 the Republic fell and the Nazis (National Socialist Party) came into power. The myths of force and nationalistic supremacy were again to control the destinies of the nation.

Liberal tendencies were immediately crushed. The Unification Act of 1933 and a law in 1934 transferred all powers of government to the Reich, including the powers formerly exercised by the states in educational matters. The people were to give unquestioning obedience to the Fuhrer and his Third Reich.

It became a matter of prime importance to imbue the younger generation with the spirit of the new regime. Education was the instrument to be used. The system established reflected strongly the views of Fichte and Hegel, both of whom emphasized the absolute state above the individual.

At first the Nazis favored the denominational school for the simple reason that mixed schools had been championed by Liberals and Socialists whom they opposed. A Concordat with the Vatican was arranged between Hitler and Pius XI (1933), in which the denominational principle was upheld. "The retention of Catholic denominational schools," states Article 23 of the Concordat, "and the establishment of new ones are guaranteed." Article 21 reads in part: "Catholic religious instruction in elementary, senior, secondary and vocational schools constitutes a regular portion of the curriculum and is to be taught in accordance with the principles of the Catholic Church."[13]   Both parties to the Concordat seemed to have made important concessions. Whereas the Catholic Church agreed that religious instruction should foster "patriotic consciousness," the interests of the Church were safeguarded by the fact that the "patriotic consciousness" was to be within the spirit of the Christian faith, not only in religion but in all subjects.[14]

The Concordat, of course, was not adhered to by the Nazis. True religion and political totalitarianism do not mix, and soon a systematic drive against denominational schools was organized by the Party. Sham plebescites were arranged, and these, by a process of adjustment, allegedly showed a majority of parents in favor of abolishing denominational schools. Catholic leaders protested vigorously. Pius XI's encyclical "With Deep Anxiety" stated succinctly the Catholic view of the situation. Unfortunately, the Evangelical churches sometimes tended to vacillate and compromise.[15]   The process of abolishing the denominational schools went on. Between 1931 and 1938 the number of publicly-controlled Catholic schools dropped from 15,256 to 9,637. During the same period the number of Evangelical schools dropped from 29,020 to 24,329.[16]   War conditions in 1939 were used as a pretext for closing the rest of the public denominational schools and all the private church-related schools. The same fate befell practically all the denominational secondary schools, Catholic and Evangelical.

So-called German Community schools were established in place of the elementary denominational institutions. They were ostensibly mixed, religion remaining nominally in the curriculum, but subtle -- and not-so-subtle -- efforts were put forth to undermine and curtail the religious teaching. The religion class was put during the last period of the school day where it could easily be omitted; the total number of hours allowed for instruction was greatly reduced; teachers were under pressure to refuse to give the instruction. Nazi-oriented teachers gradually replaced others not so pliant. When religion was taught, efforts were made to bring it in line with Nazi ideology. Religion was to be "supra-denominational." The highest task of the school, it was stated, was the "training of youth for service to nation and state in the National Socialist spirit." Eventually in most schools the religious instruction was discontinued and replaced with a study of "basic theories of Nazi faith," which simply amounted to indoctrination in Nazi ideology.

Central control of all education was implemented by the establishment of a National Ministry of Education and Youth Welfare, which prescribed the curriculum, determined the schools' procedures, and selected textbooks. In fact, it controlled all aspects of the school system, giving its most assiduous attention to teacher-training. A bust of Hitler was set up in every classroom; crucifixes were banned in Catholic schools. The goal of the school became "the formation of the National Socialist man," that is, a willing, submissive and uncritical servant of the will of the state.

Again the policy of force and militantly aggressive nationalism resulted in war and final defeat for its advocates. Germany surrendered unconditionally to the allies, May, 1945.

With the downfall of the Hitler regime, the defeated country was divided into four zones governed respectively by the four conquering powers -- United States, Great Britain, France, and Russia, with joint control of Berlin. The sovereign power of Germany was vested in the Allied Control Commission in Berlin on which sat the military governors of the four zones. Prussia, which had dominated the rest of the country for so many years, had in effect disappeared, part going to Russia, part to Poland, and the remainder divided among the four zones.

When the allies entered Germany, education in the country was virtually at a standstill. Most of the school buildings were in ruins. In Cologne, for example, 93 percent had been destroyed or damaged. The Nazi-slanted textbooks were now unusable; supplies such as pencils, pens, and paper were unavailable. Hundreds of thousands of children had been removed

from the large towns under evacuation schemes; they had received little or no instruction under the improvised conditions.
Pupils over fifteen for the most part had been conscripted as
auxiliaries and practically all university students had disappeared in various sections of the armed forces. Teachers
were scarce or non-existent. In short, the educational situation was chaotic when surrender came.

For some years the conquerors attempted to re-educate
the Germans by imposing their own educational traditions upon
them. Denazification and democratization were primary aims
at first. The religion-education question came quickly to the
fore. In November, 1945, the Central Control Council made
a tentative decision on the issue, which was to be applied until
the Germans could freely and decisively express their own
wishes on the matter. The principal point of the decision is
summed up in the words of a passage which states that in

> . . . matters concerning denominational schools
> drawing on public funds and religious instruction in
> German schools which are maintained by various
> religious groups the appropriate allied authority
> should establish in each zone a provisional regula-
> tion adapted to local conditions. This would take
> into consideration the wishes of the German popu-
> lation in so far as their wishes can be determined
> and conform to the general directions governing the
> control of education.[17]

There was also the stipulation that "no school drawing on public funds should refuse to children the possibility of receiving
religious education nor making it compulsory for a child to
attend religion classes."[18]

Gradually there developed the tendency, most marked in
the British and American zones, to leave considerable responsibility for education to the Germans themselves. The British
zone authorities, for example, handed control back to the
people in their zone in 1947. Russia, of course, disregarded
the decision of the Central Council and proceeded with its
communization tactics, which included eliminating religious

instruction and putting all schools completely under the control
of the state.

Since the question of single denominational schools versus
mixed schools had not been settled, it became a matter of controversy in several areas. In the British zone it was resolved
by plebiscites, which had varied results. In general throughout the three zones, when the wishes of parents were ascertained, there was evidence of a wide desire for denominational
education except in a number of large towns. In predominantly Catholic areas, such as Bavaria, there was strong insistence
on the single confessional school. The Evangelical church
was divided on the subject. While the orthodox Lutheran
clergy contended for the single school, the confessional church
seemed willing to accept the mixed school with religious instruction supervised by the church as an integral part of the
curriculum.[19]

In May, 1949, the West German Federal Republic consisting of the three Western zones, was established. The Republic is actually a federation of nine independent lander or states
with a population of 45,000,000. The capital is located at
Bonn. Russia followed with the establishment in the East of
the German Democratic Republic with a population of
15,000,000 and its capital in East Berlin. This meant a partition of the country with educational policies developing independently in East and West. These followed the pattern of
the two opposing divisions: the trend toward democratization
continuing in the West, while totalitarianism became the
dominant characteristic of education in the East. From this
point in Germany's post-war development, our concern in the
pages below will be with the educational situation in West Germany only.

A Basic Law or Constitution was drawn up for the Federal
Republic. Articles 6 and 7 relate to education. Section 2 of
Article 6 guarantees that "the care and upbringing of children
shall be the natural right of parents. . ." The first four
sections of Article 7 read:

1. The entire educational system shall be under the
supervision of the state.

2. Those entitled to bring up the child shall have the right to decide whether it shall receive religious instruction.

3. Religious instruction shall form part of the curriculum in the state schools with the exception of non-confessional schools. Religious instruction shall, without prejudice to the state's right of supervision, be given according to the principles of the religious societies. No teacher may be obliged against his will to give religious instruction.

4. The right to establish private schools shall be guaranteed. Private schools as substitute for state schools shall require the sanction of the state and shall be subject to Land legislation. The sanction must be given if the private schools, in their educational aims and facilities, as well as in the scholarly training of their teaching personnel, are not inferior to the state schools and if a separation of the pupils according to the means of the parents is not encouraged. The sanction must be withheld if the economic and legal status of the teaching personnel is not sufficiently assured.[20]

Liberty of choice in elementary education is somewhat restricted by Section 5 of Article 7, which reads:

5. A private elementary school shall be permitted only if the educational administration recognizes a specific pedagogic interest or, at the request of those entitled to bring up children, if it is to be established as a general community school (Gemeinschaftsschule), as a confessional or ideological school or if a state elementary school of this type does not exist in the Gemeinde.[21]

The German Solution in Operation

GENERAL FEATURES OF THE SYSTEM. Of first significance in an analysis of the West Germany system of education is the fact that it is not the Federal government but the individual lander and their respective ministries who are responsible for the administration and financing of the educational system. Thus there are really nine systems of education in the Republic. The Basic Law declares that the lander possess supreme supervisory authority in education. There is, consequently, no national ministry of education and the Bund has no authority to legislate in the sphere of education.

However, the Basic Law does, as noted above, contain some general regulations binding upon and restricting the respective lander. On analysis, it is seen that the relevant sections lay down several basic principles: the persons entitled to bring up a child have the right to decide whether it shall receive religious instruction and to determine the kind of religious instruction; religious instruction must form part of the ordinary curriculum in state and municipal schools except in definitely established secular ones (bekenntsnisfrei); and the right to establish private schools is guaranteed.

Beyond the restrictions and regulations of the Basic Law, complete control of educational affairs rests with each of the lander respectively. Obviously, the varieties of cultural traditions were considered of great advantage to the intellectual life of the nation and were preserved for that reason. The disappearance of Prussia changed the earlier situation in which one large state dominated most of the others.

The Federal Republic now consists of nine lander: Baden-Wurtenberg, Bavaria, Bremen, Hamburg, Hessen, Lower-Saxony, North Rhine Westphalia, Rhineland-Pfalz, Schleswig-Holstein, and, in addition, West Berlin, which, although closely bound to West Germany, does not de jure belong to it. Each of the lander has organized its own system of education, the basic principles and regulations of which are found in the respective constitutions and laws.

Despite the fact that the lander have complete autonomy in the field of education, there are many similarities throughout the Republic. Each land has its own Ministry of Education, although the titles given it may differ. Each gives recognition to the right of equal educational opportunities for all pupils, irrespective of economic position, social status or religion.[22]   In regard to financing, usually the lander bear staffing costs while the communes pay building and maintenance charges.

In general, the organizational pattern of education is the
same in all lander. Compulsory education begins at the age
of six. Full time attendance is required until the age of fourteen; part time, until age eighteen. All children attend the
basic school (grundschule) for four years which is the same
for all. After completing this, three paths are open to the
child. He may continue at the elementary school for another
four or five years. During these years the elementary school
tries to provide pupils, some 75 percent, with a training
which will enable them to embark upon an apprenticeship. Or
the child may enter a six-year "middle school" (mittelschule),
emphasizing preparation for professions in business administration, trade, commerce, engineering or domestic economy.
About ten percent choose this alternative. Finally, he may
enter the gymnasium or regular high school of nine years duration, which prepares for entrance into the universities and
professions of medicine and law. Approximately seventeen
percent of all school age children are attending gymnasien.
School buildings in West Germany are new, modern, efficient,
and replete with excellent equipment.

RELIGIOUS EDUCATION AND THE STATE. The constitutions of the lander vary greatly in their statements with respect to religion. Some of the constitutions do not mention
this aspect at all; some stipulate that the schools must be
inter-confessional; others stress the single confessional
character of the school, but have provisions for the establishment of inter-denominational schools.

There is separation of church and state, but this principle as interpreted in Germany does not preclude cooperation
between the two societies. There is a special guaranty for
the autonomy of the Catholic Church under various Concordats
with the Vatican signed by the lander and one by the Reich,
which has been recognized by the Federal Government as
binding on itself. The Evangelical church enjoys the same
status as a result of historical development, the provisions
of the Constitution, and various ecclesiastical contracts.
More than 96 percent of the population belong, at least nominally, to one or the other of the two church denominations.
In the Federal Republic the proportions are almost equal.[23]

From the aspect of support and control, the schools in
West Germany may be designated as (1) state or public, and
(2) private. The state schools from the viewpoint of their
policy on religion are classified as (1) confessional or denominational, (2) inter-confessional, and (3) secular. The confessional school is a public school in which all the teachers
except specialists in certain subjects are of the same denomination as are all or a majority of the pupils; the principles and
doctrines of the majority denomination are formally taught and
the instruction in all other subjects is in harmony with them.
A mixed or inter-confessional school is one which children of
various denominations attend; the teachers are appointed without regard to their denominational allegiance, although it is
usual to select a numerical proportion similar to the denominational distribution of the pupils. The children are segregated only for religious instruction, which is an integral part
of the syllabus, and are taught the Catholic or the Protestant
religion in accordance with the wishes of their parents. In
all other subjects, teaching is on a strictly non-denominational
basis. The secular school is a public school in which no religious instruction is given; the teachers, as a rule, claim allegiance to no particular creed and give instruction in a course
designated as "philosophical instruction," which deals with
truths and ethical principles of a natural order. This type of
school has never been popular in West Germany.

With the exception of the negligible number of secular
schools, in all public schools in Germany from grundschulen
through the universities, religious instruction has a legally
recognized and important role. In every time-schedule and
in every syllabus the subject of religion is placed first. The
unsettled question is whether the schools are to be confessional or inter-confessional, but this issue affects the elementary
schools almost exclusively. Part-time vocational and almost
all public secondary schools are inter-confessional. The
Evangelical church, in general, is not opposed to the elementary inter-confessional school as long as it provides sufficiently for instruction of the child in religion. The Catholic Church
demands confessional schools as a matter of principle.

The Federal Constitution did not settle the question; it

simply demands that religion be a compulsory subject in the
public schools, except in those definitely organized as secular.
In 1948-49, at a meeting of the Parliamentary Council to draw
up basic statutes for West Germany, the Catholic bishops had
argued for an inclusion of an article that would recognize the
provisions of the Concordat of 1933, which called for the establishment of single confessional schools throughout Germany.
It was argued that the establishment of confessional schools
was a necessary development of the right of parents to determine the education of their children, which was an accepted
principle. The Council sidestepped the issue as to types of
schools by simply stating that religion was to be a regular
subject of the curriculum and should be given according to the
principles of the specific religious societies.

After the adoption of the Bonn Constitution it was left up
to each land to determine whether schools were to be organized
on the single or mixed denominational basis. There were
lengthy discussions on the question in some states and the issue is still being debated in several areas. Relevant to the
controversy in the lander was the question whether the provisions of the 1933 Concordat applied to the lander or only to the
Federal Government. The highest court of Germany made the
decision May 26, 1957, in which it upheld the 1933 Concordat
as part of basic German law and binding on the present Federal
Government as the successor of Germany's pre-war government. But it also ruled that the lander are not bound by the
Concordat and, since the Constitution gives the lander control
over education, they are free to pass educational laws which
conflict with the Concordat.

As a result there are differences in the way in which the
issue of confessional schools was settled. There are four
states where only inter-confessional schools exist: Bremen,
Hamburg, Schleswig-Holstein and Hessen; four states where
there are both single and inter-confessional schools: North
Rhine-Westphalia, Rhineland-Palatinate, and Bavaria. In addition Baden-Wurtemberg, which is divided, has one region having only inter-confessional schools and another region now
called Tubingen having both single and inter-confessional
schools.[24]

Lower Saxony, which is about 80 percent Protestant, until recently had only inter-confessional schools except in one district, Oldenberg, in which only confessional schools were legal. A similar situation exists in the Saar. In February, 1965, the legislature of Lower Saxony, despite the protests of some students, teachers, and opposition leaders, ratified a Concordat with the Holy See. Christian Democrats and some Socialists joined forces to push the Concordat through by a margin of 96 votes for as against 25 opposed. The Concordat permits Catholics the right to transform inter-confessional schools into confessional schools in all areas where Catholics make up 80 percent of the population. It includes guarantees for religious training in other public schools.

Several of the other lander have their own concordats with the Holy See. The Bavarian Concordat, for example, makes definite provision for state schools that are Catholic for Catholic children and gives assurance that religious instruction given in them will meet the demands of the Church. Where Catholics are too few to have a school of their own and the child must attend a school in which he receives no religious instruction, the state promises to give the use of the school room for religious instruction outside school hours and to provide light and heat at public expense. The inspection and direction of Catholic religious instruction are assured to the Church. The same privileges are afforded Protestant children and Protestant churches when the opposite situation exists.[25]   On the other hand, the socialist governed states -- Hesse and Bremen -- have, in general, refused to give parents a legal right to new single denominational schools when needed. New schools in these states are of the inter-confessional type.

Wherever they exist the single confessional schools, whether Catholic or Protestant, are completely supported from public funds, state and local. At the same time they are completely under the control of the state except in regard to those aspects of religious instruction that are clearly the function of the churches to supervise and regulate. The state determines the curriculum, the examinations, length of terms, and so forth. The public authorities select the teach-

ers, but where single confessional schools are concerned they
must follow the pattern which the confessional school by its
very definition implies, that is, Catholic teachers are selected
for Catholic schools and Protestant teachers for Protestant
schools. All the teachers are of the laity.

It may be asked: Do the single confessional schools find
it possible to maintain their essential religious character,
given the extensive control by the state? The concensus disclaims any real difficulty. The Catholic schools can be truly
Catholic in purpose and spirit, and likewise the Evangelical
schools truly Evangelical.[26]   In fact, it is pointed out, the
government cooperates in a positive manner toward the attainment of the schools' religious aims rather than merely toler-
ating them. Those close to the situation declare that the general idea behind German education is to permit the influence
of religion to carry over into all activities.[27]

Adequate time is allowed for formal religious instruction,
which emphasizes doctrine. In Catholic schools the instruction is given by a priest in clerical garb or by a teacher who
has been prepared for the work in a Catholic training college;
in Protestant schools, by the minister or lay person who has
been specifically prepared for this teaching. The school day
begins with a brief prayer. The great Christian festivals --
Christmas, Easter, Whitsuntide -- are also important school
holiday periods. Religious symbols, such as the crucifix,
adorn the walls of classrooms. There seems to be, in short,
no opposition to all those nuances which make for a Christian
atmosphere in the school.

Whereas most of the elementary schools in Germany are
single confessional, practically all the professional schools
(Berufsschulen) and secondary schools are inter-confessional.
The part-time vocational schools (for pupils between fourteen
and eighteen) may also be regarded as inter-confessional since
recently religious instruction has been added to the schedule
of courses. The inter-confessional school, as noted above,
takes no account of denominational affiliation in the admission
of students or in the appointment of teachers. Jewish, or even
unbelieving, applicants for teaching positions are not barred.
Nevertheless, in these schools also religion stands first in the

schedule of classes and is regarded as of supreme importance.

At fixed hours the children are segregated for religious instruction in accordance with parental wishes or, in some instances, the students' preference. Qualified and approved representatives of the two major creeds conduct the courses. Each class is taught by a teacher of the same faith as the children he instructs. The religion teacher may come in for this specific purpose from outside the school, or he may be a regular teacher, and if this is the case, the course or courses in religion which he teaches are considered part of the regular teaching load for which he receives compensation. It is usually a priest who instructs Catholic children.

A Reich law of 1921 gave children who had completed their fourteenth year the right to decide their religious affiliation and attendance at school instruction in religion. All the lander still enforce this law except Bavaria and Rhileland-Pflaz, where the deciding age has been raised to eighteen. Religious denominations other than the two major creeds -- Catholic and Evangelical -- constitute less than three percent of the population. The lander laws make no provision for these groups to give religious instruction to their adherents in the schools but the children may withdraw from the instruction at the request of parents or guardians.

The inter-confessional secondary schools are completely supported from public funds. Likewise, they are subject to the educational regulations of the Basic Law and are under the control and management of their respective lander.

Although theoretically inter-confessional, many secondary schools, especially in Bavaria and the Rhineland, are in practice single denominational because of tradition, teaching staff, or the religious homogeneity of the children who attend them.

The specifically secular school has never found favor among the Germans. The few, where they do exist, teach an ethics-religion course based on the natural law.

West Berlin, which has been under socialist influence, does not recognize religion as a regular subject of the curriculum, but leaves it to the religious organizations to make arrangements for instruction in the schools. The city government allows time in the daily schedule and provides classroom facilities. The present law, which nullified a previous stipulation that the religious instruction could be given only before or after school hours, allows the subject to be taught within the school day and credits public school teachers who give instruction up to four hours a week of the regular teaching load.

PRIVATE SCHOOLS. In contrast to East Germany, which prohibits all private schools, the Federal Republic permits no monopoly of education by the state. Private schools have a constitutionally guaranteed right to exist.[28] In the implementation of the provisions of the Basic Law, however, a distinction is made between the elementary and the secondary schools. Permission of the authorities in the respective lander is required to establish any kind of private school, but in the case of private secondary schools the permission must be granted if the school in question meets required standards. Private elementary schools, on the other hand, may be established only if they fill one of the special needs which are specified by the Basic Law in Section 5 of Article 7, which is quoted above. As a consequence there are very few private elementary schools in Germany.

On the other hand, private schools of middle grade (mittelschulen) and secondary level (hohere schulen) are found in all sections of West Germany. They are owned and established by religious denominations, religious orders, corporations, and private groups. Many are under the auspices of the Catholic Church. Some twelve percent of all intermediate and high school pupils attend a private school, the majority of which are boarding institutions.[29] Private part-time vocational schools are frequently conducted and maintained by large industrial enterprises for their employees.

The Basic Law states that private schools "shall be subject to land legislation." They are, therefore, under the supervision of the land in which they are located. Their aims, standards, and the professional preparation of teachers must be equal to those of the public schools. Having met these requirements, the private schools have great freedom to manage their own affairs.

The Concordat of 1933, binding on the Federal Government,

does not touch on the question of private schools. There is no national law providing for financial assistance to these schools and whatever they receive by way of aid must be arranged with the local authorities of the nine lander. In practice, practically all the private schools are generously subsidized from public funds, the subsidies varying from 60 to 85 percent of costs, according to the individual land. Hamburg, for example, is particularly generous to the Catholic private schools. Teachers' salaries up to 90 percent and all equipment and supplies are provided for from public funds. Even socialist-ruled states aid the private schools. West Berlin, which is under a socialist government, grants subsidies to the private schools up to 50 percent and plans are under way to raise the subsidy to 70 percent.

In 1961, out of 30,005 elementary schools in West Germany only 155, or 0.5 percent, were private. About one third of these are under Catholic auspices. But in this connection it should be remembered that most of the state elementary schools are in practice run along denominational lines, that is, are single confessional schools. Of Germany's 940 middle schools, 170 were privately operated. Most of the private middle schools are Catholic. There were 1,710 high schools, 362 of which were private, and of these 234 were Catholic.[30]

TEACHER TRAINING COLLEGES. The majority of teacher-training institutions are inter-confessional and under the control of public authorities. Courses in religious doctrine and pedological methods are taught by official representatives of the religious denominations to their respective adherents. All costs are defrayed from public funds. There are, however, in addition a large number of single confessional teachers' colleges, that is, separate institutions for Catholics and non-Catholics. This type predominates in North Rhine-Westphalia, Bavaria, Wurtenberg-Baden, and Rhineland-Pfalz.[31] Bavaria by special legislation makes provision for the training of teachers for Catholic schools and gives assurance that only such teachers will be appointed to the Catholic schools as are ready to teach in the spirit of the Church. All single confessional colleges are supported completely from public funds.

There is no Catholic university in Germany, but some of the twenty universities have faculties of theology.

West Germany's Solution Appraised

The German Federal Republic sees no conflict between separation of church and state and the national need for giving religion a respected and significant role in public education or in subsidizing private religious schools. It has done both with a minimum of opposition. It has been intent upon preserving its cultural and religious traditions, as expressed in both the Basic Law and in the constitutions of the <u>lander</u>: "The public schools are Christian schools."

No general statement appraising West Germany's solution to the religion-education issue from the viewpoint of Christian philosophy can be made since the arrangements vary from <u>land</u> to <u>land</u>, but those who hold to the principles laid down by Pius XI in the encyclical "The Christian Education of Youth" would say the single confessional schools come near the ideal. The question of single <u>versus</u> mixed schools is still debated in Germany. As a rule opposition to the single confessional school has come from socialists and other leftist groups, Catholics and orthodox Protestants standing firm in its favor.

It is difficult to estimate the effectiveness of either type of confessional school since so many other factors enter into and influence life in West Germany, as elsewhere. The German pupil is reported to be an orderly and obedient learner, who does what his teachers tell him to do. The schools have no severe disciplinary problems. There is practically no truancy. A friendly atmosphere prevails in the classrooms and an agreeable rapport exists between children and teacher.[32]

From the broader view of life and living, observers report a growing secularism and a too great eagerness in the pursuit of material values. On the other hand, in relation to the traditional conflict between force and freedom, freedom seems now on the ascendancy. The West German people are giving evidence of a desire for true democracy and for peaceful relations with other nations. They have shown regret for, and willingness to amend, the errors of the past.

It is impossible to estimate the extent to which any of

these changes can be marked to the credit or discredit, as the case may be, of the schools, or more specifically to the German solution of the religion-education issue. In any case, West Germany has found a way of solving the question which avoids the two extremes -- a wall of separation between church and state on the one hand and union on the other. In between the two is a way wherein religious-minded parents can give their children a religious education without forfeiting any of the benefits the state offers its citizens.

Chapter 10

Holland: "AN IDEAL SOLUTION"

Many observers of the Dutch solution of the school issue are of the opinion that it is the most just to be found on the European continent; some, indeed, have expressed the view that it comes the nearest to an ideal arrangement. The people of the Netherlands themselves seem to have found their settlement to be eminently satisfactory.

The Dutch solution is not a compromise but a well-thought out policy designed to meet the demands of justice, freedom, and efficiency in education. Basically, the policy derives from the Dutch peoples' traditional love of independence and freedom. This feature has marked the national character for centuries and seems to have found its fullest expression in a school system which harmoniously combines the benefits of both a centralized and a decentralized system of educational administration, nicely balances freedom and efficiency, and accords due recognition to the respective rights of the three societies concerned with education -- the family, the churches, and the state. Article 208 of the national Constitution states in part: ". . . the freedom of private education concerning the choice of means of instruction and the appointment of teachers shall, particularly, be respected." The same Article emphasizes the solicitous care and concern of the government for the education of its citizens. This concern manifests itself in prescribing standards of efficiency in education, while at the same time it makes generous grants to all schools, public and private. State authorities not only authorize the creation of independent schools, practically all of which are church-related, but give them complete financial support while allowing full autonomy, provided only that guarantees are given that the instruction in the schools will meet adequate standards.

This solution, so generally acknowledged to be eminently satisfactory, was reached only after a long struggle for the rights of private education. During the mid-nineteenth century, the situation relative to the school issue in Holland was

similar to that in the United States during the same period.
Catholics had in earlier times been denied even the right to
educate their children at all. In the struggle for freedom of
education in Holland, Dutch Protestants did not capitulate to
neutralism or secularism, but joined with Catholics in their
demands for religious schools. A prominent Dutch authority
in the educational field makes the pertinent observation:

> Holland has been the scene of a long and fervent
> fight, but dogged tenacity and solid action of all
> advocates of denominational education among which
> our Protestant brothers must be specially men-
> tioned -- have led to the victory of our principle.[1]

The experiment in complete freedom of education which
the Dutch entered upon with the Education Act of 1920 has now
well passed the testing stage. The satisfaction which it has
afforded the vast majority of the Dutch people and the efficiency
of its operation have been fully manifested for almost fifty
years. This is partially because the nation still subscribes
to the principles upon which the solution was built: first, that
the education of their children is the primary concern of parents and not of the state; and secondly, that since school taxes
are paid by all the people, all parents have a right to their
share for building and maintaining the kind of schools they
want for their children.

It is instructive to examine the history of the hard fought
struggle which won for the people what the majority always
wanted, and still cherish, a school system which satisfies the
religious conscience of all parents without imposing extra financial burdens on any group because of its views.

The Testimony of History

The geographical section of Europe now known as the
Netherlands was in the early centuries of the Christian era on
the fringes of the Roman Empire. The land was inhabited by
several Germanic tribes. Christianity was brought to the
natives gradually. Educational developments in this northern
section of Western Europe followed fairly closely the pattern

set in the earlier Christianized sections of the continent. Parish, song, monastic and cathedral schools sprang up as churches were established, education here, as elsewhere, suffering a decline when the ravages of war laid waste the land.

The immediate effects of the Protestant Revolt on the schools in Holland, as in other sections of Europe were adverse, although in the early stages the country suffered less from the ravages of the religious catastrophe and the wars which followed it than did Germany. Lutheranism obtained practically no hold in the Netherlands but various dissident groups, offshoots of earlier misdirected reform movements, defected from the Catholic Church. These were known as the National Reformers. Later, as we shall see, Calvinistic influence penetrated into the country, its adherents assuming for themselves the title of Reformed Church of Holland when they had become sufficiently powerful. The majority of the Dutch people for the present continued staunch in the old faith.

The Netherlands at this time was still part of the Holy Roman Empire. In the year 1558 Ferdinand I succeeded his brother Charles V on the throne. Three years earlier Charles had placed the regency over Spain and Holland in the hands of his son Philip II, thus practically putting Holland under the rule of Spain. In 1568 the Dutch rebelled against Spanish tyranny. The revolt was due primarily to social and political considerations, but religious issues were also at stake. The king, a Spanish Catholic, was desirous of preserving the Catholic faith in the country. In pursuing his aim, he resorted at times to harsh measures, thus incurring the hostility of the Protestants and of some Catholics, who were as opposed to constraint in matters of conscience as were the Protestants. Neither the Catholics nor the National Reformers were sufficiently organized to assume separately leadership of the revolt and they were too divided among themselves to join forces. Leadership then passed to the Calvinists, the followers of a movement which had spread from France and Switzerland and had been gaining influence in the Low Countries. Thus it happened that the Calvinist creed and the national cause became more or less identified.

Resistance lasted eighty years, during which time the Calvinists succeeded in usurping step by step the supreme authority in the nascent state. In those areas where the King's troops held their ground, the population remained Catholic; in the provinces where the revolt was successful Calvinism, sternly supported by the authority of the new government, became the established religion. By the time a truce was signed in 1609 a definite pattern of religious allegiance in Holland had taken shape. It has changed little during the succeeding centuries. The southern provinces were, and have continued to be, almost completely Catholic; the north and northwest have remained predominantly Protestant, while remaining areas are somewhat mixed as to religious affiliation.

When in 1648 by the Peace of Munster Holland was proclaimed independent, the Calvinists, although a small minority of approximately ten percent of the population, found themselves in complete control of the government. From then until the end of the eighteenth century they managed by dint of strong organization and harsh legislation to maintain a tight hold on all affairs of the country. In the interests of preserving their power, they immediately began a severe persecution of dissident religious groups, particularly of Catholics, who at the time comprised a two-thirds majority.

Everywhere the Catholic Church was oppressed.[2] Catholic worship was proscribed by edict. In many places Catholic bishops and priests were put to death, thrown into prison, exiled, or were economically ruined by heavy fines. The churches were dispoiled and plundered; liturgical objects and ornaments were desecrated. Convents and monasteries were confiscated. Catholic education was interdicted. Catholic parents had either to send their children to hostile Calvinist schools or let them remain illiterate. Catholics were excluded from all public offices and denied other opportunities of employment.

In accordance with Calvin's political views the government was organized as a sort of semi-theocracy -- a union of the Reformed Church and the state, with the church as the stronger element of the union. Ministers held most of the public offices. The administration of justice was in their hands; military power was under their management. Through the imposition of heavy taxes upon the population, the authorities obtained the funds which were indispensable for preserving and consolidating their power. Oppressed, divested of influence, and unorganized, the Catholic majority remained powerless to resist the tyranny. Fault, too, lay with some of the Catholic clergy and bishops. Corrupt morals led them to abandon their faith and go over to the Calvinists, carrying with them whole parishes. In addition religious lukewarmness was rife among a portion of the laity.[3]

Local authorities established schools, the only ones allowed. In these institutions indoctrination in Calvinist beliefs was compulsory. Some of the funds for the support of the schools came from former holdings of the Catholic Church. Although lay teachers were employed, the ministers of the Reformed Church exercised the dominant influence in the committees appointed by the town councils to control education.[4] Many of the secondary schools were continuations of schools formerly taught by the Brothers of the Common Life, but now the Brothers had disappeared and Calvinist ministers inculcated the doctrine of the Reformed Church in the institutions which they had seized.

The persecution lasted almost two hundred years. It is remarkable that under its pressure the authorities did not succeed in completely uprooting the Catholic Church from the land. As it was the number of Catholics dwindled from an overwhelming majority to one-third or less, while the Reformed Church reached almost a majority. When Catholic bishops died or went into exile, there were none to take their places and the Catholic hierarchy gradually ceased to exist in Holland. Catholics were thus left without shepherds. A Vicar was eventually appointed and given the necessary jurisdiction by Rome.

Ultimately, these unhappy experiences produced some advantageous results. Dutch Catholics learned from them the necessity of organization. In succeeding years they worked unitedly in their efforts to secure their rights. A Catholic press was established and its publications were consistently read.

The invasion by the French in 1795 finally brought an end to Calvinist control of the government. Regardless of the violence and brutality which the Revolution had engendered in France and of the misuse which the Revolutionists had made of their slogan -- Liberty, Equality, and Fraternity -- the new government set up by the invaders in Holland curtailed Calvinist tyranny and the autocracy of the Reformed Church. It issued a proclamation of liberty in religious matters. Theoretically every citizen of whatever belief could henceforth be appointed to any public office. In practice Calvinist influence remained so strong that political positions for a long time continued to be held by Calvinists only.

Nor was liberty of education immediately achieved. Inspired by the rationalistic philosophers of the eighteenth century and the views of the Revolutionists, the new rulers set up a system of state-controlled, secular schools, which all children were obliged to attend. The result was a virtual monopoly of education by the state. Some relief for the religious-minded population was proffered by an Education Act of 1806, which permitted associations of parents to build their own schools provided that the approval of the government was obtained. Requests for approval, however, were rarely granted. Moreover, the government, with its board of inspectors, meddled in every aspect of education and the few private schools allowed to exist were heavily restricted in their operation by official controls over textbooks and curricula. Under exclusive governmental control, the public schools of the country could scarcely avoid becoming tainted with the rationalism of the Revolutionary philosophy. Henceforth Catholics and orthodox Protestants were united in their opposition to the state monopoly of education. It endured, nevertheless, even after the French were driven out of the Netherlands in 1813 and Holland was united with Belgium.

The struggle for educational freedom was to continue throughout the nineteenth and into the twentieth century. From the vantage point of time, two phases of the struggle are discerned. In the first phase, religious-minded people contended for freedom of denominational education as against the state monopoly. By 1848 this objective had been achieved. In the second phase of the struggle, equality of position of the private and the public schools concerning public support became the objective. This was achieved in 1920.

Organized and determined, the Dutch Catholics had by the fourth decade of the last century become sufficiently influential to voice their views and to have them heeded. Against the state monopoly of education they argued that such a policy left the care of the child to the mercy of a public body in which now this political party, now that, seized the reins of government. It meant placing the child under the care of a group of officers incompetent to exercise the functions of the Church or to implement the natural rights of parents in the education of their children. The government, they agreed, had a legitimate interest both in the adequate training of its future citizens and in the highest development of their powers. It was just therefore that the government should see to it that its citizens were properly educated and that no schools would be opened which might be dangerous to the commonwealth. The state could and should assist educational efforts by pecuniary means. But as long as parents and the churches performed their educational functions properly so that the common good and the welfare of the child were protected and enhanced, there would be no legal title for a government to interfere or to monopolize the national educational system.[5]

Furthermore, so insisted the advocates of parental and church rights, whoever intends to educate a child ought at the very least, to satisfy these conditions: to love that child and to be himself a person of staunch principle. The government could give no guarantees that it possessed such qualifications: love was foreign to it and its character varied with the characters of the persons of whom it was formed.[6] The training of the child must not be left to such haphazard circumstances.

These were the motives which impelled the Dutch Catholics to action and a majority of Dutch Protestants joined with them in their hopes and efforts. Their first victory was gained in 1848. In that year an amendment to the Constitution made education "free." Free, as the Constitution used the term, meant that now schools could be built and controlled by non-government agencies. The state-monopoly was broken.

An Education Act passed in 1857, which implemented the amendment, gave full powers to associations of parents and church authorities to establish denominational schools without governmental licensing. These schools were not free in the sense that they were maintained by the state and open without charge to students. On the contrary, the sponsors of private schools had to build and maintain them out of their own private resources. Schools established by the government or municipalities continued to be wholly supported out of public funds, but private schools received not a cent. Their sponsors, however, were obliged to pay taxes for the building and maintenance of the public schools, which, with a good conscience, they could not use. Dutch Catholics were thus put in a position similar to that in which Catholics in the United States find themselves today as regards their schools. They could have them, but at the penalty of a double burden of support. This was, of course, true of Dutch Protestants also, most of whom wanted church-related schools.

Nonetheless, the 1848 enactment was an important landmark in the struggle for educational freedom. By it the Dutch people recovered that primary and fundamental principle without which there could be no further development.

The Act also made provision for religious teachers to make use of public school rooms for religious instruction. Heretofore religious instruction had been given only out of school hours in churches or buildings rented for the purpose. Section 23 of the Act read: "Religious instruction shall be confined to clerical boards. For this purpose, rooms of the school building may, out of school time, be placed at the disposal of the pupils attending the establishments of learning concerned."[7]

The Dutch Christians, both Protestants and Catholics, were not satisfied with these gains. For them, neutral schools, even though religious instruction could be given within the buildings, were not acceptable and they saw no reason why their denominational schools should not have financial equality with the public schools. So the second phase of the struggle, beginning in 1857, was for equality of position of the private schools and of public schools concerning support out of public money, an objective which the Dutch Christians called "Pecuniary Parity of Position." Efforts to achieve this ideal were to continue for almost seventy years more, that is, until 1917 and 1920, when by constitutional amendment and statutory enactment Holland finally resolved the issue of the church-state relationship in education with a formula which, as we have seen, is regarded by many as the most satisfactory and fairest in the Western world.

In the meantime the struggle went on. Relying on the help of God and on their own limited resources, Dutch Catholics and orthodox Protestants, at the price of heroic sacrifice, began establishing their own schools everywhere in the country. The task was gigantic. Frequently wealthy benefactors made generous contributions to poor schools. Religious congregations of Brothers and Sisters were founded to supply trained teachers for the Catholic schools. Qualified lay persons came forward to fill insufficiencies in the ranks of religious teachers, willingly giving their services in return for mere pittances in order that the cause of Christian education might prosper.

The Catholic hierarchy had been restored to Holland in 1853. In 1868, the five bishops of the Netherlands jointly issued a pastoral letter pointing out the dangers to Catholic children of neutral schools and urging united efforts on the part of Catholics to obtain parity of position for their schools. Profiting by the lessons of the years between 1568 and 1848, the Catholic body organized itself for the battle. A Catholic political party was founded in 1881 to represent the Catholic viewpoint in Parliament. Its objective having been clearly defined, efforts to obtain the goal were intensified on all fronts. In fact, for many years the school issue superseded both in Parliament and out of it nearly all other political questions.[8]

In the struggle Catholics worked closely with orthodox Protestants, who had become alarmed at the effects of the liberal religious teaching given in the state schools. Finally, in the interest of pursuing their common objective, the Catholic political party formed a coalition with the Protestant parties, the earliest of which had been formed in 1848. However the groups might differ on other subjects, they were united in their views on the necessity of religious and moral education for their children. Whereas each party separately maintained its own proper statutes and its own special program, together they formed within the Dutch Parliament what was called the Right, dedicated in general to the principle of a government oriented toward God and the divine and natural laws, and in particular to the principle of a financial parity of denominational schools with public schools.

In line with the coalition's objectives, an Act in 1878 liberalized the opportunity for religious instruction in public schools, permitting it to be given during the regular school hours. Section 22 of the Act read:

> In fixing the time-tables care shall be given that during hours expressly stated for that purpose, those children who are under an obligation to attend school may receive religious instruction, which is to be imparted to them by religious teachers.[9]

The coalition wielded a strong, steady influence in Parliament for complete equality of all schools. It obtained a majority in the Second Chamber for the first time in 1887, a result which permitted the formation of a Cabinet of the Right. The same year the so-called Mackey Law was enacted, which provided that, under determined conditions, aid in money could be granted to private schools. The grants were modest, not the equality demanded, but a point had been gained -- public funds could be given to private schools.

The Right did not rest after attaining this advantage. The struggle for full parity went on, the goal becoming ever nearer. By successive enactments the grants-in-aid were augmented in 1901, 1905, 1907, 1910, and 1912. During these years Right and Left in Parliament changed places to suit the exigencies of politics, but the Right never desisted in its efforts towards achieving its objective -- "Parity of Position."

Gradually opposition began to break down. Some members of the so-called Left of the Chamber came to recognize the fact that private denominational education was what a large

proportion of the Dutch people wanted and that these desires
could not be ignored forever. A sense of fairmindedness in-
duced them to see that a wrong had been done by depriving the
sponsors of denominational education of their just share of
public taxes. At a meeting of the Socialists in Gronengen in
1902 a motion was accepted in which they acknowledged that a
"great part of the working classes in the Netherlands are
claiming denominational school teaching for their children."
They declared that they did not consider it "commendable to
put obstacles in their way, since indeed the Social Democrats
are not willing to undermine (because of some theological
points of contention) unity among the working classes in the
social domain."[10]   But the achievement of the final goal had
to await more general acceptance.

In the meantime the number of private schools had been
increasing remarkably, particularly since the passage of the
Mackey Act allotting them grants-in-aid. In that year there
were in the Netherlands 2,959 public schools with 454,926
pupils. Private schools the same year numbered 1,252 with
188,052 pupils. In 1912 the figures were: public schools
3,313 with 566,868 pupils; private schools 2,121 with 365,887
pupils. In other words, within the 25 year period, the public
schools had an increase of 354, whereas the private schools
had an increase of 869, more than twice the number of new
public schools.[11]   It was evident the people wanted their own
religion-oriented schools. Despite grants-in-aid, the sponsors of the private schools were finding the burden of supporting the ever increasing number an onerous burden indeed. As
a matter of fact, the subventions of the central government
covered but a small percent of the total cost of building and
maintenance. The municipal councils, which made up the deficiencies for public schools out of local taxes, gave nothing to
the private schools. The struggle for parity would have to go
on.

The arguments of its advocates were direct and conclusive: If the state authorities established and fully maintained
"neutral" schools out of public resources, the freedom to establish private schools would be a mockery on liberty if public
funds on an equal basis were not placed at their disposal for

their support. Otherwise, many children of poor parents who
could not afford to pay for private schools would be obliged to
attend neutral schools or remain illiterate. Such a situation,
it was reiterated, was not liberty. Basic to the whole question, however, was the traditionally accepted principle that
the parent, by the natural law, has the inalienable right and
duty to have his child educated according to the parental conscience and that the state has the corresponding duty to protect
and assist all parents in this without discrimination.[12]

The school struggle had firmly cemented the parties of
the Right. Resistance from the Liberals had weakened. The
time seemed appropriate to take the final step. By 1913 a
Cabinet of the Right had drawn up a revised Constitution, the
so-called Heemskerk-Revision, which would have guaranteed
the desired parity of position and established as the norm the
Rights' principle: Private education is normal; public education is supplementary.[13]   However, as a result of unfavorable
election returns the same year, the members of the Cabinet
of the Right found themselves obliged to abdicate, and their
work on the revised Constitution came to a close.

As it eventually turned out that disappointment served
the cause of the private schools more effectively than a victory
at the polls would have done. Parity of position would never
have been so deeply recognized by the people as a necessity
of equity had not the Left of Parliament (Liberals and Socialists) cooperated so thoroughly for its realization, as they
eventually did.

The new Liberal Premier, Cort van der Linden, set up a
State-Commission, known as the "Commission of Pacification,"
under the chairmanship of another Liberal, Dr. Bos, and composed of two members of each political party. To this Commission was given the mandate to draft a bill giving the private
schools financial equality with the public schools and to consider whether the Constitution should be revised accordingly.

The Right expressed its willingness to cooperate only
after it had received clear evidence of a sincere willingness
on the part of the Commission to put an end to the school
struggle and to work toward the achievement of financial equality for the private schools. Under its leader, Dr. Kuyper,

it had set forth three conditions over which there must be no bargaining: [14]

(1) a total pecuniary parity of position as concerns provision out of governmental and municipal moneys on behalf of school-buildings, school-furniture and teachers' salaries;
(2) no conditions which would be in violation of our pedagogical principles; and
(3) simultaneous voting on both articles of the Constitution (192 and 80).

The Premier gave his assurance:

> The government desires, nay, it conceives it even
> as a duty, to satisfy, whenever it may be possible,
> the sentiments of equity with which The Right is
> filled. . . I suggest that, now I stand at the head
> of the Government, it will be a guarantee for The
> Right that I am desirous of effecting that reform in
> the domain of education. . .[15]

A year before the Premier had made a declaration subscribing to the principle of parental rights in education: "The education of the child is, in the first place, the duty of the parents."[16]

The Commission set to work January 18, 1914. In his opening speech the Premier reminded the members:

> The work with which this Commission will charge
> itself is of the utmost importance for the future of
> our country. If you succeed therein, a basis will
> be laid down upon which our nation may develop
> their mental forces, solidly and durably, and our
> national unity will be strengthened. . . Now you
> have to face the fact that your different opinions
> are to be kept within certain bounds. The public
> and private education are for you two values to be
> judged of in their historical evolution. You are
> looking for means to make them both flourish and

to secure for both of them their independence.[17]

Outside the meetings, the Press, representing the various parties and viewpoints on the educational issue, showed remarkable moderation. There was little or no evidence of bitterness of feeling, bigotry, or animosity, although there was by no means complete unanimity of opinion on the issue. The liberal Handelsblad, for example, stated: "Good public and private instruction, that is what everybody desires, and, moreover, no meddling with the pedagogical independence of private education."[18]

The report of the Commission appeared in print April 12, 1916. A section entitled "General Considerations," which was drawn up in the second meeting and later became the guiding line for further discussion, set the tone of the whole. Jonkheer de Savornin Lohman had opened that conference with a speech in which he underlined the erroneous general notion that public and private education should be based on conflicting principles. Stress, he declared, ought rather to be laid on the fact that the state has an interest in the education of the people as such, no matter to what group it belongs. The state and private persons, he insisted, must not compete with one another but must cooperate for the same end; the government has to support both groups in such a manner that he who prefers one of those groups should not be obliged to pay more than he who prefers the other. Freedom of education has to be brought within certain limits in order to guarantee good compulsory education.[19]

The report contained a revision of Article 192 of the Constitution, the section which had reference to education. It became Article 200 of the new Constitution. The pertinent provisions of the Article are worth quoting:

(1) Education shall be an object of constant solicitude on the part of the Government.

(2) The imparting of education shall be free, saving superintendance by the Government and, moreover, insofar as general education, elementary as well as secondary is concerned, saving the examination with regard to

ability and morality of the teacher, the whole to be
regulated by law.

(3) Public education shall be regulated by law, every
person's religious views being duly respected.

(4) In each municipality the authorities shall impart
sufficient public general elementary education in an adequate number of schools.

(6) These standards (of efficiency) shall be regulated
for general elementary education in such a manner as
to guarantee equally well the efficiency of the private
education defrayed entirely from public funds, and public education. In these regulations the freedom of private education concerning the choice of means of
instruction and the appointment of teachers shall, particularly, be respected.

(7) Private general elementary education fulfilling
conditions to be imposed by law shall be defrayed from
public funds, according to the same standard as public
education. The conditions upon which private general
secondary education and preparatory university education shall be granted contributions from public funds
shall be fixed by law.

The revision represented a compromise concluded
among the Parliamentary parties without, however, any sacrifice of fundamental principles. The Left's bias for public
education received consideration in paragraph 4. The
principle of the Heemskerk revision "Private education is the
normal, public education the exception" was given up.
There was no favoritism toward private schools, but only
equality as concerned their rights to share in public moneys.

The State-Commission of Pacification concluded its report to H. M. the Queen with the following words:

The realization -- that the injustice which has been
borne for so long a period will be removed; the
conviction -- that the cooperation which is necessary to raise the level of the development of our
people will be feasible; the prospect -- that improve-

ments will be the results of such cooperation; . . .
and, finally, the strong belief -- that an arrangement such as proposed has become inevitable:
these are the various considerations which have
been encouraging the members of this Commission
to recommend that these their proposals should
become law.

The whole Article was accepted with eleven votes for as
against one negative vote.

In October, 1920, three years after the education Article of the Constitution had been revised in favor of the private
schools, a Cabinet of the Right, presided over by Jonkheer
Ruys de Beerenbrouch, passed an Education Act which gave
explicit effect to the principles enunciated in the education
Article. The provisions of the Act applied only to elementary
education. The financial needs of the secondary schools were
provided for by an Act passed in 1922.

The specific features of the 1920 Statute are analyzed in
detail in the discussion below, which deals with the practical
operation of the Act. It will be sufficient here to point out
some general results of the Constitutional revision and of the
1920 Act. These legislative changes put an end to the struggle
for parity of position of public and private schools. They
guaranteed once and for all an equality of the two systems in
regard to their provision out of public funds. They left the
private schools free to arrange their teaching in the secular
and religious subjects while accepting certain reasonable regulations which the state authorities set in the interests of preserving efficiency for all schools receiving public funds.

That the law-makers had made no mistake in the supposition that the majority of the people wanted private schools
which would meet the demands of their religious conscience
is clearly testified to by the subsequent growth of these
schools. In 1917 the majority of Dutch children were by
necessity attending public schools -- 575,000 to 433,000 in
private schools, or 57 percent. In less than a decade the
proportions were reversed. By 1934 the number of children
in public schools had declined to 466,000, while the number in

private schools had risen to 811,712 or more than 64 percent of the total.[20]   The trend toward private education still continues.

The Dutch Solution in Operation

As a result of the complete freedom of education provided by the Constitution, two types of schools work side by side in Holland. The schools which are founded and controlled by government authorities, state or municipal, form the public school system. The second type comprises those established, owned, and managed by private persons or groups. These are referred to as private or voluntary schools. The vast majority of them are church-related, sponsored by either the Catholic Church or the Dutch Reformed Church.

It is, however, the relationship of the private schools to the state which makes the situation in Holland unique and memorable. This relationship is founded on the principle that parents shall be given an opportunity to provide their children that kind of education which is in harmony with their own view of life and with their religious convictions, or with their preference for certain methods of teaching. This principle, in turn, finds its motive in the belief that education should be an integral part of the upbringing of the children and that education is in the first instance a natural right and duty of the parents.[21]

On this basis, the task of government authorities is to provide the possibilities for the adequate accomplishment of parental responsibilities. An official publication states the case:

> If parents desire public education for their children, then the authorities must arrange for the establishment and maintenance of public schools; if, however, parents want private education, either denominational or non-denominational, then in principle it is the duty of the authorities to make the means available for such private schools to be established and maintained. Moreover, the subsidizing of private education must be of such a nature that as far as financial arrangements are concerned there

shall be no competition between public and private schools.[22]

In 1965 almost three-fourths of all the children enrolled in primary and secondary schools in Holland were in private schools. That is obviously where their parents wanted them to be and Holland has geared its educational system to parental wishes.

A brief look at the general administrative set-up of education in Holland will be helpful in clarifying the government's relation to the private schools. On the national level a Ministry of Educations, Artis, and Sciences, headed by a Minister, regulates and supervises the system. The Minister is assisted by a Council of Education, an advisory body appointed by the Crown. To enable him to carry out his duties effectively, the Minister has an inspectorate consisting of a chief inspector and fifty-six others assigned to different districts. The function of the Ministry is to maintain uniformity in standards in private as well as in public schools. All schools must follow regulations as to curriculum, the minimum number of hours prescribed for each subject, and the length of the school term. The Ministry pays the salaries of all approved teachers.[23]

In order to assist Catholic school authorities in fulfilling the provisions of the Education Acts, the Dutch hierarchy in 1920 established the Catholic Central Bureau of Instruction and Education in The Hague. The Bureau has a large specialized staff including lawyers, doctors, and educational experts. It acts as the intermediary between school managers and the government, providing necessary information. It publishes a monthly magazine Het Schoolbestuur (School Management) and a detailed Year Book.[24]   Protestant schools as well as the non-denominational private schools also have a national educational center. The work of the three centers, among which it is said there is excellent cooperation, is subsidized to an ever increasing extent by the government authorities.

In the analysis given below of the church-state relationship in education, the four educational levels -- pre-primary, primary, secondary, and higher -- are considered separately

since distinct and different laws apply to the separate levels
of the educational ladder.

In Holland, the kleuterscholen, or infant schools, care
for children between the ages of four and six or seven years.
They usually have their own buildings and are independent of
the primary schools. Before 1955 there was no legal instrument regulating the pre-primary school, although many such
institutions were in existence before that time. The new law,
put into operation in 1956, set down rules for their establishment and for the granting of subsidies, which are available
equally to both public and private infant schools.

Any person or private group may establish an infant
school. No government approval is needed except that the
building must meet the requirements of governmental sanitary
inspectors. Private groups wishing to receive governmental
subsidies must meet certain specifications with regard to curriculum, number of pupils and qualifications of teachers.
Practically all the private infant schools are denominational
in character.

The agency intending to set up an infant school must produce evidence to the Minicipal Council that at least thirty
pupils are willing to enroll for a community of 50,000; sixty,
when the population is 50,000 to 100,000; and ninety, for
communities over 100,000. The agency must deposit twenty
percent of the founding costs in the municipal treasury as a
guarantee. This is repaid at the end of twenty years if the
school proves to be needed. The teachers must possess a
certificate qualifying them for their position as well as a certificate of good conduct. The teachers, however, are appointed or dismissed by the operators of the school. When these
conditions have been fulfilled, the Council is obliged to cooperate with the founding society.

The private infant schools are on a complete financial
equality with the public institutions. The government subsidy
includes full reimbursement for the cost of building the school.
In some cases the government places at the disposal of the
group an existing building. The school is then given an annual
grant, which amounts to full payment of operating costs. The
salaries of teachers are fixed by law and are the same for both

public and private school teachers. They are paid to the
operators by the municipal government, which in turn, is reimbursed by the national government. Medical and dental
services are available to children and staff. Clothes are supplied to needy children. Milk is provided at cost for all.
Parents of exceptional children, the retarded or disturbed,
may seek the help of a medical-educational bureau consisting
of specialists such as children's physicians, psychologists,
and social workers, who cooperate to solve the child's problem.[25]

There are public and private training schools to prepare
personnel for teaching in the infant schools. Most of these
are under private control, though financed by public funds.

The vast majority of children who attend infant schools,
estimated to be about 70 percent of the total five-year olds,
are in private institutions. In 1958 there were a total of
3,942 infant schools in the country. Of this number, 699 were
public, 1,485 were under Catholic auspices, 1,161 under
Protestant control, and 592 of the private, non-denominational
type.[26]   In January, 1959, out of a total of 372,794 children
attending pre-primary schools, 312,000 or approximately 90
percent, were in non-public institutions.[27]

Regulations relative to primary or elementary education
are set down in Article 208 of the present Dutch Constitution
and in the Education Act of 1920, which covers both private
and public primary schools. Article 208 states that the municipality must provide public schools in sufficient quantity, but
that under circumstances to be established by law, divergence
from this principle may be permitted. As a matter of fact, in
predominantly Catholic areas, no public schools are needed.
It was reported in 1950 that 30 percent of the 1,016 municipalities had no public elementary schools.[28]   On a national average, almost three-fourths of all children of primary school
age, seven to fifteen, are in private elementary schools, but
the proportion varies from area to area, depending upon the
religious affiliation or non-religious alignment of the respective populations.

No fees are now required for education during the compulsory education period, which extends through a period of

eight years, usually from the ages of seven to fourteen. Primary education includes several stages and types. The first six years, which constitute ordinary elementary education, emphasize the elements of learning and are approximately the same for all children. About 35 percent of the pupils completing this course continue on in a division called advanced or extended primary education, which is really secondary in nature and purpose, but comes under the Dutch primary system and the primary school inspectors. The course covers three or four years. The pupils who complete it usually go on to teacher training institutions, technical schools, or higher secondary schools. Supplementary primary education is a lower form of extended education. It is designed particularly for the children who are not passing to a secondary school or to specialized training at a technical school. Two years of work are offered with particular attention to subjects of practical use. About 25 percent of the pupils take this course. Others, perhaps 30 percent, go to technical schools, five percent to agricultural and horticultural schools, the latter being under the responsibility of the Minister of Agriculture. More than 35 percent of the girls are moved up after six years of primary education to home economic schools. These stages and types of primary education are found in both the public and the private systems.

So much for the general organization of primary education in Holland. With regard to the teaching of religion in public schools, provision is made for such instruction, but attendance is never compulsory. According to the Constitution public education must be given "with full respect to everyone's feelings and beliefs." The principal or the school board may offer students an opportunity to study the religion of their preference. This is the practice in almost all public schools, since most of the principals realize and appreciate the value of what they call "a transcendental view of life." Classrooms in the school building are made available for this purpose and local clergy -- Catholic priests and Protestant ministers -- are permitted to come into the school at stated times during regular school hours to instruct those of their persuasion who desire the instruction. The public school teachers themselves do not engage in such teaching and are expected to maintain a neutrality in regard to creeds. The law states that the teacher should refrain from teaching, doing, or permitting anything that is contrary to the respect demanded by religious convictions. Nevertheless, much of the Christian tradition enters into the public school's atmosphere. Christian festivals, such as Christmas and Easter, receive recognition, plays and dramas of a religious nature are presented. Some observers, however, state that the general spirit of the public school is at best religiously indifferent, at worst subtly atheistic.

We have seen that the majority of children in Holland attend non-public schools. In accordance with the Dutch sense of educational freedom, every juridical person -- an association, foundation, ecclesiastical body or any individual or group of persons -- intending to establish a school is entitled to cooperation by town authorities. As a matter of fact, practically all the private schools are owned either by the Catholic Church or by the Dutch Reformed Church. A small number have been founded by groups who want their own schools but desire that they be neutral in regard to religion. In 1959, private schools enrolled 72 percent of all primary school children in Holland: 43 percent in Catholic, 27 percent in Protestant, and two percent in neutral schools.[29]

If certain conditions specified by law are fulfilled, the municipality must aid in the erection and maintenance of the school. First, to obviate the multiplication of small, inefficient schools, a written statement must be signed by a specified number of parents declaring that they will send their children to this school. The number of prospective pupils required varies with the total number of residents in the town. For primary schools, the figure is 125 for towns with more than 100,000 inhabitants; 100 in towns ranging from 50,000 to 100,000; 75 in places 25,000 to 50,000; and in small towns, only 50 prospective pupils are required. For complementary primary education, the numbers of pupils are 91, 71, 51 respectively for the categories listed above.[30] In special cases, less than the specified number will suffice.

Having ascertained that the requisite number of pupils

will be forthcoming, the association which plans to establish
the school must deposit in the municipal treasury, as a guarantee of good faith, a sum equivalent to 15 percent of the cost
of building and equipping the school. If at any time during the
first twenty years of the school's existence the number of pupils in the school falls below one-third or one-half of the required number, the guarantee will be partially or wholly retained by the local authorities. Otherwise, it is returned with
interest to the founders. No deposit has yet been forfeited by
any Catholic school.

When these conditions have been fulfilled, the society
desiring to establish the new school automatically receives
the money to build it from the municipality. Nevertheless,
the ownership of the property is retained by the founding
group. A school board is then formed, which obtains the
services of a principal and qualified teachers, selects its own
textbooks and other teaching materials. In the case of Catholic schools, most of the instructional personnel will be members of a religious congregation dedicated to teaching. The
costs of running the private school are borne partly by the
national government and partly by the municipality. The
national government pays the salaries of the principal and
teachers; the municipalities pay the material operating expenses -- heat, light, repairs and so forth -- in addition to
the original cost of the building. The municipality is under
obligation to spend per pupil the same amount as is spent per
pupil in its public schools. In special cases, at the discretion
of the Minister of Education, a higher sum may be allotted.
This could happen when the voluntary school is considerably
smaller than the public school and the costs per pupil are consequently higher. No tuition fees may be charged by the subsidized schools.

The financial equality of teachers in public and private
education was established by the Primary Education Act of
1920 so that both forms of education receive grants from public funds according to the same standards. The annual remuneration is fixed by the national government and no higher
or lower salaries may be paid. This procedure is intended to
prevent unfair competition between the two types of schools.

The managers of the private schools actually pay the salaries to the teachers, but they are reimbursed by the national government for what they have paid out up to the number of teachers fixed by law for both public and voluntary schools of that size. The salaries of teachers hired above the quota allowed must be paid by the private agency. The state is also responsible for teachers' pensions, which are available to retired teachers of both public and private schools.

Under Section 13 of the Act, the local authorities may provide transportation or pay in whole or in part the traveling expenses of children who attend a school more than two and a half miles from their home. In judging all applications, the local authority must so far as possible give consideration to the wishes of parents when a question of choosing a denominational school is at issue.

The Minister of Education and the state inspectors, as seems reasonable, watch the way in which the subsidized schools observe the terms under which funds have been granted, but refrain from any direct interference. The state inspectors supervise instruction and offer advice and assistance, but each private school is free to accept or reject it as desired.[31]   With regard to specified educational standards in the secular subjects, the government is entitled to insure compliance with legal requirements. The teachers in private schools must have the same qualifications as those in public schools; they must satisfy the same moral standards. Certain curriculum requirements must be met, and the subjects must be properly distributed over various classes. If it is the opinion of the state inspectors of primary education in the area concerned that the curriculum does not satisfy the requirements of adequate and regularly progressive education, at their request the Education Council gives an opinion on the matter and the school governors have to abide by that decision on penalty of loss of subsidies.[32]   To the normal program, however, can be added subjects which relate to the religious denomination conducting the school.

All this leaves the private agency with great freedom to manage its school in complete harmony with its own philosophy of education. The teachers are appointed by the managers

without the slightest interference from public authorities.
Members of religious congregations, to the extent that they
are available, are appointed to Catholic schools. Lay teachers are protected from aribitrary dismissal. If a teacher is
dismissed, that is, if his consent is not asked, he has a right
of appeal to a commission provided by law. This commission
is composed of six members, three of whom are appointed by
the private school management, three others by the private
school teachers themselves, and these six members together
must choose a seventh person as the president, who has a vote
as any other member. Such a commission must be composed
of persons of the same denomination as that of the school to
which staff the teacher belongs. The private school is also
completely free in the choice of textbooks, educational aids
and teaching methods.

Complete freedom is especially guaranteed the private
schools in everything pertaining to their denominational character. The Catholic schools are as a rule establishments of
a parish and are under the direction of the pastor and his cur-
ates, who keep in personal contact with the children confided
to their care. The religious instruction given in the school
is a regular part of their pastoral duties. Holland has a history of zeal and care in the preparation of Catholic catechisms
and graded textbooks in religion for use at home and in the
schools. Recent editions incorporate the best findings of
modern educational psychology.

A considerable number of the Catholic schools are the
property of religious communities and are under their management. The teachers, whether in parish or community-owned
schools, cooperate with the local pastor or pastors in giving
religious instruction. Care is taken that the teachers of religion are adequately prepared for this responsibility. In the
first place, they are graduates of a Catholic Teachers' College.
In addition, every teacher of religion, religious or lay, must
possess a certificate to teach religion. In the course of his
four years training, the future teacher must gain the "Higher
Diploma A" of religion. After his normal studies he may, and
usually does, continue his studies and obtains the "Diploma
B," which requires a more detailed knowledge of religious

doctrine and methodology.[33]   The ordinary of the diocese appoints special inspectors to supervise the application of the
rules concerning teaching that have been laid down by the
Church. Despite the fact that religious instruction takes place
regularly in the schools, parents are warned that they still
have the sacred duty to instruct their children in the home and
to form them in the Christian way of life.

There is nothing to prevent the Catholic schools from
being completely and thoroughly Catholic in spirit and atmosphere. Most of them are located near their parish churches.
A cross surmounts the buildings. The children frequently
attend the daily Mass and receive Holy Communion. A statue
of the patron saint of the school most likely has a place in a
niche near the entrance. In every classroom there is a crucifix on the wall; perhaps a shrine of the Blessed Mother has an
honored place in a corner of the room. Lessons are opened
and finished with a prayer. Religion is the integrating element of all instruction. "All lessons" says Dr. Verhoeven,
former director of the Catholic Central Bureau, "from time
to time, present an opportunity to speak of God's wisdom, His
magnificence, His beauty, and His foresight and care for all
His creatures. This does not appear hitherto to have checked
the progress of Catholic children in any way; nay, it not seldom occurs that they excel their companions in 'neutral'
schools in all subjects."[34]

What has been said above about Catholic primary schools
applies equally to any of the types of prolonged primary education -- supplementary, technical, or advanced. About forty
percent of all these schools are under Catholic auspices. Religious and moral training receives its due emphasis in every
one of them. Likewise, religious instruction and a religious
atmosphere characterize the Catholic schools for special children, such as the retarded and physically handicapped. These
schools also are financially on the same footing as those of the
same type under public control.

Religious instruction by Catholic priests is given in public schools only in areas where no Catholic school exists.
This is true also of those technical schools owned and conducted
by businesses or mining concerns.

In the Protestant schools the doctrines of the Dutch Reformed Church are regularly taught. In the few non-denominational private schools there is neutrality in relation to religious creeds, but in them also an effort generally is made to give some moral instruction based on a natural philosophy.

After this look at the manner in which the Dutch solution operates in its relation to private elementary schools, a glance at the statistics of their growth will be of interest. We have noted that in 1917 before the passage of the historical Education Act, the majority of children attended public schools -- 57 percent as against 43 percent in private schools. Every year after 1920 there was a steady, sometimes a sharp, increase in private school attendance. By 1948 the proportions were reaching a plateau since by that time denominational schools were sufficiently available so that almost every child could be in the kind of school his parents desired. The percentages stood at 28 percent in public schools and 72 percent in private schools, the distribution in the latter being 43 percent in Catholic, 27 percent in Protestant, and one percent in neutral schools. In 1963 the figures were: 569,549 children, or 26 percent, in public schools and 1,620,006 children, or 74 percent, in private schools.[35] The distribution of the children among the various types of private schools was approximately what they had been for a number of years: 27 percent in Protestant, 44 percent in Catholic, and three percent in non-denominational schools.

Teachers for primary schools in Holland are prepared almost exclusively in teacher training colleges specifically for that level. In relation to control, they are of two types: those owned and controlled by public authorities and those owned and conducted by private groups, the latter again being almost entirely the Catholic and the Dutch Reformed churches. Many Catholic religious congregations have their own colleges for the training of their own members. There are some diocesan colleges for the training of Catholic lay teachers. In 1963 the state conducted 24 colleges; Protestants, 26; Catholics, 42; and there were two colleges of the non-denominational type.[36]

The course covers four or five years beyond the advanced

elementary level. Since 1952 these colleges have had their
own statutory provisions, which, following the precedent of the
Education Act of 1920, grant full financial equality to public
and private institutions. The local authorities have no obligation or duties in their regard. All costs are reimbursed by
the national government, that is, the interest and capital re-
payments on the building loan and salaries of teachers. For
maintenance expenses the voluntary colleges receive the same
amount per pupil as the government spends for each pupil in
its own colleges. The private groups have great freedom in
the management of their institutions. They grant their own
diplomas which are endorsed by the state. Examinations
qualifying teachers for advanced primary education are made
up by a committee of the Ministry of Education.

In the Dutch system there are two basic kinds of secondary schools: the high school proper, a five-year course with
Latin and Greek; and the so-called gymnasium, a six-year
course, somewhat analogous to the British grammar school,
which offers a full curriculum in the humanities, including
poetry and rhetoric. A combination of both types called the
lyceum is gradually becoming more common. A diploma from
any of these secondary schools automatically admits into a
university. There are, in addition, secondary schools for
girls and commercial schools, which are more or less termi-
nal in character. A modest tuition fee is charged by the
government in secondary schools for the last two years, that
is, for pupils fifteen years and older.

Holland has no comprehensive legislation outlining the
financial relationships of secondary schools to the state such
as the Act of 1920 provides for primary education. Much is
left to the discretion of the Ministry of Education. However,
recognition of parental rights and the same freedom in regard
to the establishment of the schools are provided for. The
secondary schools, like the primary schools, are publicly
controlled, or are owned and operated by Catholics or by the
Reformed Church. In 1917 when the new Constitution came
into force, Holland possessed ten Catholic high schools of the
preparatory type. In 1948 there were 152 public secondary
schools, 71 Catholic, and 94 conducted by other private groups.

Religion classes are allowed in public schools but only in free periods. The instruction is given by local clergy, Protestant or Catholic. Catholic bishops permit priests to teach these classes when there is no Catholic secondary school available for Catholic children.

In the financing of private secondary schools the principle of "financial parity" does not apply in the same way it does for the lower schools; instead there is a system of subsidies, which are allocated by acts of Parliament when it approves the budget for the Ministry of Education. Since 1954 the state reimburses all expenses, that is, the interest and capital repayment on the building loan, the teachers' salaries, and maintenance costs. In regard to the last item, the private secondary school receives the same amount for each school, classroom, and pupil as the government spends on its own public schools.

Of course, several conditions have to be fulfilled before an institution is considered qualified to receive subsidies. A school must maintain a recognized standard of excellence. The subjects taught and the approximate number of hours to be devoted to each of them are prescribed and little variety from the program is allowed. The requirements for the final examinations are specified by law and the questions are drawn up by a central board. Teachers must be qualified either by the possession of a university degree or by a certificate indicating success in an examination before a government-appointed board of examiners. A school board independent of the teaching staff governs the school. The state reserves to itself the right of surveillance by means of its secondary school inspectors.

Ample freedom is left the denominational secondary schools to control absolutely all matters concerned with religion and to maintain the spirit essential to the attainment of their ultimate purpose. The school board has a free hand in appointing the teachers. For Catholic schools, these are to a large extent members of religious congregations or orders. The government can never force the school to take or to dismiss any qualified person. Likewise the government has no jurisdiction over the selection of textbooks or methods of

teaching. Regular periods of formal religious instruction are
provided in the daily schedule. The religion professor is
recognized by law and receives payment as a master of his
subject. The nuances constituting the atmosphere of a religiously-oriented school can be maintained to the degree desired by the administration and staff of the school.

There are six institutions of higher learning in Holland
and four institutes for specialized studies. Of the six universities, one, located at Nijmegen, is Catholic; one is Protestant; the other four are publicly controlled. Catholics also
conduct a school of economics at Tilburg. The proportionate
share which the respective universities have in educating on
the higher level is indicated by the division of graduates. Approximately 79 percent are graduated from the public universities; 7.5 percent from the Protestant, 9.0 percent from the
Catholic University, and 4.5 percent from other private institutions.

The degrees given by all the universities are recognized
as valid. There is splendid cooperation among the institutions,
so that students may transfer to a similar department at a
different university without difficulty. The public universities
show an eagerness to cooperate with the churches. A chair
has been granted to the Catholic hierarchy at all four public
institutions; the bishops appoint a lecturer of their own free
choice to teach Catholic philosophy and theology. The Catholic
students also have their own groups on each campus and a
priest is assigned as the moderator.

The denominational universities receive subsidies from
the government, although the principle of financial equality is
not completely recognized. When establishing the amount of
financial support to be given by the state allowance has been
made for the fact that for a university the costs entailed by
some faculties are higher than those of others. For that reason, the Catholic school of Economics at Tilburg receives
subsidies covering 70 percent of costs; the Catholic University
of Nijmegen, 85 percent of expenses; the Free University of
Amsterdam (Protestant) is given 90 percent of costs. Deficits
are made up by tuition fees charged students. Scholarships
given by the government are available to competent students no

matter which university they attend. The private universities have, of course, retained complete freedom in the management of their affairs.

Has the Dutch Solution Been Successful?

Perhaps the best criterion of the success of the Dutch solution is the satisfaction it has given the people of the Netherlands, a satisfaction which has been expressed in the utilization of the opportunity it has given them to provide the kind of education they want for their children. A staff member of the Catholic Central Bureau expresses the matter this way:

> The solution of the education question in the Netherlands, in 1917, was a political fact, supported by all the existing parties of that moment. Since 1917, this solution has been maintained and the principle of financial equality has progressively been applied to all levels of education. This fact in itself is, we think, the best answer to the question, since such a development is only possible if supported by the Nation as a whole.[37]

No one in the Netherlands argues against public schools or shows an animus toward them. It is recognized that the system is necessary and has a place and that because of religious pluralism in the nation such schools must maintain a neutrality among religious denominations. If religious neutrality is what some people in Holland want, they can have it. But there are many others whose view of life demands an education which integrates the secular elements with religious and moral training; they, too, can have this without the penalty of an additional financial burden. The arrangement patently is just; it gives practical recognition to the primacy of parental rights in education; it gives full consideration to the most precious of liberties -- freedom of religion in education; it allows all to share equitably in public educational funds.

There were some people, and perhaps a few remain, who objected to the solution. Against it they leveled such criticisms as duplication of buildings, teachers, teaching materials, and consequent waste of money. Some few others saw the solution as an instrument segregating the Dutch people along religious lines. A closer examination of these arguments often betrayed in their proponents a basic prejudice against denominational schools as such and perhaps against religion itself. There may still be a few die-hards who retain these attitudes but one hears little from them today. The fallacy of the financial argument has been laid bare. There is no real duplication of costs. If the children now attending private schools should be transferred to public schools, approximately the same number of buildings would have to be built and the same number of teachers hired. Further, there is proof that the running expenses of private schools are lower than those in public schools.

There is no evidence that the great increase in private education has jeopardized the general well-being of the nation or tended to sharpen divergencies among the people. On the contrary, the more faithful a Dutchman is to the moral teaching of his church, the better citizen he is, as an unbiased observation of the situation in the country clearly demonstrates. Nor has the existence of different types of schools resulted in a segmentation of the population into hostile, unfriendly or isolated groups. There are differences in religious viewpoints in the nation. That is a cherished right in a democracy. The church-related schools have taken practical cognizance of these differences, but not augmented them to a point of intolerance. Right-minded religious teachers have respect for the religious consciences of others, without, however, necessitating the acceptance of the proposition that one viewpoint is as good as another. Democracy in Holland again exemplifies its essential nature by manifesting unity in diversity. The Dutch people, whatever be their religious convictions, are united in love of and devotion to their native land. All observers admit that a splendid spirit of cooperation exists among the various types of schools and between the educational authorities and the managers of the private schools. Comradeship among pupils follows natural lines. A clergyman of the Reformed Church summarized the situation:

The visitor to the Netherlands is rather surprised
at the many different churches and the numerous
denominations, and the religious disunity and individualism of the Dutch. But as he becomes better
acquainted with Dutch religious life, he finds that
religious questions are taken very seriously (the
Dutch have indeed been called a nation of theologi-
ans). And he finds, too, that though religious
differences have led to fierce conflicts, there is
still, in spite of all outward divisions, a background
of mutual respect and spiritual liberty. If he
speaks with leaders of the various denominations,
he will detect a passionate concern to protect and
preserve religious values, now threatened from
various sides. . . [38]

The arrangement the Dutch have made for religious instruction in the public schools seems to be the most satisfactory possible in a pluralistic society. Those who wish to
receive religious instruction have an opportunity to obtain it
from a representative of their faith without the inconvenience
of leaving the school building. Those who want no religious
instruction are perfectly free to refrain. This arrangement
appears to many thinking people who are concerned about the
need of religion in public schools to be more in harmony with
religious freedom than the plan of submitting all pupils, voluntarily, of course, as is done in England, to an agreed syllabus,
which may or may not be in accord with the creed taught them
in the churches or in the home.

The Netherlands, too, in granting full support to the private schools without tying its acceptance to forced control by
the government has displayed a high regard for parental rights
and religious freedom in education. This stands in contrast
to the recent legislation passed in France, which grants subsidies to the hard pressed Catholic schools on condition that they
relinquish freedom in degrees corresponding to the amount of
the subventions and to the extent that the very raison d'etre
of the Catholic schools is seriously jeopardized or destroyed.
All in all, Holland's solution, as so many observers have declared, is "very near the ideal."

Epilogue: SUMMARY VIEW

A study of history verifies the fact that the religious and moral training of the young has been a matter of great importance and concern since the beginning of the Christian era. In its origin Western education was essentially God-centered. Before it was possible to establish anything like a complete system of education and while persecution by pagan Rome raged, the early Church, putting first things first, instructed her catechumens in Christian truths and the Christian way of living in schools specially designed for this purpose. Later, for those prepared for more advanced instruction, she established her catechetical schools, many of which, notably the school at Alexandria, became centers of Christian learning.

From the fall of Rome to the sixteenth century, the Church provided and controlled practically all educational efforts. Her parish, monastic, cathedral schools, and finally her universities formed a far-flung system over the whole continent of Europe, embracing her children from elementary through the higher levels of learning. Provincial and general councils decreed the obligation of local churches to provide elementary education. Religious and moral training had always a place of primary importance. The pattern which education was to take was established. There is no modern educational system which does not to a greater or less extent bear the influence of its ecclesiastical origin.

With the Protestant Revolt came changes -- and problems. The multiplying Protestant sects, unable or unwilling to undertake the cost of supporting schools, looked to the ruling princes for aid. Religious rivalries, deepening into hatred and persecution, were rampant. Through it all, the traditional Christian principle stood firm: religious instruction was the most important element in the school's program. But now the concept was alloyed by its mixture with the politics

414

of the time. To solve the question of religious rivalry in the Germanic countries, the so-called Peace of Augsburg (1555) had formulated the liberty-destroying principle: <u>cujus regis illius religio</u> (the ruler's religion is to be that of his subjects). The religion of the ruler was the only one taught in the schools and the schools became the humble servant of the state. Confessions of faith, symbols, catechisms embodying the state's religious and civic creeds took the place of the free interpretation of the Scriptures which the leaders of the Revolt had at first advocated. The state entered into a close alliance with the church in order to make the school an instrument of religious and political control.

With the rationalistic movement of the eighteenth century deeper chasms were cut into religious thinking and beliefs. Scholastic philosophy gave way to the thinking of Descartes. The hold of religion began to weaken in most sections of Europe, but there was no thought of its elimination until after the French Revolution. The leaders of the Reign of Terror, drunk with power and imbued with fanatic hatred of the Catholic Church and everything religious, established the principle of a monolithic system of education, completely secularized and under the absolute control of the state. Eventually this principle exerted great influence and spawned many problems.

Political, economic, and social developments in the nineteenth century had their impacts upon education. The changes wrought by the industrial revolution and the movement toward greater democracy with its concomitant expansion of the franchise made churchmen and rationalists alike aware that participation of the state in providing educational facilities was inevitable. State aid and some kind of compulsory education were obviously necessary. The distinct problem emerging from this development was not the entry of the state into the business of education, but the fact that the great financial and coercive powers of the state should back the secular ideal in its compulsory schools. Yet, since the state took up the function of education in a world in which unity of belief had been disrupted by the Protestant Revolt, the problem of its relation to religious instruction was a real one. In a pluralistic society what religion, if any, was to be taught in the public schools? What relationship should the state establish with church-related schools: aid them, ignore them, control or destroy them? The attempt to answer these questions, history shows, occasioned some of the most bitter political contentions in the Western World. It was an issue important enough to cause governments to stand or fall; for statesmen and politicians knew that it was a struggle for the minds of generations to come. No western nation was free from the problem. Within Catholic countries the battle waged between clericals and anti-clericals. In Protestant countries, the views of divergent sects had to be contended with. Throughout the course of the ensuing struggles in most cases emotion and prejudice played a large part.

Gradually, the majority of western democracies realized that a rational resolution of the religious education issue would have to be designed. The motives underlying the attempts to provide a satisfactory solution varied from the more pragmatic or practical -- political expediency, attainment of greater national unity and peace, the country's need of adequate educational opportunity for all children of the nation -- to genuine recognition of parental rights, of true religious liberty in choice of education, of equity to all citizens in the distribution of government benefits.

The compromise or settlements finally arrived at may be classified under several categories, which, for greater clarity, must be considered under the two correlative aspects that the issue entails: first, the function of public schools in the area of religious and moral education; and, secondly, the relation of the state to church-affiliated schools. For the first aspect, we may distinguish six types of settlements. There is some overlapping here with the classifications under the second aspect.

1) An agreed syllabus or sort of common denominator of religious truths which, supposedly, the various religious groups are willing to accept is taught in the public schools, children whose parents so request being excused from the instruction. Great Britain has adopted this arrangement in her county schools.

2) Denominational religious instruction is given by official representatives of the various churches in the public school building to the children of their persuasion, the public school itself and the teachers remaining completely neutral in regard to the creeds. Several Canadian provinces, notably Manitoba; most of the Australian states; France, in her boarding lycées (with limitations), and Belgium follow this plan. The practice was declared unconstitutional for the United States by the United States Supreme Court in the McCollum case, 1949.

3) A preferred religion is taught in public schools. This happens when the overwhelming majority of the population profess a common religious creed, as is the case in Catholic Italy.

4) Within the public school system, schools are established on a denominational basis, the specific creed of each denomination being taught in its own schools. The confessional school system of West Germany, the separate schools of several Canadian provinces, the school system of Scotland, though they differ in the details of the plan, may be classified under this category.

5) Religious instruction of any kind is absolutely prohibited in the public schools, which are secularized in teaching and spirit. This seemed to the American states in the mid-nineteenth century to be the easy way out of the difficulty. The policy, however, generated many additional problems. Extreme limits of the secular concept have been reached in the public schools of the United States and in the elementary schools of France.

6) A final type of solution exists when the schools remain under the ownership and control of the respective churches and retain their denominational character intact. The state's function is limited to providing full or partial support and laying down minimum regulations to insure efficiency. Such, in general, is the arrangement in Holland, Ireland, and Newfoundland,

with minor variations. Holland also conducts public schools, which are neutral, whereas all the schools in Newfoundland and Ireland are denominational.

In regard to the second aspect of the issue, namely, the relationship of the state to church-related schools, the policies which have evolved also fall into several patterns:

1) An arrangement which overlaps with (6) above. The function of the state in regard to church-affiliated schools is limited to support and minimum essential regulations. In Holland complete support is provided for all church-related schools; in Ireland practically all expenses are underwritten by the national government; in Newfoundland up to 90 percent of costs is paid out of public funds.

2) Church-related schools are incorporated into the public school system. They are managed in all their secular aspects as public schools and are likewise completely supported while keeping their denominational character intact. The schools of Scotland, all of which are church-related; the separate schools of several Canadian provinces; with qualifications, the schools of Quebec, and the confessional schools of West Germany may be classified in this category. Integration with the public school system was offered the Catholic schools in France in 1959. They rejected the proposition since its acceptance meant the loss of their real character as religion-orientated schools.

3) Church-related schools constitute a separate system, keep their denominational character, and are financially supported on the principle: more aid -- more more state control. Great Britain has adopted this policy for her voluntary schools; and, since the passage of Loi Debré (1959), French libres écoles, practically all of which are under Catholic auspices, may by voluntary contract elect this pattern. Control by the French government over the schools under contract is highly extensive.

4) Church-related schools form an entirely separate
   system, have liberty to manage their affairs independently of the state, but are denied public aid of any
   kind. With some specific differences, this pattern
   prevails only in the United States, Australia, and
   British Columbia. Among the Western democracies,
   the respective American states, abetted by opinions
   of the U. S. Supreme Court, have carried the no-aid
   policy to its greatest limits. The Australian states
   give generous indirect aids to their church-related
   schools.

The significant point is that our Western allies, as a
whole, have shied away from the policy of secularized education for their children, have recognized the value of religion-
oriented schools in the economy of the nation, and through
regular democratic processes have evolved policies on the
school issue which seem, in general, to give satisfaction.
Given good-will among the people, democracies, it would
seem, can always find a way to satisfy the legitimate desires
of their citizens.

Some of the Western democracies still have established
churches. Most of them adhere to the principle of separation
of church and state. All are vitally concerned with complete
religious freedom. They found no conflict between the need
to safeguard the liberty of the individual conscience and the
need to give official recognition to the importance of religious
training in the educational process by providing it a role in
the public school system and by giving financial aid to church-
related schools. Quite possibly behind the more immediate
reasons which urged the statesmen to find a solution was the
conviction that the ultimate welfare of the nation was tied to a
citizenry influenced by deeply held religious beliefs and that
a thorough religious education was the most effective way to
develop responsible and law-abiding citizens.

FOOTNOTES

INTRODUCTION

[1]Cf. Edmund G. Drouin, The School Question: a bibliography on Church-State relationships in American education, 1940-1960 (Washington: The Catholic University of America Press, 1963).

[2]Cf. James M. O'Neill, Religion and Education Under the Constitution (New York: Harpers, 1949); Wilfrid Parsons, The First Freedom (New York: D. X. McMullen Company, 1948).

[3]Journals of the Continental Congress, 1774-1789. Edited from the original records in the Library of Congress by John C. Fitspatrick (Washington: Government Printing Office, 1933), XXVIII, 378.

[4]George H. Martin, The Evolution of the Massachusetts Public School System: A Historical Sketch (New York: D. Appleton and Company, 1894), p. 230.

[5]New York, Laws of 1842, Chap. CL, Sec. 14.

[6]Sherman M. Smith, The Relation of the State to Religious Education in Massachusetts (Syracuse, N. Y.: Syracuse University Book Shop, 1926), pp. 210-11.

[7]Carl F. Zollman, American Church Law (St. Paul, Minnesota: West Publishing Company, 1933), p. 82.

[8]Illinois Constitution (1870), Art. VIII, Sec. 3.

[9]Cf. References in Drouin, op. cit.

[10]Cf. Edward S. Corwin, "The Supreme Court as a National School Board;" Charles Fahy, "Religion, Education, and the Supreme Court;" John Courtney Murray, "Law or Prepossessions?" in Law and Contemporary Problems (Winter, 1949), XV, 1-22; 73-91; 23-43.

[11]Everson v. Board of Education, 330, U.S. 1 (1947).

[12]Loc. cit.

[13]McCollum v Board of Education, 333 U.S. 203 (1948).

[14]Cf. Edward Corwin, op. cit., passim.

[15]Zorach v. Clausen, 343 U.S. 306 (1952).

[16]Steven I. Engel et al. v. William J. Vitale, 370 U.S. 421 (1962).

[17]Torcaso v. Watkins, 367 U.S. 488 (June, 1961).

[18]Cf. Holy Trinity Church v. United States, 143 U.S. 457 (1892)

[19]Mormon Church v. United States, 136 U.S. 1 (May, 1890).

[20]School District of Abington Township, Penn., et al. v. Shempp et al; and Murray et al. v. Curlett et al., constituting Board of School Commissioners of Baltimore City, 374 U.S. 203 (June, 1963).

[21]National Education Association, Moral and Spiritual Values, Report of Education Policies Committee (Washington: National Education Association, 1951), p. 3.

[22]American Council on Education, The Function of the Public Schools in dealing with Religion, Report of the Committee on Religion and Education (Washington: The American Council of Education, 1953), p. 6.

[23]Cf. National Catholic Welfare Conference, Legal Department, The Constitutionality of the Inclusion of Church-Related Schools in Federal Aid to Education (Washington: The National Catholic Welfare Conference, 1961) passim.

[24]Cf. Richard J. Gabel, Public Funds for Church and Private Schools, Doctoral dissertation (Washington: The Catholic University of America, 1937).

[25]"How U. S. Will Help Church Schools," United States News and World Report (May 3, 1965), LVIII, No. 18, p. 51.

[26]Ibid., p. 52.

[27]Cited by James J. Murray, "What is the Real Issue?", in America (March 25, 1961), CIV, p. 818.

[28]Register (Denver) April 16, 1965.

[29]Catholic Standard (Washington, D. C.), May 10, 1963.

CHAPTER I

[1]H. C. Dent, The Educational System of England and Wales (London: University of London Press, Ltd., 1961), p. 13.

[2]Cf. A. F. Leach, English Schools at the Reformation (Westminster: A Constable, 1896), p. 5; _____, The Schools of Medieval England (London: Methuen and Company, Ltd., 1915), pp. 329, 330-332; _____, Educational Charters and Documents (Cambridge: University Press, 1911), p. XVI.

[3]J. A. Gasquet, Parish Life in Medieval England (London: Methuen and Company, 1906), p. 73.

[4]William T. Kane, S.J., Revised by John J. O'Brien, History of Education (Chicago: Loyola University Press, 1954), pp. 157-58.

[5]Patrick J. McCormick and Francis P. Cassidy, History of Education (Washington: The Catholic University of America Press, 1953), pp. 389, 404-405; Thomas L. Jarman, Landmarks in the History of Education (London: Cresset Press, 1951), p. 161.

[6]Cf. E. P. Graves, History of Education during the Middle Ages (New York: The Macmillan Company, 1910), p. 195; A. F. Leach, English Schools at the Reformation, op. cit., p. 5; Stanley J. Curtis, History of Education in Great Britain (London: University Tutorial Press, Ltd., 1950), p. 81.

[7]H. G. Good, A History of Western Education, 2nd Ed. (New York: The Macmillan Company, 1960), p. 160.

[8]Dent, op. cit., p. 14.

[9]Good, op. cit., p. 347.

[10]The Case for Catholic Schools, 2nd. Ed. (London: The Catholic

Education Council, 1955), p. 21

[11] Loc. cit.

[12] Ibid., p. 23

[13] Cf. George Beck, "Bishops, Schools and General Education,"
Tablet (London) CLXXXXV (January 14, 1950) 27-28.

[14] The Case for Catholic Schools, op. cit., p. 23.

[15] Mary H. Allies, Thomas Wilson Allies (New York: Benziger
Brothers, 1907), pp. 89-91.

[16] The Case for Catholic Schools, op. cit., p. 7.

[17] H. G. Good, op. cit., p. 539.

[18] A. C. F. Beales, "The Scottish Concordat and Its Applicability
to England and Wales," The Dublin Review, No. 472 (Winter 1956-57) 171.

[19] The Case for Catholic Schools, op. cit., p. 24.

[20] Beales, op. cit., p. 171

[21] Cf. Chapter II.

[22] Beales, op. cit., p. 173.

[23] The Case for Catholic Schools, op. cit., p. 18.

[24] Ibid., p. 25.

[25] Ibid., pp. 28-29.

[26] Ibid., p. 26.

[27] Ibid., p. 30

[28] Ibid., p. 42.

[29] Loc. cit.

[30] Facts relating to the negotiations leading to the passage of the
Education Act, 1959, have been obtained from account given by Most
Reverend George A. Beck, A.A., "Background to the Education Act,
1959," Catholic Education (December, 1959), No. 7, 1-26.

[31] Parliamentary Debates (Hassard), House of Commons, Official
Report (Thursday, 11th June, 1959), Vol. 606, No. 123, 1189.

[32] Ibid., 1188

[33] Parliamentary Debates (Hassard), House of Commons, Official
Report (Monday, 22nd June, 1959), Vol. 607, No. 130, 884.

[34] Ibid., 902

[35] The Times (London), June 12, 1959.

[36] Ministry of Education, Statistics of Education, Part I, 1964
(London: H. M. Stationery Office, 1965).

[37] Cf. H. R. Chetwynd, B.A., Comprehensive School: The Story of
Woodberry Down (London: Routledge and Kegan Paul, Ltd., 1960).

[38] S. Leeson, Christian Education Reviewed (London: Longmans,
Green, 1957), p. 90, citing "Report of Research Committee of the Institute
of Christian Education, 1955."

[39] Education in Great Britain (New York: British Information Services, 1960), p. 14.

[40] "A National Agreed Syllabus?" The Sower (Notes) (October,
1945), CLVII, 2-3.

[41] Loc. cit.

[42] Education in Great Britain, op. cit., pp. 14-15.

[43] Leeson, op. cit., p. 21.

[44] Interview by author with secretary of Catholic Education Council, London.

[45] Denver Register, March 18, 1960.

[46] Church and School (Education Committee of England and Wales, 1961), cited in Denver Register, December 22, 1961.

[47] Interview by author with secretary of Catholic Education Council, London.

[48] Loc. cit.

[49] Loc. cit.

[50] Ministry of Education, Statistics of Education, 1964 (London: H. M. Stationery Office, 1965).

[51] Loc. cit.

[52] Education in Great Britain, op. cit., p. 12; Catholic Education in England and Wales, (London: The Catholic Education Council, 1954), p. 5.

[53] New York Times, July 16, 1961, p. 7.

[54] Catholic Education in England and Wales, op. cit., unpaged summary of total figures.

[55] Teacher Training in Great Britain (New York: British Information Services, 1962), pp. 4, 6.

[56] Interviews by author with Mother Richardson, President, Digby-Stuart Teachers' College, Roehampton, London, and with administrators of several other teachers' colleges.

[57] Cardinal Vaughn, Letter to The Times (London), 1895, cited in Foreword to The Case for Catholic Schools, op. cit.

[58] Times' Educational Supplement (London), February 6, 1959, reprinted in Voluntary Secondary Schools (London: The Catholic Education Council, 1959), p. 9.

[59] Beck, op. cit., p. 25.

[60] Denver Register (June 5, 1962), citing statement by Anglican Archbishop Ramsey after his return from Delhi meeting of the World Council of Churches, 1962.

[61] The Case for Catholic Schools, op. cit., p. 58.

[62] Francis Summerville, S.J., "Christianity in English schools", citing a remark of Anglican Bishop Carey in a letter to The Times (London), Lumen Vitae (October - December, 1949), IV, 705.

[63] Ibid., p. 707.

[64] Ibid., p. 708.

[65] Most Reverend Bishop George Beck, "Thoughts on the Crowther Report," Tablet (London) (December 19, 1959) CCXIII, 1109.

[66] Loc. cit.

[67] Remark of Archbishop Downey of Liverpool in an address in Liverpool Stadium, February 12, 1950, cited in Tablet (London), (February 18, 1950) CLXXXXV, 136.

[68]Yorkshire Post, editorial (May 6, 1959), cited in Voluntary Secondary Schools, op. cit., p. 2.

[69]Denver Register (July 28, 1961).

CHAPTER II

[1]Cf. P. F. Quille, "The Scottish System in Practice--An Unqualified Success," Dublin Review (Winter, 1956-57), No. 47^2, 185.

[2]Sister Mary Bonaventure Dealy, O.S.B., Catholic Schools in Scotland, Doctoral dissertation (Washington: The Catholic University of America, 1945), p. 32, citing Acts of Parliament, II, 235.

[3]William Barry, "Catholic Education in Scotland," The Catholic Educator (December, 1952), XXIII, 200.

[4]Dealy, op. cit., p. 39.

[5]Barry, op. cit., p. 200.

[6]Ibid., p. 201; A Bellesheim, History of the Catholic Church in Scotland, trans. by David Oswald Hunter-Blair (Edinburgh: William Blackwood and Sons, 1887), IV, 128.

[7]James Mulhern, A History of Education: A Social Interpretation, 2nd Ed. (New York: The Ronald Press Company, 1959), p. 376.

[8]Ibid., 377.

[9]Barry, op. cit., (January, 1953) 246.

[10]Loc. cit.

[11]Barry, op. cit., 248.

[12]John F. Cramer and George S. Browne, Contemporary Education: A Comparative Study of National Systems (New York: Harcourt, Brace and Company, 1950), p. 80.

[13]Barry, op. cit., (February, 1953), p. 283.

[14]Ibid., p. 281; Cf. Dealy, op. cit., pp. 151-53.

[15]Cf. Scottish Education Department "Memorandum with Regard to the Provisions Made for Religious Instruction in the Schools of Scotland" (Edinburgh; H. M. Stationery Office, 1943), p. 5; Barry op. cit., pp. 280-281.

[16]Education (Scotland) Act, 1872, Preamble.

[17]Ibid., Sec. 67(2).

[18]Barry, op. cit., p. 282.

[19]Scottish Education Department, op. cit., p. 8, citing Report of Education Department, 1878-79, p. 173.

[20]Rev. Brother Kenneth, M.A., "Catholic Education in Scotland, 1878-1917," Scottish Catholic Herald, XV, 1956.

[21]Loc. cit.

[22]Loc. cit.

[23]Barry, op. cit., p. 283.

[24]Cf. Parliamentary Debates, 100 H.C., Deb. 5s., (December 17, 1918), pp. 1655 ff.

[25]Glasgow Herald, March 1, 1918, p. 3.

[26]"The Education Bill: Secretary for Scotland Replies to Critics," The Educational News (January, 18, 1918) XLIII, 48.

[27]Quille, op. cit., pp. 185-86.

[28]"The Holy See and the Scottish Bill," Tablet (London) (April 27, 1918), CXXXI, 552.

[29]Parliamentary Debates, Official Reports, op. cit., (Nov. 8, 1918) Col. 394.

[30]Education (Scotland) Act, 1918, 8 and 9 Geo. V, Chap. 48.

[31]Barry, op. cit., p. 288.

[32]Local Gov. (Scotland) Act, 1929, 19 and 20 Geo. V, Chap. 25, Sec. 12.

[33]Quille, op. cit., 187-8.

[34]Ibid., p. 194.

[35]Scottish Education Department, Edinburgh (typed report sent to author), May, 1964.

[36]Quille, op. cit., 194-195.

[37]Barry, op. cit., (March, 1953), p. 342.

[38]Edinburgh Corporation Education Committee, Handbook, Sec. 10, p. 74, cited by Quille, op. cit., p. 195.

[39]Quille, op. cit., p. 190.

[40]The Education (Scotland) Act, 1918, 8 and 9, Geo. V, Chap. 48, Sec. 7.

[41]Dealy, op. cit., p. 299.

[42]Ibid., pp. 299-300.

[43]A. C. F. Beales, "The Scottish Concordat and Its Applicability to England and Wales," The Dublin Review, no. 47[2] (Winter, 1956-57), p. 167.

[44]Ibid., p. 168, citing J. Grant Robertson, The Education (Scotland) Act, 1918 (Catholic Truth Society of Scotland, 1937).

[45]Quille, op. cit., p. 196.

CHAPTER III

[1]British North American Act, reproduced in J. G. Bourinot A Manual of the Constitutional History of Canada (Toronto: The Copp, Clark Company, Ltd., 1901), pp. 211-212.

[2]"Reference Paper," No. 45 (Ottawa, Canada: Information Division, Department of External Affairs, 1960), Typescript, p. 3.

[3]Ibid., pp. 4-5.

[4]C. E. Phillips, The Development of Education in Canada (Toronto: W. J. Gage and Co., Ltd., 1957), p. 301.

[5]W. L. Grant, History of Canada (Montreal, 1899), pp. 135-6.

[6]Edward A. Connaughton, "A Study of the Provisions Made for the Catholic Elementary Schools of the Province of Ontario." Unpublished Master's dissertation (Washington: The Catholic University of America, 1940), p. 2.

[7]Franklin A. Walker, Catholic Education and Politics in Upper Canada (Toronto: J. M. Dent and Sons, 1955), p. 37, citing Dr. Charles Duncombe, "Report on the Subject of Education" (Toronto, 1836), pp. 50-51.

[8]Connaughton, op. cit., p. 5, citing W. L. Grant, op. cit., p. 167.
[9]Ibid., p. 7.
[10]George W. Ross, The School System of Ontario (New York: 1896) pp. 142-3.
[11]Charles B. Sissons, Church and State in Canadian Education (Toronto: Ryerson Press, 1959), p. 15.
[12]Ibid., p. 25.
[13]Walker, op. cit., p. 113.
[14]Loc. cit.
[15]The Banner, Nov. 28, 1844.
[16]The Globe, July 9, 1850.
[17]The True Witness, Aug. 5, 1853
[18]The Globe, May 22, 1855.
[19]Walker, op. cit., p. 267.
[20]The True Witness, March 13, 1863.
[21]The Globe, March 14, 1863.
[22]Cf. pp. 161-162.
[23]John Lewis, "George Brown" in Makers of Canada Series, Vol. XIX (Toronto: 1910) pp. 122-123.
[24]H. E. Egerton and W. L. Grant, Canadian Constitutional Development (London: John Murray, Albemarle, 1907) p. 422.
[25]Connaughton, op. cit., p. 19.
[26]Law Reports, Repealed Cases, 1928.
[27]Connaughton, op. cit., pp. 20, 51.
[28]Regulations and Programs for Religious Education in the Public Schools (Ontario: The Minister of Education, 1960), p. 5.
[29]Ibid., pp. 5-6.
[30]Ibid., p. 9.
[31]The Schools Administration Act, Revised Statutes of Ontario, 1960, Chap. 361 (Toronto: Frank Fogg, Queen's Printer, 1961), Sec. 22 (c), p. 19.
[32]Report of the Minister, 1964 (Ontario: Department of Education, 1964), p. S.2.
[33]Data from correspondence with officials of Catholic schools.
[34]Loc. cit.; Report of the Minister, op. cit., pp. S. 160-S. 167.
[35]Report of the Minister, op. cit., pp. IX-X.
[36]The Separate Schools Act, Revised Statutes of Ontario, 1960, Chap. 368 (Toronto: Frank Fogg, Queen's Printer, 1961), Sections 16-44,

pp. 16-21.

[37]Ibid., Sec. 22, p. 19.

[38]Connaughton, op. cit., p. 52.

[39]The Separate Schools Act, op. cit., Sec. 53, (1) and (2), p. 26.

[40]Ibid., Sec. 59 (1), p. 28-29.

[41]Connaughton, op. cit., p. 62.

[42]Ibid., pp. 63-64.

[43]Canadian Register, Nov. 10, 1962.

[44]Cf. Edward Wakin, "The Catholic College that Disappeared."
The Sign (August, 1965) XLV, No. 1, 31.

[45]Loc. cit.

CHAPTER IV

[1]Franklin Walker, Catholic Education and Politics in Upper Canada
(Toronto: Dent and Sons, 1955), p. 15.

[2]Ibid., pp. 15-16.

[3]Report of the Superintendent of Education (Province of Quebec:
Roch Lefebre, Queen's Printer, 1961), p. 60.

[4]Ibid., p. 66.

[5]Information submitted in correspondence from H. B. Billings,
Director of Protestant Education, Department of Education, Quebec,
March 5, 1963, citing the 1962 Canada Year Book.

[6]Donald A. MacLean, The Catholic Schools in Western Canada:
Their Legal Status (Toronto: The Extension Press, 1923), p. 53-55.

[7]Our Sunday Visitor, May 6, 1961.

[8]Ibid., December 6, 1959.

[9]Charles B. Sissons, Church and State in Canadian Education
(Toronto: Ryerson Press, 1959), pp. 165-166.

[10]Statistics kindly supplied by R. W. Dalton, Director of Administration, Department of Education, Manitoba, March 1, 1963.

[11]MacLean, op. cit., p. 77.

[12]North-West Territories Act, 1875, Sec. 11.

[13]Canadian Legislative Debates (Hassard) p. 8082, cited by MacLean,
op. cit., p. 93.

[14]Based on information kindly supplied by H. Janzen, Director of
Curricula, Department of Education, Saskatchewan, November 28, 1962.

[15]Sissons, op. cit., p. 277.

[16]Ibid., p. 296.

[17]Ibid., p. 297.

[18]Based on information kindly supplied by H. Janzen, op. cit.,
February 28, 1963.

[19]Revised Statutes, Saskatchewan, Chap. 172 (Regina: Queen's
Printer, 1963) Sections 20-23, pp. 3001, 3003.

[20]Information kindly supplied by H. Janzen, op. cit., February 28,
1963.

[21]Sissons, op. cit., p. 341

[22]Based on information kindly supplied the writer by the Deputy Minister of Education, Province of Alberta, March 6, 1963.

[23]Loc. cit.

[24]G. A. Frecker, Education in the Atlantic Provinces (Toronto: W. J. Gage and Company Limited, 1956), p. 32.

[25]Ibid., p. 111.

[26]Sissons, op. cit., pp. 217, 246.

[27]Based on information kindly furnished the writer by O. V. B. Miller, Education Services Director, Department of Education, New Brunswick, February 28, 1963.

[28]The School Act, Revised Statutes of Prince Edward Island, Chap. 145 (Charlottetown, Department of Education, 1961), p. 48.

[29]Based on information kindly supplied by M. MacKenzie, Deputy Minister of Education and Director of Education, Prince Edward Island, February 28, 1963.

[30]Cf. Fred W. Rowe, The History of Education in Newfoundland (Toronto: The Ryerson Press, 1952), p. 131.

[31]Sissons, op. cit., p. 403, citing Education Act, 1903, Sec. 106.

[32]Act of Union, 1949, Clause 17.

[33]Loc. cit.

[34]Based on information kindly supplied by Sister Basil McCormick, R.S.M., St. Bride's College, Littledale, St. John's, Newfoundland, April, 1963.

CHAPTER V

[1]Cf. pp. 233-34 of this chapter.

[2]Ronald Fogarty, F.M.S., Catholic Education in Australia, 1806-1950 (Melbourne: Melbourne University Press, 1959), Vol. I, p. 19.

[3]William Keane, "Australia: A Study in Courage," America (April, 23, 1949), LXXXI, 117.

[4]Fogarty, op. cit., p. 150, citing views expressed by Mr. Cohen in educational debates on 1872 bill: Parli., Deb. (Vic), 1872, p. 1674; and views expressed in liberals journals of the period.

[5]Cf. Fogarty, op. cit., pp. 140

[6]Ibid., p. 143

[7]"The Catholic School in Australia," Current Affairs Bulletin (August 25, 1956), XXII, 133.

[8]Fogarty, op. cit., p. 143.

[9]Loc. cit., citing Freeman's Journal (April 6, 1872), p. 11, b.

[10]"The Catholic School in Australia," op. cit., p. 134.

[11]Fogarty, op. cit., p. 198, citing Act, 43 (Vic.) no. xxiiii, Chap. 7, 1872.

[12]Loc. cit., citing Education Act, 1880.

[13]Fogarty, op. cit., pp. 134-135, citing Report of Royal Commission on Education, 1875, p. 202.

[14]"The Catholic School in Australia," op. cit., p. 133.

[15]Ibid., p. 134.

[16]Cf. Keane, op. cit., p. 118.

[17]"The Catholic School in Australia," op. cit., p. 134.

[18]John F. Cramer and George S. Browne, Contemporary Education: A Comparative Study of National Systems (New York: Harcourt, Brace and Company, 1956), p. 335.

[19]Schools, 1964. Social Statistics: Australia, No. 29 (Camberra: Australia: Commonwealth Bureau of Census and Statistics, 1965), Table II, p. 6.

[20]Ibid., Table I, p. 4.

[21]"The Catholic School in Australia," op. cit., p. 135.

[22]Ibid., p. 136.

[23]Cf. Chap. I, pp. 58-61.

[24]Australian Encyclopedia, Vol. III, p. 355.

[25]"Government Scholarships for Secondary Education," Bulletin No. 13 (Sydney: Commonwealth Office of Education, 1958).

[26]Education Act, 1910, Sec. 60.

[27]Keane, op. cit., p. 118.

[28]"The Catholic School in Australia," op. cit., p. 134.

[29]Ibid., 137.

[30]Keane, op. cit., p. 118.

[31]"The Catholic School in Australia," op. cit., p. 137.

[32]Ibid., p. 144.

[33]Catholic Standard (Washington, D.C.) December 31, 1962.

[34]Denver Register, September 28, 1962.

[35]"The Catholic School in Australia," op. cit., p. 135.

[36]Catholic Universe Bulletin (Columbus, Ohio), July 27, 1962.

CHAPTER VI

[1]Robert Ulich, The Education of Nations (Cambridge: Harvard University Press, 1961), p. 143.

[2]Sister Justine Redmond, Laïcism in the Schools of France. Doctoral dissertation (Washington: The Catholic University of America, 1932), p. 7.

[3]Pierre J. Marique, History of Christian Education (New York: Fordham University Press, 1932), III, p. 236.

[4]Clarence E. Elwell, The Influence of the Enlightenment on the Catholic Theory of Religious Education, 1750-1850 (Cambridge: Harvard University Press, 1944), pp. 69-71.

[5]Cf. Frank Maloy Anderson, Constitutions and Other Select Documents Illustrative of the History of France, 1789-1907, 2nd Edition (Minneapolis: University of Minnesota, 1908; W. H. Wilson, 1908).

[6]Cf. W. H. Kilpatrick, Source Book of the Philosophy of Education (New York: The Macmillan Company, 1926), pp. 8-11.

[7]William T. Kane, S.J., Revised by John J. O'Brien, History of Education (Chicago: Loyola University Press, 1954), p. 307.

[8]Ibid., p. 316.

[9]Redmond, op. cit., p. 13, citing Maurice Legot, Laïcisme et Laïcite, p. 18.

[10]Evelyn M. Acomb, The French Laïc Laws (1879-1889). Doctoral dissertation (New York: Columbia University, 1941), p. 23, citing P. Pagnelle de Follenay, Vie du Cardinal Guibert (Paris: 1896).

[11]H. G. Good, A History of Western Education, 2nd Edition (New York: The Macmillan Company, 1960), p. 345.

[12]Acomb, op. cit., p. 176.

[13]Ibid., pp. 144-46.

[14]Redmond, op. cit., p. 19, citing Legot, op. cit., p. 75.

[15]Loc. cit., citing Legot, op. cit., p. 76.

[16]Redmond, op. cit., p. 20, citing Y. de la Brière, Lettres presentes de l'Eglise, Premiere Series, pp. 319-320.

[17]Ibid., p. 26.

[18]Sister Alphonsus Liguori Cyrier, O.P. Developments in Church-State Educational Relations in France between the Two World Wars. Unpublished Master's dissertation (Washington: The Catholic University of America, 1950), p.11, citing Journal Officiel de la Republique Francaise. Senat Documents Parlementaires, July, 1901, p. 4026.

[19]Mother Bernardine Hoban, R.S.H.M., Present Day Catholic School Problem in France and the Adequacy of Its Temporary Solution: La Loi Barangé. Unpublished Master's dissertation (Washington: The Catholic University of America, 1958), p. 15 citing Henri Chatreix, Au dela du Laïcisme ou la paix scolaire (Paris: Paris Editions du Seuil, 1946), p. 42.

[20]Journal Officiel de la Republique Francaise. Senat Documents Parlementaires, 1904, p. 208.

[21]Lettre Pastorale des Cardinaux Archeveques et Eveques de France, 1901.

[22]Redmond, op. cit., p. 28.

[23]Charles L. Souvay, "The Catholic Church in Contemporary France," in The Catholic Church in Contemporary Europe, 1919-1931, edited by Peter Guilday (New York: J. P. Kenedy and Sons, 1932), II, pp. 74-76.

[24]Cited in Redmond, op. cit., p. 31.

[25]Cf. Reverend Leo Rummel, "The Anti-clerical Program as a Disruptive Factor in the Solidarity of the Late French Republic." The Catholic Historical Review (April, 1948), XXXIV, 17.

[26]Redmond, op. cit., p. 36, citing Legot, op. cit., p. 99.

[27]"Revival of Anticlericalism," Tablet (London) (July 29, 1939), CLXXIV, p. 144.

[28]Journal Officiel, Sept. 17, 1940, pp. 5033-34.

[29]"History of France" (New York: French Cultural Service, No d.), p. 16.

[30]"Deeper Cleavage in France: the Religious Issue Which Split the Government Last Week" Tablet (London) (May 22, 1948), CLXXXXI, 317.

[31]Good, op. cit., p. 538.

[32]Marguerite Bousquet, Le Probleme de l'Enseignement primaire prive en France dupuis 1947 (Lyon: Universite de Lyon, 1956), p. 220.

[33]Le Monde (Paris), le 22 mars, 1951.

[34]Le Monde (Paris), le 6 juin, 1951, p. 12.

[35]Private Education in France (New York: French Cultural Services of French Embassy, no d.), p. 2.

[36]Loc. cit.

[37]Loc. cit.

[38]Cf. McCormick-Cassidy, op. cit., p. 622; John F. Cramer and George S. Browne, Contemporary Education (New York: Harcourt, Brace and Company, 1956), p. 281; I. L. Kandel, The New Era in Education: A Comparative Study (Boston: Houghton Mifflin Company, 1955), p. 165; Edmund J. King, Other Schools and Ours (New York: Rinehart and Company, 1958), p. 42.

[39]Robert Barrat, "The School Question in France," Commonweal (December 25, 1951), LXXI, 372.

[40]Loc. cit.

[41]Loc. cit.

[42]Cf. p. 337

[43]Cf. Liberté d'Ens, (September, 1963), Nos. 256-57, p. 29.

[44]Law No. 59-1557 of December 31, 1959. Article I, reproduced in "Private Education in France," op. cit., p. 5.

[45]Frank Macmillan, "A Settlement in France; The Confessional Schools," Tablet (London) (Jan. 2, 1960), CCXIV, 6.

[46]George F. Kneller, "Education in France" in Arthur H. Moehlman and Joseph C. Roucek, Comparative Education (New York: The Dryden Press, 1953), p. 197.

[47]Hoban, op. cit., p. 13.

[48]"The Secularizing Influence of the Neutral Official Schools," Lumen Vitae, No. 1. (January-March, 1950), V, 11-14.

[49]Moehlman, op. cit., p. 211.

[50]Redmond, op. cit., pp. 56-57, citing A. Bayet, Lecons de Morale, Preface pp. 1-2, 149 ff.

[51]Ibid., p. 58, citing E. Durkheim, La Division du Travail, 1893.

[52]"The Secularizing Influence of the Neutral Official Schools," op. cit., p. 13.

[53]Cf. Robert Ulich, op. cit., p. 164.

[54]French System of Education (New York: French Cultural Services of the French Embassy, no d.), pp. 5-7.

[55]Private Education in France, op. cit., p. 1.

[56]Loc. cit.

[57]Cramer and Browne, op. cit., p. 104.

[58]Private Education in France, op. cit., pp. 2-3.

[59]Loc. cit.

[60]Loc. cit.

[61]Cf. Frank Macmillan, "Back to School in France: A New Deal for the Catholic Parents," Tablet (London) (September 10, 1960), CCXIV, 813-14.

[62]Ibid., p. 812.

[63]"Chaplaincies in the State Schools of France," Tablet (London) (September 17, 1960), CCXIV, 852-53.

[64]Cf. Ulich, op. cit., pp. 154-157; Gwendolin Carter et al., Major Foreign Powers (New York: Harcourt, Brace and Company, 1952), p. 247; Cramer and Browne, op. cit., pp. 86-7; King, op. cit., pp. 35-36.

[65]Pius XI, The Christian Education of Youth (Washington: National Catholic Welfare Conference).

[66]Cited by Hoban, op. cit., p. 16.

[67]Acomb, op. cit., p. 25, citing Journal Officiel, May 5, 1877, p. 3286.

CHAPTER VII

[1]A. C. F. Beales, M.A., "Forward" to John Mescal, M.A., L.L.B., Religion in the Irish System of Education (Dublin: Clonmore and Reynolds, LTD., 1957), p. 7.

[2]C. Keenan, "Ireland's Fair Deal in Education," America (August 20, 1949), LXXXI, 540.

[3]James Mulhern, A History of Education, Second Edition (New York: The Ronald Press Company, 1959), p. 376

[4]Edward J. Power, Main Currents in the History of Education (New York: McGraw-Hill Book Company, Inc., 1962), p. 215.

[5]John Healy, Ireland's Ancient Schools and Scholars (Dublin: Sealy, Bryers, and Walker, 1912), p. 201-221, 369.

[6]Benedict Fitzpatrick, Ireland and the Making of Britain (New York and London: Funk and Wagnalls Company, 1927), p. 75.

[7]Cited in Nicholas Hans, Comparative Education: A Study of Educational Factors and Traditions (London: Routledge and Kegan Paul Limited, 1961), p. 142.

[8]Report from the Select Committee on Foundation Schools and Education in Ireland, p. 6. Cited in Sister Anthony Marie Gallagher, O.S.F., Education in Ireland. Doctoral dissertation (Washington: The Catholic University of America, 1948), p. 41.

[9]Quoted in Patrick J. McCormick, Ph.D., D.D. Revised by Francis P. Cassidy, Ph.D., History of Education (Washington: The Catholic Education Press, 1953), p. 409.

[10]Michael Tynan, "General Review of Education in Ireland," Lumen Vitae (Jan-March, 1949) IV, 380.

[11]Loc. cit.

[12]Acta et Decreta Synodi Habitae Apud Maynutian, 1900. Appendix, pp. 327-31. Cited in Gallagher, op. cit., p. 75.

[13]"Legislation Affecting Education in Ireland" (Washington: Irish Embassy, no d.). Typescript, p. 2.

[14]W. J. M. Starkie, Recent Reforms in Irish Education (Dublin: Blackie and Son, Ltd., 1902), pp. 25-6.

[15]"Legislation Affecting Education in Ireland," op. cit., p. 2.

[16]The Draft Constitution, Supplement to Irish Press, June, 1937, 127.

[17]"Legislation Affecting Education in Ireland," op. cit., p. 1.

[18]Case for the Catholic School (London: The Catholic Education Council, 1955), p. 90.

[19]Tynan, op. cit., p. 387.

[20]"Notes on the Education System in Ireland" (Washington: The Irish Embassy, no d.) Typescript, p. 1.

[21]Ibid., p. 2.

[22]Tynan, op. cit., pp. 392-93.

[23]Ibid., p. 393.

[24]Mescal, op. cit., p. 123, citing Programme of Primary Instruction, 1926, p. 2.

[25]Department of Education, Dublin. Typescript, December, 1965.

[26]Interview by author with Very Reverend Fergal McGrath, S.J., Dublin.

[27]Ibid.

[28]"Outline of the Education System of Ireland" (Dublin: Department of Education, no d.) Typescript, p. 5.

[29]Tynan, op. cit., p. 403.

[30]"Notes on the Education System of Ireland," op. cit., p. 3.

[31]Interview by author with Mother Superior of Mercy Sisters, Dublin.

[32]"Notes on the Education System of Ireland," op. cit., p. 3.

[33]Loc. cit.

[34]Interview with Very Reverend Fergal McGrath, S.J., Dublin, June, 1956.

[35]Mescal, op. cit., p. 100.

[36]Cf. Chap. II.

[37]Michael Tynan, "Catholic Schools in Ireland: Contrast of North and South," Dublin Review (Winter, 1956-57) No. 47[2], 204.

CHAPTER VIII

[1]Vernon Mallison, Introduction to the Study of Comparative Education (London: William Heineman, Ltd., 1960), p. 14.

[2]Gommar A. De Pauw, The Educational Rights of the Church and Elementary Schools in Belgium. Doctoral dissertation (Washington: The Catholic University of America, 1953), p. 55.

[3]Ibid., p. 57.

[4]Pierre J. Marique, Ph.D., History of Christian Education (New York: Fordham University Press, 1932), Vol. III, p. 237.

[5]De Pauw, op. cit., p. 83.

[6]Marique, op. cit., p. 238; De Pauw, op. cit., pp. 86-87.

[7]DePauw, op. cit., 90.

[8]Paul De Bevere, "Church-State Relationships in Belgium." Unpublished Master's dissertation (Washington: The Catholic University of America, 1953), p. 6.

[9]Ibid., p. 6.

[10]Ibid., p. 7.

[11]De Pauw, op. cit., p. 117.

[12]Loi Collard, 1955, Sec. 6.

[13]G. G. Steckler, "Vast Designs of Belgian Socialists," America (April 23, 1955), XCIII, 99.

[14]"Fight for Belgian Schools Continues," America (August 13, 1955), XCIII, 461.

[15]"Church and Government," Tablet (London) (May 19, 1955), CCV, 187.

[16]"Bishops' Declaration," Tablet (London) (August 6, 1955), CCVI, 140.

[17]M. Grammans, "Elections in Belgium," Tablet (London) (May 31, 1958), CCXI, 508.

[18]M. Grammans, "New Groupings in Belgium," Tablet (London) (May 6, 1961), CCXV, 435.

[19]"Belgium's New Bill -- Parents' Choice" Times Educational Supplement (May 22, 1959), MMCCXCVI, 937.

[20]Ministry of Education, Enseignement Primaire, 1961 (New York: Belgian Government Information Center, 1961), Tableau III.

[21]Mallinson, op. cit., p. 21.

[22]George A. Male, Teacher Education in the Netherlands, Belgium, Luxembourg, Bulletin No. 4 (Washington: U. S. Department of Health, Education, and Welfare, 1960), p. 107, citing Ministere de l'Instruction Publique, Lois Coordonnees sur l'Enseignement Normal, 1957, p. 8-11.

[23]Interview by author with Most Reverend Rector of Louvain University, His Excellency Msgr. Honore van Waeyenbergh, May, 1956.

[24]"General Survey of Religious Teaching in Italy," Lumen Vitae (January-March, 1949), IV, 156-157.

[25]Loc. cit.

[26]Fausto Montanari, "Indirect Action Exercised by Religious Teachers in the State Secondary Schools Run in Italy," Lumen Vitae (January-March, 1950), V, 36.

[27]Ibid., p. 35.

[28]"General Survey of Religious Teaching in Italy," op. cit., p. 157.

[29]Leicester C. Webb, Church and State in Italy, 1947-1957 (Melbourne: Melbourne University Press, 1958), p. 5.

[30]Washington Post, June 27, 1964.

[31]Arthur H. Moehlman, Comparative Education (New York: The Dryden Press, 1953), p. 264.

[32]John J. Doyle, Education in Recent Constitutions and Concordats. Doctoral dissertation (Washington: The Catholic University of America, 1933), p. 113.

[33]Statement drawn by author from interviews with educational leaders and observation of school conditions in Italy, 1956.

[34]National Catholic Welfare Conference News Service, July 17, 1961.

[35]Signor Fausto Montanari, "Observations on the Religious Formation of State School Pupil," op. cit., p. 141.

CHAPTER IX

[1]Cf. p. 372 for definitions.

[2]Arthur H. Moehlman, Comparative Education (New York: The Dryden Press, 1953), pp. 299-300.

[3]Cf. Christopher Dawson, The Making of Europe (London: Sheed and Ward, 1938).

[4]F. Paulsen, German Education, Past and Present. Translated by T. Lorenz (New York: Charles Scribners' Sons, 1908), p. 54.

[5]James Mulhern, A History of Education: A Social Interpretation. Second Edition (New York: The Ronald Press Company, 1959), p. 374.

[6]Ibid., 375.

[7]I. L. Kandel, History of Secondary Education (Boston: Houghton-Mifflin and Company, 1930), p. 239, citing Allgemeine Landrecht, 1794.

[8]Erick J. Hylla and Friedrich O. Kegel, Education in Germany. 2nd Edition (Frankfurt/am Main: Hochscule fur Internationale Pedagogische Forschung, 1958), p. 44.

[9]Cf. Chap. VI.

[10]R. H. Samuel and R. Hinton Thomas, Education and Society in Modern Germany (London: Routledge and Kegan Paul Limited, 1949), p. 100.

[11]Ibid., p. 99-100.

[12]Ibid., p. 106.

[13]Ibid., p. 107.

[14]Ibid., p. 107-108.

[15]Ibid., p. 104.

[16]Loc. cit.

[17]Ibid., 168.

[18]Loc. cit.

[19]Ibid., 170.

[20]Alena M. Lindegren, Germany Revisited: Education in the Federal Republic (Washington: U. S. Department of Health, Education, and Welfare, Office of Education, 1960), p. 4.

[21]Loc. cit.

[22]"Science and Education," Extract from book Germany Reports (Wiesbaden: Press and Information Office of the Federal Government, 1961), p. 14 (750).

[23]Helmut Arntz, Facts About Germany (Wiesbaden: Press and Information Office of the Federal German Government, 1960), p. 80.

[24]Ernst Helmreich, Religious Education in German Schools (Cambridge: Harvard University Press, 1959), p. 237; Hylla and Kegel, op. cit., p. 44.

[25]John J. Doyle, Education in Recent Constitutions and Concordats. Doctoral dissertation (Washington: The Catholic University of America, 1933) pp. 117-118.

[26]Interview with Catholic educational authorities of West Germany, 1963.

[27]Theodore Huebener, The Schools of West Germany (New York: New York University Press, 1962), p. 130.

[28]Cf. p. 369.

[29]"Science and Education," op. cit., p. 22.

[30]National Catholic Welfare Conference News Service (June 5, 1961).

[31]Hylla and Kegel, op. cit., p. 52.

[32]Huebener, op. cit., p. 93.

CHAPTER X

[1]Denver Register, August 12, 1960, citing Msgr. Frans Op de Coul, Director of the Catholic Bureau for Information and Education, The Hague, Holland.

[2]The Netherlands' Solution of the Education Question (The Hague: Het Rooms-Katholick Centraal Bureau Voor Onderwijs En Opvoeding. Printed as a manuscript, 1940), pp. 21-23. Referred to hereafter as The Netherlands' Solution.

[3]P. Albers, "Holland," The Catholic Encyclopedia (New York: Ròbert Appleton Company, 1910) Vol. VII, 387.

[4]The Netherlands: A Guide to the Academic Placement of Students from the Netherlands in Educational Institutions in the United States of America (World Education Series, 1961), p. 1.

[5]The Netherlands' Solution, op. cit., p. 27.

[6]Loc. cit.

[7]Ibid., p. 14.

[8]Ibid., p. 31.

[9]Ibid., p. 14.

[10]Ibid., pp. 50-51.

[11]Ibid., p. 64.

[12]"The Dutch Solution," The Case for the Catholic School, Second Edition (London: The Catholic Education Council, 1955), p. 80.

[13]The Netherlands' Solution, op. cit., p. 69.

[14]Ibid., pp. 111-112.

[15]Ibid., p. 107.

[16]"The Dutch Solution," op. cit., p. 82.

[17]The Netherlands' Solution, op. cit., pp. 124-5.

[18]Ibid., p. 131.

[19]Ibid., pp. 139-140.

[20]Ibid., p. 58.

[21]Dutch School System (The Hague: The Ministry of Education, Arts, and Sciences, 1960), p. 7.

[22]Ibid., p. 8.

[23]The Netherlands, op. cit., p. 2.

[24]"The Dutch Solution," op. cit., p. 86.

[25]Digest of the Netherlands, Part 4. Education and Cultural Aspects (The Hague: Netherlands Government Information Service, 1959), pp. 9-11; Dutch School System, op. cit., pp. 19-21.

[26]Ibid., p. 10.

[27]Dutch School System, op. cit., p. 7.

[28]George A. Male, Teacher Education in the Netherlands, Belgium, Luxembourg (Washington: U. S. Department of Health, Education, and Welfare, 1960), p. 6.

[29]Dutch School System, op. cit., p. 25.

[30]Ibid., p. 24.

[31]Ibid., p. 10.

[32]Digest of the Netherlands, op. cit., p. 4.

[33]"The Educational System and Religious Teaching in Holland," Lumen Vitae (April-June, 1949), IV, 372.

[34]The Netherlands' Solution, op. cit., p. 57.

[35]Statistics, 1963 (The Hague: Het Rooms-Katholick Centraal Bureau Voor Onderwijs en Opvoeding) Typescript.

[36]Loc. cit.

[37]Statement contained in correspondence with A. J. de Beurs, Head of Foreign Relations' Department, Het R. K. Centraal Bureau Voor Onderwijs en Opvoeding, The Hague, Feb., 1964.

38William Banning, "Religion in the Netherlands." A reprint
from Delta, Vol. I, No. 4 (Winter, 1958-59). Distributed by the Netherlands Embassy, Washington, D. C.